Transactions of the Royal Historical Society

FIFTH SERIES

37

LONDON 1987

British Library Cataloguing in Publication Data

Transactions of the Royal Historical Society.
—5th series, vol. 37 (1987)
1. History—Periodicals
I. Royal Historical Society
905   D1
ISBN 086193–115–7

Made and printed in Great Britain by Butler & Tanner Ltd, Frome and London

CONTENTS

TRANSACTIONS OF THE
ROYAL HISTORICAL SOCIETY
PRESIDENTIAL ADDRESS

By G. E. Aylmer

COLLECTIVE MENTALITIES IN MID SEVENTEENTH-CENTURY ENGLAND: II. ROYALIST ATTITUDES

READ 21 NOVEMBER 1986

ANY attempt to apply the same approach in the case of Cavaliers as I did with Puritans last year may seem doomed to inevitable failure.[1] It will be considered futile to search for particular varieties of human temperament which inclined individuals towards adopting particular ideas and beliefs of a broadly conservative persuasion. Left-wing intellectuals, historians included, have sometimes been reluctant to admit that instinctive, emotional conservatism can be held to constitute a system of ideas at all, as opposed to a welter of prejudices and vested interests. Correspondingly, for many people of conservative views, acceptance of the world of order, hierarchy and inequality broadly as they find it—not necessarily as the best of all possible worlds but as the least bad of all realisable ones—is so obviously sensible as to need no intellectual defence or justification. None the less, not all the royalists of 1641–2 and after were unthinking conservatives, with the smallest of small 'c's, or at any rate not in the same sense. Not all professed the same religious tenets; not all adhered to the same constitutional principles; not all came to be royalists in the same way and at the same time. So some modest analysis of the Cavalier party in terms of what may be called ideological temperament is, I hope, worth undertaking. Not that the royalist cause has lacked its apologists, from the greatest of seventeenth-century historians to our own day. Few, however, have paused to consider the kind of people who became Cavaliers and their probable motivation.

[1] I am grateful, far beyond the normal indebtedness of authors to librarians, to the staff of the Bodleian for all their help, during what has been for them an exceptionally difficult year.

I

One problem for the historian is their relative lack of articulacy compared to their Puritan–parliamentarian counterparts. Naturally I am not going to suggest that no royalists kept diaries or compiled journals. Of course they did. But on examination a number of these turn out to be not quite what we might expect, or else in other instances do not strictly provide evidence for what people felt and thought at the time, especially during the early to mid-1640s. To start with the best known case of all, Clarendon's *Life ... written by himself,* although a primary source of great importance, is not nearly so contemporary with the events in question as the first Books of his *History,* written on the Island of Jersey in the years 1646–8.[2] Thus, while what Clarendon tells us about himself may fairly be taken to be more deliberately self-justificatory when he was writing in his second exile and therefore perhaps less reliable, he was prepared to be critical of his own colleagues in the wartime royal government, even of his royal master, after the monarchy had been safely, if not miraculously restored, more than he had been when writing earlier in the shadow of defeat. This may seem more a matter for a historiographical discussion, but as will be seen it has relevance for my subject this afternoon. Also near the apex of the administrative hierarchy, Edward Nicholas's autobiographical notes read more like a skeleton *curriculum vitae,* which is particularly unfortunate in that with him we certainly have someone who, whatever the course of events might have been in 1640–42, could never have been other than a loyal servant of the King, whereas even if we agree that Hyde did not 'change sides' in 1641, he only appeared openly in the King's service after the parliamentary recess of that year.[3] Nicholas's political and less easily his religious standpoint can reasonably be inferred, but it is a matter of inference not of what he tells us.[4]

Clarendon's famous passage about Sir Edmund Verney, the King's standard-bearer, is a case in point about contemporary evidence. It is to be found in the *Life,* written around 1669, and not in the corresponding part of the *History,* first drafted about 1647. So when

---

[2] On the composition of the *History,* the best authority is still C. H. Firth's article in *EHR,* xix (1904); see also B. H. G. Wormald, *Clarendon: politics, history and religion 1640–1660* (Cambridge, 1951), which unfortunately stops short of the writings during his second exile (1667–74).

[3] Professor Conrad Russell has reminded me that Hyde recorded being introduced to the King in June or July 1641 (*The Life of Edward, Earl of Clarendon ... written by himself* (Oxford, 1759), folio edn. 42, octavo edn. 82–4). S. R. Gardiner, however, pointed out that, if the meeting did take place then, the intermediary could not, as Hyde says it was, have been Henry Percy who was in hiding throughout the summer (*History of England ... 1603–1642* (10 vols. 1883–4), ix, 387–8).

[4] B.L., Additional MS 31954, 18th-century transcripts and abstracts of papers then in the Evelyn collection.

Sir Edmund is reported as having told Hyde that he did not like the quarrel, especially concerning the Bishops, wished that the King would give the parliamentarians what they desired, and only followed the King because he had 'eaten his bread' and served him for thirty years, we have to weigh the fallibility of memory or the desire to embroider a good story against the absence of any possible motive for falsification.[5] Only a month or so before Sir Edmund's death at Edgehill, his younger son, Edmund Verney junior, wrote from Ireland to his then parliamentarian elder brother, Sir Ralph, reproaching him for causing 'a greate griefe to my father'. He continued:

> I beseech you consider that majesty is sacred; God sayeth, 'Touch not myne anointed'; it troubled David that he cutt but the lapp of Saul's garment; I believe yee will all say yee intend not to hurt the King, but can any of yee warrant any one shott to say it shall not endanger his very person? I am soe much troubled to think of your being of the syde you are that I can write no more, only I shall pray for peace with all my hearte, . . . (etc.)[6]

As we shall see, many were ready at almost all stages to profess their desire for peace; but as with consensus or unity, it was invariably a matter of peace on their own terms.

Sir Henry Slingsby of Scriven near York, a future martyr for the royal cause, provides us with another contemporary witness for attitudes towards the bishops. 'I went', he writes

> with the Bill for the taking of their votes in the house of Peers, and for medling with temporal affairs but I was against the Bill for taking away the function and calling of Bishops; . . .

While he did not believe that church government, as it was then established, by archbishops and bishops was of absolute necessity, he considered that their removal at that juncture 'may bee of dangerous consequence to the peace of the Church'. He regarded episcopacy as an ancient custom with at least some basis in apostolic times and considered that the common people were guided by ancient usage; and he foresaw future conflicts between learned and unlearned ministers without the framework of episcopal authority.[7]

The best known Anglican-Cavalier diarist of the century presents us with a very different picture. Both in his *de Vita Propria* and in his Diary John Evelyn explains how he turned up complete with horse and arms to join Prince Rupert for the assault on London in the late autumn of 1642, but how when the King's forces withdrew to the

[5] Clarendon, *Life*, folio edn. 69, octavo edn. 134–6.
[6] *Memoirs of the Verney Family during the 17th century . . .*, ed. Frances Parthenope Verney and Margaret N. Verney (2nd edn. 2 vols. 1907), I, 282–3.
[7] *The Diary of Sir Henry Slingsby of Scriven, Bart. . . .*, ed. D. Parsons (1836), 66–9.

west, he went back to his home in Surrey, and during the following year obtained the King's permission to travel abroad. He asserts that since all his property lay in areas controlled by Parliament's forces, the loss to the royal cause from its expropriation would have been greater than any possible gain to the King from Evelyn fighting in the royal army. In the summer of 1643 he crossed to the Continent in order to avoid having to take the Solemn League and Covenant (which incidentally was also to precipitate Sir Ralph Verney's change of sides), but at the same time sent a potential cavalry charger, with a relative to ride the animal, to join the King's forces in Oxford.[8] What are we to make of this? Evelyn's attendance at Anglican services during the Protectorate and the second Commonwealth of 1659 proves that he had the courage to take risks because of his beliefs. And it would be a cheap crack to say that with many friends like that King Charles didn't need enemies. None the less without at all imputing cowardice to Evelyn, that is not the end of the matter, for his case was by no means unique. Among other well known compilers of autobiographical materials, Elias Ashmole's reactions look on the surface almost diametrically opposite to those of Evelyn. The future antiquary, astrologer and free-mason appears for some time to have taken no part at all in the conflict, living mainly in Cheshire, partly in London exercised with his personal affairs. Yet Ashmole joined the King at Oxford at the end of 1644, when as events were soon to show the outcome of the war was all but decided; he had already by whatever means—he does not really tell us—obtained office as a Commissioner of Excise. If, as is at least possible, he was led to commit himself in this way by his own astrological predictions, these were to cost him dear in the short run but to guarantee him an exceptionally lucrative post in the Excise from the Restoration to the end of his days. Perhaps he always was a royalist by conviction; but from 1642 to 44 seems a long time to take to decide upon any action.[9]

It is striking how many other cases we have of obviously committed Anglican royalists who did not fight for the King or in some way opted out. Such who lay low or seem to have been primarily concerned to avoid seizure of their property and for whom there is clear documentation include John Bramston, son of the King's ex-Chief Justice,[10] Christopher Guise of Elmore in Gloucestershire,[11] George son and

---

[8] *The Diary of John Evelyn*, ed. E. S. de Beer (6 vols. Oxford, 1955), i, 53–5, ii, 79–80, 81, 81–2.

[9] *Elias Ashmole (1617–1692) His Autobiographical and Historical Notes . . .*, ed. C. H. Josten (5 vols. Oxford, 1966), 18–20, 29–31, 339–58.

[10] *The Autobiography of Sir John Bramston, K.B. . . .*, ed. Lord P. Braybrooke (Camden Soc., xxxii, 1845), 103–4, 107.

[11] *Autobiography of Thomas Raymond and Memoirs of the Family of Guise of Elmore, Glos.*, ed. G. Davies (Camden 3rd ser., xxviii, 1917), 123–32.

heir of Christopher Wandesford, the King's last pre-war Lord Deputy of Ireland, and—up to a point—Sir Humphrey Mildmay of Danbury, Essex and Queen Camel, Somerset.[12] Poor George Wandesford seems to have been somewhat accident-prone according to the account given by his deeply pious sister Alice, later Mrs Thornton. Although he was nineteen at the outbreak of war, he was 'sent into France by his guardian for education, as most of our English gentry was'; unfortunately young Wandesford and his Scottish tutor ran out of money and he had to come back to Yorkshire in 1644. He was on his way to collect a younger brother from school in York on the fatal day 2 July 1644 and was actually seen crossing Marston Moor before or during the battle in which he took no part; but on suspicion of having been in arms for the King that day he was after all sequestered, although some of his difficulties appear to have arisen from his father's unpaid debts. Like other royal servants who died at the wrong moment Lord Deputy Wandesford left his family severely encumbered. George was also in trouble, this time genuinely for his principles, because he deliberately appointed a non-presbyterian cleric to the family living of Kirklington. His sister clearly felt that some kind of apologia was called for, and goes on to explain:

> It must not be denied that my dear brother's affections and conscience carried him in judgment to serve his King, the church and state, by way of armes. Yet as things then fell out, such was his prudence for the preservation of his family, according to his gracious majestie's command to his friends, that he saw all was lost, and that they should sitt in quiet, and preserve themselves for the good of himselfe or soone afterwards. So he saw that it was in vaine to strive against that impetuous streame, and involve himself in utter ruine willfully, when noe good could possibly be don by his service to the King, otherwaies then by our praiers and teares for him. This was the reason made him decline the ingaging into that warre.

Alas he was to be carried away by another impetuous stream, being drowned trying to ford the river Swale when it was in flood on his way to transact some family business in 1651. And it was a brother, not a son, for whom the Wandesford estate or what remained of it was to be preserved.[13]

[12] The Earl of Derby's justification for his having withdrawn to the Isle of Man in 1643 or 4, leaving his wife to defend Lathom House, is perhaps rather different; even so he felt it necessary to defend himself from the charge of having become 'a neuter' (*The Stanley Papers*, Part III (Chetham Soc., 70, 1867), 6–10).

[13] *The Autobiography of Mrs. Alice Thornton of East Newton, co. York* (Surtees Soc., lxii 1875), 40, 57–68.

Sir Humphrey Mildmay deserves fuller consideration on various counts. Here at last we seem to have an unpublished 'Cavalier' diary, of absolutely contemporary authenticity, to set against comparable Puritan remains. His twentieth-century biographer interprets numerous entries in the diary as indicating repeated marital infidelities as well as frequent and eventually chronic drunkenness. Certainly Sir Humphrey pretty often records that he was 'foxed', that is the worse for drink. His text is one of those deceptive manuscripts which look regular and straightforward, but in fact is in many places well-nigh illegible. And I am not convinced that all the entries in question do indicate what contemporaries often called 'drabbing' and we would call casual adulteries. More important for our purposes, Mildmay, who was fifty when war began, had been sheriff of Essex back in 1636–37 in unpopular ship money days; and his principal house and estate were in an ultra-Puritan-parliamentarian area. Some of his passing comments leave us in no doubt of his sympathies and later in the war he did in fact help the King's forces from his secondary landed base down in Somerset. He was more than once plundered and had to borrow a large sum in order to pay his composition fine; but what is astonishing and tells us, I think, a good deal about conditions during the war, is the frequency with which he was able to move about the country between London, Essex and Somerset, and his apparent ability to keep himself afloat financially speaking, whether living in London lodgings or at home in hostile territory. As his biographer has pointed out, not the least unexpected thing about Sir Humphrey was his long-lasting friendship with the notorious Dr Dorislaus, the disgruntled ex-Cambridge history lecturer who later drafted the charge against the King and was soon afterwards assassinated for his pains. In truth, however, Mildmay's diary is not a very 'political' document and the expressions of religious interest and belief while sincere are thinly sprinkled. His real obsessions were with the weather, with his time of getting up in the morning, and with his family, in particular his eldest surviving son, 'Nompee' who was wounded´ in the war but survived. Not being a Catholic he lacks the consolation of confession, and his diary—it may be surmised—provided an alternative outlet for his constant, almost morbid self-criticism. He records his return to Queen Camel in the summer of 1642 'where I hope I maye finde tyme and occasion to shake off my fooleinge'. It would be harsh to condemn Sir Humphrey for not having sacrificed all and gone to serve in the royal army as a gentleman volunteer with no means of support. And it would be all too easy to pontificate about the demoralisation of defeat which his diary exemplifies. The surviving portion ends in 1651, so we cannot tell whether he rallied at the Restoration or was by then too far gone in the descent into alcoholism.[14]

By contrast, Gervase Holles, historian of his family and second cousin of the more famous Denzil, leaves us in no doubt as to his sympathies, which his war service equally attests. Unfortunately for our present purposes, however, his *Memorials* tells us nothing about his own feelings during the 1640s, and even the date at which he decided to take up arms for the King has to be inferred by his editor.[15]

In one sense the royalists lost the Civil War because not enough people felt enough loyalty to King Charles I for him to crush the rebellion. Yet, if the King's cause failed for lack of men and of the other necessary 'sinews of war' (above all money and munitions), it hardly did so from lack of support in the form of the printed word. While the total output of royalist pamphlets, sermons, newsbooks and so on was certainly less than that emanating from Parliament's presses, it was still very considerable. And much of it remains, in my submission, a somewhat under-used source by historians. There is of course the perennial question with seventeenth-century pamphlets of who read them and how much impact they had. Curiously this objection is more often raised by scholars concerned to deflate the significance of the Levellers, Diggers and the more extreme religious sects. However it seems fair to suggest that what is sauce for the radical goose should also be so for the royalist gander. Granted that caveat, a preliminary and superficial survey of this literature may be rewarding.

Some of these works and their authors have been discussed by historians of political thought,[16] others by students of religion and the Church.[17] I have tried rather to assess them as propaganda, as

[14] B. L., Harleian MS 454, fols. 4–107. See Philip Lee Ralph, *Sir Humphrey Mildmay Royalist Gentleman: Glimpses of the English Scene 1633–1652* (New Brunswick, N.J., 1947).

[15] *Memorials of the Holles Family 1493–1656 by Gervase Holles*, ed. A. C. Wood (Camden 3rd ser., lv, 1937), vii–xi, 186–8.

[16] See J. W. Allen, *English Political Thought 1603–1660*, vol. i, *1603–1644* (1938; no other volume was ever published); Margaret Atwood Judson, *The Crisis of the Constitution, An essay in constitutional and political thought in England 1603–1645* (New Brunswick, N.J., 1949); Perez Zagorin, *A History of Political Thought in the English Revolution* (1954), which brilliant as it is is devotes only 13 out of 200 pages to the Royalists apart from Hobbes; Andrew Sharp (ed.), *Political Ideas of the English Civil Wars 1641–1649 A Collection of representative texts with commentary* (1983) is an excellent anthology, doing justice to Royalists and neutrals; and, since this paper was written, see also David Wootton (ed.), *Divine Right and Democracy* (Harmondsworth, 1986), which while covering the whole century is valuable for 1640–60.

[17] See P. E. More and F. L. Cross, *Anglicanism: the thought and practice of the Church of England, illustrated from the religious literature of the 17th century* (1935); G. W. O. Addleshaw, *The High Church Tradition: A study in the liturgical thought of the 17th century* (1941); R. S. Bosher, *The Making of the Restoration Settlement, The influence of the Laudians 1649–1662* (1951); H. R. McAdoo, *The Spirit of Anglicanism* (1965). I have deliberately excluded titles primarily to do with the Restoration church settlement of 1660–62.

statements making a case for the King's side or—more often—against the Parliament's.[18] And effectiveness as propaganda is not of course at all the same thing as originality in political theory, profundity of theological scholarship or acuteness of ethical sensibility. Even a cursory study of these publications reveals some of the contradictions, or at least the cross-currents, in the arguments which were deployed. At its simplest and most extreme the royalist case asserted kingly power to be of divine authority, that positive or active resistance was in all circumstances tantamount to the mortal sin of rebellion against God; likewise the authority of bishops was of apostolic and thus, at one remove, of divine origin and institution. According to taste and judgment, this left little or much space for more specific issues such as the King's relation to the law and to parliament, likewise the actual system of episcopacy, ecclesiastical jurisdiction and the liturgy as they had existed under William Laud or very briefly and uneasily in 1641 after the overthrow of the Archbishop and his system. In respect of both the religious and the secular issues at stake we find a no doubt predictably wide range of positions, from those who would concede nothing to those whose emphasis on the very substantial concessions which the King had made in matters of church and state constituted a vital part of their argument in his favour from 1642 onwards.

Another way of looking at this material would be in relation to the specific circumstances including the changing fortunes of war which brought it into being. Thus from late in 1642 until well into the following year many of the political pieces produced on the King's behalf were direct or indirect responses to Henry Parker's *Observations*. Among Parker's opponents, since his intellectual standing was a matter of total disagreement between the authors of two standard histories of political thought produced earlier in this century, it would be evasive of me not to include Dudley Digges junior and most notably his work *The Unlawfulnesse of Subjects taking up Armes against their Soveraigne, in what case soever* of 1643, rather than his earlier and more narrowly anti-Parkerian *An Answer to a Printed Book Intituled, Observations upon some of His Majesties Late Answers and Addresses* (1642). Granted that Digges must have acquired a copy of Hobbes' *De Cive* by the time that he wrote the second and longer of these two treatises, in cogency and coherence of argument I find it as impressive as Margaret Judson did and am amazed at J. W. Allen's cursory dismissal of its intellectual merit; even Professor Perez Zagorin's judicious assessment, bracketing Digges and the Revd. Dr Henry Ferne as competent polemicists, seems a shade too cool.[19]

[18] Besides the standard bibliographical aids, I have been particularly dependent on F. Madan, *Oxford Books*, vol. 2, *Oxford Literature 1450–1640, and 1641–1650* (Oxford, 1912).
[19] Allen, 404; Judson, 393–6; Zagorin, 74–5, 195.

Among the more eloquent of these anti-Parkerian pieces is Bishop John Bramhall's *The Serpent Salve, or, Remedie For the Biting of an Aspe*, in which he wrote 'It is not twins but litters of Hereticks that struggle in the wombe of the Church'; and a little later 'If you make a strict survey of the Parliaments party, I believe you will find as many Courtiers as Countrymen (proportion for proportion).'[20]

More characteristic of this genre just because it is less original and less powerfully argued is *A View of a Printed Book Intituled Observations* ascribed to Sir John Spelman, arguing that the King alone is superior to the two Houses alone. The author is familiar with Bodin. He maintains that the leaders of the two Houses have already turned the monarchy of England 'into an arbitrary boundlesse Oligarchy'; the author goes on to warn his readers that 'Tis not prerogative that is now contending with the subjects libertie, but libertie struggles with Ochlocracie, the established protestant Religion with scism and here-sie': an early example of the contention that Parliament's rebellion against the King was but the prelude to the rule of the 'Many-headed monster'. Yet the author seems elsewhere to waver on the crucial issue of whether resistance can ever be justified, and his own preferred sovereign is clearly the King in Parliament.[21] This might be cited as an example of a propagandist who weakened his case by his honesty, namely by conceding too much. To grant that the members of the two Houses still sitting at Westminster were a valid parliament was to fight on Parker's own ground, and to suggest that resistance could ever be justified was to invite the answer that this was precisely such an occasion. By contrast the principle of unqualified non-resistance to a divine-right king or queen required only that every one should know who was the rightful monarch and, unlike the case in the civil wars of the fifteenth century, this was not in serious dispute.

The most authoritative statements of the King's case were naturally those contained in his own declarations, and sometimes more suc-cinctly in his proclamations, which were mainly penned for him by Hyde, Falkland and Colepepper. The only one of these three whose works were published under his own name was Falkland, but neither his speech on the judges (pre-1642 by the old calendar) nor that 'concerning Episcopacy', also with a 1641 imprint, can be called

---

[20] John Bramhall, *The Serpent Salve* ... (1643), 116, 126.
[21] [Sir John Spelman] *A View* ... (Oxford, 1642), 5–6, 10, 20, 28–9, [34–5, 37]. On this theme see C. Hill, 'The Many-headed Monster', in *Change and Continuity in 17th-century England* (1974). For other responses to Parker, see various works by Henry Ferne, Griffith Williams, John Maxwell, John Bramhall, and the anonymous *Christus Dei, Or, A Theologicall Discourse, Wherein is proved, that Regall or Monarchicall Power is not of Humaine but of Divine Right* ... (Oxford, 1642).

royalist in the normal sense, despite the latter's opposition to Root and Branch. In the Dedication to the 1644 Oxford edition of his 1641 speech on episcopacy appears the famous encomium:

> That it was that made Tew so valued a Mansion to us: For as when we went from Oxford thither we found ourselves never out of the Universitie.[22]

And it is worth reminding ourselves, because this bears on an issue which we shall shortly have to consider more fully, that Falkland's most extended work was his *Discourse of Infallibility*, written in the 1630s, first published in the 1640s and reprinted in 1660—an attack, albeit of the most measured urbanity, on the pretensions of the Roman Church.[23]

There were some early expressions of what we might call the offensive, as opposed to the defensive statements of the royalist case. One such is found in a genuine or spurious work ascribed to the famous antiquary, Sir Robert Cotton, which sought to demonstrate that the King's physical presence was essential to the very being of a parliament; thus, by implication, the King's withdrawal from London in January 1642 automatically meant that the gathering of peers and MPs at Westminster had ceased to be a parliament, in spite of the fateful Act of May 1641 for the present Parliament's self-perpetuation.[24] This line of argument was to re-appear more explicitly in later pamphlets including some of the replies to Parker's *Observations*. The argument that the King's absence automatically invalidated parliamentary proceedings, notably legislation, was often thrown in along with others.[25] The other prong of this argument was what we may call the tumults one, that direct action to coerce Parliament by crowds or mass demonstrations likewise invalidated the very being of a parliament and brought its existence to an end. We might also call

[22] Speeches against the judges by all three were printed during the first session of the Long Parliament, before their breach with the radical leadership. For the quotation, see Falkland, *A Speech ... Concerning Episcopacy* (2nd edn. Oxford, 1644), Sig. xxx 2.

[23] Sir Lucius Cary, later Lord Viscount Falkland, *A Discourse of Infallibillitie* was written by 1635, Wat Montague's Letter in reply to it being dated from Paris 21 November (1660 edn. p. 278). For polemical purposes, dangerously much is conceded, both to Rome and to reason; the *Discourse* certainly provides support for the concept of Great Tew as a staging-post between Erasmian humanism and the Enlightenment (see H. R. Trevor-Roper, 'The Origins of the Enlightenment' in *Religion, The Reformation and Social Change* (1967). I hope to return to this theme in my fourth address.

[24] Sir Robert Cotton, Knight and Baronet, *A Treatise, shewing That the Soveraignes Person is required in the great Councells or Assemblies of the State, as well at the Consultations as at the Conclusions* (1641).

[25] *No Parliament without a King* ... (Oxford, 1642) is a different imprint of the same work. See also *A Vindication of the King. With some Observations upon the Two Houses* ... (1642), p. 6.

this a special case of the 'many-headed monster' motif in royalist propaganda, but it had particular relevance to the events of 1641, when it was first adumbrated. One of its earliest expressions—I only hesitate to say the first—is in the Revd. Thomas Warmestry's *Pax Vobis*, of which Thomason the great collector and a future presbyterian was the publisher. Its general tone is indeed restrained, one might say near neutralist; and the *DNB* article on its author may well be correct to describe him as a royalist of Puritan leanings, although he was to be sequestered in 1646 and rewarded with the Deanery of Worcester after the Restoration. He claims that the laws of England require the mutual free consent of both King and subjects, the latters' consent being given in a free parliament, and his warning against 'tumultuous spirits' and 'disorderly meetings' was intended to help protect the country against 'the tyranny and usurpation of that man of sinne, the Romish wolfe'.[26] And that brings us to one of the most glaring inconsistencies or contradictions in the whole royalist case.

The King claimed, I am sure with complete sincerity, to be fighting for the Church of England as by law established, that is for a church in the legal and ecclesiastical sense Protestant, in the generic and theological sense Catholic (as in the wording of the creed and elsewhere in the liturgy). His enemies made great play with the threat of a Catholic conspiracy or Popish plot, and tended to portray Charles as at best its unwitting dupe. Indeed, despite some disagreement among modern scholars, there seems little doubt that most English Catholics, at least nobility and gentry, were active royalists.[27] Quite why so many of them should have fought so bravely and in other ways served so devotedly in the cause of a monarchy, under which their Church had been dispossessed and sacrilegiously despoiled and they and their priests had suffered so much discrimination, not to say persecution, I find profoundly puzzling.[28] A kind of neo-Augustinian pessimism about the affairs of this world may provide an explanation at a theological or intellectual level. How far the Queen's well-known Catholicism acted as a rallying-cry for her co-religionists remains

---

[26] Thomas Warmestry, *Pax Vobis Or A Charme for Tumultuous Spirits* ... (London, printed for George Thompson, 1641), p. 41 [sic. = p. 31]; he was also the author of *An Answer to Certaine Observations of W. Bridges, concerning the present Warre against his Majestie* ... (1643). For his career, see also A. G. Matthews, *Walker Revised being a revision of John Walker's Sufferings of the Clergy during the Grand Rebellion 1642–60* (Oxford, 1948), 178.

[27] The contrary view is persuasively put by K. Lindley in 'Lay Catholics during the reign of Charles I', *Journal of Ecclesiastical History*, 22 (1971) and in 'The Part played by the Catholics', in Brian Manning (ed.), *Politics, Religion and the English Civil War* (1973). I am here following P. R. Newman, 'Catholic Royalist Activists in the North 1642–46', *Recusant History*, 14 (1977–8), 26–38, and 'Catholic Royalists of Northern England', *Northern History*, 15 (1979), 88–95.

[28] I am grateful to my colleague Dr Henry Mayr-Harting for help on this question.

uncertain; it may well have influenced some. As with the Irish Rebels of 1641–2 the most plausible argument is that English papists took up arms for the King chiefly through fear of much worse things being in store for them and their religion in the event of a Puritan victory. This explanation can certainly be found in at least one pamphlet published in 1643, which also suggested that the fear of Popery on one side was balanced by the fear of atheism, rebellion and profaneness on the other.[29] The ascription of atheism to the Puritans may appear one of the more far-fetched extravagances of mutual denunciation; it can, however, be bracketed with the royalist slogan, frequently repeated, that 'rebellion is as the sin of witchcraft', the reasoning here being that both involved taking the Devil's part against God.[30]

Be that as it may, the active participation of so many Catholics on the King's side, even leaving out of account Charles's damaging agreements with the Irish Catholic Confederacy, raised ideological difficulties for other royalists. Some extreme anti-Puritan polemicists went so far as to equate sectaries and Papists because of their allegedly similar anti-monarchist tenets; others were careful to distinguish Jesuits or 'Jesuited Papists', who did indeed advocate and practise resistance and even tyrannicide, from other Catholics who could be and normally were perfectly loyal subjects.[31] This was so frequently repeated that among some strongly Anglican apologists for the King's cause it may almost be described as an orthodoxy. A characteristic specimen of this genre likewise exemplifies a much-used seventeenth-century dialectical device: the tract or pamphlet cast in the form of a fictional or imaginary dialogue. It is also very typical in that the full title tells us nearly all that is worth knowing about its contents. That is

A Discourse Discovering some Mysteries of our New State, and remembering some Fatall Daies on both parties, The Loyall and Rebell: Betwixt a Protestant, a Puritan, and a Papist: shewing the Rise and Progresse of Englands Unhappinesse, Ab Anno illo Infortunato 1641. Si Populus vult decipi, decipiatur.

[29] N. R., *Englands Petition to the Two Houses Assembled in Parliament* (London and Oxford, 1643), 7–8.
[30] For example I. S. Generosus whose abode is in the King's Army, *The Publique Confider* (Oxford, 1643); see also Nathaniel Bernard, *Ezoptron The Antimaxias, Or A Looking-Glasse for Rebellion*, a sermon preached before the members of the two Houses in St Mary's Church, Oxford, 16 June 1644 (Oxford, 1644), p. 1, on the text 1 *Samuel*, XV, 23.
[31] *A Dialogue or Discourse Between a Parliament-man And a Roman Catholick, Touching the present State of Recusants in England* (1641), 22. Other works categorizing Catholics in this way include Warmestry's *Ramus Olivi*, and D.O., *A Persuasion to Loyalty* ... (1642), see Table of Contents, 'Puritan-Jesuitisme'.

I need hardly say that in the simulated debate Protestant succeeds in winning over Papist by driving a wedge to divide Bellarmine and his like from non-Jesuited Catholics. He goes on to explain how 'these New Statesmen', that is the leaders of 'the Faction', Lord Saye and more surprisingly the Duke of Hamilton, have duped their followers. Puritan is persuaded that his support for the rebellion requires him to 'scorne and vilify the Gentry'; Papist is made to disavow the Irish Rebellion. Finally both profess themselves contented with Protestant's case: by 1645 an example of whistling in the dark.[32] Perhaps it was a little more than mere pulpit rhetoric when the Anglican vicar of Stepney, preaching before the King in Christ Church, exclaimed '. . . the zealous Sectarie . . . is now Jesuite enough'.[33] We may certainly agree that it was an honest, commonsense response to parliamentarian accusations to draw a distinction between different kinds of Catholics. But it didn't entirely meet the 'Popish Plot' argument and failed to answer their opponents' propaganda about the Queen and other Roman Catholic (open or concealed) in positions of influence around the King.

I have found it less easy than I expected to select a representative, contemporary voice of what one might call main-stream English Catholicism. Thomas White, *alias* Blacklo, is too untypical, both in his viewpoint and his intellectuality; and he will, as I hope, feature in my fourth address. A better spokesman for the loyalism, i.e. royalism, of the English Catholic community was too young to be writing during or immediately following the events of the Civil War. Cuckolded by his King, Roger Palmer, Earl of Castlemaine, has had an indifferent press from historians both lay and professional. However, as the *DNB* correctly points out, his *Catholique Apologie* is far from despicable in either form or content. With the various additions it constitutes a lengthy and detailed defence, demonstrating that all the way from Elizabeth to Charles II the overwhelming majority of Catholics had served king (or queen) and country with complete loyalty. Castlemaine was no theologian, and for most of his text he sensibly avoids the ecclesiastical and doctrinal issues dividing the two communions. If anything, in the passages dissociating the English Catholics from the Irish 'rebels' of the 1640s, he may be thought to have conceded too much. By contrast in deflating the absurdly high figures then widely accepted for the number of Protestants massacred and dying in other ways as a result of what he (in common with other Englishmen then and now) calls the Rebellion, when he might equally fairly have styled it a national uprising (or what we would call an unsuccessful War of Liberation), he may be thought to have spoilt a good case by

[32] *A Discourse* . . . (Oxford, 1645), especially pp. 3, 19–20, 34, 38–42.
[33] William Stampe, *A Sermon* . . . (Oxford, 1643), 9.

overstatement, reducing the grotesquely exaggerated total of 300,000 to only 3,000. Setting this aside, it is an effective work for those who like their polemic in a fairly low key; by the 1670s however such voices were again increasingly unheeded.[34]

The now fashionable contention, to which I referred last year, that the outbreak of Civil War was due primarily to religious issues[35] seem to be borne out on the royalist side, in that the Bishops and the Prayer Book were defended openly in print sooner than the cause of monarchy as such. It may still be thought that there is an element of tautology in this, in that Root and Branch together with the Commons' resolutions on religious innovations posed a much more open and explicit threat to the Church than even the Ten Propositions or the Grand Remonstrance did to the monarchy. Moreover it was mainly clerics who rallied to the defence of the Church. With the exception of Sir Thomas Aston of Cheshire (something of a 'one-man-band'?) and Lord Falkland if indeed he counts here, these champions of episcopacy and the Prayer Book were almost without exception Anglican divines. Other obvious exceptions to this generalisation are two of the early 'side changers': Thomas Lechford, who went to New England as a quasi-refugee but was so disgusted by what he found there, especially at being hindered in following his profession as a lawyer, that on his return he wrote trenchantly in defence of episcopacy and condemned the religious-based franchise then operative in the colony of Massachusetts Bay;[36] and poor Sir Edward Dering, who had been gulled or bullied into actually moving the Root and Branch Bill in the summer of 1641, but who tells us that he had always believed in 'primitive episcopacy', whatever he thought he meant by that.[37] This does not make them any less sincere, but it does add interest to pure

[34] 'A Person of Honour' [Roger Palmer, Earl of Castlemaine], *The Catholique Apology with a Reply to the Answer* ... (3rd edn. 1674): for Ireland see esp. pp. 52–65. Only in the P.S., p. 531 *et seq.*, does he get into theology. The earliest part of the text, dated 11 Nov. 1666, entitled '*To All the Royalists that suffered for His Majesty ... The Humble Apologie of the English Catholicks*', comprises only pp. 22–37, and the next earliest section only pp. 1–22, of what had by 1674 become a duodecimo volume of over 600 pages in all.

[35] A. Fletcher, *The Outbreak of the English Civil War* (1981), and J. S. Morrill, 'The Religious Context of the English Civil War', *TRHS*, 5th ser. 34 (1984), 155–78, and 'The Attack on the Church of England in the Long Parliament' in *History, Society and the Churches*, ed. D. Beales and G. Best (Cambridge, 1985), 105–24.

[36] *Note-Book kept by Thomas Lechford, Esquire, Lawyer, in Boston, Massachusetts Bay From June 27, 1638, to July 29, 1641*, ed. E. E. Hale and J. Hammond Trumbull (Archaeologia Americana. Trans. & Colls. of the Am. Antiq. Soc., vii, Cambridge, Mass., 1885); Thomas Lechford, of Clement's Inne in the county of Middlesex, Gent., *Plain Dealing: Or, Newes from New England ... A Short View of New Englands present Government, both Ecclesiasticall and Civil* ... (1642). The best modern account is T. G. Barnes, 'Thomas Lechford and the Earliest Lawyering in Massachusetts, 1638–1641', *Colonial Soc. of Mass.*, 62 (1984), 3–38.

[37] *A Collection of Speeches made by Sir Edward Dering knight and Baronet, in Matter of*

principle as a motive for the line that they took and also raises the question of how many laymen actually took up arms for the King, or supplied him with the sinews of war, of their own volition because of the threat to the Church, except where this merged in their perceptions with a wider threat to the whole established order.

The King's acceptance of the Bill removing the Bishops from the House of Lords and banning the exercise of any civil jurisdiction by ecclesiastical persons (of February 1642) raised special difficulties for royalist propaganda. To defend the King's action as a reluctant but necessary tactical concession, with the strong implication that it would be revoked as soon as better times permitted, which was probably how Charles intended it, was to raise the whole question of his trustworthiness. In his *History* Clarendon simply says that

> those of greatest trust about the King and who were very faithful to his service, though in this particular exceedingly deceived in their judgments, and not sufficiently acquainted with the constitution of the kingdom

sought to persuade him to pass the Bill in order to save the Church. In his *Life* he is more explicit and tells us that it was Sir John Colepepper who advised the King to give way on this but to stand firm on the Militia Bill, whereas Charles himself and Hyde favoured rejection by the royal veto of both measures. What the 1646–7 and the 1669 accounts share in common lies in identifying the Queen's influence as decisive in having persuaded the King to accept the Exclusion Bill, firstly because of her generally low view of the Anglican Church and secondly because she feared that otherwise Parliament would somehow prevent her from leaving the country to seek foreign help while preserving herself from impeachment or attainder.[38]

Clarendon's point about the constitution brings us back to the contrast between the 'high' and 'low', or offensive and defensive versions of the case for the King. If, contrary to the King's Answer to the Nineteen Propositions, the Bishops were one of the three estates of which parliament was composed, then an Act to remove them was ipso facto ultra vires and actually rendered the body sitting at Westminster a non-parliament, a mere assemblage of peers and MPs. Since the Bill preceded the Answer to the Propositions by four months, it seems most unlikely that this point was anticipated on the earlier

---

Religion. Some formerly printed, and divers more now added: All of them revised ... (1642), 2–4, 26–7, 27–35, 71–88, 89–94, 94–6. It is clear from the text that not all the speeches were ever delivered in the House.

[38] Edward Earl of Clarendon, *The History of the Rebellion and Civil Wars in England begun in the year 1641*, ed. W. D. Macray (6 vols. Oxford, 1888), I, 565–8 (Book IV, paras. 297–304); contrast with Clarendon, *Life*, folio edn. 50–2, octavo 98–102.

occasion unless we are to envisage an identical disagreement between Hyde and Colepepper in both February and June.[39] Once again, in so far as it had been passed both by the Lords and by the King under the threat of direct action by the London crowds, the argument that 'tumults' automatically made a parliament unfree, and so not a parliament at all, could again be invoked.

The King's trustworthiness was indeed the crux of the whole issue behind the political debate. If the King could be trusted, then the royalist case was a very strong one in view of all the concessions he had made by the summer of 1641, as a number of royalist publications were to emphasise over the following years. There was then a compelling case for giving him the benefit of the doubt and an opportunity to prove that the reformed system could be made to work; correspondingly those who were demanding further concessions from him as in the Grand Remonstrance, let alone the Nineteen Propositions, could fairly be represented as the innovators, seeking to overturn the traditional order, if not to destroy monarchy as it had ever been known in England. If the King could not be trusted, if the reforms which he had accepted were mere tactical devices to be revoked or reversed as and when they could be, then no amount of further constitutional debate would serve any purpose. The reluctance of many spokesmen on both sides to address this issue directly gives an air of 'shadow-boxing' to much of the debate. Parliament, it should be remembered, claimed to be fighting for the King, in order to liberate him from evil councillors. Only after the capture of his papers and subsequent publication of *The King's Cabinet Opened* in the summer of 1645 do we find explicit attacks on Charles's honesty. As some royalists pointed out, the evil councillors argument led to ridiculous conclusions, that the King was *non compos mentis*, defective or imbecile.[40] Correspondingly, if the King could not be trusted, then Parliament's further demands were amply justified, in order to protect the country and themselves against a ruler who was, to put it bluntly, a liar and a tyrant as well as a would-be absolutist acting in the Catholic interest. And that case could in turn only be met by the high royalist argument for total unqualified non-resistance, or at most for strictly passive resistance being taken to the ultimate stage of martyrdom under even the worst of tyrants. Some royalist writers may be felt to have spoilt

[39] On this compare Corinne C. Weston and Janelle R. Greenberg, *Subjects and Sovereigns. The Grand Controversy over Legal Sovereignty in Stuart England* (Cambridge, 1981) and M. Mendle, *Dangerous Positions. Mixed Government, the Estates of the Realm, and the Making of the Answer to the xix Propositions* (Alabama, 1985).

[40] [D. Digges] *An Answer to a Printed Book Intituled, Observations ...* (Oxford, 1642), 41; [? Mr Doughty of Merton College] *The Kings Cause Rationally, briefly, and plainly debated ...* (1644), 4, 6.

their case by indulging in a kind of intellectual 'over-kill', arguing simultaneously that the King had made many concessions, that he could be trusted, but that resistance was in no circumstances justified. If Charles was a good Protestant and a good constitutional ruler in the sense of knowing and governing by the laws of the land, then why was it necessary to harp on non-resistance?

The purely pragmatic argument against rebellion or revolution, so fashionable in our own time, seems to have been largely absent in the seventeenth century. The nearest we find to the conviction that things have to be almost unbelievably or impossibly bad for us to be sufficiently confident that the remedy will not be worse than the disease, was the well-worn cliché that anarchy was even worse than tyranny. But this was so far from having been a specifically royalist argument during the Civil War and after that we find the Levellers at least purporting to accept it. Pursued further its proponents would be led into debate about definitions: who was a tyrant, what was a state of anarchy? The other familiar royalist platitude, that rebellion never prospered can have had little persuasive power, at least from the stage at which the King had clearly lost the War until the eve of his son's return, say between 1645 and 1659 inclusive. Used as a warning in 1642–3 it may have had more force with some waverers. About the nearest that we can find anyone getting to this position, namely the generic argument against change, is—rather surprisingly—John Taylor the 'Water-Poet', who wrote in 1645:

> the nature of an Englishman is, not to know when things are well, which if we would have knowne, things had not been so bad as they are.[41]

Or maybe this should be seen more as a variant of that other well-worn theme that prosperous times lead to troubles.

The view that the King's difficulties arose from his having conceded too much rather than too little was widely held. Clarendon and Hobbes shared at least that much in common, while lesser Cavalier historians can be found expressing similar views.[42] Charles I himself, and this we can hardly think invented by Gauden or anyone else, was to express much more acute contrition for his assent to Strafford's attainder and execution than for his acceptance of the Bishops'

---

[41] *The Generall Complaint of the most oppressed, distressed commons of England. Complaining to, and Crying out upon the Tyranny of the perpetuall Parliament at Westminster* (n.d. ? 1645), Sig. A2V.

[42] See George Bate, *Elenchus Motuum Nuperorum in Anglia* (Paris, 1649; London, 1661; 1st English translation, 1652), as well as the better known works by Sir Edward Walker, Sir William Dugdale, and Sir Philip Warwick, besides Hobbes's *Behemoth* and Clarendon's *Rebellion*.

Exclusion Bill.[43] The former had involved him in breaking a solemn promise and left him with the Earl's blood on his conscience; however the latter was less excusable in that neither he nor his wife and family were under direct physical duress in February 1642 as they had been in May 1641.

As the War progressed, some of the issues naturally changed, others remained much the same. Predictably enough this is reflected in the propaganda of both sides. Besides the argument about tumults, we find it frequently hammered home how the two Houses had allowed themselves to fall under the control of a small and narrow clique, what many royalist spokesmen were fond of calling 'a' or 'the faction'. An early criticism of Parliament's system of penal taxation, imposed on neutrals as well as on royalists, continues by focusing on the relative poverty of the parliamentarian leaders and their consequent habit of rewarding themselves and their relatives with lucrative offices. They are contrasted with the wealthy (and impeccably Protestant) peers and commoners to be found on the King's side who, the author cannot believe, would 'induce arbitrary government'.[44] This may be compared with *A Complaint to the House of Commons*, also dated 1642 but probably early 1643 by our reckoning, which is a densely packed attack on Parliament's excesses, showing a close knowledge of events inside the two Houses: it is unusual in not engaging with Henry Parker or any other pro-parliamentarian spokesman; the author instead concentrates on all that the leaders of the two Houses have done wrong. Priority is given to political over religious aspects; it is very much the work of a constitutional royalist, and the legalistic tone makes it possible that it emanated from someone in Hyde's own circle.[45] By 1644 we find Cromwell being singled out for attack, but for the profanation and desecration of churches rather than for political or religious extremism. The famous Oliverian nose also became a target of propaganda in the same year, as when the poet Cleveland wrote

He should be a Bird of prey too, by his bloody Beake: his Nose is able to try a young Eagle, whether she be lawfully begotten. But all is not Gold that glisters: . . .[46]

[43] *Eikon Basilike. The Portraiture of His Sacred Majestie in His Solitudes and Suffering* (1649), ed. P. A. Knachel (Ithaca, N.Y., 1966), 41–2, 101, 186 on the bishops, and 7–9 on Strafford.
[44] T.R., *A Honest Letter to a Doubtfull Friend*, addressed to his friend and kinsman, Sir H.W., at Westminster, dated 28 Dec. 1642.
[45] The author is well informed about happenings inside Parliament, and gives political considerations priority over religious.
[46] Francis Quarles, *The Loyall Convert* (1644) describes him as 'that profest Defacer of Churches ... and Rifler of Monuments of the Dead ...'; this is echoed in *Mercurius Aulicus* for 16 September 1644; [John Cleaveland] *The Character of a London Diurnall*

The Solemn League and Covenant and the entry of the Scots into the War on Parliament's side must have been recognised by the more realistic of the King's supporters as a heavy, perhaps fatal, setback to his cause. But it provided preachers and pamphleteers with a veritable field day on which to display their invective and polemical talents. Anti-Scottish prejudice, the two-faced wording of the document itself, the now overt designs of the Presbyterian party were all brought into play.[47] Some of the more effective statements of the Anglican position were made too late to influence the outcome of the war. Such was Isaac Basire's *Deo et Ecclesiae Sacrum: Sacrilege arraigned*, dedicated to the King on Ascension Day 1646, ten days after he had fled from Oxford. It contains a trenchant definition of the essentially 'Catholic' nature of the Anglican Church. Basire's main purpose is to explain why the King cannot agree to the secularisation of church property. If anyone still believed that by sacrificing episcopal, or even capitular lands, he would satisfy the Presbyterian party, they were sadly out of touch.[48] Presumably there were fears in some circles that Charles might give way over church lands as he had over bishops' votes in the mistaken belief that he could thereby salvage episcopacy itself. The Revd Jasper Mayne's *Ochlo-maxia*, as its title suggests concerned with the danger of popular anarchy, appeared fittingly in the summer of 1647. The author draws an interesting distinction between the illegitimacy of any offensive religious war, even for example against a country inhabited by virtuous atheists, and a defensive war for religion, which he felt might apply to Fairfax's army resisting the Presbyterians; yet against a legitimate prince only passive resistance was ever justified.[49]

I have already suggested that the most eminent figures, measured by their moral and intellectual distinction, do not always make the most effective propagandists. The 'ever memorable' John Hales' tract '*Of Scisme*' was so lame a piece of pro-Anglican apologetic that Izaack

(1644), 5–6. As early as 1643 he had been quoted in *Sober Sadnes*, 35, to illustrate what the sub-title calls *The Proceedings, Pretensions, and Designes of a prevailing party in both Houses of Parliament*; in 1644 he was also included in some execrable verse on various parliamentarian leaders both living and recently dead: [? Hausted] *Ad Populum: Or, A Lecture to the People*.

[47] See John Bramhall, Bishop of Derry, *A Sermon Preached in Yorke Minster ... January 28, 1643* (York, 1643/4); *England and Scotland, Or, The Proceedings of the Parliament of England, The Confession of the Church of Scotland ...* (Oxford, 1644); [Dr Gerard Langbaine] *The Anti-Confederacy, Or, A Discovery of the iniquity and hypocrisie of the Solemne League and Covenant, as Concerne the Law: Proving it to be destructive of the Lawes of England both ancient and moderne* (Oxford, 1644); *The Anti-Confederacie: Or, An Extract of certaine Quaeres ...* (Oxford, 1644).

[48] (Oxford, 1646), esp. p. 16.

[49] *Or, The Peoples War* (Oxford, 1647). It is interesting that such a work could still be published in Oxford a year after the surrender of the city.

Walton in his uncompleted fragment of biography explains that Hales was conned into publishing it by none other than Lord Saye and Sele.[50] William Chillingworth, although he virtually died a martyr for the Anglican Church, was remarkably ineffective as an anti-Puritan spokesman. Henry Hammond's fifth casuistical *Tract*, 'Of Resisting the lawfull Magistrate under colour of Religion', is by any standards over-elaborate and academic, and seems at times as if the author were conducting an argument with himself, or at most a private debate with Stephen Marshall and one or two other individual Puritan divines.[51] Robert Sanderson, the future Bishop of Lincoln, who was together with Hammond crucial in maintaining the Anglican communion under Puritan domination, was likewise too much of a pastoral and theological casuist. Indeed his letter of 10 April 1649 to 'N.N.' would have been extremely damaging to the royalist-epis-copalian cause if it had been published at any time before the Res-toration. Presented as a rebuttal of the Scottish presbyterian Robert Baillie's *Dissuasive from Error*, the letter argues that one can with more logic and consistency be an Independent or Brownist, even an Anabaptist, than a Presbyterian. This is like suggesting today that someone might as well or better be Fascist as Tory, pari passu as well be Communist as Labour: a most impolitic line of argument, to say the least. Despite his profession to live and die as an 'honest, downright, sober English Protestant', Sanderson could not refrain from telling his unknown correspondent

> I find no security at all, either in Popish or Puritanical principles. Yet of the two, Popery hath this advantage, that it keeps the Proselyte, though with insufferable tyranny, yet confined within some limits and bounds, like water shut up within the banks of a muddy unsavoury lake. Whereas this wild thing, for want of a more proper name commonly called Puritanism, like a sea-breach, runs itself into a thousand channels, and knows not where to stop.

And later in the 1650s he seems to have been as much concerned to criticise the unfortunate Jeremy Taylor as to express a clear, simple defence of episcopalian Anglicanism. Moreover, his own definition of the Protestant position, in the letter already quoted, leaves unan-swered the vital questions who is to interpret the word of God, who

[50] S. R. Gardiner (ed.), 'Collections by Isack [sic] Walton for his Life of John Hales of Eton', *EHR*, ii (1887), 751.

[51] Henry Hammond, *Tracts* (Oxford, 1645), no. 5 (1st published Oxford, 1644); also available in *The Workes of the Reverend and Learned Henry Hammond D.D.* .... (4 vols. folio, 1659–84), i, 53–70.

is to define essentials as opposed to accidentals, and who is to identify the proper civil and ecclesiastical governors.[52]

It may be thought that I should have said something more about Anglican moral theology, to balance my discussion of Puritan morality last year. The reasons for my not doing so are three: firstly, my own lack of the necessary qualifications, intellectual let alone ethical, to assess the great casuists and theologians of the time: second, that whatever else may be said about them, this aspect of their writings seems to have little or no direct bearing on their royalism; third, and closely related to this, the large overlap in substance with similar writings by Puritan moralists which only strengthens my view—already expressed—that Puritanism was a temperament more than it was a doctrine. Casuists and preceptors of the two parties are for the most part saying the same things, but with differences of tone and mood.

Lesser men than such as these, with coarser, more conventional minds could sometimes do the job better. Crude anti-Puritanism, the mirror image of anti-Cavalierism, can be found in Sergeant-Major Kirle's *Copy of a Letter to a friend in Windsor*, celebrating his own change of sides. He attacks what he calls the 'pseudo-clergy'

> who while they are severe (and therein they do well) against drunkennesse and adultery, and they make robbery, rebellion, sacriledge and murder become vertues, because they are in order to effect their designe ...[53]

Among the more temperate expressions of the opposite view, from the other side, is a work entitled *The Zealous Magistrate*, suitably dedicated to Arthur Upton and Francis Rouse MP. The author exhorts the younger gentry who are born of religious (i.e Godly) families

> To give over Ben and Shakespeare and fall upon Moses and the Prophets, to be better read in St. Peter than in Sir Philip, and not to read Msr. Balzac's Letters with more delight than they do St. Pauls Epistles.[54]

Once more it would be grotesque to take these stereotypes at their face value; none the less they can tell us something about contemporary attitudes.

---

[52] *The Works of Robert Sanderson, D.D., Sometime Bishop of Lincoln, now first collected by William Jacobson, D.D.* (6 vols. Oxford, 1854), vi, Appendix v, 368–71; see also nos. xi and xiii, 381–3, 386–9. Sanderson at first tried to avoid getting involved in the dispute with Taylor, pretending not to know what Socinianism was about. His *Lectures on Conscience and Human Law*, ed. C. Wordsworth (Lincoln, London, Oxford, Cambridge, 1877) are more to the point, especially nos. 5–10, but they were delivered as a lecture course in Latin and were not published in English until the 18th century.

[53] (n.d. [1642]), signed R.K.

[54] John Trescot, *The Zealous Magistrate* ... (Oxford [sic], 1642), Sig. C2 [= p. 11].

As a specimen of episcopalian-royalist propaganda, Matthew Griffith's sermon, *A Patheticall Perswasion to pray for Publick Peace*, is unremarkable. If, however, it was actually delivered in St Paul's cathedral, as dated on the 2 October 1642, this must have taken considerable moral and physical courage, even though the author's overt attacks are on Anabaptists, 'phanatick Sectaries', and Papists especially the Irish Rebels, rather than on mainstream Puritans. This is a very early example of Anglican-Cavalier success in annexing the term 'fanatic' as a label for their more radical opponents, a practice which was to be systematised and carried to absurd excess after 1660. It is not surprising to learn that Griffith was shortly to be sequestered from his London parish living, nor that he was later to be captured in arms at the fall of Basing House near Winchester in 1645.[55]

Although so famous, and moderate an Anglican as 'Tom' Fuller was for a time a chaplain with Hopton's army in the south-west, most of the surviving royalist sermons are from formal occasions in Oxford. As an author, Fuller was so far from being a hard-line polemicist that he was later to be savagely criticised by that truly hard-line, 'high' royalist, Dr Peter Heylyn.[56] A more obscure figure, the Revd Edward Symmons provides a notable exception to what has just been said. His '*Militarie Sermon*', preached at Shrewsbury in May 1644 to Rupert's army before they went on to the North, contains the famous definition, which although it has been quoted before, by Rupert's biographer in the nineteenth century and by Professor Hardacre in our own time, not only will bear but positively demands repetition here today:

A complete cavalier is a child of honour ... because of a more Loyall Heart ... He is the only reserve of English gentility and ancient valour, and hath rather chosen to bury himself in the tomb of honour than to see the nobility of his nation vassalaged.[57]

---

[55] M. Griffith, Rector of St Mary Magdalens, near Old Fish Street, London, *A Patheticall Perswasion* ... (1642), especially 24, 28; see also *DNB*, and Matthews, *Walker Revised*, 49.

[56] Peter Heylin, *Examen Historicum*: ... (1659), Part I, *Containing Necessary Animadversions on the Church-History of Britain. And the History of Cambridge. Publisht by Thomas Fuller For Vindication of the Truth, the Church and the injured Clergy*, parts of which read like a 17th-century anticipation of a deliberately unfair book review in a 19th- or 20th-century literary journal. Heylin's own interpretation can be seen to best advantage in his *Observations on the Historie of the Reigne of King Charles: Published by H.L. Esq.* [= Hamon L'Estrange] ... (1656), rather than in his *Short View of the Life and Reign of King Charles* ... (1658).

[57] Edward Symmons, Chaplain to the Lifeguard of the Prince of Wales, *A Militarie Sermon* ... (Oxford, 1644), esp. 3, 12–13, 16, 18–19, 25, 28–9, 32. His other principal publication was the re-issue in 1642 of four sermons from the years 1632–41, when he was a minister in Essex. For the passage quoted, see B. E. G. Warburton, *Memoirs of*

This might fairly be added as a postscript to Dr Mervyn James's highly original *Past and Present* supplement on the Concept of Honour of a few years ago, and to another slightly earlier article.[58] Symmons spells out the equation of rebellion against the King with that against God; he calls for the severest punishment of the guilty, but warns his listeners against atrocities and the wreaking of private vengeance; in addition he implies that all is far from well with the conduct of the King's soldiers, and he appeals to both the civil and military authorities to rectify this. Warburton and Hardacre were surely correct to single out this memorable sermon. It seems to come as near to what we might call grass-roots Anglican-Cavalierism as anything we can find.[59] I must by the way confess to a certain scepticism about measuring the religiosity of parishes by the quantity of communion wine consumed. Anyone who served on the Lower Deck of the Royal Navy before the abolition of the rum ration will appreciate the fine distinction between 'sippers' and 'gulpers'. May there not have been a primitive belief among some of the unlettered in bygone times that the bigger the swallow, the more efficacious the sacrament?

Something more needs to be said as to how far either the tone or content of royalist propaganda was affected by the course of the war. In 1642 and into the earlier part of the next year, the primary concern of polemicists was to show why the rebels were in the wrong and to win waverers or neutrals over to the King's side. From the summer of 1643 until the summer of 1644, many royalists probably believed that they were winning the war. From Marston Moor to Naseby they were uncertain to say the least but still hopeful. From June 1645 on, it was increasingly difficult to keep up the pretence that they were other than on the losing side. And from 1646–7 until the eve of the King's trial and execution it was a matter of attempting to salvage by negotiation, or persuasion, or the exploitation of the differences among their opponents, what had been lost in battle. This reaches its most extreme form after the institution of the Commonwealth with the often bitter debate among the new King's advisers whether to go for an Irish or a Scottish alliance as a springboard for the recovery of England, and—as in Hyde's famous paper submitted to the Queen

Prince Rupert and the Cavaliers ... (3 vols. 1849), I, 414; P. H. Hardacre, *The Royalists during the Puritan Revolution* (The Hague, 1956), p. 3, n. 13.

[58] Mervyn James, *English Politics and the Concept of Honour 1485–1642* (Past & Present Supplement, no. 3, 1978); Jerrilyn Greene Marston, 'Gentry Honour and Royalism in Early Stuart England', *Jnl. of British Studies*, xiii (1973–4), 21–43, where another work by Symmons is quoted but not this one (p. 37, n. 58).

[59] On popular royalism in the south-western counties (excluding Cornwall) see now David Underdown, *Revel, Riot and Rebellion: Popular Politics and Culture in England 1603–1660* (Oxford, 1985), and for popular Anglicanism J. S. Morrill, 'The Church in England, 1642–9', in Morrill (ed.), *Reactions of the English Civil War 1642–1649* (1982).

Mother—whether it would be better to make a tactical alliance with the Presbyterians or with the Levellers, the future Lord Chancellor on opportunist grounds preferring the latter.[60] From the King's escape after Worcester until the very eve of the Restoration the main debate was between those who favoured direct action—insurrection, invasion or whatever, and those like Hyde who believed in 'waiting on events', i.e. until their enemies tore each other apart and the King's was invited back as the only solution to a total political impasse. As it turned out, the latter policy was triumphantly successful. And on the determinist view this could not have been otherwise. Historians, on the other hand, who believe in the importance of contingent circumstance will naturally reserve judgment. Of course for those who see Divine Providence as the first cause of all things, apparently random happenings and chances of personality, like the hopeless inadequacy of Richard Cromwell, could be and were perceived as the way in which God allowed the English to come back to their senses after what Clarendon was to call 'the prosperous wickedness' of the intervening times.

Most historians would agree that considered as propaganda for the royalist cause, the *Eikon Basilike*, or 'the King's Book' should have pride of place, even though it was produced after Charles I's defeat and execution. No matter how much of it was written in his own words, how much by Gauden, Duppa, or whoever else, judged by the number of imprints alone its popularity is beyond dispute. If one attempts to apply any kind of intellectual or historical analysis, its substance is by turns feeble and disingenuous, with the King portraying himself as an injured innocent from first to last. Yet in helping to create and propagate the image of King Charles the Martyr, as a martyr that is alike for the law and liberties of the land and for the Protestant religion as by law established since 1559, the *Eikon* was a superb success. But I submit that it could not have had the impact that it did without the regicide; indeed without that, could it have come into existence at all? Charles deposed and then either banished abroad or securely imprisoned at home would have been a continuing problem no doubt, perhaps even a menace, but could never have served the cause of monarchy with such powerful effect as he did decapitated.

Is it possible to be more systematic? I am aware that episodic history, *histoire événementielle* to dignify it as our French contemporaries do, can all too easily degenerate into anecdotal history.[61] The categ-

[60] *The Nicholas Papers. Correspondence of Sir Edward Nicholas, Secretary of State*, vol. I, *1641–1652* (Camden Soc., new ser. 40, 1886), 138–47.
[61] I am grateful to Professor Gwyn A. Williams for a timely reminder of this when we were colleagues in the 1960s.

ories which I would like to put forward for your consideration hardly merit the designation of a typology. They are simply meant as different ways of thinking about royalists; and, up to a point, so long as we do not make these labels of convenience into rigid entities, of classifying them; each is more of an axis or spectrum than a strict antithesis or dichotomy.

1. First the religious division into Roman Catholic and Protestant, the former being in turn sub-divided between Jesuit and secular (or in whatever other way best expresses the undoubted distinctions which existed among them); the latter between Arminian and Calvinist, or in later terminology 'high' and 'low' church, with room having to be left (as on the parliamentarian side) for a few irreligious materialists. As we have already seen, the Catholics were an embarrassment to the royalists, glad as they were of them on the field of battle. The King himself was to offer an explanation of their presence on his side, clearly perceiving that there was a question to be answered.[62] The *Iniunctions concerning the Garrison of Oxford, in Order to Religion*, issued in 1645, go into great detail about Sunday services, regimental chaplains, etc., even requiring that there should be a special chaplain to instruct the King's Welsh soldiers in their own language. But nothing at all is said about Catholic officers or other ranks.[63] Presumably they were tacitly excused attendance; there must have been Catholic priests available to celebrate mass privately in Oxford and other major royalist centres.

2. Some historians have been tempted to classify the King's advisers and supporters according to their political preferences and objectives, into constitutionalists and absolutists. At the top this does seem to help explain some of the tensions between Hyde on the one hand, and Digby and some of the Queen's circle on the other. Some such distinction is also visible, as I have indicated, among the preachers and pamphleteers. However, in the last resort political circumstances, and above all the nature and completeness of a hypothetical royalist victory, would determine the balance of absolute and constitutional monarchy more than rivalries between the King's advisers, or differences of emphasis among those preaching and writing in support of the royal cause. In confirmation of this may be adduced the fact that Charles II came nearer to being an absolute ruler in the last phase of his reign (1681–5) than in the immediate post-Restoration years.

3. Closely linked to this, and of undoubted consequence within the King's counsels at Oxford, was the distinction and sometimes disagreement between soldiers and civilians. Again it is easy to point out a well-defined demarcation, sometimes also involving antipathy, even animosity, between the men of the sword—Rupert, Wilmot,

[62] *Eikon Basilike*, ed. Knachel, 88–9.
[63] *Iniunctions* ... (Oxford, 1645. 5 pp.).

Astley, Goring—and those of the pen—Hyde and Nicholas. There turn out to be as many exceptions as cases conforming to any such rule. Hyde's real rivals for influence over the King were surely (at different times) Digby and the Queen, rather than Rupert, let along Goring, however much he may have resented the former and dis-approved of and disliked the latter, while he invariably wrote later with respect and even affection of another military commander, Ralph Lord Hopton. Moreover this leaves us with the problem of how to classify some of the great nobles who were regional commanders-in-chief but not professional soldiers—Hertford and Newcastle.

4. More promising is the contrast, recently illuminated with effect-ive examples by Dr Ronald Hutton, between established members of the aristocracy or upper gentry and self-made men for whom the war provided a crucial means of upward social mobility. These *novi homines* would include younger sons of gentry families as well as some from below that social level.[64] These is more than a hint at times in his discussion that this can be correlated with the constitutionalist-absolutist antithesis. It is certainly true that on the King's as on Parliament's side, successful military careers brought rapid social advancement to a number of mostly youngish men, though by no means all (perhaps not even a majority) were younger sons. I am not however persuaded that, even in that event of a royalist victory, this would have been of comparable significance to the prominence of lesser gentry and non-gentry in places of power from 1647 to 1660. On the king's side such men would have been absorbed into the traditional upper class, rather than forming a new and partially different ruling elite as they did under the republic.

5. These ways of classifying different sorts of royalists may be said to overlap with another dichotomy which is of course far from being peculiar to the years of the Civil War and Interregnum. Indeed it was arguably of less consequence then than either before 1640 or after 1660. There is a meaningful sense in which seventeenth-century land-owners, lawyers, merchants, even physicians and other professional men can be described as belonging to the Court or to the Country. Among articulate royalists, in the sense of those who have left us any record of their views and feelings during these years, William Blundell of Crosby, Lancs., a Catholic and John Oglander of Nunwell, Isle of

[64] R. Hutton, 'The Structure of the Royalist Party, 1642–6' *Histl. Jnl.*, 24 (1981), and subsequent articles by P. R. Newman, 'The Royalist Officer Corps, 1642–60', *ibid.*, 26 (1983), by J. Daly, 'The implications of Royalist politics, 1642–6', *ibid.*, 27 (1984), and—since this paper was written—P. R. Newman,' The Royalist Party in arms: the Peerage and Army Command 1642–1646', ch. 5 in C. Jones, M. Newitt and S. Roberts (eds.), *Politics and People in Revolutionary England Essays in honour of Ivan Roots* (Oxford, 1986).

Wight, a Protestant, together with Sir Henry Slingsby, whom I have already cited, may fairly be regarded as spokesmen of the country; while not only Hyde and Nicholas but such secondary figures as John Ashburnham, Sir John Berkeley, Sir Christopher Hatton and Henry Jermyn were essentially men whose careers lay within the Court, in the wider sense of embracing central government as well as the royal household. The second Lord Aston of Tixall, Staffs, whose father had been Ambassador in Madrid, may be cited as an instance of the transposition from Court to Country; his father's conversion to Rome appears to have disqualified Aston from command of a regiment, even of a company, in 1642–3, although he fought for the King as a volunteer.[65] Incidentally, though it should be taken more as an indication of opinion than as objective fact, Blundell records being told by Lord Brandon of Macclesfield, in front of several other witnesses, in 1663, that

> the late King had 900 servants, whereof no more than twenty-seven engaged with him in the late war. He said there were very few lawyers that adhered to the King, and spoke ill as to the same thing of the nobility in general that were made before the war. He said at the same time, that the King's cause was truly and constantly maintained by the English gentry.[66]

It is tempting to suggest that the Cavalier ladies who have left us memoirs of themselves or of their husbands can be classified in some similar way. They certainly merit consideration in their own right. The recent surveys of female diarists and authors by Drs Mendelson and Crawford[67] convey the same impression of Puritan and later Quaker preponderance, numerically speaking, as with their male contemporaries. None the less some of the same nuances are discernible as we have seen with other autobiographers in the works of Margaret Duchess of Newcastle,[68] Lady Ann Fanshawe, Lady Anne Halkett whose story has almost picaresque touches,[69] Mrs Alice Thornton, and the less well-known Lady Anne Harcourt later Waller.[70] Alice

[65] *Tixall Letters . . .*, ed. A. Clifford (2 vols. 1815), ii, 115–22.
[66] *Crosby Records: A Cavalier's Note Book Being Notes, Anecdotes and Observations of William Blundell of Crosby, Lancs, Esquire . . .*, ed. T. Ellison Gibson (1880), 264. Charles Gerrard, later 1st Earl of Macclesfield, was born *c.* 1618, and so can be counted a contemporary witness.
[67] Mary Prior (ed.), *Women in English Society 1500–1800* (1985), chs. 6 and 7 and Appendices.
[68] Margaret Duchess of Newcastle, *The Life of William Cavendish Duke of Newcastle . . .*, ed. C. H. Firth (2nd edn n.d. [*c.* 1900]).
[69] *The Memoirs of Anne, Lady Halkett and Ann, Lady Fanshawe*, ed. J. Loftis (Oxford, 1979).
[70] E. W. Harcourt, *The Harcourt Papers*, i (privately, Oxford, n.d.), 169–99.

Wandesford, later Thornton, might almost be bracketed with Mary Rich, *née* Boyle, later Countess of Warwick, as the daughter of someone highly placed in the pre-Civil War regime who married into a Puritan family, except that from all the evidence she provides for us Alice Wandesford was already fervently religious, more so than her husband whom she persuaded to admit his doubts about the policies of his own side on agreeing to marry him, virtually as a condition of their becoming formally engaged.[71] Dorothy Osborne, later Temple, came from a long-established 'upper middle' Exchequer family of committed royalists and married into a Puritan one whose Irish background was more like that of the Boyles than the Wandesfords.[72] Among all of these, Anne Murray, later Halkett, is much the liveliest, as might be expected of one whose companion was the notorious double-agent Colonel Joseph Bampfield, whom she assisted in effecting James Duke of York's escape from St James Palace and then out of the country. Whether, if the parliamentarians had kept James in their power, they would have declared both Charles I and his eldest son deposed and have tried to flatter or pressurize his second son into accepting the Crown can only be speculation. The implications of James II succeeding to the throne in 1648 or 1649 are indeed 'mind-boggling'! Bampfield repeatedly deceived Anne Murray, at first concealing his wife's existence, then pretending that she was dead; he went on with this so long, and as we must suppose so persuasively, that in despair she eventually made out that she was married to Halkett when she had not yet even agreed to marry him.[73]

6. Some of the remaining possible ways of trying to distinguish between different royalists are what we may call generic or functional. We might classify them generationally, by age-groups. There does appear to be a heavy concentration of prominent figures born between 1600 and 1613, that is who were aged from 42 to 29 at the outbreak of war.[74] Here the royal nephews, still in their early twenties, stand out at one extreme;[75] Patrick Ruthven, Earl of Brentford and Forth, Sir Robert Heath, Sir Jacob Astley, and the Earl of Bristol at the other, as having been born before the 1580s and thus being well into their sixties by 1642. It has sometimes been suggested that younger sons had less to lose and so were readier to commit themselves, on

---

[71] *Autobiography of Mrs Alice Thornton*, 78–9, note.

[72] *Letters from Dorothy Osborne to Sir William Temple 1652–1654*, ed. G. C. Moore Smith (Oxford, 1928).

[73] *Memoirs, passim*, esp. p. 82.

[74] Sir John, later 1st Lord Colepepper born 1600; Henry Jermyn 1600s; Sir Christopher Hatton 1605; the 4th Earl of Southampton 1607; George Goring junior 1608; Edward Hyde 1609; Arthur Lord Capel *c*. 1610; Lord Falkland *c*. 1610; George Lord Digby, later 2nd Earl of Bristol, 1612.

[75] Rupert born 1619; Maurice 1620.

both sides, in the Civil War, while heads of families or heirs apparent were more likely to try to remain neutral or to opt out. Some of those quoted at the beginning of this paper do appear to provide a little evidence for the latter part of this proposition. But I must leave to other researchers the questions of whether anything systematic can be established as to either age or place in the family in determining the extent or the nature of men's royalism. In so far as 'interest' was the decisive motive, then by definition younger sons did have proportionately more to gain and less to lose; whether it followed that more of them were in arms or took a more extreme, high line as preachers and writers, is a very different matter, and one on which I can only return a verdict of non-proven.

7. Then there is the geographical classification, according to where individuals had their main residences and estates, in relation to the areas held by the forces of the King or those of Parliament or disputed between them. For someone to go against the prevailing trend of his region or district would seem to argue a greater measure of commitment to whichever side he took. Correspondingly, some very tepid loyalties or reluctant takings of sides can perhaps best be explained by a desire not so to stand out but to go with the trend. But in neither case does this work both ways round. It would be absurd to rule out the existence of ardent royalists who came from predominantly royalist areas, nor the possibility of lukewarm or wavering ones hailing from parliamentarian or disputed territory. Moreover, as has been pointed out before, there is a partially 'circular' character to this whole argument; for in many instances it was only the prior existence of individuals with strong commitments which gave a predominant character to a district one way or the other.

8. Finally there is a very crude distinction among royalists (as of course among neutrals and parliamentarians) by social standing, between those of noble and gentle and those of plebeian origin. How far this might be found to correspond with some of the differences of attitude which have been my main concern here must remain unknown, due to the paucity of first-hand, contemporary evidence about those at the lower social levels. This is not to deny the existence of popular royalism, only to express some scepticism about it as a subject for historical research.

9. So perhaps we are after all forced back on to temperamental differences, which I have so far eschewed today. The most helpful contrast here may be between intellectual rationalisers and those whose actions were chiefly determined by instinct and emotion. Sir Edmund Verney would be an excellent case of someone whose instinctive loyalty overcame his intellectual disapproval of royal and episcopal policies. Not that the Revd Edward Symmons's 'complete

Cavalier' was meant to be, or should be thought of as having been, a brainless or even an unthinking oaf. Falkland's heroic, although futile death in battle, or that of Hobbes's friend Sidney Godolphin, or among the survivors the career of Sir Charles Cavendish, mathematician and lieutenant-general of horse in the Yorkshire army, or indeed the case of Montrose should be sufficient reminders to the contrary.

In conclusion, many strong arguments were deployed on the King's behalf from 1641–2 on. For all that, the strength and fighting spirit of his supporters may well have owed more to the concepts of honour and loyalty than to the force or validity of these arguments.

RECONQUEST AND CRUSADE IN SPAIN
c. 1050–1150
By R. A. Fletcher

READ 31 JANUARY 1986

IN THE summer of 1898 the entire Spanish fleet was destroyed in two successive engagements with the navy of the United States: the most comprehensive, catastrophic and humiliating naval defeats of modern history. Not only did these reverses shear Spain of the last shreds of transatlantic empire: they also inflicted a severe psychological blow to the Spanish nation at large. Already a stranger to most of the invigorating developments in economic, cultural and political life which had transformed western Europe in the course of the nineteenth century, Spain found that her backwardness and feebleness had now been devastatingly exposed to the gaze of the world. Spain had become a laughing-stock among the nations. What had gone wrong? The 'Generation of '98' was the name given to the group of intellectuals and public men who set themselves to ponder this question. They conceived of their task in large terms. It was not just a matter of diagnosing and treating present and local sickness—to employ the medical imagery of which they were so fond—but of taking account of the whole organism which was so visibly ailing; and this involved examining its early growth. An historical dimension was built into their deliberations from the outset. It is for this reason that 1898 is a significant date for the historian of medieval Spain.

Twentieth-century debate on the nature of the Spanish past and the shape of the Spanish identity which that past delineated was thus begun in a mood of anguish and heart-searching. It continued against a background of mounting social and political turmoil culminating in civil war. These conditions were not conducive to dispassionate scholarship. Furthermore, Spanish academic discussion was then—and in some quarters still is—conducted in a rhetorical tradition which is foreign to our own habits of scholarly discourse. We should be prepared for the results of this intellectual activity to look a little odd. Debate is hardly the appropriate term for what occurred during the ensuing period of general Franco's regime. At home, the victors permitted only that version of the Spanish past to be disseminated of which they approved. Scattered in exile abroad the defeated were able to work in a less constricting atmosphere, but their labours tended

31

to suffer from the perennial difficulties which exiles encounter when contemplating the history of their native country.[1]

It is this background which renders intelligible that interpretation of Spain's medieval history which has proved the most acceptable, not just in official or intellectual circles, but much more widely in the peninsular social community. Briefly summarised, it runs along these lines. The overrunning of nearly all the Iberian peninsula in the early eighth century by the forces of Islam was owing in large part to the decadence of the Visigothic regime which was overthrown. It was, in a sense, a punishment visited upon Spain for her shortcomings thus to be trampled upon by alien, non-Christian enemies. Yet even out of monstrous evil good can come. Spain suffered for Christendom. She saved western Europe from being engulfed beneath a tidal wave from Africa and the Orient.[2] Purged by this ordeal, the Christian refugees in the north were able to undertake the task destined for them—'destiny' being another much-favoured concept—of reconquering the land of Spain from the Moors.

At this point let Ramón Menéndez Pidal (1869–1968) take up the story—an exceptionally long-lived member of the generation of '98, an acute scholar and felicitous stylist, and a medievalist who achieved in his own country a singular and well-merited degree of public renown. I quote from his celebrated essay on Spanish history published in 1947:

The pure unfettered religious spirit which had been preserved in the north gave impetus and national aims to the Reconquest. Without its strength of purpose Spain would have given up in despair all resistance and would have become denationalized. In the end it would have become Islamized as did all the other provinces of the Roman Empire in the east and south of the Mediterranean. In the period from the eighth to the tenth centuries Islam appeared so immensely superior in power and culture to the West that it was amazing that Spain did not succumb as did Syria and Egypt when they were Arabized, in spite of their more advanced Hellenistic culture; and as did Libya, Africa and Mauritania, likewise Arabized. What gave Spain her exceptional strength of collective resistance and enabled her to last through three long centuries of great peril was her policy of fusing into one ideal the recovery of the Gothic states for the fatherland and the redemption of the en-

[1] P. E. Russell, 'The Nessus-shirt of Spanish history', *Bulletin of Hispanic Studies*, xxxvi (1959), 219–25, is an acute critique of the historical writing thrown up in the wake of 1898; A. MacKay, 'The Hispanic-*Converso* predicament', *TRHS*, Fifth series, xxxv (1985), 159–79, contains a perceptive discussion (at pp. 171–3) of the difficulties experienced by Spanish historians during the Franco era.
[2] It is a pity that Spain is neglected in E. W. Said, *Orientalism* (1978).

slaved churches for the glory of Christianity. This fusion of ideals was solemnly declared as a national aim in the *Epitome Ovetense* of the ninth century ... The proposal to recover all the soil of the fatherland, which never ceased to appeal to the mass of the people, was felt to have been accomplished in the thirteenth century, and both the people and the kings considered the great work terminated, and were convinced that it had been the united enterprise of all Spain.[3]

Spain's medieval past, then, is a tale of suffering and endurance, followed by the epic triumph of a glorious, national, crusading reconquest. This is the Ariadne's thread which will guide the explorer through the labyrinthine complexities of her history between the ninth and the thirteenth centuries.

Of course, such a vision or myth of Spain's medieval achievement was not expressed for the first time by Menéndez Pidal. In one form or another it has been current since the thirteenth century itself. I cite him because his expression of the vision was authoritative, passionate and influential: also—and I trust not mischievously—in the hope of indicating something of the manner in which Spanish historiographical concerns differ from ours. The essay from which I quoted was composed as an introduction to the first volume of the *Historia de España* of which Menéndez Pidal was the founding editor. Would not an English reader of today be a little disconcerted if on first looking into Collingwood and Myres he found himself confronted by an essay in that vein by the late Sir George Clark?

We are faced, thus, by a long-cherished, movingly-articulated interpretation of Spain's medieval past. Over the last twenty years or so it has come to seem steadily less satisfying to ever larger circles of scholars within Spain and without. It is to give some account of why this should be so that I am here today. What I have to say will not, I fancy, be of any interest to scholars who are specialists in Spanish medieval history, for they will be familiar with it already.[4] It is addressed rather to other medievalists among whom the interpretation which I call in question still retains some potency.[5]

The notion that from an early date the Christian rulers of the Asturian kingdom were committed to an ideology of reconquest rests

<hr />

[3] R. Menéndez Pidal, *The Spaniards in their history*, translated with a prefatory essay on the author's work by Walter Starkie (1950), 143–4, 188.

[4] My indebtedness to these scholars will sufficiently appear in later footnotes, but I should like to take this opportunity of drawing attention to the particularly stimulating essay of P. A. Linehan, 'Religion, nationalism and national identity in medieval Spain and Portugal', *Studies in Church History*, xviii, ed. S. Mews (Oxford, 1982), 161–99, reprinted in P. A. Linehan, *Spanish Church and Society 1150–1300* (1983).

[5] Here is a small but telling example. In the index to E. Siberry's *Criticism of Crusading 1095–1274* (Oxford, 1985) there is an entry (p. 256) reading 'Spain, crusades, *see Reconquista.*'

principally upon a passage in the so-called *Crónica Albeldense*, composed in about 881 quite probably at the instance of king Alfonso III.

> They [the Saracens] take the kingdom of the Goths, which until today they stubbornly possess in part; and against them the Christians do battle day and night, and constantly strive; until the divine fore-shadowing orders them to be cruelly expelled from here. Amen.[6]

This chronicle is one of a cluster of texts produced at the royal court of Oviedo towards the end of the ninth century, designed to celebrate the great days of the Visigothic kings of the past and to usher in the restoration of Gothic order through the victories of Alfonso III. It has frequently been asserted, as for example by Menéndez Pidal, that this programme of reconquest once enunciated remained the dominant concern of Spanish rulers, especially those of the successor-states to the Asturian kingdom in León and Castile, until the process was complete.[7] This view cannot be accepted. These aspirations, prophecies and prayers belong to a precise political context in the reign of Alfonso III. Were they of interest subsequently? Surviving manuscripts show that they were being copied, sometimes with adjustments, a century later.[8] In certain places, at any rate, they were still seen as having relevance in the late tenth century. Later on, in the period which is my main concern, this was apparently not the case. No manuscripts of these texts have come down to us from the period between about 1000 and about 1140.[9] To rest an argument on negative evidence is always hazardous. However, I would suggest that this hiatus is noteworthy. Such as it is, the evidence—or lack of it—suggests that Spaniards of the eleventh and early twelfth centuries were not interested in a programme of reconquest.

If we cannot use these early texts to shed light on the aspirations of eleventh- and twelfth-century Christian Spaniards, what can we use?

[6] M. Gómez Moreno, 'Las primeras crónicas de la reconquista: el ciclo de Alfonso III', *Boletín de la Real Academia de la Historia*, c (1932), 562–628, at p. 601.

[7] For a strident re-affirmation of this theme in one of the last published works of Claudio Sánchez-Albornoz, see his *La España cristiana de los siglos VIII al XI* vol. i (Madrid, 1980), xxi–xxii. This forms a first part of volume vii in the *Historia de España* whose founding editor was Menéndez Pidal. See also J. A. Maravall, *El concepto de España en la edad media* (3rd ed., Madrid, 1981), 252–3, 262–3.

[8] The three most important MSS. are Escorial d.I.2., and Madrid, Real Academia de la Historia 39 and 78. On these MSS. see the important codicological studies of M. C. Díaz y Díaz, *Libros y librerías en la Rioja altomedieval* (Logroño, 1979), 32–42, 63–70, 165–73.

[9] The series picks up again in the middle years of the twelfth century with Madrid, Biblioteca Nacional, MSS. 1358, 2805, 8831. See also M. C. Díaz y Díaz, 'Bibliotecas en la monarquía leonesa hacia 1050' in his *Códices visigóticos en la monarquía leonesa* (León, 1983), 149–246.

In the first place, we can look at the actual conduct of relations between Christians and Muslims and attempt, with all due circumspection, to infer motive from action. Consider, to start with, the alliance made—or, strictly speaking, renewed—in 1073 between Sancho IV of Navarre and his neighbour al-Muqtadir, independent ruler of a Muslim principality in the Ebro valley governed from Zaragoza. The text of their treaty has survived, and a most remarkable document it is.[10] The Muslim ruler bound himself to pay an annual tribute of 12,000 gold pieces to the Christian, or their equivalent in silver. In return, Sancho was to intercede with the Christian king of Aragon, his second cousin, in an attempt to persuade him to withdraw from certain territories which he had seized from al-Muqtadir; if it should prove necessary, Sancho was to use force against his kinsman. For the future, if al-Muqtadir should require military aid Sancho was to provide it, but the Muslim was to pay the wages of his troops. Whenever necessary, the two rulers were to assist one another with military aid 'whether against Christians or against Muslims' (*tam super christianos quam etiam super muzlemes*). There was nothing that was unusual, at that time, about the features of this relationship. During the sixty-odd years that elapsed between the final extinction of the caliphate of Cordoba in 1031 and the Almoravide invasion of Spain in the 1090s, several Christian rulers systematically exacted tributes, known as *parias*, from the petty principalities into which Muslim Spain had fragmented.[11] Fernando I (1037–65) and his son, Alfonso VI (1065–1109) of León-Castile were the most prominent among these tribute-takers, but the rulers of Aragon, Catalonia and—as we have seen—Navarre profited too. Tribute took diverse forms: coin, bullion, jewellery, textiles, ivories and the mortal remains of St Isidore. Its exaction was a traditional and glorious role for a king; its lavish and devout bestowal, for example upon the monastery of Cluny, bought prayer and renown. Of course, the condition upon which the system of *parias* depended was the continued existence and economic vitality of the tribute-payers. It would have been foolish to kill the geese which laid the golden eggs. In contemplating the use of military force against his Aragonese cousin in the interests of a Muslim prince, Sancho of Navarre was not behaving in an unusual fashion. The Aragonese king's father, Ramiro I, had been defeated and killed in 1063 by a combined force of Christian Castilians and Muslim Zaragozans in a similar three-cornered territorial squabble. Neither was it unknown

[10] J. M. Lacarra, 'Dos tratados de paz y alianza entre Sancho el de Peñalén y Mocatdir de Zaragoza, 1069 y 1073', in *Homenaje a Johannes Vincke*, i (Madrid, 1962), 121–34.
[11] The latest study of this period is by D. Wasserstein, *The rise and fall of the party-kings. Politics and society in Islamic Spain 1002–1086* (Princeton, 1985).

for Muslim rulers to hire Christian mercenary troops. ʿAbd Allāh of Granada tells us casually in his extraordinarily interesting autobiography how ʾIbn Ammār, the famous poet then in the service of the ruler of Seville, hired an army from Alfonso VI.[12] Rodrigo Díaz, *El Cid*, spent the years between 1081 and 1086 in the service of the Muslim ruler of Zaragoza on whose behalf he waged war against the Count of Barcelona and the king of Aragon.[13]

The Cid was the most celebrated operator in the age of the *parias*. Through soldiering for a variety of paymasters, both Christian and Muslim, he amassed a vast fortune and ended his life as the independent ruler of a principality based on Valencia (1094–9). His career had much in common with those of the contemporary Norman adventurers in Italy and the Byzantine Empire such as Roger of Sicily, Roussel of Bailleul or Bohemond of Antioch. The Cid was certainly not, what later legend was to make him, a national and Christian hero in the struggle to liberate Spain from Islam. Legend has rendered him unique in Spanish history: but it is important to remember that he was merely the most skilful and successful, by no means the only man of his type. Comparable careers were enjoyed by, to name but two examples, Arnal Mir de Tost (*d. c.* 1072?) in eastern and Sisnando Davídiz (*d.* 1091) in western Spain.[14]

The impression we are left with is that in this age the frontier was not a hard-and-fast line between opposed camps but a permeable zone. Soldiers of fortune from kings downwards could operate within it. Treaties could link parties on either side of it. Allegiances could shift and change. All sorts and conditions of people could cross it—distinguished political exiles such as Alfonso VI himself; high-ranking churchmen such as Paterno, successively bishop in Muslim Tortosa and Christian Coimbra; trains of merchants such as the Jewish businessmen we encounter in Galicia; eccentric monks such as Anastasius of Cluny.[15] There is a degree of mutual restraint in the political dealings of Christian and Muslim with one another.

There survives one text, however, which has a different tale to tell. It is the report by the Moroccan chronicler, ʾIbn Idhārī, of a speech allegedly delivered by Fernando I to an embassy from Toledo in about 1040. The ruler of Toledo was trying to secure Fernando's help

---

[12] *El siglo XI en primer persona. 'Las "Memorias" de ʿAbd Allāh último rey ziri de Granada*, trans. E. Lévi-Provençal and E. García Gómez (Madrid, 1980), 154.

[13] The classic account remains R. Menéndez Pidal, *La España del Cid* (7th ed., Madrid, 1969).

[14] P. Bonnassie, *La Catalogne du milieu du Xe à la fin du XIe siècle*, vol. ii, (Toulouse, 1976), 789–97; E. García Gómez and R. Menéndez Pidal, 'El conde mozarabe Sisnando Davídiz y la política de Alfonso VI con los Taifas', *Al-Andalus*, xii (1947), 27–41.

[15] On the last named see most recently B. Z. Kedar, *Crusade and Mission. European approaches toward the Muslims* (Princeton, 1984), 44–6.

against the principality of Zaragoza. Fernando refused, and 'Ibn
Idhārī reported his reasons as follows:

> We seek only our lands which you conquered from us in times past
> at the beginning of your history. Now you have dwelled in them
> for the time allotted to you and we have become victorious over
> you as a result of your own wickedness. So go to your own side of
> the straits [of Gibraltar] and leave our lands to us, for no good will
> come to you from dwelling here with us after today. For we shall
> not hold back from you until God decides between us.[16]

How trustworthy is this report? I am not competent to say, but the
following features strike me as significant. First, the attitude of mind
expressed is at variance with what we know of Fernando I's policies.
Second, 'Ibn Idhārī is a very late witness; he was writing in about
1310. Third, although he was usually scrupulous in citing sources for
his account of the eleventh century, he gave no indication of source
for the statement ascribed to king Fernando. I do not think that we
can accept 'Ibn Idhārī's account for what it purports to be without
misgiving.[17]

Fifty years after this alleged encounter, 'Abd Allāh of Granada, a
strictly contemporary witness, allows us a revealing glimpse of the
policies of Fernando's son, Alfonso VI, as related to him—or so he
claimed—by Sisnando Davídiz. Tribute-taking was still the paramount aim, but it was envisaged as a means of sapping the vitality
of the Muslim princes preparatory to a Christian takeover of their
territories. A shift in the terms of Christian–Muslim relations was
taking place.[18]

There is general agreement that the state of affairs which I have
tried to sketch did indeed undergo important changes in the second
half of the eleventh century.[19] While it is incontestable that changes
occurred, I am inclined to locate them in time rather less precisely:
from rather than *in* the second half of the eleventh century. The
implications of certain developments were not immediately obvious
and the mental readjustments entailed were necessarily slow. The

[16] Wasserstein, 250 and cf. also 264, 275.
[17] Does Dr Wasserstein think so too? He finds it necessary to assure us not once but
twice on a single page (275) that the passage is 'highly likely' to be genuine; from
which I infer that he has his doubts.
[18] *Memorias de 'Abd Allāh*, 157–9, 197–8.
[19] See for example J. A. García de Cortazar, *La época medieval* (Madrid, 1973), ch. 3;
C. J. Bishko, 'The Spanish and Portuguese Reconquest 1095–1492' in *A History of the
Crusades* (gen. ed. K. M. Setton), vol. iii ed. H. W. Hazard (Madison, 1975), ch. 12; A.
MacKay, *Spain in the middle ages* (1977), ch. 1; D. W. Lomax, *The Reconquest of Spain*
(1978), ch. 2; T. F. Glick, *Islamic and Christian Spain in the middle ages* (Princeton, 1979),
ch. 1; R. Collins, *Early Medieval Spain* (1983), ch. 7; Wasserstein, ch. 9.

fundamental shift was in the character of relations between Christian and Muslim. The restraint which had marked them was gradually replaced by more aggressive attitudes on both sides of the religious divide. Such drifts of mood are difficult to pin down and explain: yet it seems reasonably clear that the impulses were generated outside the Iberian peninsula. The agents of change were the incoming French adventurers, ecclesiastical as well as lay, who were establishing themselves in Spain in the period c. 1080–c. 1140; the servants of the reformed papacy, beginning to be active in Spain during the same period, and the Berber devotees of an Islamic fundamentalist sect, the Almoravides, who overran Muslim Spain between about 1090 and 1120. For the Christian authorities in Spain, these developments resulted in the replacement of a policy of exploitation of their Muslim neighbours by a programme of reconquest which was given a sharper edge by the notion of crusade.

Changes so various and so complex cannot be evenly treated in a paper such as this. The Almoravides I must leave to Islamic scholars, observing only that they deserve closer attention than they have yet received. I shall confine myself to the Christian kingdoms.

How did Spanish rulers regard their wars with the Muslims? We may begin by examining some royal charters, for here we shall encounter sentiments attributed to kings, composed indeed by the drafters but presumably acceptable to their masters. But we must pick our way with care, for where there are charters there are also interpolations and forgeries. Wars against Muslims are righteous wars in which God will fight on the Christian side. Sancho Ramírez of Aragon dated a charter of 1083 'on the fourteenth day after God gave me Graus' (a Pyrenean town north-east of Barbastro). In 1107, Ramón Berenguer III, count of Barcelona, granted an irrigation system to the monks of Sant Cugat 'because almighty God gave me the victory over the Saracens invading our borders'. Fifty years later the first independent king of Portugal, Afonso Henriques, put it on record in a letter to pope Adrian IV that he owed the conquest of Santarém to God.[20] Dozens of similar examples could be cited. There is nothing remarkable about them (though some Spanish historians have made the mistake of thinking that there is). They fit into a tradition of ecclesiastical teaching on the subject of warfare between Christians and non-Christians.

More interesting are those charters which contain a retrospective account or *narratio* of individual episodes of conquest. A famous

---

[20] *Documentos correspondientes al reinado de Sancho Ramírez*, ed. J. Salarrullana, vol. i (Zaragoza, 1907), no. xxi (p. 67); *Cartulario de Sant Cugat del Valles*, ed. J. Rius Serra, vol. ii (Barcelona, 1946), no. 794 (p. 449); *Documentos Medievais Portugueses. Documentos Régios*, ed. R. Pinto de Azevedo, vol. i (Lisbon, 1958), no. 256 (pp. 317–18).

example is furnished by Alfonso VI's grant of land and privileges to the cathedral church of Toledo issued in December 1086. The text contains what purports to be the king's own account of his conquest of the city in 1085. He tells us how:

> I took up arms against the barbarian peoples. After many engagements and innumerable enemy deaths with the assistance of God's grace I captured from them populous cities and very strong castles. And thus, inspired by the grace of God, I moved my army against this city where once my forebears, very rich and powerful kings, reigned; believing that it would be pleasing in the sight of God if what once a treacherous people under their evil leader, Muhammad, had stolen from the Christians, I Alfonso the emperor under the leadership of Christ might restore to the worshippers of the same faith...[21]

Its latest editor—to say nothing of previous commentators—regards this as a genuine charter which has come down to us in its original form. But this it cannot be: the witness-list is impossible for an instrument of 1086. The text is undoubtedly based on a genuine charter, but it has been touched up at some later date. Did the touching-up involve interpolating, recasting or even inventing the passage quoted? We have no means of telling. As an account of the devious machinations which had preceded the capitulation of Toledo, it may most charitably be described as selective. One can see how it might have appealed to the clergy of Toledo; perhaps especially to the new archbishop Bernard, a Frenchman, a Cluniac monk, the friend and legate of pope Urban II. Only with reservations can one regard the passage as accurately representing the attitude of Alfonso VI or as marking a stage in the development of a royal ideology of reconquest.

Other charters contain statements of intent about future plans of conquest. Here too, inferences have sometimes been drawn which are not justified. For instance, there survives a charter of Pedro I of Aragon drawn up in 1086 which refers to the king's projected conquest of Huesca.[22] The city was not conquered until 1096. Therefore, it is argued, Pedro had been nurturing plans for the conquest of Huesca for at least ten years. Conceivably he *had*; we do not know: for what many scholars have overlooked is that the phrase referring to the conquest of Huesca was an addition to the original charter made during the siege which preceded the city's conquest in 1096. The king

---

[21] *Privilegios reales de la catedral de Toledo 1086–1492*, ed. J. A. García Lujan, vol. ii (Toledo, 1982), no. 1 (pp. 15–20). I am grateful to Professor Bernard F. Reilly, of Villanova University, Pennsylvania, for his comments on this document.

[22] *Colección diplomática de Pedro I de Aragón y Navarra*, ed. A. Ubieto Arteta (Zaragoza, 1951), no. 1 (p. 211).

was alluding not to some deeply-meditated, far-reaching project of future conquest, but to an outcome whose realisation was imminent. Most such programmatic charters refer to immediate rather than long-term aims; for example, a charter of Alfonso VII referring to Mérida (1129), or a charter of Afonso Henriques referring to Lisbon (1147).[23]

Thus far the royal charters, where we might have expected them to utter manifestoes of reconquest, have proved less than completely helpful. But sometimes they are. Consider for example the treaty of Tudellén between Alfonso VII of León-Castile and Ramón Berenguer IV of Aragon-Catalonia.[24] (It forms an interesting contrast with the treaty between Sancho IV and al-Muqtadir of 1073). This was, among other things, nothing less than a partition-treaty sharing out between the two rulers a vast tract of the Iberian peninsula which was still in Muslim hands. The parties took it for granted that they were striving to bring Islamic dominion in Spain to an end, and confidently supposed that that end was in sight. It was the first of a series of such treaties. Observe its late date: 1150.

Chronicles should supply an additional perspective on our topic. Few were composed between 1050 and 1150, and those few are laconic and confined in point of information almost exclusively to the kingdom of León-Castile. I sample the four most significant of this meagre series. The earliest two of them, the *Cronicon Iriense* composed at Santiago de Compostela about 1090 and the chronicle of bishop Pelayo of Oviedo composed possibly in the second decade of the twelfth century, do not give the impression that their authors—or audiences—regarded wars of territorial reconquest as constituting a task of over-riding importance for Spanish kings.[25] This may have been in part a matter of region. Galicia and the Asturias are a long way from the frontier zone and the authors of these two works were men of strong local loyalties. With the so-called *Historia Silense*—which despite its name was composed not at the monastery of Silos, but in León about 1120—we move into a rather different atmosphere. The unknown author intended to write an account of the life and deeds of king Alfonso VI. Sadly, we have only the preliminaries, surveying

---

[23] *Historia Compostellana*, in *España Sagrada*, ed. E. Flórez, vol. xx (Madrid, 1765), 486; *Documentos Medievais Portugueses*, no. 221 (p. 272).

[24] *Colección de documentos inéditos del archivo de la Corona de Aragón*, ed. P. de Bofarull, vol. iv (Barcelona, 1849), no. lxii (pp. 168–74).

[25] 'El Cronicon Irense. Estudio preliminar, edicion crítica y notas históricas', ed. M. R. García Alvarez, *Memorial Historico Español*, l (1963), 1–240; *Crónica del Obispo Don Pelayo*, ed. B. Sánchez Alonso (Madrid, 1924). I suggest that the composition of Pelayo's chronicle was associated with the production of the cathedral cartulary known as the Liber Testamentorum or Libro Gótico now in the Archivo de la Catedral of Oviedo: the latest document contained therein is dated 2 December 1118 (fol. 111).

the doings of Visigothic, Asturian and Leonese monarchs from the time of Leovigild (*d.* 586) to the death of Fernando I in 1065—in itself an intriguing perspective. That part of the work dealing with Alfonso VI has either been lost or, perhaps more probably, was never composed. Still, we have a hint of how he would have presented the king:

> He displayed great energy in enlarging the kingdom of the Spaniards and in waging war against the barbarians, reclaiming provinces from their sacrilegious grasp, and turning them to the faith of Christ.[26]

This was the king's main claim to fame. We approach a little close to the spirit of the reconquest as conventionally presented. But we are not quite there. Later on, the author tells us that Fernando I attacked the Portuguese town of Viseu in 1055 in order to avenge the death of his father-in-law who had been killed while besieging it. Since that father-in-law, Alfonso V, had died nearly thirty years before, and since Fernando I had acquired León by compassing the death of his brother-in-law, its king, there is a certain implausibility about the motive ascribed. The point is, however, that the author thought that a reason was needed for attacking Muslims. You did not make war on them just because they were there. Later generations were to be less scrupulous.

The latest of this clutch of chronicles is the *Chronica Adefonsi Imperatoris*, a panegyric in prose and verse on Alfonso VII, king and emperor of León-Castile, composed shortly after 1147.[27] Consider, in the first place, its plan. The work is divided into two books. The first of them concerns itself with the internal history of the kingdom from Alfonso's accession in 1126 until his imperial coronation in 1135. The second book is devoted to his wars against the Muslims, and it culminates with an account in verse of his greatest exploit, the acquisition of Almería in 1147. This division of the work is significant. The author presented Alfonso's deeds in two distinct categories. Warfare against the Muslims was a distinctive and specially important kingly activity. A second interesting feature of the work is the quantity and particular type of biblical reference which it contains. Especially in Book II, the author had the historical books of the Old Testament and the Apocrypha constantly before his mind—particularly Judges, I and II Samuel, and the Maccabees—and quoted phrases or verbal reminiscences occur with extraordinary frequency. The work's most recent editor suggests that these 'flowed involuntarily' from his pen. Perhaps:

[26] *Historia Silense*, ed. J. Pérez de Urbel and A. González Ruiz-Zorrilla (Madrid, 1959), c. 8 (p. 119).
[27] ed. L. Sánchez Belda (Madrid, 1950).

though experience suggests that one of the things which references don't do is to flow involuntarily; they have laboriously to be assembled. There is conscious artistry here. The biblical flavour of the *Chronica* focuses Alfonso sharply as the leader of a chosen people carrying out God's holy task through battle. This is how the author wants us to see the king; and, in a Spanish context, it is a novel perspective.

The poem on the Almería campaign is rich in turns of phrase which suggests that the author thought of it as a crusade. It was meritorious in the eyes of the church, preached by bishops and promising spiritual benefits to the participants. It is time, before they fuse together, to turn from reconquest to crusade.

We must retrace our steps to 1064, the year of the so called 'Barbastro crusade'. I do not propose to linger on it because I regard it as a red herring in the history of crusading in Spain. The two pieces of evidence which can be manipulated to suggest that the Barbastro expedition was a kind of dummy-run for the crusades turn out on scrutiny to suggest nothing of the kind. 'Ibn Hayyān's phrase does not mean 'commander of the Roman cavalry', and pope Alexander II's indulgence has no connection with the campaign.[28] The Barbastro episode presents several points of interest, but that it was a 'pre-Crusade crusade' is not among them.

So when did the Spanish wars acquire a crusading character? Immediately we are faced by problems of definition. What historians call the First Crusade has been aptly characterised as a 'muddled international raid'.[29] Although worthy attempts to define a crusade have been made, what strikes one most forcibly about the early stages of the crusading epoch—say, the half-century after 1095—is precisely this atmosphere of muddle. One cannot apply hard-and-fast criteria to a given set of circumstances as a sort of litmus-test of their crusading character. However, it does make sense to ask by what date the popes had come to sanction the view that warfare against the Muslims in Spain partook of the same distinctive character as warfare against them in the Middle East. I have argued elsewhere that although certain pronouncements of both Urban II and Paschal II indicate the direction in which the popes were slowly feeling their way, it was not until 1123 that pope Calixtus II made it clear that he regarded the

---

[28] For a recent discussion with full references see A. Ferreiro. 'The siege of Barbastro 1064–65: a reassessment', *Journal of Medieval History*, ix (1983), 129–44. Working independently and on slightly different lines I had reached conclusions similar to this. I am grateful to Mr. J. S. F. Parker for help with the Arabic of 'Ibn Hayyān. Professor Ferreiro's arguments about the papal letter would have been strengthened by some consideration of the manuscript in which it has come down to us, London, British Library, Additional MS 8873.

[29] E. Christiansen, *The Northern Crusades* (1980), 48.

Spanish wars as crusades.[30] A next stage was marked at the time of the Second Crusade in the years 1146–49. Not only was the notion of 'crusade' given clearer definition in Eugenius III's bull *Quantum praedecessores*; in addition, the theatre of crusading was broadened to include the Baltic and the Iberian peninsula as well as Palestine and Syria.[31]

The pronouncements of popes and canonists in themselves tell us rather less than some scholars have supposed. We need to investigate how they were transmitted to Spain and how they were received there. The century between 1050 and 1150 was marked by a progressive thickening of Hispano-Papal contacts, from the thin gruel which trickled in the 1050s to the rich gravy which flowed in the 1140s. One indication of this was the attendance of Spanish churchmen at papal councils. The First Lateran council of 1123, for instance, at which crusading in Spain was discussed, was attended by at least three Spanish bishops or their representatives.[32]

In the light of this, we might look for incipient crusading consciousness in Spain from about the third decade of the twelfth century. And we are not disappointed. It is really rather neat—almost too good to be true—that within only a few months of Calixtus II's ruling of 1123, the archbishop of Compostela, Diego Gelmírez, had taken the unprecedented step of proclaiming a Spanish crusade 'in accordance with the lord pope's decree'.[33] Or consider an equally eminent churchman from the opposite side of the peninsula, Oleguer of Tarragona. Deeply involved in the problems of frontier defence, accustomed to accompanying the count of Barcelona on campaigns against the Muslims, a regular attender of papal councils (Toulouse and Rheims in 1119, Lateran I in 1123, Clermont in 1130, Rheims in 1131), he helped to establish the crusading order of Knights Templar in Catalonia in 1134 'to serve God and fight in our land'.[34] We move westwards once move, and onward in time to 1147. The address delivered by the bishop of Oporto to the northern seadogs who had turned up to help conquer Lisbon was not exactly, as Carl Erdmann pointed out, a crusading sermon.[35] I think it is something rather

[30] R. A. Fletcher, *Saint James's Catapult* (Oxford, 1984), 297–8.
[31] G. Constable, 'The Second Crusade as seen by contemporaries', *Traditio*, ix (1953), 213–79.
[32] Oleguer of Tarragona (see note 34 below), Pedro de Segovia and Pedro de Lugo: Segovia, Archivo de la Catedral, D/3/8; Lugo, Archivo de la Catedral, 3/2.
[33] *Historia Compostellana*, 427–30.
[34] See the two *Vitae* of Oleguer in *España Sagrada*, ed. E. Flórez, vol. xxix (Madrid, 1775), appendices xxi and xxii; Mansi, *Concilia*, vol. xxi, columns 230, 233, 256, 437, 462; *Colección de Documentos … de la Corona de Aragón*, vol. iv, no. xi (pp. 29–33).
[35] *De Expugnatione Lyxbonensi*, ed. and trans. C. W. David (New York, 1936), 68–84; C. Erdmann, *A idea de cruzada em Portugal* (Coimbra, 1940), 23.

more interesting, the sermon of a man who had his doubts about crusading—as well he might have done, faced by such a crew. At any rate, it belongs in the moral territory of the crusades.

The first bishop of reconquered Lisbon was an Englishman, Gilbert of Hastings. In 1150 we encounter him back in England, recruiting for a campaign against Seville.[36] It reminds us that people outside the Iberian peninsula were being encouraged to look upon it as a theatre of crusading warfare. It was a lesson that was reiterated inside the peninsula by the emissaries of the pope. For example, at the council of Valladolid in January 1155 held under the presidency of the legate cardinal Hyacinth, the opening canon was a restatement of the doctrine of crusading indulgences. The cardinal himself took the cross and prepared to lead a crusade against the Muslims, though this expedition never actually took place.[37]

Another ecclesiastic who visited Spain on several occasions as a papal legate (1119, 1121, 1138) was Guy, bishop of Lescar in southwestern France. In 1134 he had accompanied the Aragonese army to the disastrous battle of Fraga, in the course of which he had the misfortune to be captured. After a humiliating imprisonment he was released for a substantial ransom. William of Malmesbury had a more exotic tale to relate: bishop Guy was liberated miraculously after prayers to the Virgin Mary and St Anne.[38] The appearance of the new and fashionable Marian devotion in this context of armed confrontation between Christian and Muslim is of interest. The Virgin was not the only saint who was displaying concern for Christian warriors in Spain and their clergy. It was at very much the same time that St James began to be widely associated with warfare against Islam. The town militias of Avila, Segovia and Toledo invoked St Mary and St James on their campaigns. A share in booty captured from the Muslims could be despatched to Compostela. It was on St James's day that Afonso Henriques of Portugal won his great victory at *Aulic* in 1139, and in the following year Alfonso VII recorded that

[36] John of Hexham, *Historia*, in *Symeonis monachi opera omni*, ed. T. Arnold (Rolls Series), vol. ii (1885), 324.

[37] The Valladolid decrees were printed by C. Erdmann, *Das Papsttum und Portugal im ersten Jahrhundert der portugiesischen Geschichte* (Berlin, 1928), appendix v (pp. 55–63). For Hyacinth's crusading plans see *La documentación pontificia hasta Inocencio III*, ed. D. Mansilla (Monumenta Hispaniae Vaticana, Registros, vol. i: Rome, 1955), no. 98 (pp. 116–17). The letter is undated but the reference to master Robert shows that it belongs to Hyacinth's first Spanish legation of 1154–5 rather than to this second of 1172–4: Robert drafted a document for him at Burgos on 24 February 1155 (Lugo, Archivo de la Catedral, 3/5).

[38] This has been interestingly discussed by P. Carter, 'The historical content of William of Malmesbury's Miracles of the Virgin Mary', in *The writing of history in the middle ages. Essays presented to Richard William Southern*, ed. R. H. C. Davis and J. M. Wallace-Hadrill (Oxford, 1981), 127–65.

he had conquered Coria with St James's help. His son Fernando II styled himself St James's standard-bearer (*vexillifer*) in a charter of 1158.[39]

St James, of course, became the patron of the most famous of the Spanish military orders—the Order of Santiago, which emerged in the early 1170s with the assistance, among others, of cardinal Hyacinth.[40] The order was modelled upon the international order of the Temple. The slightly earlier Spanish order of Calatrava, which emerged between 1158 and 1164, orginated in an initiative by a Cistercian abbot, Raymond of Fitero. We should remember that it was a more famous Cistercian, Bernard of Clairvaux, who had helped to codify the Templars' rule in 1128 and had composed the pamphlet *De laude novae militiae* for the order's first master, Hugh of Payns.[41] Cistercian expansion into Spain got under weigh in the 1140s. Their first foundation was at Fitero in Navarre in 1140, and the ensuing fifteen years saw the establishment of such famous houses as Sacramenia (1142), Valparaiso (1143), Huerta (1144), La Espina (1147), Rioseco (1148), La Oliva, Poblet and Santes Creus (1150) and Alcobaça (1153).[42] It was also from the third decade of the twelfth century that the Templars began to acquire property and responsibilities in the Iberian peninsula, first in Portugal (1128), then in Aragon and Catalonia (1131–2) and finally in León-Castile (1144–6). As is well-known, Alfonso I of Aragon attempted to leave his kingdom in the joint care of the orders of the Temple, Hospital and Holy Sepulchre. This extraordinary will was never implemented, but the settlement in 1143 of the Templars' claims arising from it gave them a major role in the Aragonese reconquest over the next two generations.[43]

The appearance of the international military orders in the peninsula and the subsequent foundation of native orders such as Calatrava and Santiago were preceded by the establishment of other communities, experimental and, in the event, ephemeral, but of interest none the less. The one about which we are best informed was the military confraternity of Belchite, founded by Alfonso I of Aragon in 1122 and surviving until shortly after 1136.[44] The knights who enlisted in the confraternity, whether permanently or temporarily, undertook 'never

[39] For these examples see Fletcher, *Catapult*, 296–7.

[40] D. W. Lomax, *La Orden de Santiago* (Madrid, 1965), ch. 1.

[41] See most recently M. C. Barber, 'The social context of the Templars', *TRHS*, Fifth series, xxxiv (1984), 27–46.

[42] M. Cocheril, *Études sur le monachisme en Espagne et au Portugal* (Lisbon-Paris, 1966), especially ch. 5.

[43] For details see A. J. Forey, *The Templars in the Corona de Aragon* (1973), ch. 2.

[44] P. Rassow, 'La cofradía de Belchite', *Anuario de Historia del Derecho Español* 3 (1926), 200–27. For the date of foundation see A. Ubieto Arteta, 'La creación de la cofradía militar de Belchite', *Estudios de Edad Media de la Corona de Aragón*, v, (1952), 427–34.

to live at peace with the pagans but to devote all their days to molesting and fighting them'. There has been much discussion of the possible debt of the confraternity of Belchite to the Muslim institution of the *ribat*. I cannot enter into this debate here, and will observe only that such a borrowing seems to be inherently implausible.[45] What especially interests me about Belchite is first the date of the foundation and secondly the persons involved in forwarding the king's plans. There are some familiar names among the witnesses to the foundation charter of 1122: Bernard of Toledo, Oleguer of Tarragona, Diego of Compostela, Guy of Lescar. It was a small world. Oleguer himself founded a somewhat similar confraternity for the defence and restoration of Tarragona a few years later.[46] In 1129 he recruited Norman military entrepreneurs under Robert Burdet for the same purpose. There are suggestive verbal parallels between Oleguer's charter for Burdet in 1129 and his charter for the Templars in 1134.[47] Norman adventurers and monks of war were engaged in a single enterprise. Already there were some who set that enterprise in a larger vista. In his foundation-charter for the military confraternity of Monreal, probably to be dated between 1126 and 1130, Alfonso I of Aragon spoke of overcoming the Saracens of Spain and opening a way to Jerusalem.[48] Whether he received the idea, through his bishops, from the pope; or from the Frenchmen such as those named in this document, count Gaston of Béarn and archbishop William of Auch; or whether he made it out for himself, we cannot tell. What matters is the timing and the tone.

The present generation of medievalists in Spain is engaged upon a long overdue reassessment of the character of those centuries between *c.* 800 and *c.* 1300. We are invited to consider that the Christian expansion of that period was rather a conquest than a reconquest, and that it was propelled by more earthy impulses than earlier and more fastidious scholars chose to contemplate: demographic pressure, climatic change, developing military technology, the needs of an

---

[45] A. Noth, *Heiliger Krieg und heiliger Kampf in Islam und Christentum* (Bonn, 1966), 66–87; E. Lourie, 'The confraternity of Belchite, the Ribat, and the Temple', *Viator* 13 (1982), 159–76; A.J. Forey, 'The emergence of the Military Order in the twelfth century', *Journal of Ecclesiastical History*, xxxiv (1985), 175–95.

[46] L.J. McCrank, 'The foundation of the confraternity of Tarragona by archbishop Oleguer Bonestruga, 1126–1129', *Viator*, ix (1978), 157–77.

[47] L.J. McCrank, 'Norman crusaders in the Catalan reconquest: Robert Burdet and the principality of Tarragona, 1129–1155', *Journal of Medieval History*, vii (1981), 67–82; *Cartas de población y franquicia de Cataluña*, ed. J.M. Font Rius, vol. i (Madrid-Barcelona, 1969), no. 51 (pp. 87–9); and see above, note 34.

[48] 'Documentos para el estudio de la reconquista y repoblación del valle del Ebro (segunda serie)', ed. J.M. Lacarra, in *Estudios de Edad Media de la Corona de Aragón*, iii (1947–8), 499–727, no. 151 (pp. 549–50).

emergent aristocratic elite, the appetites of sheep and cattle.[49] I suspect that they would regard the preoccupations of this paper as ludicrously antiquated, its author engaged in tilting at windmills (an activity not without honoured Hispanic precedent).

Obsession with social forces may lead the revisionists unduly to neglect the power of ideas. Ideas *were* important in the messy and long-drawn-out process which we call for convenience the Spanish reconquest. However, we should study to be cautious in identifying their formation, character and bearing. The emergence of a programme of reconquest was rather more hesitant than some scholars have argued. In acquiring definition, it drew sustenance from notions about warfare between Christian and Muslim which may loosely be described as 'crusading'; and these notions were not native to Spain, but imported. Emergence and definition were gradual: the process was stretched out over some three generations. Looking at the convergent fragments of evidence, of which I have presented a sample here, I am inclined to think that the second quarter of the twelfth century marked a crucial stage. It is then that a new grid or pattern of ideas is for the first time clearly discernible. It is after that, in the Spanish kingdoms and in Portugal, that things would never quite be what they had been before.

---

[49] For the ideas of the revisionists see A. Barbero and M. Vigil, *Sobre los orígenes sociales de la reconquista* (Barcelona, 1974) and their *La formación del feudalismo en la península ibérica* (Barcelona, 1978); J-L. Martín, *Evolución económica de la península ibérica (siglos VI–XIII)*, (Barcelona, 1976); S. de Moxó, *Repoblación y sociedad en la España cristiana medieval* (Madrid, 1979); J. A. García de Cortázar and C. Díez Herrera, *La formación de la sociedad hispano-cristiana del Cantábrico al Ebro en los siglos VIII al XI* (Santander, 1982).

'A PARTY FOR OWNERS OR A PARTY FOR EARNERS?' HOW FAR DID THE BRITISH CONSERVATIVE PARTY REALLY CHANGE AFTER 1945?

By John Ramsden

READ 7 MARCH 1986

THE period spent in opposition between 1945 and 1951 has generally been thought of as a key to the understanding of the activities of the post-war British Conservative Party. Autobiographies of the Party leaders of the time began to appear at the end of the Fifties, already looking back to a period in which the Conservatives had decisively changed their approach. So for example, Lord Woolton's *Memoirs* reviewed not only a term as Party Chairman which had been a highlight of his own crowded career, but also his sharing in a major act of transformation, a transformation that had led on to Conservative success since 1951: 'the change was revolutionary'.[1] Other key figures in the organisation reached similar conclusions as their own accounts appeared: David Maxwell-Fyfe argued that the new Party rules which he had drawn up had not only decisively widened the political base of British Conservatism, but that events since had confirmed the importance of the change.[2] R. A. Butler's account of *The Art of the Possible* argued in 1971 that 'the overwhelming electoral defeat of 1945 shook the Conservative Party out of its lethargy and impelled it to re-think its philosophy and re-form its ranks with a thoroughness unmatched for a century'.[3] The effect was to bring both the policies of the Party and 'their characteristic mode of expression', as he puts it, 'up to date'. As recently as 1978, Reginald Maudling—a key figure behind the scenes in 1945–51 as a speechwriter from Eden and Churchill and as the organising secretary of the committee which produced the *Industrial Charter* of 1947—reached much the same view: 'We were at that time developing a new economic policy for the Conservative Party ... It marked a substantially different approach for post-war Conservative philosophy.'[4] Memoirs of other senior politicians less closely involved in organisational and policy-making

[1] Earl of Woolton, *Memoirs* (1959), 346.
[2] Earl of Kilmuir, *Political Adventure* (1964), 164–6.
[3] Lord Butler, *The Art of the Possible* (1971), 126.
[4] Reginald Maudling, *Memoirs* (1978), 44.

matters—Anthony Eden, Harold Macmillan and many others—do
not challenge the broad view that 1945 marked a sea change in the
Party's history and in its identity. In the short term, politicians of
the Fifties and Sixties could make similar claims with even greater
emphasis; Iain Macleod—whose whole career was on occasion seen
to embody the broadening of the Party's social base and the leftward
shift of its policy—regularly looked back to 1945–51 as the foundation
stone of later success. The key to an understanding of that success, he
argued in 1962, lay in the Party's way of reacting to defeat; in 1945
the Conservatives had not responded by blaming unfair electioneering
and had not assumed that the electorate must be wrong to have
rejected them. Instead, the Party had acknowledged that the customer
is always right and changed the product accordingly.[5] Through all of
these views then, there runs a single thread, a recognition that the
Conservatives saw in their 1945 defeat something more than the loss
of a single election, accepted the need to 'modernise' their Party's
structure and policy. The changes they made were of lasting consequence.

To a large extent, historians have accepted at face value much of
the Party's self-evaluation. The outpouring of charters and other
policy documents emerging in and after 1947 have been painstakingly
analysed and deemed to show a shift of philosophy as well as a change
of programme. The outburst of organisational reforms was described
at length by J. D. Hoffman, whose early account of a move into a
new age of mass, participatory politics has not been subsequently
challenged.[6] Lord Blake's Ford Lectures of 1968 and their subsequent
publication then conferred the authority of the Party's pre-eminent
historian on this received view, which has since been adopted by
politicians, researchers and contemporary journalists alike.[7] Paul
Addison's *The Road to 1945* did not focus on the post-war period or on
the political Right, but his findings did nonetheless shed much light
on the Conservative position. He may be thought to have added a
variation on the received view, by placing the decisive point of change
in 1940 and 1942 rather than in 1945, but he also emphasised the
large shift that the war years produced in the whole character of
British politics at the elite level. The date of change was questioned
but not its magnitude.[8]

[5] Iain Macleod at the 1962 Party Conference, quoted in Lord Butler, ed., *The Conservatives* (1977), 425.
[6] J. D. Hoffman, *The Conservative Party in Opposition 1945–1951* (1964)
[7] Robert Blake, *The Conservative Party from Peel to Churchill* (1970), 256–62; T. F. Lindsay and M. Harrington, *The Conservative Party 1918–1970* (1974), 146–62; Nigel Harris, *Competition and the Corporate Society* (1972), 77–145.
[8] Paul Addison, *The Road to 1945: British Politics and the Second World War* (1975), especially 270–9.

What then has been thought to be the Conservative Party's response to the twin impulses of war in 1939–45 and electoral defeat in 1945? Basically two-fold. On the one hand the Party has been shown to have greatly enlarged its membership to an all time high in the early 1950s, a vast influx of new blood that provided not only an effective workforce for electioneering and fund-raising purposes, but a far broader social base in keeping open channels of communication with the electorate. This was seen as much as a social as a political phenomenon; Tony Hancock's thoughts about joining the Young Conservatives in 1961 revolved around table tennis and the possibility of finding a wife.[9] More seriously, the creation of the Conservative Political Centre with branches for policy discussion in every constituency allowed for the two-way movement of ideas; the constituency rank and file would be kept informed of the views of the leaders and Central Office would be able to take the views of the Party faithful into account. At the top level, the formation in 1949 of the Advisory Committee on Policy brought together representatives of the parliamentary and voluntary wings to coordinate advice to the leaders in all issues of policy, and to sound their opinions on proposed policy changes.[10] The same broadening of the base could be detected in the adoption in 1949 of the Maxwell-Fyfe reforms on financial relationships between candidates and their local supporters, and between constituencies and Central Office.[11] Henceforth it was impossible to buy safe Conservative seats; one of the bitterest pre-war critics of the system of large candidates' contributions, Ian Harvey, became a Conservative MP and a junior minister in the 1950s. The large number of new Conservative MPs of 1950 and 1951, the so-called 'class of 1950', was therefore scrutinised very carefully and adjudged to demonstrate the advent of a new character for the Party in parliament, a period in which more grammar-school educated meritocrats would be coming to the fore— evidenced by the arrival all at once of Enoch Powell, Iain Macleod, Edward Heath, Robert Carr and Reginald Maudling. The rapid promotion of this new generation into minor and then leading governmental posts in the Fifties seemed to show that the revolution had not stopped at the back-benches. Similarly, the published lists of annual quota payments from constituencies to Central Office after 1949 showed the participation of the wider rank and file. Most standard works on British politics saw this as an important development.[12]

[9] Alan Simpson and Ray Galton's script for *The Blood Donor*, first broadcast on BBC Television, 1 October 1961.
[10] John Ramsden, *The Making of Conservative Policy: The Conservative Research Department since 1929* (1980), 131.
[11] Nigel Birch, *The Conservative Party* (1949), 43.
[12] See for example Robert McKenzie's *British Political Parties* (2nd edition, 1963), 653–4.

The second area of change was adjudged to lie in the Conservatives' acceptance of what Paul Addison called 'Attlee's consensus', a policy package that included a mixed economy of both public and private sectors co-existing side by side, a more interventionist welfare state with a National Health Service, a commitment to full employment and an acceptance of Keynesian methods for economic management. These various policy commitments by Conservatives were apparently misunderstood by the other parties, as is evidenced by Labour's absolute conviction in 1951 and 1955 that a Conservative Government would imperil all that had been done since 1945.[13] Conservatives themselves were fairly clear about the degree to which they accepted what the Attlee Government had done; Churchill told the US Congress in 1952 that British socialism and Tory free enterprise gave plenty of room for argument, but 'fortunately overlap quite a lot in practice... Our complicated society would be deeply injured if we did not practice what is called in the United States the bipartisan habit of mind.'[14] In the same year, the *Economist* merged the names of the old and new Chancellors of the Exchequer to create in 'Mr. Butskell' a shorthand for the post-war political consensus.[15] But, as Churchill had admitted to Congress and as he emphasised rather more when addressing audiences of British Conservatives, overlap between practical policies did not imply a convergence of overall goals between the parties. The phrase most canvassed as summing-up the Conservatives' own aspiration was 'a property-owning democracy'.[16] The phrase was much used by Anthony Eden, encompassing as it did both the widening of the Party's ranks and of its policy objectives, but it was a phrase that neatly obscured too the potential conflict between the long-term interests of those whose income was earned and those whose income derived from ownership. The advent of democracy was completed with the destruction of business votes and graduate votes in 1948; at the same time, the emergence of a mass-membership Party, more democratically run at the grass roots, and the acceptance of larger public sectors both in the economy and in social policy drove the Party to consider the interests of wage and salary earners with limited wealth. Through the spread of ownership envisaged in the 'property-owning democracy', the potential conflict between owners

[13] David Butler, *The British General Election of 1951* (1952), 126.

[14] Churchill's comment to Congress compares nicely with an earlier Conservative leader's similar comment, also favouring bipartisanship as a necessary characteristic of the British political system: Arthur Balfour's introduction to Walter Bagehot's *The English Constitution* (1928 edition).

[15] Alan Thompson, *The Day Before Yesterday* (1971), 95.

[16] F. W. S. Craig, ed., *British General Election Manifestoes 1918–1966* (Chichester, 1970), 146.

and earners could be headed off. Power for an uninterrupted period of thirteen years after 1951 appeared to validate the basic assumption that the sum of these organisational and policy changes had been to reverse what might have been a terminal decline.[17] That the Party had, as Macleod argued, taken its medicine in defeat and become a changed man in the process.

As the 1980s sees the retirement from politics of the last of the generation who took the Party through the post-war reconstruction, and as we see a Conservative Government conceived on very different lines to the 'bipartisan frame of mind', it may be appropriate to test the assumptions on which previous accounts of '1945 and all that' have been based. It seems appropriate too that we should ask three questions of the material now available and with the benefits of a longer hindsight. I shall seek to show first that the events of 1945 to 1950 were far more predictable for the Conservative Party in the light of pre-war trends than has been generally assumed, that changes during the Second World War were at least as important as reactions to defeat in 1945, and that events after 1951 demonstrate that the scale of change has been at the least exaggerated.

The clearest extent to which pre-war practice can be seen to foreshadow post-war 'changes' is to be found in the Party's internal affairs. I have shown in *The Age of Balfour and Baldwin* the extent to which reforms introduced by Baldwin in 1924 and pushed ahead by J. C. C. Davidson as Party Chairman between 1926 and 1930 had blazed this trail.[18] Baldwin sought to mobilise the considerable moral authority at his disposal after the *victory* of 1924 to stop the sale of safe Tory seats to the highest bidder. We can see that many local constituency parties had relieved their candidate of all or part of the costs of election campaigns before the war, and that quite a number had also ceased to depend on their candidates for money to meet normal running costs too.[19] During the 1920s, there was a great influx of new membership into the Party as in the 1940s, there was a great influx of new membership into the Party as in the 1940s, especially into the new women's sections created since the 1918 Reform Act. The official Party now effectively took over the role of the Primrose League as the mobiliser of large numbers, and especially of women and the young.[20] (In passing though, it may be noted that the Primrose League in its Edwardian heyday could teach most modern parties a number of

[17] Conservative Research Department file, '1955 Election: Bouquets', quoted in Ramsden, *Making*, 177.

[18] John Ramsden, *The Age of Balfour and Baldwin, 1902 to 1940* (1978), 218–62.

[19] Ramsden, *Balfour and Baldwin*, 247.

[20] Ramsden, *Balfour and Baldwin*, 250–1.

lessons about mass-membership politics.[21]) As membership rose in the Twenties, involvement of members in policy debates also increased and Party conferences became quite different from their earlier character, not significantly different from what they were to be in the Fifties. In the same period there was a determination to provide an effective youth wing for the Party through the Junior Imperial League, though there was also a recognition that both its name and its structure was something of an anachronism in the Thirties. In 1938 and 1939 a committee was already looking at the problem and making recommendations similar to those carried out when the Young Conservatives were launched in 1947—a change delayed rather than occasioned by the war.[22] The wish to involve the Party membership in social as well as political events was well understood in Baldwin's day, perhaps another legacy from the Primrose League and its contemporaries. Unfortunately, records of the national Party for this period are fragmentary at most; it is not possible to produce full national membership figures for any year before 1947, if indeed such figures were even collected, which seems unlikely. Nonctheless, the investigation of numbers of constituency records which survive for the inter-war years does prove that many local parties had already adopted modernising methods that are often associated with the later period. What had certainly not happened was a universalisation of such methods or any real attempt to compel the reluctant to come into line; for this the Party had to wait for Woolton and for Maxwell-Fyfe. But in the Conservative Party change cannot be enforced on independent constituency associations by the Party hierarchy, as Michael Pinto-Duschinsky has shown for a more recent period.[23] The enforced changes of the 1940s rested then on previous decades of persuasion as least as much as on any short-term influences of the time. At the least it can be assumed that the new Maxwell-Fyfe rules of 1949 would not have had either an easy passage to the rule book or a quick implementation, were it not for the fact that many local parties already practised what was now being preached and the rest had quite a longstanding sense of guilt for not doing so.

A similar case can be argued in relation to policy; Paul Addison has already laid much of the groundwork for this view. Conservatives in government between the wars were sceptical about government intervention in the economy but by no means were they unanimously hostile. The rationalisation of the steel industry in the early 1930s took

[21] M. I. Ostrogorski, *Democracy and the Organisation of Political Parties*, (English edition, translated by F. Clarke, 1902), i, 370–419.

[22] Ramsden, *Balfour and Baldwin*, 359.

[23] Michael Pinto-Duschinsky, 'Central Office and "Power" in the Conservative Party', in *Political Studies* (1972).

place under the auspices of the Bank of England rather than the Government but there was in practice quite a large governmental involvement in such interventions and quite a lot of them. The actual format for public ownership, the 'Morrisonian public corporation' owed a great deal to pre-war examples which had been set up or re-formed by the Conservatives—the prime example being the British Broadcasting Corporation. If the BBC is thought of as a special case as a new industry with a potent influence on public opinion, it can be matched with other examples—the Central Electricity Generating Board of 1926, the London Passenger Transport Board of 1933 and the creation of BOAC in 1939.[24] The concept of public ownership was then not unacceptable in principle to those Conservatives who held office between the wars; in even such a politically-sensitive case as the coal industry they were prepared to accept a far greater degree of intervention by 1935 than even ten years earlier. The 1935 manifesto included a pledge to unify coal royalties and although the implemen-tation of that pledge caused serious parliamentary difficulties for the National Government, it was eventually pushed through; it was indeed only the sacking of a National Liberal Minister and his replace-ment by a Conservative that ensured that the Bill went through in 1938, so allowing the unification of royalties, though too late for amalgamations to go far before the war intervened.[25] Conservative research officers investigated a whole series of industries for their political masters; they rejected out of hand Harold Macmillan's radical proposal for an enabling bill to give the Government open-ended powers to intervene in industry, something no Conservative Government contemplated until 1972, but they were far from rejecting intervention where it could be pragmatically justified. Meetings of Conservative Ministers in the National Government agreed with enthusiasm to a set of criteria for intervention that established that Government should take a leading part only if the industry could not be restored without compulsion; the control should then be vested in a representative body drawn from the industry itself.[26] In view of the acceptance of industries nationalised after 1945 on ground of the needs of the industries themselves, and with the at least tacit acquiscence of the industries' leaders, it can be seen that much of the groundwork for this approach already existed in 1939.

It was much the same in social policy. No account of the political life of Neville Chamberlain (except, oddly enough the biography of Chamberlain by Iain Macleod?) ignores or underestimates his contribution to the development of social policy. Nonetheless, most

[24] E. E. Barry, *Nationalisation in British Politics* (1965), 247–8, 298, 320, 360.
[25] Barry, *Nationalisation*, 354; Ramsden, *Making*, 71–5.
[26] Ramsden, *Making*, 79–80.

books on his government do underestimate the extent to which the
normal planning of domestic policy continued right up to the brink
of war.[27] One reason for that planning was the anticipated general
election of 1939–40, and the belief was already current among the
Party's advisers that a more advanced social policy would be needed
if power was to be retained. Drafts for a manifesto included commitments to advances in education, mainly in the technical field (so
foreshadowing one of the legs on which the Butler Act of 1944 was to
stand), and plans for family allowances and the inclusion of the
dependents of insured persons in health and pension cover.[28] In July
1939 the Government regretfully announced that plans for improve-
ments in pensions were now financially impossible because of the level
of defence spending. In effect they had recognised the desirability of
various policy advances that are associated with Beveridge or with
the Butler Act, but had also asserted the primacy of national security
in 1939; this was not far from Churchill's 'victory first' response to the
Beveridge report itself,[29] nor indeed from the Party's later view of
NHS costs in the context of the Korean War of 1951.[30]

There is thus no real doubt that a Conservative election manifesto
for a peacetime general election of 1940, had one ever been held,
would have included at least some social policy proposals in advance
of existing practice; finance was still the paramount argument and
was to remain so as the scale of the proposed advances increased. In
one area of domestic policy in particular does pre-war practice come
very close to what is generally associated with post-war experience,
and that is housing. Chamberlain's first statute of importance was the
Housing Act of 1923 (itself owing something to plans made before
1914), investing large sums of public money in private house-
building.[31] In the Thirties, the government whose financial policy
Chamberlain effectively dominated presided over the biggest ever
sustained house-building boom, comparable only to the Macmillan
building boom of the Fifties. Much of the success of the building
programme before 1939 can be attributed to factors beyond the
Government's control and to the accidental consequences of its overall
economic policy—cheap land, cheap money and mass unemployment.
Nonetheless it would be a mistake to conclude that Conservatives
between the wars did not appreciate the political value of housing

[27] Ramsden, *Balfour and Baldwin*, 362–3.
[28] Ramsden, *Making*, 91–2; this can be compared with Conservative support for
pension proposals during Joseph Chamberlain's Tariff Reform crusade or with the
refusal of Conservative MPs to vote again such proposals even in such financially
difficult times as 1923, Ramsden, *Balfour and Baldwin*, 174.
[29] Addison, *Road to 1945*, 220–1.
[30] Ramsden, *Making*, 155–6.
[31] David Dilks, *Neville Chamberlain* (1984), i. 311–14.

too. Chamberlain himself had told the House of Commons during the debate on the Wheatley Housing Bill that 'I am quite certain that the man who owns his own home is generally a good citizen too.' Local politicians could make the same point rather less guardedly, as when the local Conservative leader in Leeds told the Labour Party in 1926 that 'It is a good thing for the people to buy their own houses. They turn Tory directly. We shall go on making Tories and you will be wiped out.'[32] Even the phrase 'the property-owning democracy' is rooted in the inter-war years, and appears to have originated with Noel Skelton in a *Spectator* article of 1924. Skelton, like many of his friends in the 'YMCA' acknowledged the case for intervention in industry, but he argued too for a wider ownership of property, in industry as well as in spheres like housing.[33] In this field as in many others, the radical Conservatives of the Twenties were nearer to the centre of the Party by 1939, especially with Chamberlain the *Unionist* as Leader of the Party. The first test would seem to show that the scale of change after 1945 has been overstated.

An examination of the events of the Forties demonstrates never-theless just how strong were short-term influences too. For the Party organisation, the war provided both an eclipse and a spectacular recovery. It was precisely because the Party had already adapted to changing expectations that it was hit so hard by the war. A Party that had become dependent on long lists of subscribers and large numbers of voluntary fund-raisers in order to sustain large estab-lishments both at Central Office and in the constituencies was extremely vulnerable to the six-year cessation of activities that the war brought about. Most constituency associations had simply gone out of business by about 1943, offices had been closed and staff discharged; Central Office was run from a couple of rooms in place of the large suite of offices on several floors which had kept going even through the First World War; policy-making machinery vanished altogether. There is evidence enough of awareness as to how vul-nerable this made the Party, not least as seats were lost at by-elections; there were regular urgings to keep things going, but no sign that the urgings were heeded.[34] Any organisational recovery that took place after 1945 was bound to look spectacular when compared to the depths to which things had sunk by 1945. It was also to be expected,

[32] R. Finnigan, 'Housing Policy in Leeds between the Wars' in J. Melling (ed), *Housing, Social Policy and the State* (1980), 174.

[33] *Spectator*, 28 Apr. 1924 to 19 May 1924.

[34] Ramsden, *Making*, 97–9; Islington East Conservative Association minutes, Feb-ruary and April 1940; Totnes Conservative Association minutes, 29 Mar. 1941; Dulwich Conservative Association minutes, 9 Dec. 1943. (All these local party records held in constituency offices.)

with the benefit of a longer hindsight, that the very existence of a Labour Government would lead to an improvement in the Conservative Party's membership and finances. That has been the Conservatives' good fortune on all five occasions when Britain has had a Labour Government, and there is no reason to expect anything different of the years after 1945 when the *first* majority Labour Government was in office and Conservative supporters were getting their first ever taste of legislation passed by a Labour House of Commons. In this perspective, the organisational recovery after 1945 seems to need less explanation; even so its sheer scale and speed remain impressive. After a short period of collective shock in 1945–6 during which the scale of defeat seemed to be an insuperable problem in itself, things advanced very quickly. Structural changes were carried through by 1949 and with overwhelming agreement (compare with the mayhem that followed defeat in 1906!) and local evidence suggests that the letter of the Maxwell-Fyfe reforms was followed. Finances boomed and membership accumulated in millions.[35] Membership was levelling off at a level of just over three millions when the Party re-entered office in 1951, perhaps ten times the number who had been actual subscribers at the end of the war. It is not surprising that the local leaders of these newly-revived structures, often people who were themselves men and women with little or no experience of the Party before 1939, should have assumed that they were doing things never done before. They were indeed actively encouraged to think so by leaders like Woolton who had not even joined the Party until after its 1945 defeat and then become Party Chairman within a year.[36]

The adjustment of policy was a more difficult and more complex operation. The first point to stress is the extent to which the accommodation to 'Attlee's consensus' was not just a matter of one party moving towards the other, but of mutual convergence. The basic programme of the Attlee Government was after all based heavily on the reconstruction plans made by all parties together as the members of Churchill's wartime coalition. Labour Ministers took the lead in the planning process both because of the offices that they held and because of their greater interest in domestic and social policy, but Conservatives and Liberals were involved just the same. Many key influences came from outside the world of politics, as in the development of education policy, or from individuals like Keynes and Beveridge who were neither Conservatives nor socialists.[37] While the war lasted, Conservatives as a whole certainly paid less attention to these developing policies than did Labour MPs and were perceptibly less

[35] Hoffman, *Conservative Party*, 83–90.
[36] Woolton, *Memoirs*, 330.
[37] Addison, *Road to 1945*, 41–2, 171–4.

enchanted with them in detail. Nevertheless all the main features
of the policy developments of 1940 to 1945 were accepted by the
Conservative leaders as well as by other parties and are to be found
clearly set out in the Conservative manifesto of 1945: this contained
an unequivocal pledge to introduce a National Health Service in the
next parliament, a specific commitment to the 1944 proposals on
National Insurance, full employment, and a more guarded reference
to industrial policy which promised to deal with each industry pragmatically.[38] *The Times* talked of 'the great national programme' and
congratulated the electorate in being free to judge between teams of
men who agreed on the basis of what must be done.[39] That no doubt
overstated the case, for the 'agreed programme' would certainly have
been put into effect in very different ways by the different parties,
but it corrects the myth that Labour alone was proposing a bold
programme of reconstruction in 1945. On the other hand evidence of
the time certainly bears out the view that Labour alone convinced
people at large that their words and their intentions were in
harmony.[40] In the event, since what Labour did in office was to carry
out what all parties had proposed in 1945 at least in principle, it is
clear that the Conservatives did not need a very radical re-think of
policy to keep up with the course of post-war events. Churchill's well-
known resistance to policy-making in opposition was overborne by
the vociferous demands of the Party rank and file and the result was
the setting up of the committee which drew up the *Industrial Charter*.[41]
This was conceived by its framers as an important new departure for
Conservatism, so much so that R. A. Butler declaimed the Tamworth
Manifesto to the Committee at its first meeting to emphasise that they
like Peel were breaking new ground; a perceptive historian might
have pointed out that Peel himself was more concerned to demonstrate
the acceptance of changes that had already occurred than to make a
new departure. In any case, judged by such elevated hopes, the
outcome was signally disappointing, since the text said very little that
was specific and practically nothing that was not inherent in the 1945
manifesto. The real success of the *Industrial Charter* was twofold, neither
part relying on the words in the text. As a 'charter' and the first of
many produced between 1947 and 1950, it could be made into a
public relations event of the first order and so help to repair the Party's
credibility problem with the electorate. Equally its status as a major
policy statement, the first produced by the Party as opposed to Con-

[38] Craig, *Election Manifestoes*, 87–97.
[39] Butler, *Conservatives*, 424.
[40] See for example, Burton on Trent Conservative Association minutes, 25 June 1945;
Lichfield Conservative Association Annual Report, 1945 (constituency offices).
[41] Ramsden, *Making*, 109.

servative Ministers since 1931, meant that it would have to go through a long process of consultations and would then be published in the end with a far greater degree of authority than either the 1945 Manifesto or pledges given by shadow ministers. The real purpose then was not to shift philosophy but to line up the Party behind the philosophy that had been emerging since 1931. One such convert was Churchill himself, whose public support was vital in giving the new document public credibility. Wide consultations did take place in 1947, rather more successfully than the document's authors expected, and it was approved by an overwhelming majority at the 1947 Party Conference. At that point Churchill seems to have read the document for the first time, disliked it but accepted it and loyally supported it thereafter.[42]

The charters and the subsequent policy documents were of course only one part of policy formulation in opposition, for the tide of legislation after 1945 also required the Party to commit itself in more detail than in the *Industrial Charter* either for or against items of Attlee's policy. Over time the Conservatives gradually recovered from the heavy shock of 1945 and became a fighting opposition again by about 1949. Under the guidance especially of Butler and Eden they managed to avoid giving many hostages to fortune. Much legislation was opposed more in detail than in principle and very few pledges were made to repeal acts that the Government passed or undo the general direction of the Government's achievements.[43] This is after all one of an opposition's greatest temptations and one of the most dangerous, especially for a Party more concerned with its credibility than with its actual policy. Taking a long view, the Conservative acceptance of much of the nationalisation measures, and the tendency of Labour spokesmen to defend their measures on the low ground of pragmatism rather than from the high ground of ideology, created a bigger long-term problem for Labour than for the Conservatives. Conservatives were quick enough to respond to cries for help from industries which wanted to resist state ownership, notably in the cases of sugar, iron and steel and road haulage, but it seems to have been the industries as much as the Party which decided which cases to fight.[44] Having fought and lost in Parliament, the Party did in these few cases promise repeal, promises that were at least partly carried out after 1951. By making no such dangerous pledges in relation to the other energy and transport bodies set up by Labour, the Conservatives held to the pragmatic line of the Thirties; they also left the way open for their own party to argue in the 1955 and 1959 General Elections that coal,

[42] Maudling, *Memoirs*, 45; Hoffman, *Conservative Party*, 162–6.
[43] Craig, *Election Manifestoes*, 140.
[44] Ramsden, *Making*, 119.

for example, had been nationalised only because of the industry's weakness but that continuing large losses reported annually by the National Coal Board proved that the experiment should not be extended to other more profitable industries. An election record produced in 1964 included a song called 'Nationalisation nightmare', ending with the words: 'Is this the way to run our Steel/Which we sell the whole world over?'[45] Pragmatism meant the chance to have it both ways in the future as in the past. But in the long run the policy issues that helped the Conservatives to recover power in 1951 were the ones that had the least to do with the charters and other documents of 1947 to 1949. The two issues most stressed by candidates in 1950 and 1951 were housing and freedom. Housing came back to the top of the agenda as a result of public demand rather than party calculation, and the policy offered in 1951 was not very different from that of 1945 or 1935. The idea of setting the people free was not prominent in the *Industrial Charter* (and was indeed in one sense in conflict with its philosophy of interdependence), and freedom as a concept was only inserted into the 1949 Policy Statement in a late draft. Once again the central electioneering issue owed more to traditional ways of opposing Labour and to public demand than to any shift of philosophy by the Conservatives.[46]

These changes of policy and organisation must now be set against subsequent experience. In organisation, the most that can be said is that the scale of change has not been spectacular. Membership fell after the heady days of Lord Woolton and—perhaps most significant of all—national membership figures were no longer published. When reliable figures were again available in 1970, it seems that the total was less than half that of 1951, probably not far above its level in the Thirties.[47] There it has more or less remained. The Maxwell-Fyfe rules have been observed and it can fairly be said that Harold Macmillan's Conservative Party did not contain the physical and financial barriers to equality that existed when he himself entered Parliament. But even without barriers in the rules, the practical effect was limited. In 1963, W. L. Guttsman's *The British Political Elite* demonstrated just how little the educational, social and occupational character of the Party had changed; at the same time, Anthony Sampson demonstrated more impressionistically how far the great cousinhood still prevailed; in the same year, Enoch Powell and Iain Macleod, associated more than any other two Conservatives with the

---

[45] 'Songs for Swinging Voters', Election record published by Conservative Central Office, 1964.

[46] Butler, *General Election of 1951*, 55–6.

[47] David Butler and Michael Pinto-Duschinsky, *The British General Election of 1970* (1971), 279.

social changes in their Party, found it impossible to serve under a new Prime Minister in the House of Lords.[48] In policy terms too, Conservatives in government in the Fifties were pragmatic; there was little attempt to disturb the balance in industry or the rest of the public sector, only token concessions to the idea of denationalisation and greater freedom, as with the advent of commercial broadcasting.[49] The idea of the property-owning democracy was honoured through the housing boom of the Fifties, though as the 1951–1964 Government went on there was a good deal of public housing built too, by Conservative as well as Labour authorities. Affluence allowed for a widespread extension of consumer durables and cars, but suggested campaigns to extend share-ownership or co-partnership, described with enthusiasm by Eden in 1955 and announced again in 1959, never came to much.[50] Nothing perhaps would have done more to tilt the balance between owners and earners than wider ownership of industry, a positive alternative to Labour's plans for state ownership. Nonetheless it was still an aspiration in the Fifties as it was between the wars.

A re-evaluation of the 1940s in the history of the Conservative Party seems to show that its importance for the Party's policy and organisation was rather less than has been generally assumed. The point stands out rather more clearly if the long period of incremental change between 1924 and 1964 is compared to the developments that began in 1965. In that year, the Party came close to committing itself to the introduction of a wealth tax, intended specifically to enable a Conservative Chancellor to make major reductions in income tax for earners, at the expense of the owners of inherited wealth.[51] Within two years more it had committed itself to a sweeping programme of denationalisation and the dismantling of the municipal housing empires in a crash programme to extend ownership. It was at last moving towards actual changes in its social character at the top, signalled by the election of a Leader from a grammar school.[52] It would be premature to reach any conclusions about such recent

[48] W. L. Guttsman, *The British Political Elite* (1963), ch. 10; Anthony Sampson, *The Anatomy of Britain* (1960); David Butler and Michael Pinto-Duschinsky have argued that social character has not really mattered in practice to electoral prospects, in Z. Layton Henry (ed), *Conservative Politics* (1980), 186–204.

[49] This view has been put forward recently by such unlikely allies as Kenneth Morgan, in the process of building up the Attlee Government in *Labour in Power 1945–1951* (1984), 490, and John Biffen, in arguing how feeble were Conservative Governments before that of Margaret Thatcher, in *Forward from Conviction* (1986), 4.

[50] Ramsden, *Making*, 201.

[51] Ramsden, *Making*, 245.

[52] Andrew Roth, *Health and the Heathmen* (1972) *passim*; Peter Riddell, *The Thatcher Government* (1985), 10–11.

events, but even a superficial glance makes the 'revolutionary' change of the Forties look very small indeed. If this is so, it remains to ask why the earlier version, based so heavily on the views of participants, has had so wide a currency. The answer to that probably does lie in reactions to defeat in 1945. The problem was that in the 1945 election the Party campaigned on a policy about which many in the Party had doubts; the policy pledges of the manifesto were therefore lost in doubts about the willingness of the Party to carry them out. In defeat they could hardly turn directly away from policies that they helped to frame and which had helped to put Labour into office by a landslide. Nor could they just say the same again without expecting to lose again. The strategy that solved this problem was to keep the same policy in essentials—though it was propagated with more conviction in order to convince others—while saying at the same time that the policy was new and different. Continuity of content was needed alongside a change of packaging and style; to a large extent that was what happened, though changing political fashions helped to restore such issues as freedom and housing on which Conservatives felt safer. R. A. Butler described the changes as 'impressionistic', that is a paint-ing with a broad brush for appearance, rather than the more natu-ralistic policy-making in which parties usually engage. He also called it 'a cosmetic exercise' and this seems even nearer to the truth. Behind the cosmetics there were major elements of continuity alongside cumu-lative and gradual change.[53]

[53] Butler, *Art of the Possible*, 145–6.

DISRAELI'S POLITICS

By Paul Smith

READ 18 APRIL 1986

'COULD I only satisfy myself that D'Israeli believed all that he said, I should be more happy: his historical views are quite mine, but does he believe them?' Lord John Manners, who wrote these words at the height of the Young England episode in 1843,[1] has never lacked for company in his puzzlement. 'The question', says Lord Blake, 'echoes emptily down the years. We can answer it no more certainly today than Lord John Manners could then.'[2] Yet if the answer is elusive, so, in a sense, is the question: that is, the question which will most help us to understand the character of Disraeli's ideas and their relation to the form and conduct of his career. The question whether Disraeli believed in the literal descriptive and moral truth of the views he propounded, if that is what Manners was asking, is not only unanswerable but also, perhaps, unimportant—unimportant, that is, if what we are concerned with is the genesis and instrumentality of Disraeli's political postulates rather than their status as 'principles'.

It is of course by the test of their authenticity as principles related to an overriding concept of the public good that they have sometimes been judged and found wanting. Disraeli has often seemed to lack conscience, and, still worse, seriousness. Archbishop Tait had 'a painful feeling' that the author of *Endymion* considered 'all political life as mere play and gambling'.[3] For Wilfred Scawen Blunt, Disraeli was 'a very complete *farceur* ... you cannot persuade me that he ever for an instant took himself seriously as a *British* statesman, or expected any but the stolid among his contemporaries to accept him so'.[4] Disraeli's ideas become in this reading the mere patter of the charlatan,

---

[1] C. Whibley, *Lord John Manners and His Friends* (2 vols., Edinburgh & London, 1925), i. 149.

[2] R. Blake, *Disraeli* (1966), 175.

[3] Diary, 12 Dec. 1880, in R. T. Davidson and W. Benham, *Life of Archibald Campbell Tait, Archbishop of Canterbury*, 3rd ed. (2 vols., 1891), ii. 429.

[4] To W. Meynell, Sept. 1903, in W. S. Blunt, *My Diaries: Being a Personal Narrative of Events 1888–1914* (2 vols., 1921), ii. 71–2. In November 1910, Blunt had it from Rivers Wilson, who had been Disraeli's private secretary in 1867–8, that his master 'was in those days still the *farceur* he had been in his youth, having his tongue in his cheek and not pretending to be serious when behind the scenes. . . . It was not till after the Congress of Berlin, ten years later, that he began to take himself *au grand sérieux*' (*ibid.*, ii. 325–6).

at best extravagant nonsense, at worst cynical and impudent deceit. The political persona dissolves into its medium, the 'infinite glitter of language', in which nothing more can be discerned than 'the aspirations of megalomania in search of a career . . . a rhetoric which neither commanded nor expected belief', designed 'to enrapture rather than to convince'.[5]

Even when they emanate from political opponents, such strictures are hard to dismiss. In dealing with so blatant a careerist as Disraeli, there is an obvious difficulty about envisaging his ideas as anything other than the rhetorical crampons donned in order to get a firm grip on the greasy pole. Yet to say that they were adapted to his needs is not the same thing as to demonstrate that they were either fraudulent or foolish, and it is by no means incontestable that Disraeli neither took them seriously himself nor expected others to do so. If they are nothing like a system of political philosophy, they represent nonetheless a more extensive and coherent set of observations on English history, character, and destiny than has been exposed to public view in his lifetime by almost any other party leader and prime minister, expressed with remarkable pertinacity over fifty years. In the extent of their elaboration, the provocativeness of their content, and the openness and even arrogance of their display, they went much further than was necessary or prudent for the mere purpose of rising—indeed, from that point of view, sometimes threatened to be counterproductive.[6] It is impossible to sweep them aside as a mere bag of burglar's tools for effecting felonious entry to the British political pantheon.

Nor is it obvious that we are bound to follow Lord Blake or others in separating them out into the product of youthful rhodomontade on the one hand and genuine, operative principles on the other. Lord Blake acquits Disraeli of the charge of insincerity and lack of principle by treating the 'Tory idea' he elaborated in the 1840s (and earlier) as unconnected with his practical career as a front-rank politician.

[5] G. Watson, *The English Ideology: Studies in the Language of Victorian Politics* (1973), 130.

[6] The views on race, religion, and the Jews expounded in *Coningsby*, *Tancred*, and *Lord George Bentinck*, and in the debates on Jewish disabilities, are a prime example. Russell once praised Disraeli's tenacity in a speech on Jewish emancipation, 'tho' he knows that every word he says is gall and wormwood to every man who sits around and behind him' (a recollection by Gladstone, in J. Morley, *The Life of William Ewart Gladstone* (3 vols., 1903), iii. 476). Perhaps Disraeli's writings did not percolate far enough through his party to cause much perturbation, if we accept his own complaint that 'they never read . . . and did not understand the ideas of their own time' (Stanley's journal, 9 Feb. 1853, in *Disraeli, Derby and the Conservative Party: Journals and Memoirs of Edward Henry, Lord Stanley 1849–1869*, ed. J. Vincent (Hassocks, 1978), 96). Yet it is the life of Bentinck that Jawleyford is found reading in c. 15 of *Mr. Sponge's Sporting Tour*.

'The truth is', Lord Blake assures us, 'that Disraeli had principles
when he led the party and believed in them sincerely, but they were
not the "principles", if that word can be used at all, of Young
England'. They resided essentially in a profound belief in the
supremacy of the landed interest as the guarantee of the greatness of
England and the liberties of her people.[7]
    Mr P. R. Ghosh has aggregated this view with the opinions of other
students of nineteenth-century Conservative politics—Maurice
Cowling, R. M. Stewart, myself—to constitute what he characterises
as the 'neo-opportunist' interpretation of Disraeli's career, according
to which Disraeli 'may have had principles sufficient to justify his
personal integrity', but yet they 'were not *efficient*, they did not determine his actions in any detailed or specific sense'. On the plane of
practical politics, he remained an opportunist. Ghosh himself bids to
show that *from the late 1840s* Disraeli's career displays a coherent
development in which policy is guided by principles resting on such
bases as 'Francophilism and his estimate of the political value of low
taxation' and achieving 'their final, coherent formulation centring
round the maxim that "expenditure depends on policy"' at the end
of the 1850s. His Disraeli is a competitor with Gladstone for the
Peelite mantle of economical finance and moderate progress, whose
appearance in the late 1870s as 'an aggressive patriotic *and* imperial
minister' was a 'deviation' provoked by the success of the Bulgarian
atrocities agitation and existing 'almost solely in the realm of the style
and presentation of policy'.[8] Apart from making Disraeli sound dull,
this thesis reproduces a key feature of Lord Blake's position by operating a divorce between the professions of the 1830s and 1840s and
the mature political career. But the banal precepts which it parades
cannot do duty for the fundamentals of Disraeli's political outlook,
and Ghosh's implication[9] that they might have provided a satisfying
resolution of the search for an intellectually-based Conservative creed
manifested in *Coningsby* places on them a weight they will not bear.
    It is questionable whether the disjunction which the views just
summarised introduce into their subject's life would have been understood by Disraeli himself. He was perfectly capable in later life of
attempting to obliterate youthful extravagances, but he never tried
to distance himself from the pronouncements about Toryism, religion,
English history, and English society which he had broadcast in the
1830s and 1840s. On the contrary, he went on saying the same things,

---

[7] Blake, 761-3, and cf. 211.
[8] P. R. Ghosh, 'Disraelian Conservatism: a Financial Approach', *English Historical
Review*, xcix (1984), especially 268, 293-5. The maxim 'expenditure depends on policy'
has also impressed Harold Wilson (*The Governance of Britain* (1976), 70).
[9] Ghosh, 294, n. 2.

or at least using the same terms of reference; and in 1870, when he had been twenty years a party leader and very recently prime minister, he went out of his way, in the preface to a new edition of his novels, not merely to draw attention to his early professions but to assert that, in his famous trilogy of the 1840s, *Coningsby*, *Sybil*, and *Tancred*, he had provided a systematic exposition of, respectively, the political, social, and spiritual condition of the English nation.[10] Disraeli wanted people to think, and, more important, wanted to think himself, that the politics of the mature statesman were still those, minus a few exaggerations, of the mentor of Young England.

That might have been the result simply of vanity, of a desire to give a specious consistency to a career in fact sharply divided into a 'Tory Radical' and Young England extravaganza and thirty years of Peelite pragmatism in the name of the 'aristocratic settlement' and the 'territorial constitution'. But there is a case for considering seriously Disraeli's claims to unity in his political life and for regarding the stance evolved in the 1830s and 1840s as the core of his politics, indeed *as* his politics, rather than as a colourful but more or less irrelevant prologue to his 'real' political career. To adopt such an approach is not to contest the view that he was an 'opportunist' or 'adventurer': he was undoubtedly both, and would have regarded the latter epithet, at least, as in one sense a title of honour. Nor is it necessarily to assert a close operative relationship between a scheme of thought and the details of day-to-day political action. But it is to suggest a wholeness of political conception which possessed a force quite independent of its literal fidelity to the facts or of its practical application to the conduct of Conservative politics or British government, the key to the understanding of which lies in the consideration of the personal imperatives it evolved to answer.

The functional analysis required to expose its inner logic cannot be conducted simply in the terms of that crude model which sees professions of political belief as pragmatic and tactical, the necessary rhetorical devices to articulate the strategies of personal, sectional, and party advancement and to cope with the practical exigencies of government. While not excluding their possible status as principles or denying their instrumentality as elements of manoeuvre, we have to look at Disraeli's ideas as the means of resolving a problem of personal integration, the integration of the elements of Disraeli's personality and inheritance one with another, and the integration of what Disraeli conceived to be his 'genius' into English society and history, in terms which should be intellectually coherent, emotionally tolerable, and aesthetically harmonious, as well as operationally viable.

---

[10] 'General Preface to the Novels' (1870), in the *Bradenham Edition of the Novels and Tales of Benjamin Disraeli, 1st Earl of Beaconsfield* (12 vols., 1926–7), i. xiii–xv.

That problem was an acute one for a christianised Jew with a boundless sense of his own abilities but no natural line of ascent to the summit of British public life. It will not do to talk as though, once baptism had removed the disqualification for sitting in parliament, there was no special obstacle to Disraeli's career. 'To enter into high society', runs the familiar quotation from his first novel,[11] 'a man must either have blood, a million, or a genius.' Disraeli had neither wealth nor assured social position, and he did not undergo in youth the processes of socialisation that were becoming standard in the production of the country's political elite—a fact of which he was ruefully aware, as the fascinated references in his novels to the public school and university life he had not experienced suggest.[12] There was only the 'genius', the sense of supereminent powers, of special election and destiny, that had somehow to command the recognition of a society to which Disraeli's relation was doubly oblique, by the fact of his descent and the character of his vision, that is by virtue of his Jewishness and his romanticism.

It is commonplace to acknowledge both Jewishness and romanticism as primary ingredients of the quality of strangeness which characterised Disraeli in English political life, but commonplace also to underestimate their role in the shaping of his political outlook and career, as though they were nullified as matters of practical moment, the one by the fact of baptism and the second by the prosaic realities of life in the Conservative party. Lord Blake's classic study may seem to undervalue the formative power of the one and to overlook the instrumental importance of the other. Romanticism is hardly discussed. Jewishness is virtually dismissed as a matter of serious importance in a single page, where we are told that 'it is not so much the Jewish as the Italian streak in Disraeli that predominated'. The

[11] *Vivian Grey* (5 vols., 1826–7), bk. I, c. 8.
[12] The point is made twice by him and his sister in the jointly authored *A Year at Hartlebury or the Election* (2 vols., 1834, under the pseudonyms of 'Cherry and Fair Star'): 'In this country where the art most sedulously fostered is the art of making a connection numerous are the established means of arriving at the great result. A public school, a crack college, the turf if you are rich, are all good in their way—but to travel on the Continent is a highly esteemed mode' (i. c. 2; cf. ii. c. 8). If Disraeli told Rowton thatat Higham Hall 'the whole drama of public school life was acted in a smaller theatre' (Blake, 13), his longing for the real thing is strongly suggested by the Eton chapters in *Coningsby: or the New Generation* (3 vols., 1844), bk. I, cc. 8–11. But he convinced himself that his upbringing in his father's library had given him intellectual advantages over his more conventionally educated competitors in public life. A student of Bayle, he once noted how that author had introduced Sir George Lewis (and by implication him) to 'a kind of knowledge, unknown to the Universities, & which marked out Lewis from the Gladstones, Lytteltons & all those, who, as far as general knowledge was concerned, were only overgrown schoolboys' (*Disraeli's Reminiscences*, ed. H. M. and M. Swartz (1975), 101).

justification for this is apparently that Disraeli failed to behave with the circumspection and reserve typical of the wealthy and influential portion of Anglo-Jewry in his day, and indeed of his own family, and was 'financially incompetent to a high degree'; while on the other hand he displayed in abundance 'the traits associated, though perhaps not always fairly, with the Mediterranean character'—pride, flamboyance, theatricality, and so on.[13] It is true that if you are thinking of David Ricardo, Lionel de Rothschild, or Moses Montefiore, Disraeli was not a typical Anglo-Jew. But he was a Jew all the same, and scholars as acute as Israel Zangwill, Philip Rieff, and Isaiah Berlin have not been wrong to see Jewishness as a central determinant both of his situation and of his mode of response to it.[14] Indeed, Lord Blake, in discussing *Tancred* and in the account of the 'Grand Tour' which forms a pendant to his main work, does finally acknowledge Disraeli's need to find a means of integrating his Jewish identity into the role he aspired to play in English life.[15]

It is important to stress that the insertion of Disraeli's genius into English public life was more than a matter of the accommodation of a few mild aberrations or youthful flourishes. 'My mind', he wrote in the so-called 'Mutilated Diary' in 1833, 'is a continental mind. It is a revolutionary mind.'[16] Both epithets require more pondering than they have always received from Disraeli's biographers. The second of them evidently worried Monypenny, who devoted an uneasy passage to trying to reconcile it with a Conservative career.[17] It is not clear

[13] Blake, 49–50.
[14] I. Zangwill, *Dreamers of the Ghetto* (1898), c. 10, 'The Primrose Sphinx'; P. Rieff, 'Disraeli: the Chosen of History', *Commentary*, xiii (1952), 22–33; Sir I. Berlin, 'Benjamin Disraeli, Karl Marx and the Search for Identity', *Transactions of the Jewish Historical Society of England*, xxii (1970), 1–20. See also C. Roth, *The Earl of Beaconsfield* (New York, 1952), c. 6, 'Disraeli, Judaism and the Jews'; M. C. N. Salbstein, *The Emancipation of the Jews in Britain: the Question of the Admission of the Jews to Parliament, 1828–1860* (1982), c. 5, 'Benjamin Disraeli, Marrano Englishman'; H. Fisch, 'Disraeli's Hebraic Compulsions', in *Essays Presented to Chief Rabbi Israel Brodie on the Occasion of His Seventieth Birthday*, ed. H. J. Zimmels, J. Rabbinowitz, and I. Finestein (1967), 81–94. Buckle's statement that 'The fundamental fact about Disraeli was that he was a Jew' (W. F. Monypenny and G. E. Buckle, *The Life of Benjamin Disraeli, Earl of Beaconsfield* (6 vols., 1910–20), vi, 635) would not have been contested by Gladstone, who thought Disraeli's 'Judaic feeling' was, after his wife's death, 'the deepest and truest ... in his whole mind' (Morley, ii. 553, and cf. ii. 558, iii. 475–6), or by Wilfred Scawen Blunt, who accepted Disraeli's 'semitic' politics as 'genuine enough' (ii. 72). A comprehensive study of the role of Jewishness in the formation of Disraeli's mind and career is badly needed.
[15] Blake, *Disraeli*, 204; *Disraeli's Grand Tour: Benjamin Disraeli and the Holy Land 1830–31* (1982).
[16] *Benjamin Disraeli Letters: 1815–1834*, ed. J. A. W. Gunn, J. Matthews, D. M. Schurman, M. G. Wiebe (Toronto, 1982), 447.
[17] Monypenny and Buckle, i. 244–5.

whether either of them worries Lord Blake, for he does not quote them. But to ignore them is to ignore the extra-territorial springboard from which Disraeli assaulted the summit of English life and the extent of the tension he had to resolve in finding the terms of composition between his consciousness and his environment. It is tempting to relate them simply to the grandiose enterprise on which he was engaged of turning himself into the Homer or the Milton of his age by producing an epic poem designed to embody its spirit, the *Revolutionary Epick*, inspired by the spectacle of the French Revolution and of the man of supernatural energies, Napoleon, emerging from it, and centring on the struggle between the two principles of government which he saw as contending for the mastery of the world, the aristocratic on the one hand and the revolutionary and democratic on the other, represented by the continents of Asia and Europe respectively. But 'continental' and 'revolutionary' applied to more than the scope and nature of Disraeli's poetic preoccupations. They signalled his sense of being born into a world in which, to borrow from George Steiner's brilliant characterisation of it, the French Revolution and the Napoleonic wars had 'quickened the pace of felt time' and opened up apparently boundless and immediate prospects of individual and social liberation.[18] Yet by the time Disraeli was growing to manhood, the 'great ennui' was already setting in, as political reaction and social consolidation left ardent young men, in despair at the impossibility of emulating the recent past, to stalk in frustration 'through the bourgeois city like *condottieri* out of work. Or worse, like *condottieri* meagrely pensioned before their first battle'.[19] The sense of continental perspectives and revolutionary opportunities, merged in the young Disraeli with the consciousness of supreme powers, beat ceaselessly against the constraints of life without fortune or high connection. What relieved the tension between limitless aspiration and circumscribed prospects was the romantic mode of thought and feeling, whose cult of introspection, fascination with 'genius', and sense of preternatural vision presented Disraeli not simply with a handy set of stylistic conventions but with a pattern of self-realisation and with the means to transcend the limitations and frustrations of his position through the power of the romantic imagination to transform the terms of relation to the external world. To Disraeli, with that sense of apartness from his fellows which he seems to have acquired very early in life, romanticism offered a home, membership of a European confraternity, a sense of special election and spiritual aristocracy which may

[18] G. Steiner, *In Bluebeard's Castle: Some Notes Towards the Re-definition of Culture* (1971), 18–21.
[19] Ibid., 21–2.

have been a translation of the chosenness he felt, or came to feel, as a Jew.[20]

In the frenetic efforts to achieve success which marked Disraeli's start in life, the essential object was to define and materialise his genius in anticipatory response to the Nietzschean injunction to 'become that you are'. This dedication to subjective authenticity as a fundamental moral goal and to the living of life as a process of *Bildung* differentiated him sharply from the exponents of the ideal of 'character', seen as the strenuous cultivation of desirable moral qualities.[21] His relation to a different value scheme than that which was taking an increasing, though not (by J. S. Mill and Arnold, for example) unchallenged, grip on the England of his day[22] accounts for much of the incomprehensibility which he presented in his own time and afterwards, and the difficulty of catching his moral drift was intensified by the particular style in which his search for the true revelation of self was conducted. In his speculations, dandyism, love affairs, but most especially in his novels, the young Disraeli sought to locate himself through the acting out of the possibilities of being inherent in him, a series of impersonations which were to some degree fantasies of wish fulfilment but were in large measure dress rehearsals, designed more

[20] The nature and function of romanticism in Disraeli's thought is another subject demanding a thorough treatment. The references to it in pt. I, c. 4 ('Au "Sanctuaire de la Sensibilité"') of what is otherwise the most extensive and searching study of Disraeli's personality and ideas, R. Maitre, *Disraeli: Homme de Lettres* (Paris, 1963), are unsatisfying. More can be gleaned from the sensitive probing of Disraeli's mental world in C. Richmond's unpublished Oxford University M.Litt. thesis, 'The Development of Disraeli's Conservatism 1820–1835' (1982), which gives weight to the German influences—imbibed largely through Madame de Stael's *Germany*—that helped to render the 'continental' mind elusive to its English audience, touched as it was by Kantian and Fichtean notions of the transcendental role of the mind in the apprehension of the world. Disraeli read in translation Goethe, Heine, and Wieland (at least), and was himself admired as an author by the first two: see, e.g., *Letters: 1815–1834*, 192, 426, 427; *Letters: 1835–1837*, ed. J. A. W. Gunn, J. Matthews, D. M. Schurman, and M. G. Wiebe (Toronto, 1982), 51 & n. 20, 124; J. S. Hamilton, 'Disraeli and Heine', *Disraeli Newsletter*, 2 (1977), 8. His *Contarini Fleming: a Psychological Auto-Biography* (4 vols., 1832) was among several English novels, including his friend Bulwer's *The Disowned* (1828), modelled on Goethe's *Wilhelm Meister* (author's preface to the 1845 edition of *Contarini Fleming*, Bradenham Edition, iv, ix; R. Ashton, *The German Idea: Four English Writers and the Reception of German Thought 1800–1860* (Cambridge, 1980), 22).

[21] On the contrast of the two concepts, see S. Collini, 'The Idea of "Character" in Victorian Political Thought', *T.R.H.S.* 5th series, xxxv (1985), 37–8, who notes the debt of the former to German romanticism. The antagonism between Disraeli and Gladstone could almost be summed up as *Bildung* versus 'character'.

[22] Collini points out (40, 43–4) that the advance of 'character' was linked with a rejection of the 'ethics of the *salon*' and of the eighteenth-century language of politeness and sociability. Disraeli's social and intellectual persona was in some ways out of date by mid-century.

as a preparation than as a surrogate for actual performance.[23] The exercise was conducted in full view of an audience needed both to accommodate the instinct of performance and—as purchasers of the novels—to meet the heavy overheads of pseudo-Byronic living, but once Disraeli had abandoned the raw and naive self-exhibition embodied in *Vivian Grey* he was careful to interpose between himself and the paying customers that distancing irony whose function was to protect the romantic ego from too naked an exposure and to avoid a premature commitment to any of the postures through which its manifold potentialities were being tried out—the irony which throughout his life was to breed among the baffled and the offended a conviction of his insincerity which rested on incomprehension of his artistic purpose. He made it easy to interpret his self-search as vulgar self-seeking.

Following the Carlylean view of the man of letters as 'our most important modern person', it was in literature that Disraeli first sought to vindicate his claim to greatness.[24] But the disappointing reception in 1832 of *Contarini Fleming*, his ambitious *Bildungsroman* designed to provide the definitive analysis of the development of the poetic mind, helped to tip the balance of aspiration towards politics, where perhaps—if one accepts at face value his description of his first novel, *Vivian Grey*, as portraying his 'active and real ambition'[25]—his fondest dreams had always lain. Contarini Fleming had in any case, like his inspiration, Wilhelm Meister, concluded that the time for introspection was over and that 'genius' must be put to practical effect in the world. Yet, whereas in the spheres of literature and dandyism, and within the conventions of romanticism, Disraeli had been able to operate in a European rather than a merely national frame, the assimilation of the continental and revolutionary consciousness into the political life of England, with its settled institutions, its aristocratic elite, and its historic parties, posed a different and more specific problem. The limitless expansion of self, subversive in principle of all established forms, had now to be confined within the bounds of time, place, and tradition: the genius must compound with the *genius loci*.

Seen against this background, the function and formation of Disraeli's politics become clearer. They were the politics of denization,

---

[23] Though he invested it with uncommon panache, the process is a common one, familiar to students of the 'dramatistic' aspects of mental and social life. See, e.g., S. M. Lyman and M. B. Scott, *The Drama of Social Reality* (New York, 1975), c. 5. Literary specialists have been cleverer than historians at recognising what Disraeli was doing, notably D. R. Schwarz, *Disraeli's Fiction* (1979), c. 1 and 151–2.

[24] The artist as (in Hugo's word) magus was often the first heroic role for the romantic sensibility. The young Marx wrote romantic poetry and contemplated a career as a *Dichter* (S. S. Prawer, *Karl Marx and World Literature* (Oxford, 1976), 2).

[25] 'Mutilated Diary', 1833, in *Letters: 1815–1834*, 447.

of settlement, the means by which Disraeli could achieve a sense of home. They were the politics of a stranger, a sojourner, whose attitudes and responses could not be the predictable outgrowth of a settled position and the unstudied inheritance of a native tradition. 'I am not in a condition', he said in 1846, 'to have had hereditary opinions carved out for me and all my opinions, therefore, have been the result of reading and thought.'[26] He was, in other words, obliged—or privileged—to create them, in an effort on the one hand to reconcile within a coherent political persona the diverse strains of conservative instinct and continental and revolutionary sensibility, of English allegiance and Jewish identity, on the other hand to reconcile that strenuous synthesis itself with the conditions of ascent to the peak of political life.

It is with the logic and method of that endeavour that the remainder of this paper must be concerned. Disraeli's technique in establishing a stance and a role consistent with the dictates of his nature remained, whether in print or on the platform, that of dramatic experimentation which had served for the realisation of self in the early novels. The initial radicalism of 1832–4 was another of his theatre workshops of personality, neither naive witness of political conviction nor merely cynical vehicle of political manoeuvre, but rather the opening bid in a process of political self-materialisation.[27] The integration of the elements of the political self under the freedom of a radical umbrella was, however, quickly complicated by the need to integrate the whole into the collectivities of party and nation. From the definition of self, Disraeli's political creativity was drawn into the definition of a Tory party and an English nation in which that self could occupy a leading place, a transformational exercise of the romantic vision achieved, principally in the *Vindication of the English Constitution* and in the novel trilogy of *Coningsby*, *Sybil*, and *Tancred*, through the assumption of the role of the magus, possessing a special insight into the historical character and destiny of both. This progressive enlargement from the individual to the collective focus of vision—or rather fusion of the

---

[26] Monypenny and Buckle, ii. 371, citing *Hansard*, 8 May 1846. Perhaps that underestimated the influence of his father.

[27] Re-creating in *Hartlebury* (ii. c. 2) his Red Lion speech of June 1832, Disraeli refers to his hero, Bohun, as 'a perfect master of stage effect', and many similar metaphors witness to his sense of the theatrical nature of politics as of life in general. He was almost certainly aware of the ambition to create a drama of national self-consciousness entertained by the German romantics, e.g. Friedrich Schlegel, the title and Spanish setting of whose tragedy, *Alarcos* (1802) he reproduced in his own *The Tragedy of Count Alarcos* in 1839. Yet the capacity to involve a national audience in the dramatic projection of politics on the grandest scale was to elude him: if we follow John Vincent (*Pollbooks: How Victorians Voted* (Cambridge, 1967), 47), it was Gladstone who 'created a national theatre for England as Verdi did for nineteenth-century Italy'.

two—would be complete only, in *Tancred* and *Lord George Bentinck*, with the final assertion of the racial and religious propositions appropriate to perfect Disraeli's credentials as a seer and to integrate his sense of Jewishness into his Christian and national sphere of operations by exposing the racial foundations of historical process and nominating the British empire as the legatee of the spiritual mission of his people.[28]

From the outset, Disraeli's pronouncement bore the impress of the organic view which sees politics as a matter of practical wisdom within the sometimes narrow constraints of history and culture, and of the romantic view which regards them as the sphere not of mechanical analysis and contrivance but of imagination and *Fingerspitzengefühl*, not of logic but of art.[29] He stood for Wycombe in 1832, however, unencumbered by much in the way of developed political theory. His first task was to find a seat and a standpoint. When, in 1833, he published his pamphlet, *What is He?*, he was trying to answer the question less for the bemused spectators of his early political gyrations than for himself.

His appetite for politics had been reawakened by the reports of the Reform Bill crisis that had reached him on his way back from his Eastern tour in 1831. When he came two years later to write with his sister the pseudonymous novel *Hartlebury*, in which he evoked his first election contest, he described how his hero and *alter ego*, Bohun, was prompted to return from abroad by the Reform Bill, which had caused England to be seen from afar as in a state of critical instability. 'At the prospect of insurrection, he turned with more affection towards a country he had hitherto condemned as too uneventful for a man of genius'—he felt 'all was stirring'.[30] Disraeli's remark to Austen on his return to England in November 1831—'The times are damnable. I take the gloomiest views of affairs, but we must not lose our property without a struggle'[31]—suggests an expectation of convulsion. It also hints at a fundamentally conservative attitude to it, but not at commitment to a Tory party too much in the doldrums for a young

[28] The process may be seen as the progressive generalisation of the self-presenting individual's need to try to control the response of others to him by 'influencing the definition of the situation which the others come to formulate ... the object of a performer is to sustain a particular definition of the situation, this representing, as it were, his claim as to what reality is' (E. Goffman, *The Presentation of Self in Everyday Life* (English ed., 1969), 3, 74).

[29] The second aspect is rarely well assimilated into attempts to give a systematic account of Disraeli's political ideas, but see W. Stafford, 'Romantic Elitism in the Thought of Benjamin Disraeli', *Literature and History*, vi (1980), 43–58.

[30] *Hartlebury*, i.c. 14.

[31] *Letters: 1815–1834*, 207.

man on the make.[32] If there was to be a storm, such as might offer
opportunities of fulfilment to frustrated young talent, Disraeli was
prepared to risk running before it.[33] Radicalism, in the loose and often
eccentric meaning of that term in the 1830s,[34] gave him a standpoint
of independence from which he could pursue the national and popular
politics that seemed more fluidly adapted to an epoch of rapid political
alteration than the current shibboleths of the parties. The main aim
of his political self-development was to gauge the wind, to attune
himself to the requirements of the times and the needs of the country.
The aristocratic principle of government, he suggested in *What is He?*,
was outworn and the democratic must replace it under the guidance
of a national party in which Tories and Radicals should coalesce.[35]
The idea of a national party was an obvious vehicle for an aspirant
who, without connection in either of the established groups, needed
to transcend them in the name of a new political force which he could
himself claim to define and control. Years later he was to tell Bright
that 'the politics and principles to suit England must be of the "English
type"',[36] and already in 1832, in the anonymously published *England
and France: a Cure for the Ministerial Gallomania*, he was disavowing
either Whig or Tory allegiance and declaring: 'I have confidence in
the genius of the people.... My politics are described by one word,
and that word is ENGLAND.' Government must follow not the
dictates of the 'Doctrinaire Clique' but those of the national character.[37]

Disraeli denied from the first that either the democratic principle
or the national character was safe with the Whigs. Bohun found what

[32] 'Toryism is worn out', he told Austen in June 1832, 'and I cannot condescend to
be a Whig' (ibid., 285). His letters during his wooing of Wycombe hint at a Tory
penchant but show readiness to tack in any direction to gain the seat (ibid., nos. 133–
4, 141–2, 144, 163, 167–8, 173, 179, 184, 188, n. 1, 198–9, 202). The tactical considerations are well outlined in R. W. Davis, *Disraeli* (1976), 28–34. Disraeli's abortive
start for the county in December 1832 struck a stronger Tory note.
[33] Like Bohun, who 'had too great a stake in the existing order of society to precipitate
a revolution', but 'intended to ride the storm, if the hurricane did occur' (*Hartlebury*,
ii. c. 1).
[34] A point well made by Blake, *Disraeli*, 90–1. His friend Bulwer's example no doubt
influenced Disraeli's adoption of a radical posture.
[35] His Wycombe address of 1 Oct. 1832 had already called on Englishmen to 'rid
yourselves of all that political jargon and factious slang of Whig and Tory' and unite
in a great national party (*Letters: 1815–1834*, 305).
[36] *The Diaries of John Bright*, ed. R. A. J. Walling (1930), 130.
[37] *England and France: a Cure for the Ministerial Gallomania* (1832), 13, 50–1. Bohun
follows the same progressive but national line. Change in the relations between the
governors and the governed must occur, but 'he thought it the duty of a great statesman
only to effect that quantity of change in the country whose destiny he regulated which
could be achieved with deference to its existing constitution'. He, too, meant to guide
the 'movement' through a new party (*Hartlebury*, ii. c. 1).

Disraeli always subsequently maintained, that the Reform Act of the Whigs was a rigging of the constituency designed to perpetuate their power.[38] Perhaps if the Whigs had given Disraeli passage at Wycombe he would have felt differently. But he could hardly expect to rise in the tight circles of grand Whiggery. 'A Whig', said Sir Francis Baring, 'is like a poet, born not made. It is as difficult to become a Whig as to become a Jew.'[39] As for low Whiggery, his experience with the 'sectarian oligarchy' of High Wycombe led him to characterise them as 'the least human of all the combinations of human matter', naturally hostile to the man of genius who made them 'ashamed of their dead, dunghill-like, existence'.[40] Under pretence of making changes required by the spirit of the age, the Whigs had set out to destroy the balance of parties, and had created a situation in which the only way to get rid of them was to 'expand the Whig constituency into a national constituency' by the further prosecution of reform.[41]

In combating the Whigs at Wycombe in 1832 and 1834–5, Disraeli was glad to enrol the support of Tories. A degree of fundamental conservatism in his deference to established national institutions, and no doubt the influence of the father whose volumes on Charles I had been Tory enough in tone to earn him an honorary DCL from the University of Oxford, made it easy for him to contract such an alliance. But the integrating bent of his mind, the compulsion both to feel and to exhibit intellectual consistency, made it necessary for him also to justify it. His invocation of the support of a Tory tradition embodied in the names of Wyndham and Bolingbroke for such Radical devices as triennial parliaments needed to counter the designs of the Whigs[42] was in fact a less bizarre synthesis than it has sometimes seemed. His Radicalism was of a peculiar kind, not that of the Birmingham men, whom he despised,[43] but more akin to the high-toned, independent line of Sir Francis Burdett, whom Byron thought the only reformer in whose company a gentleman would be seen.[44] Burdett, a supporter of equal electoral districts, annual parliaments, and a direct taxation franchise, adopted a 'patriot' stance which linked him to the 'country' ideology of the late seventeenth and early eighteenth centuries,

[38] Ibid.
[39] Quoted in B. Mallet, *Thomas George Earl of Northbrook G.C.S.I.: a Memoir* (1908), 33.
[40] *Hartlebury*, ii. c. 1.
[41] Ibid.
[42] Apparently first heard in the speech of November 1832 at Wycombe quoted in Monypenny and Buckle, i. 219.
[43] See his remarks on them to his sister, 26 May 1832, in *Letters: 1815–1834*, 280–1.
[44] Byron to Hobhouse, 26 June 1819, in *Byron's Letters and Journals*, ed. L. A. Marchand, vi (1976), 166. Cf. Disraeli's 'the greatest gentleman I ever knew' (*Reminiscences*, 37).

described his political creed as that of a Tory of the reign of Queen
Anne, and owed a substantial intellectual debt to Bolingbroke.[45]
Disraeli compared his views to those of Wyndham and Cotton and
called him a Jacobite who had been mistaken for a Jacobin.[46] A figure
like Burdett conferred living reality on Disraeli's effort to link Radical
professions with Tory traditions, and his case points up what Disraeli
was trying to do. He was attempting to create a suitable political and
intellectual vehicle for himself by reviving the 'country' opposition
politics of Bolingbroke's era, as the counter to what he saw as a new
Whig oligarchy comparable to that under the early Hanoverians.

If he exaggerated for partisan purposes the wickedness and rapacity
of the Whigs,[47] it is not at all certain that he much exaggerated the
extent to which a genuine tradition of Tory engagement in radical
and popular opposition politics existed, even if it had hardly emerged
in vigour from the age of Pitt and Liverpool. Recent scholarship has
made his drawings on eighteenth-century history seem less profligate
than Whig historiographical tradition would have them. John Brewer
has suggested that the country party platform of the early eighteenth
century supplied in its 'ideology of the excluded' perhaps the only
Hanoverian species of radicalism before Wilkes,[48] and Linda Colley
has shown extensively how before 1760 'A common hatred of the
whig regime encouraged tory MPs to identify themselves at least
rhetorically with the socially and politically dispossessed, and the
electorate to regard a tory vote (like a liberal vote a century or more
after) as a means to vex the mighty'.[49]

[45] J. R. Dinwiddy, 'Sir Francis Burdett and Burdettite Radicalism', *History*, lxv
(1980), 17–31.
[46] *Reminiscences*, 37. He canvassed for Burdett in the 1837 Westminster by-election, in
which the latter was effectively the Tory candidate. Another Radical figure describing
himself as 'a Tory of Queen Anne's reign' with whom Disraeli later had dealings was
David Urquhart (O. Anderson, *A Liberal State at War: English Politics and Economics
During the Crimean War* (1967), 142, 145, 147–8).
[47] Grey in 1830 had, however, provided government places for eight of his nearest
relatives and friends; and it was Gladstone who remarked in 1855 that the 'prizes' of
public life were 'air, light, heat, electricity, meat and drink and everything else to that
which meets at Brooks's' (quoted in D. Southgate, *The Passing of the Whigs 1832–1886*
(1962), 201).
[48] J. Brewer, *Party Ideology and Popular Politics at the Accession of George III* (Cambridge,
1976), 19.
[49] L. Colley, *In Defiance of Oligarchy: the Tory Party 1714–60* (Cambridge, 1982), 173.
Cf. her 'Eighteenth-century English Radicalism Before Wilkes', *T.R.H.S.* 5th series,
xxxi (1981), 1–19. Increasing Tory dependence on open constituencies was a factor in
bringing closer involvement with popular opinion and participation. There was an
obvious tension between encouragement of popular ferment and the Tory belief in
social subordination, and the ending after 1760 of the Tories' exclusion from power
and place made their attitudes more conservative, yet there was still a significant Tory
contribution to the Wilkite movement.

By the time he came to write the *Vindication of the English Constitution* in 1835, however, Disraeli needed to do more than simply confect an anti-Whig creed reconciling his Radical and Tory strands.[50] Having finally taken lodgings in the reviving Tory party, he had to convert it into a suitable home. In moving from the realisation of self to the realisation of an environment in which the self could operate with assurance, he moved from the individual to the collective mode of introspection, to history, through which the special faculty of the seer could claim to discern the true character and destiny of organisms such as parties and nations and, by peeling away excrescences and errors, restore to them the knowledge of their identity and mission.[51] The reconceptualisation of the Tory party to supply a possible vehicle and a viable role for an outsider who sought no less than to command it was an exercise perilous to attempt without a powerful spiritual sponsor, and he fashioned one from the shade of Bolingbroke, whose career he clearly felt paralleled and validated his own. Disraeli's Bolingbroke, 'opposed to the Whigs from principle, for an oligarchy is hostile to genius', was saddled with the reputation of inconsistency because he maintained 'that vigilant and meditative independence which is the privilege of an original and determined spirit', contemplated (Disraeli supposes) 'the formation of a new party, that dream of youthful ambition in a perplexed and discordant age, but destined in English politics to be never more substantial than a vision', but in the end had to choose between the Whigs and the Tories. Having 'penetrated their interior and essential qualities', he found it a choice between oligarchy and democracy, and from the moment of becoming a Tory he lent his pen to the party and 'eradicated from Toryism all those absurd and odious doctrines which Toryism had adventitiously adopted', and 'clearly developed its essential and permanent character'.[52] Wearing this convenient periwig, Disraeli took

[50] Though the reconciliation continued to be strenuously pursued in 1835, as Disraeli responded angrily to charges of ratting on a Radical past provoked by his appearance as Tory candidate for Taunton with attempts to demonstrate the congruity of the 'primitive Toryism' he was professing with his previous Radical gestures (*Letters: 1835–1837*, nos. 379, 398, 406, 409, 415, 458; Monypenny and Buckle, i. 282–4).

[51] The process was also, as with that of individual self-realisation, intended to be a purging of corruptions and a restoration of purity, which assimilated it to the idea of the salvation of the corrupt state through the exercise of civic virtue transmitted by writers such as Bolingbroke from Macchiavelli and embodied to some degree in nineteenth-century Radical criticisms of the perversion of the ancient constitution to oligarchic forms by an oppressive aristocracy. Disraeli's use of history, partly as a means to satisfy the romantic longing for a sense of community, requires a study.

[52] B. Disraeli, *Vindication of the English Constitution in a Letter to a Noble and Learned Lord* (1835), c. 31. Bolingbroke believed as profoundly as Disraeli in the power of superior spirits in public affairs. 'These are they', he wrote, 'who engross almost the whole reason of the species; who are born to instruct, to guide, and to preserve; who are

up the mission of 'labouring to replace the Tory party in their natural and historical position in this country' which forty years later he was to speak of as his life's work.[53] The *Vindication* formulated the idea of the Tory party as the national and democratic party, charged, in association with the national and popular institutions of crown and church, with resistance to the designs of a 'Venetian' oligarchy.[54] As Bolingbroke had argued that the country party was not really a party but 'the nation, speaking and acting in the discourse and conduct of particular men',[55] so Disraeli conceived Toryism as 'the proposed or practical embodification, as the case may be, of the national will and character', to the extent even that it must sometimes 'represent and reflect the passions and prejudices of the nation, as well as its purer energies and its more enlarged and philosophic views'.[56] Disraeli's Tory politics, in this version, were literally England, his country, right or wrong.[57]

The assertion of special insight into the nature of the Tory party was of course the validation of Disraeli's title to lead it, and the same device was employed in the succeeding years to support his pretensions to guide not simply the party but the nation. Like Marx, Disraeli had a good deal of the rabbi *manqué*, and his compulsion to set up as a visionary teacher was strikingly displayed in the 1840s in Young England and in the trilogy of *Coningsby*, *Sybil*, and *Tancred*. Young England contained elements both of romantic escapade and of grandiose self-delusion, as Disraeli harassed the leader who had refused him office with what Peel explicitly recognised as a further version of

---

designed to be the tutors and the guardians of human kind' (*The Works of Lord Bolingbroke* (4 vols., 1844), ii. 352). In *Sybil or: The Two Nations* (1845), Disraeli recognised a second exemplar in Burke, who 'effected for the Whigs what Bolingbroke in a preceding age had done for the Tories: he restored the moral existence of the party', suffusing their 'ancient principles' with 'all the delusive splendour of his imagination' (bk. I, c. 3).

[53] To the Rev. A. Beaven, 17 Jan. 1874, in Monypenny and Buckle, i. 222.

[54] The language emphasises the historical cast of Disraeli's vision. The image of politicians seeking to emulate the Venetian polity and turn the king into a mere Doge went back at least to the late seventeenth century: see *The Parliamentary Diary of Narcissus Luttrell 1691–1693*, ed. H. Horwitz (Oxford, 1972), 10–11 (9 Nov. 1691).

[55] *Works*, ii. 48.

[56] *Vindication*, cc. 28–32. Cf. *The Crisis Examined* (1834), 16: 'The people have their passions, and it is even the duty of public men occasionally to adopt sentiments with which they do not sympathise, because the people must have leaders.'

[57] Paradoxically, of course, the politics of the transcendence of faction *à la* Bolingbroke had to be employed by Disraeli as a strategy of partisan advantage, since, standing outside the established political elite, he was dependent on party for his rise. The elision of a national standpoint into a sectional platform was to be a central feature of the Conservative party he helped to shape.

the 'patriot' opposition techniques of the previous century.[58] But it was also the transition appropriate to Disraeli's age and aspirations away from the swashbuckling parade of his own youth towards the intellectual formation of the youth that was coming up behind, a bid to seize the political future by capturing the minds of those who would shape it. Young England linked Disraeli's 'continental' and 'revolutionary' spirit to the movements of Mazzinian inspiration which had kept alive the flame of liberal nationalism after the revolutions of 1830—Young Italy, Young Germany, even, by the 1840s, Young Ireland—not only in name but in the concept of the liberation of the national genius that formed a natural counterpart on the collective plane to the romantic obsession with the genius of the individual. The vindication of national genius did not require in England the political revolution which was often its apparent precondition elsewhere, but it did require, for Disraeli, a near-revolution in the conceptualisation of the national past, national tasks, and national destiny, in the accomplishment of which his own genius could achieve its complete naturalisation. The technique of integrating and realising the individual nature through the exploration of its psycho-history as a prelude to creative action was now to be applied to the people and the race: the trilogy was Disraeli's *Bildungsroman*, his attempted psychotherapy, of the English nation.[59] In *Coningsby or: the New Generation*, he invited the well-born youth of England[60] to recognise their country's authentic political traditions and to assume their great political responsibilities; in *Sybil or: the Two Nations*, he summoned them to the task of ending that alienation between rich and

[58] Peel to Graham, 22 Dec. 1843, in C. S. Parker, *Sir Robert Peel from His Private Papers* (3 vols., 1891–9), iii. 425.

[59] In chapter 3 of the *Vindication*, Disraeli had developed the notion that nations had characters like individuals, and, like individuals, ascertained by self-examination their principles for right conduct. It is significant that, as he pursued that collective self-scrutiny, he offered 'to the new generation' a new edition of his paradigm of the individual search, *Contarini Fleming* (see the July 1845 preface, *Bradenham Edition*, iv. xi). The realisation of the individual self was continued alongside the collective quest in the trilogy: R. O'Kell, indeed, would see *Coningsby* as concerned less with contemporary politics than with the definition of 'an ideal identity or role of heroic individualism' ('Disraeli's "Coningsby": Political Manifesto or Psychological Romance?', *Victorian Studies*, xxiii (1979), 58, 70). The frustrating nature of his parliamentary situation in the early 1840s no doubt accounts in part for Disraeli's undertaking through the novel the enterprise of teaching his contemporaries to think: literature was the way to reach the public opinion which he chose to see as more powerful and enlightened than an unrepresentative House of Commons, and to realise his idea of a great man as 'one who affects the mind of his generation' (*Coningsby*, bk. III, c. 2, bk. VII, c. 2, and preface to the 5th ed., 1849, quoted in Blake, *Disraeli*, 193).

[60] The appeal to aristocracy chimed not only with Disraeli's sense of his own aristocratic nature but with the argument of the *Vindication* that the peers were more truly representative of the people than the House of Commons.

poor which threatened to disintegrate the nation itself;[61] and in *Tancred or: the New Crusade*, he beckoned them to the reinvigoration of national faith through the rediscovery of its pristine sources.

The magisterial but external position from which he lectured his countrymen on their national character and needs was symbolised in *Coningsby* and *Tancred* by the person of Sidonia, the mysterious visionary who embodies the timeless wisdom and the detached critical eye of an ancient and superior race. With Sidonia, and with the almost truculent exhibition of his religious and racial views in *Tancred* and, a little later, *Lord George Bentinck*, Disraeli finally attacked the problem of the integration of his Jewishness into his finished political persona and his English environment. If there was no bar to a Jew's making a career in England, even in politics if he were baptised, nonetheless a Jew like Disraeli who aspired to a leading role was not untouched by the dilemmas which afflicted his continental brethren, emerging from the ghetto to face the strenuous choices of identity which full participation in the life of their states posed. The cries of 'Shylock' and 'Old Clothes' which greeted Disraeli on the hustings at Maidstone in 1837 indicated a set of hostile stereotypes (to be reinforced within a year by that of Fagin) difficult to reconcile with pretension to party and national leadership.[62] The temptation to submerge his Jewishness was perhaps momentarily strong. It is well known that one of his first acts in parliament was to cast a vote which effectively went against the relief of Jewish disabilities for municipal office, and that he wrote to his sister: 'Nobody looked at me, and I was not at all uncomfortable, but voted in the majority with the utmost *sang froid* ...'[63] But pride, and the need to situate self in a way which incorporated a sense of origin, precluded the effacement of Jewish identity. The Eastern tour of 1830–1 had been in part a successful search for origins, and in the novel of the twelfth-century Jewish hero David Alroy, published in 1833, Disraeli had embodied what he described as his 'ideal' ambition,[64] to be a leader of his people. If he wavered in 1837, it was

---

[61] The image of the 'two nations' so strongly associated with Disraeli reflects the receptivity of his mind to whatever was in the air. A character in Heine's play *William Ratcliff* (1822) speaks of 'two nations ever at war, the well fed and the hungry'. In the 1840s, Lorenz von Stein was developing on the Continent the analysis of the dangers of class cleavage in modern industrial and urban society which derived largely from Hegel, and in Britain a Tory Radical like Ferrand could speak of the division of society 'into two classes—the very rich and the very poor' (at Manchester, 14 Dec. 1843; quoted by D. Southgate, 'From Disraeli to Law', in *The Conservatives: a History From Their Origins to 1965*, ed. Lord Butler (1977), 121).

[62] For Maidstone, see Monypenny and Buckle, i. 375; *Letters: 1835–1837*, 284, n. 1. Apparently the mob offered Disraeli bacon and ham. The 'Shylock' taunt had been used against him in a broadside following the Taunton election of 1835 (ibid., 49, n. 11).

[63] Ibid., 323–4 (5 Dec. 1837).

[64] *Letters: 1815–1834*, 447.

not for long, as his later record on Jewish disabilities was to show. He
made his position clear when, in his memoir of his father, he touched
sharply on his grandmother's indulgence of 'that dislike for her race
which the vain are too apt to adopt when they find that they are born
to public contempt'.[65] The way of total assimilation, with the self-
hatred it signified or engendered, would not be his. Yet he had still
to find the means by which his origins could be a source of strength
rather than weakness in the effort to command the Tory party and
the English nation.

His problem was a special case of the difficulty which faced emergent
European Jewry in the early nineteenth century of incorporating into
the mainstream of modern life a people whose history was frozen in
the expectation of the Messiah. Disraeli's response had something in
common with that of the movement known as *Wissenschaft des Juden-
tums*, whose manifesto of 1822 he may or may not have heard of, more
perhaps with the subsequent approach of Graetz. It was essentially to
fuse Judaism with the progressive development of human history and
the world spirit, and to ascribe to the Jewish race the creation of the
fundamental values of the civilisation of the West.[66] It was the 'pri-
meval vigour of the pure Asian breed',[67] deriving its force from the
purity Disraeli stressed so insistently as to earn himself the approval
half a century later of Houston Stewart Chamberlain,[68] that had
given Europe much of its law and literature and all of its religion.
Christianity was completed Judaism; the church 'the only Jewish

[65] 'On the Life and Writings of Mr. Disraeli. By His Son'; preface to I. D'Israeli,
Curiosities of Literature (14th ed., 3 vols., 1849), i. xxiii. In *Tancred* (bk. V, c. 5), Disraeli
had written scathingly of Mlle. de Laurella, who 'felt persuaded that the Jews would
not be so much disliked if they were better known: that all they had to do was to
imitate as closely as possible the habits and customs of the nation among whom they
chanced to live', and 'really did believe that eventually, such was the progressive spirit
of the age, a difference in religion would cease to be regarded, and that a respectable
Hebrew, particularly if well dressed and well mannered, might be able to pass through
society without being discovered, or at least noticed. Consummation of the destiny of
the favourite people of the Creator of the universe!'.
[66] 'Assuming that the popular idea of Inspiration be abandoned, & the difference
between sacred & profane history relinquished, what would be the position of the
Hebrew race in universal History, viewed with reference to their influence on Man?'.
Disraeli thought in 1863 of offering a prize for the best essay on this theme, to be
judged by Gladstone, A. P. Stanley, and himself (*Disraeli's Reminiscences*, 103–4).
[67] *Coningsby*, bk. IV, c. 10.
[68] H. S. Chamberlain, *Foundations of the Nineteenth Century* (1899), trans. J. Lees (2
vols., New York, 1977), i. 271. Little has been done to relate Disraeli's harping on race
to the growth of racial ideology in his day. Sidonia's 'All is race; there is no other truth'
(*Tancred*, bk. II, c. 14) may be set beside the Edinburgh anatomist Robert Knox's 'in
human history race is everything' (*The Races of Men* (1850), quoted in Watson, 205).
It might be argued that race and the Hebrew race provided for Disraeli the conceptual
tools for the ideological transformation of a hostile environment which class and the
proletariat provided for Marx.

institution remaining'.[69] It was for Christians to recognise in Jews the progenitors of their faith, and for Jews to find in Christianity the fullest expression of theirs. As the 'trustees of tradition, and the conservators of the religious element', hostile to false notions of human equality, and gifted with 'the faculty of acquisition', the Jews were natural conservatives, unless driven into subversion by persecution.[70] They were finally a natural aristocracy, to the most noble Sephardic branch of which Disraeli convinced himself that his own family belonged. In this perspective, it was Disraeli's Jewishness that enabled him to convert himself from a middle-class parvenu into the equal, or rather the superior, of the landed aristocracy in whose service he was retained when he was set up by Bentinck money as the proprietor of Hughenden and achieved the Commons lead of the Conservative party.[71]

Plainly, in his mode of defining a Jewish identity appropriate to his pretension to lead a Christian nation, Disraeli was in some senses denaturing Judaism by stripping the heart—the messianic and national vision—out of it.[72] But in a flicker of self-revelation to Lord Stanley in 1851, when he talked of the restoration of the Jews to Palestine, he showed that he had not entirely rejected that vision,[73] and perhaps it was not beyond his imaginings, as it was not beyond Herzl's fifty years later,[74] that the most powerful empire in the world

[69] *Disraeli's Reminiscences*, 103. Here and elsewhere, Disraeli no doubt owed something to the views of his father: see I. D'Israeli, *The Genius of Judaism* (2nd ed., 1833), especially 14, 211.

[70] B. Disraeli, *Lord George Bentinck: a Political Biography* (1851), c. 24.

[71] Disraeli's position had parallels with those of Berryer (father's name: Mittelberger), the spokesman set up as a country gentleman by the 'parliamentary' legitimists in France, and the converted Jew Stahl, who led the Prussian conservatives in mid-century. His status as virtually a hired hand, Lord Stanley's man of business, rendered the assumption of aristocratic credentials all the more necessary.

[72] A propos of *Tancred*, Fisch (93) remarks: 'He was betraying his Jewish instincts, whilst at the same time he was using them as the ground for his characteristic political ideology'.

[73] Stanley's journal, *Disraeli, Derby and the Conservative Party*, 32–3. Stanley recorded this as the only instance of Disraeli's displaying 'signs of any higher emotion' than 'irritation or pleasurable excitement', and noted Disraeli's preoccupation with matters relating to the Hebrews and his ambition to write 'the *Life of Christ* from a national point of view' (cf. on the latter point, ibid., 107, 5–6 May 1853). The implication of *Alroy* seems to be that Jabaster's 'national' vision represents the true path. Blake (*Disraeli's Grand Tour*, 113, 131) holds, first, that it is impossible to envisage Disraeli's even dreaming of restoring the Jews to Jerusalem, then, that it is impossible to tell whether he did or not.

[74] 'England, mighty England, free England, England that surveys the seven seas, will understand us and our aspirations': opening address to the fourth Zionist Congress, London, 13 Aug. 1900, in T. Herzl, *Zionist Writings: Essays and Addresses* (2 vols., New York, 1973), ii. 154. Herzl put Disraeli's name first in a proposed series of literary profiles of 'representative exponents of the Zionist idea' for his new paper, *Die Welt* (15

would assist its realisation. Disraeli's musings on the Jewish race were not as outlandish as is sometimes assumed in a country where the restoration and conversion of the Jews were a lively preoccupation of protestant theology.[75] The English, too, were a people of the book, extending across the globe the values derived from Israel, to which they added that genius of their own for combining liberty with order which led Disraeli to write in a significant passage in the *Vindication* that they were in politics as the Hebrews in religion, 'a favoured and peculiar people'.[76] The final form of his imaginative reconciliation of his inheritance with his physical place on the map was to see in England the destined inheritor of the civilising mission of his race. The British empire became the translation appropriate to his needs of Jewish universalism.[77]

With the integration of Jewishness at the end of the 1840s, the political persona with which Disraeli was to operate for the rest of his career was essentially complete. The location of genius in time and place had been achieved, in terms which made intellectual and emotional sense to its possessor. How far they made sense to anyone else, and how far the ideas they incorporated connected with the realities of British and Conservative politics in the mid-nineteenth century, is a subject for another occasion. Their function was not to supply a programme of political action or a blueprint for legislative measures, but to achieve the integration of different aspects of Disraeli's personality one with another and of the whole with the cold and fog-bound island where destiny –in which Disraeli believed so firmly—had placed it.

May 1897: *The Complete Diaries of Theodor Herzl*, ed R. Patai (5 vols., New York & London, 1960), ii. 548).

[75] M. Vereté, 'The Restoration of the Jews in English Protestant Thought 1790–1840', *Middle Eastern Studies*, viii (1972), 3–50.

[76] c. 34. It was Disraeli's view that the winning of English liberties had depended on the inspiration of the Old Testament. 'Philosophically considered', he noted of the Great Rebellion, 'it might be looked upon as the influence of Hebrew literature on the northern mind—as no doubt the translator of the Bible did it all' (*Reminiscences*, 89).

[77] Cf. Zangwill, 386; Fisch, 89–90, who argues that 'Disraeli's imperialism takes its place alongside Marxist communism as one of the messianic religions or pseudo-religions of the nineteenth century. Both have their origins in a more or less perverted Hebraism'. Disraeli might have been intrigued to hear a prime minister of Israel declare that his people had learned from Britain 'how to sustain a unique national character while preserving that which is precious to humanity as a whole' (Shimon Peres to the Royal Institute of International Affairs, 22 Jan. 1986: text circulated by the Information Department of the Embassy of Israel, London).

THE KING AND THE GENTRY
IN FOURTEENTH-CENTURY ENGLAND
The Alexander Prize Essay
By C. Given-Wilson
READ 16 MAY 1986

LATE medieval English historians have recently become quite interested in the gentry, and particularly in magnate-gentry relationships. The ubiquity of indentures of retainer in the fourteenth and fifteenth centuries is evidence that the outward form of these relationships was changing; the question is, do they also indicate a change in the nature and purpose of such relationships? And if so, then why? G. L. Harriss, for example, has argued that the fifteenth-century bastard feudal affinity was

> an attempt by the traditional leaders of society—crown and nobility—to contain the increasingly diversifying armigerous class within the old traditions of lordship and chivalry.... (This) solution disintegrated not under any attack from the crown but as cumulative wealth and access to political authority gave the broad class of landowners independence from the nobility as mediators of patronage and power.[1]

This theme of gentry 'independence' from the nobility was also taken up by Christine Carpenter, who suggested that forceful monarchical government in the shires could only be achieved once 'the gentry who administered the shires could be separated from the nobility' —and this, she speculated, may have occurred as a result of the wars of the roses.[2] From there, it is but a short step to the oft-expressed view that the efficacy of Tudor monarchy was, at least in part, due to the establishment of more direct crown–gentry relationships. To quote Harriss again:

[1] K. B. McFarlane, *England in the Fifteenth Century* (Oxford, 1981), introduction by G. L. Harriss, xxvii; see also N. Saul, *Knights and Esquires: The Gloucestershire Gentry in the Fourteenth Century* (Oxford, 1981); Katherine Naughton, *The Gentry of Bedfordshire in the Thirteenth and Fourteenth Centuries* (Leicester University Occasional Papers, 2, 1976); M. J. Bennett, *Community, Class and Careerism: Cheshire and Lancashire Society in the age of Sir Gawain and the Green Knight* (1983); Colin Richmond, 'After McFarlane', *History*, lxviii (1983); see also a number of unpublished theses cited in later footnotes.

[2] Christine Carpenter, 'Political Society in Warwickshire, c. 1401–1472', (unpublished Ph.D. thesis, University of Cambridge, 1976), 310–22.

87

The study of both the royal and noble affinities in the Tudor age has scarcely begun, but separate studies are beginning to suggest that the crown was now more able to use the lesser nobility and gentry (often those with court connections) as instruments for direct royal influence within the shire.[3]

To state the problem in such terms is (as Harriss was of course perfectly aware) to beg a number of questions. Who were the gentry? What evidence is there for their enhanced wealth and authority? Why had the crown not attempted to establish more 'direct royal influence within the shire' before? The aim of this paper is to look at the problem from one particular viewpoint, that of the connections established between the king and the gentry, but in doing so it is hoped to shed some light on the general question of crown, magnate, and gentry interrelationships.

During the twelfth and thirteenth centuries, direct relationships between the king and the 'knightly class' were in the main confined to the military sphere. This is not of course to deny that knights and esquires were playing an important role in local administration, but this did not involve their active recruitment by the king in large numbers or on a regular basis. The only knights who were actually retained by the king were his household knights. J. O. Prestwich and Marjorie Chibnall have recently shown how important the knights of Henry I's *familia* were during the protracted warfare of that king's reign.[4] For the reign of Henry III, the number, duties, and rewards of the king's household knights have been established by R. F. Walker.[5] Their overriding duty to the king was military; they received robes from the king at Christmas and Whitsun, and fees at the exchequer ranging between £5 and £100.[6] The number receiving fees in any one year varied, but it was 'seldom less than thirty', and never surpassed seventy. These fluctuations are clearly related to military activity: thus the number rose noticeably, for example, in 1228–30, 1253–4, and after 1261. Some of them were foreigners, some were members of English baronial families, and others were humbler men, but what they all had in common was that they were soldiers. They were the core of the king's retinue, his nucleus of shock-troops, a force in itself, and capable of rapid expansion whenever necessary.

Edward I's household troops are even better-known. As Michael

---

[3] McFarlane, xxvi.

[4] M. Chibnall, 'Mercenaries and the *Familia Regis* under Henry I', *History*, lxii (1977); J. O. Prestwich, 'The Military Household of the Norman Kings', *EHR*, xcvi (1981).

[5] R. F. Walker, 'The Anglo-Welsh Wars 1217–1267', (unpublished D.Phil. thesis, University of Oxford, 1954), 66–90.

[6] Though £100 was quite exceptional; the majority of the 117 tabulated by Walker got £15 or less; only eleven got £30 or more.

Prestwich pointed out, their 'main duties were military', their main activity was 'of course, fighting'.[7] They were now divided into two groups, bannerets and simple knights—essentially a recognition of military rank.[8] Also, they now began to receive both their robes and fees through the wardrobe rather than the exchequer, which means that analysis of the wardrobe accounts will reveal their numbers over the whole period *circa* 1270–1360.[9] From such a list, two points emerge clearly. firstly, that the number varied very considerably, and often very rapidly; secondly, that these fluctuations are very largely related to military activity. In 1312–13, for example, the number stood at thirty-seven; for the Bannockburn campaign, however, the wardrobe account for 1314–15 shows a leap to 121. Although the king might occasionally use his household knights in other capacities, such as undertaking an embassy, or sitting on local commissions, 'such tasks as these', according to Professor Prestwich, 'were not part of the normal role of household knights'.[10] Essentially, they were still just fighting men.

[7] M. C. Prestwich, *War, Politics and Finance under Edward I* (1972), 41–66.

[8] The term *milites simplici* was often used to differentiate them from the bannerets; although initially a military rank, the term 'banneret' evolved during the fourteenth century to include wider social implications.

[9] The following selection gives some idea of the numbers of bannerets and knights of the household over this period, and of the fluctuations in those numbers:

Year	Bannerets	Knights
1284–5	14	87
Easter 1286	13	39
Whitsun 1286	21	41
1288–9	16	27
1297	10	46 (20 newly-created)
1300	23	40
1306	17	28
1312–13	5	32
1314–15	32	89
1315–16	7	45
1322–23	5	28
1327–28	15	30
1334	9	27
1340	17	45
1347	14	66
1353–54	7	12
1359–60	10	37 (11 newly-created)

References: Prestwich, *War, Politics and Finance*, 46–7; PRO, E101/352/31; E101/352/4; E101/375/8; E101/376/7; E101/378/6; E101/377/1; *Society of Antiquaries* MSS. 120, 121; BL Add. MSS. 9,951 and 17,362; BL Stowe MS. 553; PRO, E101/385/4; E101/392/12; E101/393/11; E101/398/18; *The Wardrobe Book of William de Norwell*, ed. M. Lyon, B. Lyon and H. S. Lucas (Brussels, 1984), xcii, 301–3; *A Collection of Ordinances and Regulations for the Government of the Royal Household* (Society of Antiquaries, 1790), 10, 12.

[10] M. C. Prestwich, 59.

By the mid-fourteenth century, however, this long-established system of household knights was breaking down. After 1360, none of the surviving wardrobe accounts for the remainder of the fourteenth century lists any knights of the household. Nor is the term found in other royal documents of the period.[11] It is occasionally found in the later fifteenth century, but only when used loosely, to describe men who were really knights 'of the body', or members of the king's war-time retinue.[12] In effect, the mid-fourteenth century marks the demise of the household knight of the type whose existence is so well documented for over a century prior to this time. In his place arose the chamber knight. It is difficult to be sure when the term *miles camere regis* was first used, but its use is clearly associated with that general shift from the hall to the chamber which is a well-known feature of both royal and noble households in the later middle ages, and with the increasing importance attached to the office of king's chamberlain (or under-chamberlain) from the early fourteenth century.[13] By the 1320s, this latter post was held by none other than the younger Despenser, and it may be significant that it is at about this time that the earliest references to 'knights of the chamber' occur. The author of the *Annales Paulini*, *sub anno* 1320, described Edmund Darel, who was suspected of being implicated in a plot to seize the queen, as *miles de camera domini regis*, and official confirmation of the term is given in Edward II's chamber journal for 1322–3, which refers to *monsire Giles Beauchamp chivalier de la chambre le Roi*, and to *monsire Johan Lesturmy seneschal de la chambre le Roi*.[14] The references are very scattered, however, and the number of chamber knights at this time was probably only two or three.

The first actual list of the king's chamber knights that I have found appears in a great wardrobe livery roll for 1348, followed by a second

---

[11] There are a very few references to knights *de retinentia regis* or *de familia regis* in the later years of Edward III's reign but these are clearly associated with military service, and relate to Edward III's projected campaign of 1372. Also, in 1385, John Holand and Ralph Stafford the younger are described as knights of the household (*familia*) in proceedings relating to the brawl at Mustardthorpe during which Holand killed Stafford while the royal army was travelling north for the Scottish campaign of that year, but again what is clearly meant is that they were both members of the king's military retinue. Otherwise I have not found the term used at any time in the period 1377–1413 (PRO, E403/446, 5 August, 11 August; E403/451, 27 February; *CPR, 1370–74*, 261–4; Ibid., *1377–81*, 241; Ibid., *1385–89*, 62, 99).

[12] A. R. Myers, *The Household of Edward IV* (Manchester, 1959), 240, nn. 95, 97.

[13] See generally T. F. Tout, *Chapters in the Administrative History of Medieval England* (6 vols., Manchester, 1920–33), iv. 227–348; and Natalie Fryde, *The Tyranny and Fall of Edward II 1321–26* (Cambridge, 1979).

[14] *Chronicles of Edward I and Edward II*, ed. W. Stubbs, i (Rolls Series, 1882), 287–8; J. Conway Davies, 'The First Journal of Edward II's Chamber', *EHR*, xxx (1915), 677–8.

in 1364–5. In each case they numbered twelve.[15] Each of the eleven surviving wardrobe accounts from the period 1366 to 1406 provides a further list of chamber knights. Under Edward III, between 1366 and 1377, they number between three and five; under Richard II and Henry IV, they number between eight and thirteen.[16] During the fifteenth century they came to be known as 'knights of the body', though both their number and their duties remained similar. Edward IV's Black Book, for example, makes it clear that their duties were in the chamber and hall, and assumed that there would normally be sixteen of them, but more 'yf hit please the king'.[17] What is abundantly clear is that these late fourteenth-century lists have their own internal consistency—that is, the same names tend to recur—and that what they present us with, therefore, is a small group of men closely attached to the personal service of the king, and with regular duties at court. Indeed their proximity to the king often made them thoroughly unpopular: for example, more than half the men described as chamber knights during the 1380s were either executed or dismissed from court during the Merciless Parliament of 1388.[18] And this very unpopularity affords further clues to the significance of this changeover from knights of the household to knights of the chamber. For this was more than a change of style or of domestic *mores*. The service which the king expected from his chamber knights was not only more domestic than that which he had expected from his household knights, it was also much more varied. Edward III's chamber knights were men who were used by the king in a whole variety of responsible positions besides military ones: men like John de Molyns, Guy Brian, Roger Beauchamp, Walter Manny, Richard Stury and Alan Buxhull served their king regularly as councillors, special commissioners, and diplomats as well as serving him in war. And the same is undoubtedly true of their successors, men such as (under Richard II) Richard Abberbury, Nicholas Dagworth, John Russell, George Felbridge, and Arnold Savage, and (under Henry IV) Richard Arundel, John Pelham, John Straunge, and John Tiptoft. Naturally they continued to campaign, with or without the king, but they were men of far

[15] PRO, E101/391/15, mm. 5–6; E101/394/16, m. 9.

[16] PRO, E101/396/2, 11; E101/397/5; E101/398/9; E101/401/2; E101/402/2, 10, 20; E101/403/10; E101/404/21; BL Harl MS. 318; from 1395–6 they are described as 'knights of the chamber and hall', but the addition is not significant; it is clear that some of those who were called simply knights of the chamber before 1395 in fact had duties in the hall as well as the chamber, such as William Murreres and Thomas Peytevyn (E101/400/4, m. 21; E101/400/24; E101/401/6, m. 16).

[17] Myers, *Household of Edward IV*, 106–8 and 240, n. 97.

[18] They included James Berners, John Salisbury, Nicholas Dagworth, Richard Abberbury, Baldwin Bereford, Thomas Clifford, John Clanvow, John Golafre, and Aubrey de Vere.

greater individual importance than the household knights of the thirteenth and early fourteenth centuries. Moreover, the fact that when (after 1360) the king went campaigning in person, there was no increase in the number of his chamber knights, is further proof of the fact that these men were of a different type to the earlier household knights.

In summary, what we have is an inner-group of high-ranking and trusted royal servants valued by the king for their counsel, their administrative ability and their domestic service as much as for their strong right arms. The replacement of household knights by chamber knights was naturally a gradual process, but by 1370 it had definitely been accomplished. What is more, it paved the way for an even more significant change, that is, the establishment of a body of 'king's knights' outwith the household, but attached to the king by indentures of retainer, and clearly employed by him not so much for their military value as for their local influence and authority. The term 'king's knight' begins to appear quite suddenly, at the very outset of Richard II's reign, and again it is much more than just a change in style. Although Henry III had occasionally used the terms *miles domini regis* and *miles de familia nostra* interchangeably (to describe his household knights), it is a term which is hardly ever used during the reigns of the first three Edwards. Beginning in 1377, however, and continuing through until 1413, some 290 men in all are described in various sources (mostly in the chancery rolls) as *milites regis*. It is used with considerable consistency: men who were king's knights were normally described as such whenever they were mentioned in royal documents. They did not receive fees or robes through the wardrobe like the chamber knights, but they were almost all (if not all) granted annuities at the exchequer (ranging from £20 to £100, but mostly around £40 to £60).[19] In addition to the king's knights, there were also 'king's esquires', and this term also takes on a new meaning after 1377: it is not uncommon during Edward III's reign, but it is used to describe men who were in reality esquires of the household. After 1377, although it is still sometimes used to describe esquires of the household, it is also applied to a larger number of men who were not in the household. These esquires also received annuities at the exchequer— usually between twenty and forty marks. During Richard II's reign, about 280 men who were not esquires of the household were described as king's esquires. Under Henry IV, the equivalent figure is about 140. However, the number of king's esquires under Richard is substantially distorted by the king's drive to recruit Cheshiremen during the last two years of his reign. Of these 280, only 105 were documented before

[19] Lists of the knights retained by Richard II and Henry IV may be found in C. Given-Wilson, *The Royal Household and the King's Affinity* (1986), 282–90.

1397, while at least three-quarters of those newly-recruited in 1397-8 came from Cheshire. Thus if for the moment we exclude the years 1397-9, the over-all figures for king's knights and king's esquires during the two reigns are not dissimilar: under Richard II, there were about 150 knights and 105 esquires; under Henry IV, about 140 of each.

The chief conclusion to be drawn from this evidence is that during the last quarter of the fourteenth century the crown was moving towards a system of retaining members of the gentry in a way that parallels the practice of the higher nobility much more closely than the system of the earlier fourteenth century. But two further questions need to be considered: firstly, why did the system of household knights break down? secondly, and more importantly, what was the reasoning behind Richard's and Henry's retaining policy? With regard to the first, the personal role of the king in warfare was one of the lynchpins of the old system of household knights. It was to accompany him on campaign, and to provide his personal retinue in battle, that kings from Henry III to Edward III had maintained a corps of household knights. During the second half of the fourteenth century, however, the king did not often campaign in person. Indeed the only military expedition undertaken by a king in person between 1360 and 1385 was Edward's brief and futile sortie from Sandwich in the autumn of 1372, which lasted less than two months and never progressed beyond the channel. It was, in large part, because of this military inactivity that the system of household knights was allowed to disintegrate. What this also meant of course was that very few new knights or esquires were being recruited to the service of the crown at this time.[20] Edward was no longer seeking to attach the gentry to his cause; nor was he bequeathing to his successor a body of fighting men attached to the crown. With the accession of a new king, both processes had to be begun anew.

Initially, however, there was no real attempt on behalf of the new king to rectify this situation. Richard was of course only ten when he came to the throne, so it is hardly surprising that he was not too active in this field at first. For the first decade of the reign, those who were described as king's knights or esquires (and there were about 140 of them, roughly seventy of each) were for the most part former followers of either Edward III or the Black Prince, men whom Richard had in effect inherited. Others were relatives of these men, whose attachment to the service of the crown was really a matter of personal connection or family tradition. Thus by the time of the crisis of 1387-8 the king's

[20] Two of those referred to in note 11 above were however new recruits—Gilbert Giffard and Thomas Banfeld—but they were almost certainly recruited for the 1372 campaign.

affinity must have had a rather old-fashioned look about it; more importantly, it failed to reflect the realities of local politics as they had developed over the previous quarter of a century. During the summer of 1387, there are unmistakable signs that Richard tried hurriedly to rectify this situation by recruiting more of the gentry to his cause, but his move came too late, his methods were ham-fisted, and in the event he had to fall back on his Cheshire loyalists.[21] At Radcot Bridge, and in the Merciless Parliament of 1388, he and his followers paid the price for their bungling.

After the traumatic interlude of 1387–9, Richard set out deliberately to build up his following among the gentry. This brings us on to the second question, that is, the reasoning behind Richard's and Henry's retaining policy. Political necessity was the mainspring of Richard's actions, as is amply demonstrated by both the timing of his recruitment and the type of men that he retained. It was in 1389 that Richard regained control of his government. During the next ten years, he retained a further ninety or so knights and about 200 esquires. There were two periods in particular when he was actively recruiting: from 1389 to 1393, and in 1397–8. The first was a reaction to his humiliation in 1387–9; the second was an attempt to bolster his régime following the coup of 1397. That, however, is where the similarities end. The first recruiting drive, that of 1389–93, is characterised by a desire to retain men from a broad spread of geographical areas, and by a conscious attempt to retain those men who formed the topmost layer of the gentry in their localities.[22] It was mainly knights whom Richard now recruited: of the 200 or so esquires whom he retained after 1389, only about thirty-five were retained before

[21] See for example the Westminster Chronicler's description of Richard's attempt to whip up support in the summer of 1387 by sending a royal sergeant-at-arms to East Anglia to hand out the king's livery badges to the local gentry; the sergeant-at-arms was eventually imprisoned. The charge is supported by other chroniclers and by the articles of the appeal of treason in 1388 (*The Westminster Chronicle 1381–94*, ed. and trans. B. Harvey and L. C. Hector (Oxford, 1983), 187; *Rotuli Parliamentorum*, iii, 232–3; *Chronicon Henrici Knighton*, ed. J.R. Lumby, Rolls Series 1895, ii, 291; Thomas Walsingham, *Historia Anglicana*, ed. H. T. Riley, Rolls Series 1863–4, ii. 162).

[22] There were, for example, only two counties (Derby and Rutland) from which Richard failed to recruit any of his knights, and in general it is clear that they were more or less evenly spread around the various regions of the country. More significantly, it is worth noting that whereas before 1389 only nineteen of Richard's knights had come from the northern half of the country, between 1389 and 1399 he recruited a further forty-six knights from the north. Nor is this to be explained by the concentration on the north-west after 1397, for during the early 1390s Richard was focusing his attention more on counties like Yorkshire and Lincolnshire than on Cheshire and Lancashire. From Yorkshire and Lincolnshire combined, there were only five king's knights before 1389; by 1396, there were twenty. So if Richard's government was as unpopular in the north as has sometimes been suggested, then at least during the early 1390s he was trying to do something about it.

1397. And the knights whom he recruited were of precisely the sort who could have made all the difference in 1387-8: prominent local administrators, men who had often acted as sheriffs or justices of the peace in their shires, or who had represented their shires in the parliaments of the 1370s and 1380s. Many of them, indeed, had been active in their support for the Appellants in 1387-8.[23] As a retaining policy, this was not only sensible but successful. The king was, in effect, tapping in on already established local power-structures, and the mutual strength and authority which each drew from the other helped—along with the easing of financial pressure following the French truce, and the generally more conciliatory image projected by the court—to produce the most harmonious few years of the reign.

All this makes it more difficult to understand why Richard abandoned this policy in 1397. For abandon it he certainly did. The recruiting drive of 1397-8, following hard on the heels of Richard's destruction of his chief opponents among the higher nobility, was marked by quite different characteristics. Instead of recruiting widely through the shires, Richard now concentrated his efforts almost entirely on the north-west, particularly on Cheshire.[24] Instead of bolstering the authority of the men who were already the most prominent in their localities, he retained relatively few knights but a much greater number of esquires and gentlemen.[25] At the same time of course, as is clear both from the accounts of contemporary chroniclers and the researches of modern historians, he began to interfere in a much more arbitrary way in both national and local affairs.[26] Why he did so is not easy to say: it is difficult to explain his behaviour except as a combination of his strange obsession with his new principality of Chester, and his own mounting insecurity. The result, however, was

[23] John Bussy, William Bagot, Henry Green, Edward Dalyngridge, Gerard Braybrooke the younger, Simon Felbridge, and Roger Strange of Knokyn were all supporters of the Appellants in 1387-8, and all became king's knights in the early 1390s; for these men and their connections with the Appellants see Anthony Goodman, *The Loyal Conspiracy* (1971), 19, 34, 37, 43.

[24] Of the twenty-eight new king's knights recruited by Richard during the last two years of his reign, eleven came from Cheshire or Lancashire, and of the 170 or so new king's esquires recruited during the same time, about 140 came from these two counties. For Richard's obsession with Chester in the later years of his reign see Bennett, *Community, Class and Careerism, passim*; R. R. Davies, 'Richard II and the Principality of Chester', in *The Reign of Richard II*, edd. F. R. H. Du Boulay and Caroline Barron (1971); and J. L. Gillespie, 'Richard II's Cheshire Archers', *Transactions of the Historical Society of Lancashire and Cheshire*, cxxv (1974).

[25] The crucial document for the study of Richard's Cheshire retinue is in the Public Record Office: E101/402/10.

[26] See especially Caroline Barron, 'The Tyranny of Richard II', *Bulletin of the Institute of Historical Research*, xli (1968), and Anthony Tuck, *Richard II and the English Nobility* (1973), chapter 7. Walsingham's remark that it was in the summer of 1397 that Richard began to tyrannise his people has often been quoted.

that he now began to forfeit much of that local support which had been so carefully cultivated over the previous seven or eight years, and that his affinity now ceased to reflect local power-structures, but began instead to undermine them. This must have contributed significantly to what happened in 1399.

Political expediency was also at the heart of Henry IV's retaining policy. The most politically fragile years of Henry's reign were the early years: the financial chaos was extreme, and a succession of magnate-inspired rebellions (in 1400, 1403, and 1405), alternating with bitter parliamentary disputes (in 1401, 1404, and 1406), combined to make the usurper's hold on his throne appear dangerously precarious.[27] Not surprisingly, it was during these early years that Henry sought to win support. Of the 280 king's knights and esquires recruited by him, more than half were retained during the first two years of the reign. Following the major Percy rebellion of 1403 there was a further burst of retaining by the king, particularly in the north, so that by 1406—the mid-way point of the reign—almost 250 of the 280 were already retained. Thus after 1406 Henry virtually ceased his recruitment of knights and esquires. Financial necessity probably played its part in this, for it was in 1406–7 that the king was eventually forced to make at least some of the economies which the commons had been pressing on him since 1401, and cutting back on retaining fees was one way of economising—but the main reason was surely the more peaceful political atmosphere of the second half of the reign.

Although he did it during the early rather than the later years of his reign, Henry's aims in attaching large numbers of the gentry to himself were broadly similar to Richard's (Richard's before 1397, that is). Like his cousin, he retained men from almost every county in England, and, like Richard again, the typical royal retainer under Henry was a man already prominent in local politics and administration—the sort of man who could effectively lend his weight to the government in matters such as the raising of loans, the mobilisation of local forces at short notice, and the maintenance of effective peace-keeping and administration. This was, after all, precisely what Henry had been urged to do almost at the outset of his reign. At a council meeting held in February 1400, immediately following the rebellion of the Ricardian earls in January, the king was advised that

in each county of the realm a certain number of the more sufficient and well-respected (*de bone fame*) men should be retained by the king and associated with the said commissions (of the peace), and

[27] For a very comprehensive study which shows just how chaotic royal finance was, especially during the first half of Henry's reign, see Alan Rogers, 'The Royal Household of Henry IV' (unpublished Ph.D. thesis, University of Nottingham, 1966).

charged also diligently and carefully to save the estate of the king and his people in their localities.... And that all those of the said retinue should receive a grant from the king annually, as much as shall please the king, a reasonable sum according to their estate.[28]

By the end of the month, thirteen new king's knights had been added to the list.

Henry, of course, was not drawing only on his cousin's example. His father John of Gaunt was a great retainer of men, and at least fifty of Henry's knights and esquires had been formally recruited by his father. What is also interesting to note is that about forty of Henry's knights had also been retained by Richard, and most of them were snapped up very quickly by Henry: within six months of the usurpation, more than twenty of Richard's knights had already become Henry's knights. There was obviously something of a political balancing act here: those whom Richard thought important enough to retain were also those whom Henry thought important enough to retain. There may also have been something of a geographical balancing act. Most of Henry's (and his father's) *natural* followers came from the northern half of the country, especially the Yorkshire–Lancashire–North Midlands heartland of the Duchy of Lancaster; moreover, political events during the first half of the reign made it imperative that at this time Henry should draw men from the north into his orbit in order to counter-balance the pretensions of the Percies. To balance this tendency, Henry needed to cultivate support among prominent members of the county establishments in the southern shires, and many of those who were most prominent here were those whom Richard too had patronised. Thus there seems to be a reversal of the situation under Richard: Richard's natural following (Cheshire excluded) was in the south, yet after 1389 he deliberately tried to win the support of more northerners. Henry's natural following, on the other hand, was in the north, and to balance this he wooed former supporters of Richard in the south.[29]

These knights and esquires were retained by the king principally for the support which they could give to the government in their localities. Naturally they might also be called upon to swell the king's retinue in time of war, but the evidence does not suggest that this was seen as their primary function by the king. For example, of the eighty-nine bannerets and knights who served in the king's retinue for the Irish campaign of 1394–5, only thirty-nine were king's knights, while of the 200 or so esquires in Richard's retinue, only about ten were

[28] *Proceedings and Ordinances of the Privy Council*, ed. Sir H. Nicholas (1834), i. 109.
[29] See above, n. 22. Twenty-five of Henry's knights came from Yorkshire alone, and over half of the total came from the less well populated northern half of the country.

king's esquires (although over a hundred were esquires of the house-hold). Yet Richard had over 150 knights and esquires by this time, whom presumably he could have summoned to join him had he wished them to. The fact he did not suggests that his over-all retaining policy was geared to peace-time rather than war-time needs, and that the process of gathering a retinue for a campaign was one which he saw really as a one-off exercise. For his 1399 campaign, Richard took about thirty of his knights to Ireland. It is however worth noting that many of those who went with him in 1399 had also gone with him in 1394, which might suggest that even if *most* of the king's knights and esquires were not recruited primarily for their military value, there was a small number—perhaps thirty or forty out of the total—who were.[30] For the majority, though, the service which the king required of them was less definable: like late medieval magnates, whose retaining policy was largely geared to retaining the support of the gentry in their 'countries', the king traded money and good lordship for as widespread a network of local connections as he could afford. These men were the heart of the royal affinity. Ultimately—like magnate affinities—the royal affinity is incapable of precise definition. Nevertheless, the figure of 250–300 knights and esquires retained by Richard and Henry can usefully be compared with the estimated norm of sixty to eighty followers whom the greatest members of the English nobility seem to have retained at this time.[31] Clearly too, they invite comparison with the 220 or so knights and esquires who were retained by John of Gaunt during the early years of Richard's reign, which serves to emphasise how untypical among English magnates Gaunt was, and the extent to which he geared his retaining policy to his pretensions as 'King of Castile and Leon'.[32] It is probably true to say that the number of knights and esquires retained by Richard II and Henry IV was between four and eight times greater than the number retained by most dukes or earls.[33]

If the short-term considerations which induced both Richard and Henry to retain knights and esquires were essentially political, their

[30] For the army (including the king's retinue) of 1394–5, see PRO, E101/402/20, ff. 31–40; the records for the army of 1399 are less complete, but a partial picture of it can be gained from the enrolled account of the keeper of the wardrobe (E361/5/26) and from the letters of protection issued in chancery (*CPR, 1396–99*, 22 Richard II, parts II and III).

[31] McFarlane, xi.

[32] *John of Gaunt's Register 1379–83*, ed. E. C. Lodge and R. Somerville (Camden 3rd ser. lvi, 1937), i, 6–13.

[33] It is worth noting that even for a duke and a royal uncle Gaunt seems to have been quite exceptional; his brother the Duke of York was apparently only retaining about forty knights and esquires in 1399: C. D. Ross, 'The Yorkshire Baronage 1399–1435' (unpublished D.Phil. thesis, University of Oxford, 1950), 394.

reasons for doing so are also indicative of long-term changes in English society. It is worth for example comparing their retaining policies with that of Edward II at a time when he too was eager to build up political support. In 1316–17, as J. R. S. Phillips discovered, Edward drew up a series of indentures for service in peace and war with 'a majority of the leading magnates' (nineteen have survived in full or in summary), promising a total of about £4,000 in peace-time annuities and considerably more for service in war.[34] Thus his approach in time of need seems to have been to seek the support of the higher nobility. To suggest that Richard ignored the higher nobility would of course be quite incorrect: the thoroughly aristocratic composition of his courtier clique in the 1390s, and the titles which he bestowed on his favourites in 1385–6 and 1397, are sufficient testimony to his desire either to woo the great men of his realm or, if they refused to be wooed, to elevate around them others who could vie with them in status. Yet what is also abundantly clear is that Richard felt the need to go further than this, to appeal to the gentry. And even if in the end it failed to save him his throne, Richard's retaining policy did at least have the merit of originality. Whether one chooses to see this as—in G. L. Harriss's terms—an attempt to 'contain' the 'broad class of landowners',[35] what does seem clear is that such a policy stemmed from a recognition of the crucial role played by the gentry, and of the consequent need for the king to harness their skills and influence to his cause. The part played by the gentry in English society had altered substantially since the twelfth century. The spread of lay literacy had led to a breaching of the barriers demarcating the work done by clerks and the work done by laymen: many knights and esquires were by now as much administrators (either at the county level or in the service of magnates) as they were soldiers. And from administrative involvement stemmed political involvement—at both the local level and the national. It is hardly surprising that such an important long-term development should be mirrored in the knights attached to the king, and so it is, both in the employment of chamber knights and in the retaining of king's knights and esquires.

What, however, do we mean by the term 'gentry'? A number of local studies are now beginning to point to a reasonably clearly defined stratum of 'upper (or 'county') gentry' in England, by the end of the fourteenth century at the latest. Thus Nigel Saul calculated that the real 'gentry' of mid-fourteenth century Gloucestershire consisted of about fifty families, of whom about thirty were knights. For Cheshire and Lancashire, M. J. Bennett has suggested an over-all figure of

[34] J. R. S. Phillips, *Aymer de Valence, earl of Pembroke 1307–1324* (Oxford, 1972), 148–51, 312–15.
[35] See the quotations at the start of this paper.

about 600 landowning families, but within this an upper gentry stratum of around a hundred families, comprising the knights and greater esquires. Similar studies by G. G. Astill in late fourteenth-century Leicestershire, Susan Wright in fifteenth-century Derbyshire, and Christine Carpenter in fifteenth-century Warwickshire, have pointed to 'county gentry' figures of between fifty and seventy in each county. These were the families that made up the office-holding and landholding élites in their counties, who generally had the largest estates and who between them tended to share out the greater shire offices such as sheriff, MP and, increasingly, JP. What these historians also emphasise is that there was a real gulf between them and the lesser gentry, consisting of the less wealthy and influential esquires and the gentlemen.[36] Unless those shires which have been studied are wholly unrepresentative (which seems unlikely), then it seems possible to extrapolate from this evidence a figure of about 2,300 to 2,500 'county gentry' families throughout England in the late middle ages.

What this means is that at any given time between about 1390 and 1413, roughly one in ten of England's 'county gentry' was retained by the king. It is clear that both Richard (before 1397, at any rate) and Henry sought their retainers from the top level of county society, and it was thoroughly logical that they should do so. Both kings spent a lot of money on their retainers, and obviously set considerable store by them.[37] Yet, as is demonstrated by the events of 1397–1405, it would be foolish to imagine that this gave either king the right or the ability to 'manage' local politics. County establishments must always have been to a large extent a law unto themselves, and to try to meddle with them was likely to produce precisely the opposite result to that intended. Ralph Griffiths, for example, has recently argued that in the late 1450s the court decided to adopt the midlands (from Hereford to Lincolnshire, roughly) as its 'power-base'; a series of appointments followed, designed to place administrative and political control of this area in the hands of curialists. Yet the effect of these appointments was not in fact to rally these shires to the crown, but rather to alienate the leaders of local society, who now felt thrust aside, and to throw them into the arms of the court's opponents. This

[36] Saul, *Knights and Esquires*, 260–2; Bennett, *Community, Class and Careerism*, 82–4; Carpenter, 'Political Society', 18, 22–5, 42–5, 85, 172; G. G. Astill, 'The Medieval Gentry: A Study in Leicestershire Society 1350–1399', (unpublished Ph.D. thesis, University of Birmingham, 1977), 17; Susan Wright, 'A Gentry Society of the Fifteenth Century: Derbyshire *circa* 1430–1509' (unpublished Ph.D. thesis, University of Birmingham, 1978), 9–10.

[37] At roughly £60 per knight and £20 per esquire, the annuities promised by both Richard and Henry amounted in total to over £10,000; of course annuities were often in arrears, but even so very substantial payments were made, for the king could not afford politically to allow arrears to accumulate for too long.

at least is the explanation offered by Christine Carpenter and Susan Wright, for Warwickshire and Derbyshire respectively.[38] The moral of Richard II's failure after 1397 seems to be very similar: as long as the king's patronage continued to reflect, build upon and bolster the structure of local power, that was a process from which the crown could, and probably would, draw strength, but once patronage gave way to manipulation, alienation could follow rapidly.

In conclusion, while the evidence cited here has been derived largely from the later fourteenth and early fifteenth centuries, it does, when combined with other published evidence from the earlier part of the fourteenth century, appear to point to a substantial shift in the attitude of the crown towards the gentry. It has already been seen that Edward II's political retaining policy was aimed essentially at the higher nobility, while his recruitment of knights and esquires was, in keeping with the policies of his father and grandfather, primarily designed to swell his personal military retinue. Moreover, Nigel Saul has recently pointed out that neither Edward II nor the Despensers (despite the considerable number of their retainers) made any serious attempt to intrude their supporters among the gentry into important offices or commissions in the shires—indeed Dr Saul speculates that their failure to do so might have been one of the chief causes of the collapse of their régime in the autumn of 1326. By contrast, he notes that the attempt by the court to dominate local offices and commissions was regarded as one of the major malpractices of Richard II's 'tyranny' in the years 1397–9, as indeed is suggested by the accusations made in the 1399 deposition charges.[39] While there is little doubt that Richard's attitude to local politics and administration became ever more high-handed after 1397, it is however necessary to see his actions in a late rather than an early fourteenth-century context. The point, as Richard seemed to realise from at least 1387, was that the potential usefulness of the gentry to the king was increasing. The consolidation of county establishments, their control over the major shire offices, and the developing influence of the commons in parliament, all point in this direction. There was nothing new in 1397 in Richard's attempt to influence local politics, he had been trying to do this for the last ten years. The novelty was in the methods which he now adopted, and which, by contrast with his approach during the early 1390s, were to prove so fatal to his cause. In fact, Richard received a considerable amount of support from the higher nobility in 1399. It

[38] R. A. Griffiths, *The Reign of King Henry VI* (1981), 800–2; Wright, 'Gentry Society', 221; Carpenter, 'Political Society', 46–53.
[39] Nigel Saul, 'The Despensers and the Downfall of Edward II', *EHR*, xcix (1984), 1–33.

was the gentry who failed to rally to his cause, and hence to provide his chief supporters with the means to resist Henry's invasion.[40]

If we return, then, to the question of whether the ubiquity of indentures of retainer indicates a real change in the nature and purpose of the gentry's role *vis-à-vis* the magnates and the king in late medieval England, then the answer must surely be, at least as far as the late fourteenth century is concerned, that it does. The leaders of local society were now retained primarily for their usefulness and influence in the localities rather than for their military ability—which is not to argue that they were no longer employed by the king and the magnates in a military role, nor that military ability no longer counted as a reason for retaining a knight or esquire, but merely that the balance had shifted.[41] And what is significant here, I would suggest, is Richard II's and Henry IV's attempts to secure that 'direct royal influence within the shire' which is usually seen as one of the principal aims of the early Tudor kings. Rightly or wrongly, Edward II and the Despensers seem to have thought such initiatives unnecessary. As far as can be gathered, Edward III, who (with good reason) trusted his magnates to act as his lieutenants in the regions, thought likewise. Both Richard II and Henry IV, neither of whom placed the same degree of confidence in their magnates, adopted a different policy. It is perhaps the clearest evidence that we have for the growing influence in both local and national affairs of late medieval England's 'county gentry'.

[40] Given-Wilson, *Royal Household*, 267.
[41] Ibid., 221–2, 233–4; see also Anthony Goodman, 'John of Gaunt', in *England in the Fourteenth Century*, ed. W. M. Ormrod (Woodbridge, 1986), 79.

NUMERACY IN EARLY MODERN ENGLAND

The Prothero Lecture

By Keith Thomas

READ 2 JULY 1986

IN RECENT years historians of the early modern period have given
much attention to the subject of literacy, its growth, its determinants
and its consequences. The sixteenth and seventeenth centuries in
England saw the widespread dissemination of the printed book and a
substantial increase in the proportion of the population able to use
the written word. It is possible to exaggerate the historical importance
of these developments, but there is no denying that they give the early
modern period much of its distinctive flavour.[1]

Far less attention has been paid to the closely associated topic of
numeracy. Yet the subject is of equal importance to anyone concerned
to reconstruct the mental life and cognitive apparatus of the past, for
numbers and number systems are among the most basic of all mental
categories. Even those historians who do not regard their discipline
as a form of retrospective ethnography would admit that numeracy
matters, if only because the enhanced ability to perform numerical
manipulation has underlain most of the scientific and technological
developments of modern times.

Moreover, the claims of the early modern period to have been
decisive in this area are perhaps even greater than they are in the case
of literacy. For those concerned with the history of numbers and
numerical skills, the period 1500–1700 in England is one of dramatic
transformation. It saw the replacement for most purposes of roman
numerals by arabic ones and the consequent supersession of the counting-board or abacus by arithmetical calculation on paper. It wit-
nessed the proliferation of textbooks on commercial arithmetic and
double-entry bookkeeping; the introduction of decimals, logarithms
and algebra; and the adoption of most of the arithmetical symbols
with which we are now familiar. Alongside the pure mathematics of
giants like Thomas Hariot, John Wallis and Sir Isaac Newton, there
developed the applied mathematics of military engineers, navigators,
map-makers, surveyors, gunners and other skilled practitioners. The
late seventeenth century saw the rise of political arithmetic, with its

[1] Cf. Keith Thomas, 'The Meaning of Literacy in Early Modern England', in *The
Written Word. Literacy in Transition*, ed. Gerd Baumann (Oxford, 1986).

faith in the power of statistics to resolve the problems of government and administration. Numerical analysis established itself as one of the dominant forms of intellectual enquiry.

But how widely were these numerical skills and concepts disseminated among the population at large? What sort of numerical vocabulary did they employ? How capable were they of numerical manipulation?

In the present state of knowledge it is impossible to answer such questions. There is no systematic study of the role of number and numerical thinking in England at a popular level, comparable to the many works on literacy and the written word. There is an admirable brief survey of the problem in a recent book largely devoted to the rise of statistical thinking in the United States of America;[2] and there are excellent histories of mathematics (both higher and practical), accountancy, astronomy, navigation and political arithmetic.[3] But we are still largely ignorant about the numerical skills of the population at large.

The main reason for this is that numeracy does not leave evidence which can be readily measured. For all the defects of signatures (as opposed to marks) as an index of reading capacity, they do at least provide some basis for generalisation about people's ability to write. Students of numeracy have no comparable evidence on which to draw and their conclusions have to be much more impressionistic. Another reason for the undeveloped state of the subject is that numeracy is entirely a matter of degree. In early modern England there were

[2] Patricia Cline Cohen, *A Calculating People, The Spread of Numeracy in Early America* (Chicago, 1982). See also the same author's 'The Domain of Numbers in Eighteenth-Century Popular Culture', in *Science and Technology in the Eighteenth Century. Essays of the Lawrence Henry Gipson Institute for Eighteenth Century Studies*, ed. Stephen H. Cutcliffe (1984).

[3] Helpful works include Florian Cajori, *A History of Elementary Mathematics* (New York, 1896); David Eugene Smith, *History of Mathematics* (2 vols., Boston, 1923–25); Florence A. Yeldham, *The Story of Reckoning in the Middle Ages* (1926), and *The Teaching of Arithmetic through Four Hundred Years (1535–1935)* (1936); E. G. R. Taylor, *The Mathematical Practitioners of Tudor and Stuart England* (Cambridge, 1954) and *The Mathematical Practitioners of Hanoverian England* (Cambridge, 1966); *Studies in the History of Accounting*, ed. A. C. Littleton and B. S. Yamey (1956); B. S. Yamey, H. C. Edey and Hugh W. Thomson, *Accounting in England and Scotland: 1543–1800* (1963); Francis R. Johnson, *Astronomical Thought in Renaissance England* (Baltimore, Md., 1937); David W. Waters, *The Art of Navigation in England in Elizabethan and Early Stuart Times* (1958); G. N. Clark, *Science and Social Welfare in the Age of Newton* (2nd edn., Oxford, 1949), chap. v; Peter Buck, 'Seventeenth-Century Political Arithmetic: Civil Strife and Vital Statistics', *Isis*, 68 (1977).

On the medieval background to many of the problems discussed in this lecture, see Alexander Murray, *Reason and Society in the Middle Ages* (Oxford, 1978), chaps. 7 and 8, and, for general stimulus, Karl Menninger, *Number Words and Number Symbols. A Cultural History of Numbers*, trans. Paul Broneer (Cambridge, Mass., 1969).

illiterates, but there were no innumerates. Merely to speak the language was to know that three was more than two. The ability to count, at least a little way, was regarded by contemporaries as one of those distinctive human attributes marking off mankind from the rest of the animal creation.[4] Just as a medieval burgess was deemed to be of age when he could measure cloth and reckon up to a shilling, so a Tudor or Stuart adult's inability to count twenty pence was proof of his idiocy. 'We make it an argument of a fool,' remarked a preacher, 'that he cannot count aright nor tell ten or twenty.'[5]

Yet knowing how many beans made twenty was hardly proof of great numerical dexterity. John Locke described some American Indians who, though 'otherwise of quick and rational Parts enough, could not, as we do, by any means count up to 1,000, nor had any distinct Idea of that Number, though they could reckon very well to 20'.[6] Nearer home, it was said of a Wiltshire pauper in 1618 that, though he could tell how many groats made a shilling, he did not know how many made three shillings.[7] In the sixteenth century the Cornish were reputed to count up only to thirty, after which their language forced them to start again.[8]

Although this latter aspersion may have been unjustified, it is clear that the ability to reckon did not necessarily imply any larger numerical skill. The most superficial investigation reveals that people of this period varied very greatly in their ability to perform numerical manipulations. They also varied in the numerical categories they used and in the extent to which they perceived the world in quantitative terms. A full exploration of these differences would be an enormous and indeed impossible task. I see no prospect of ever being able to map degrees and forms of numeracy, regionally or socially, in the way that some have attempted to map literacy. My aim in this lecture is more modest. I wish to identify the pressures which led some contemporaries to acquire new numerical skills and categories and to contrast them with the circumstances which deterred or prevented

[4] See, e.g. Robert Recorde, *The Ground of Artes Teachying the Worke and Practise of Arithmetike* (1551?; STC 20798), sig. a iiii; James Peele, *The Pathewaye to Perfectnes, in th'accomptes of Debitour, and Creditour* (1566), sig. *iij; John Dee, Preface to *The Elements of Geometrie of the Most Auncient Philosopher Euclide* (1570); Humfrey Baker, *The Well-Spring of Sciences* (1617), sig. A3ᵛ.

[5] *The Works of Symon Patrick*, ed. Alexander Taylor (9 vols., Oxford, 1858), vii. 533. Cf. Anthony Fitzherbert, *The New Natura Brevium* (1677), 519.

[6] John Locke, *An Essay concerning Human Understanding*, ed. Peter H. Nidditch (Oxford, 1975), 207 (II.xvi. 6).

[7] M. J. Ingram, 'Ecclesiastical Justice in Wiltshire, 1600–1640, with Special Reference to Cases concerning Sex and Marriage' (Oxford Univ. D. Phil. thesis, 1976), 82.

[8] *Andrew Borde's Introduction of Knowledge*, ed. F. J. Furnivall (EETS, 1870), 123–4. Richard Carew, however, gives the Cornish words for forty, a hundred, a thousand and ten thousand; *The Survey of Cornwall*, ed. F. E. Halliday (1953), 127.

others from doing the same. I also want to examine some of the contrasting attitudes to number and the differing forms of numerical vocabulary which co-existed within the same society. My approach will be necessarily very general, and the issues to be discussed deserve much further exploration.

It is not hard to see why many people in sixteenth-century England felt the need to acquire some knowledge of arithmetic. Anyone involved in trade was forced by self-interest to make calculations and, if his business was at all elaborate, to keep accounts. Financial records had been kept for centuries by the royal government, by landed estates and by corporate bodies, large and small. At a modest level, accounting was more likely to be done orally, but by the mid-sixteenth century even some smiths and hauliers had account books.[9] Of course, the purpose of most of these records was less to provide a basis for profit-and-loss calculations than to keep track of dealings with others and to make sure that one was not being cheated. But the motive for financial reckoning was there and it grew with the number of business transactions and the fiscal demands of government. 'Every good and discreet merchant', accordingly, was advised to 'have knowledge and cunning in reading and writing; also to be prompt and readie in his reckoning and accompt making, and most specially ... have the knowledge and feate of Arithmetike ... with penne or compters.'[10]

Arithmetic with counters was the old method, involving an abacus or counting-board and the use of roman numerals. It had obvious disadvantages. Roman numbers were very clumsy when used to express large sums; they had no fractions; above all, they had no symbol for zero and no concept of place value. They were therefore adequate for recording transactions, but useless for calculations, which had to be done with beads on an abacus or with counters on a board. The new arithmetic of the pen which spread into sixteenth-century England used arabic numerals. It was what in the Middle Ages had been known as algorism. In the Tudor period they called it 'cyphering', the cipher originally being the zero and then, by extension, any of the new figures. Its advantage was that it combined the two operations of recording numbers and making calculations. It was also quicker. 'I shall reken it syxe tymes by aulgorisme or you can caste it

[9] *Manorial Records of Cuxham, Oxfordshire circa 1200–1359*, ed. P. D. A. Harvey (Oxon. Rec. Soc., 1976), 14–15; *The Ledger of John Smythe*, ed. Jean Vanes (Bristol Rec. Soc., 1974), 17.
[10] Hugh Oldcastle, *A Briefe Introduction and Maner how to keepe Bookes of Accompts*, newly augmented by J. Mellis (1588), chap. 2.

ones by counters,' as John Palsgrave's dictionary put it in 1530.[11] At
the end of the seventeenth century John Arbuthnot declared that it
'would go near to ruine the Trade of the Nation' were arabic figures
abolished, and merchants and tradesmen obliged to go back to using
'the Roman way of notation by Letters'.[12]

Written arithmetic was thus presented as an indispensable business
technique and it was obviously better to know it oneself than to
depend on a professional clerk. The author of the first Tudor textbook
on the subject was Cuthbert Tunstall, who explained in his dedication
to Sir Thomas More that he had been forced to look more closely into
the matter after some unfortunate transactions with money-changers
which neither he nor More had fully understood.[13] The vernacular
textbooks on arithmetic which appeared intermittently during the
sixteenth century and with increasing frequency in the seventeenth
were addressed to people planning a business career. They were often
dedicated to the great trading companies; and, like the Italian and
German models on which they were based, they were unambiguously
commercial in their orientation. Most of the problems they expounded
related to buying and selling, calculating rates of interest, converting
foreign currencies into English ones or computing an individual's
share of some joint enterprise.[14] Arithmetic was, in short, 'the very
soul of trade'.[15] Lack of acquaintance with its rules could lead to
financial disaster. Gerard Malynes thought in 1636 that 'many' individuals ignorantly made usurious contracts because 'deceived' by the
rules of arithmetic, while a Lombard Street banker later in the century
declared that most bankrupt tradesmen had been ruined 'for want of
skill in arithmetic'.[16] For tradesmen and private individuals alike,
good book-keeping was a duty, both moral and prudential. Typical
of large concerns was the London brewery in the 1690s which kept
its accounts in eleven ledgers, the smallest containing eight hundred
columns of pounds, shillings, pence and farthings, with twenty-six
lines to the column.[17] Typical of conscientious individuals was

[11] (John Palsgrave), *Lesclarcissement de la langue francoyse* (1530), f. CCCxxxvi^v.
[12] (John Arbuthnot), *An Essay on the Usefulness of Mathematical Learning* (Oxford, 1701),
27.
[13] Cuthbert Tunstall, *De Arte Supputandi Libri Quattuor* (1522), sig. A2.
[14] For bibliography see David Eugene Smith, *Rara Arithmetica. A Catalogue of the Library
of George Arthur Plimpton of New York* (4th ed., New York, 1970), to which is appended
a reprint of Augustus de Morgan, *Arithmetical Books from the Invention of Printing to the
Present Time* (1847).
[15] James Hodder, *Hodder's Decimal Arithmetick* (1671), sig. A4.
[16] Gerard Malynes, *Consuetudo, vel, Lex Mercatoria* (1636), 232; *Aubrey on Education*, ed.
J. E. Stephens (1972), 103–4.
[17] Peter Mathias, *The Brewing Industry in England 1700–1830* (Cambridge, 1959), 350.
Cf. *The Educational Writings of John Locke*, ed. James L. Axtell (Cambridge, 1968), 320–
21; Daniel Defoe, *The Complete English Tradesman* (2 vols., Oxford, 1841), i. 309–11.

Jonathan Swift, who recorded all his expenses right through his adult life, down to the last halfpenny.[18]

Arithmetic was also vital for administration, essential, as a contemporary put it, for 'Auditors, Treasurers, Receivers, Stewards, Bailiffs, &c. '.[19] It was necessary for the military arts, particularly gunnery and fortification. It was also required by those engaged in navigation, ship-building, architecture, surveying, dialling and instrument-making. These were the occupations which produced most of the practitioners whose skills have been so well documented during recent decades.[20] In the mid seventeenth century the introduction of the excise enhanced the demand for people capable of measuring the contents of irregularly-shaped casks and barrels; would-be excise officers had to prove themselves qualified in the first four rules of arithmetic before being allowed to learn gauging; and there was a flurry of text-books on the subject.[21] We recall Goldsmith's schoolmaster:

> 'Twas certain he could write, and cypher too,
> Lands he could measure, terms and tides presage.
> And ev'n the story ran that he could gauge.[22]

Edmund Burke would later refer contemptuously to 'the mathematics and arithmetic of an exciseman' as something about equal in weight to 'the metaphysics of an undergraduate'. But John Graunt's pioneering exercises in demography were based on what he called 'the Mathematicks of my Shop-Arithmetick'; and the numerical expertise of some of these practical men is not to be underestimated.[23]

An infinity of other occupations required numerical skill. Bookbinders needed 'a little arithmetic'.[24] So did those engaged in gardening and laying-out grounds.[25] 'Even in hedging and ditching,' it was said, 'men ... that comprehend Lines and Numbers, ... will be Master Work-men among the other labourers'.[26] Arithmetic, in

[18] *The Account Books of Jonathan Swift*, ed. Paul V. Thompson and Dorothy Jay Thompson (1984).

[19] Thomas Lawson, *A Mite unto the Treasury, being a Word to Artists, especially to Heptatechnists* (1680), 30.

[20] See the works of E. G. R. Taylor and D. W. Waters cited in note 3 above.

[21] John Owens, *Plain Papers relating to the Excise Branch of the Inland Revenue Department, from 1621 to 1878* (1878), 111.

[22] Oliver Goldsmith, 'The Deserted Village' (1769).

[23] Edmund Burke, *Reflections on the Revolution in France* (1790), in *Works* (Bohn edn., 6 vols., 1854–69), ii. 454; *The Economic Writings of Sir William Petty*, ed. Charles Henry Hull (2 vols., Cambridge, 1899), ii. 323.

[24] Joseph Collyer, *The Parent's and Guardian's Directory, and the Youth's Guide in the Choice of a Profession or Trade* (1761), 68.

[25] Stephen Switzer, *Ichnographia Rustica: or, the Nobleman, Gentleman, and Gardener's Recreation* (2 vols., 1718), ii. p.i.

[26] Christopher Wase, *Considerations concerning Free-Schools, as settled in England* (Oxford, 1678), 49.

Locke's words, was 'of so general use in all parts of life and business, that scarce anything is to be done without it.'[27]

Yet, despite its utility, a knowledge of arithmetic was not easily obtained. In the petty schools numeration and 'cyphering' came a bad third after reading and writing. The notion that the foundation of all education was the 'three Rs' was not yet standard. The grammar school curriculum was almost exclusively literary: very few grammar schools before 1660 seem to have taught arithmetic, and then only as an extra to be done on half-days and holidays or by poor boys destined for apprenticeship.[28] The mental habits engendered by the subject were alien, even antipathetic, to the rhetorical skills which a Latin education was supposed to inculcate; and mathematics was widely regarded as an anti-social subject, making people 'unapte to serve in the world' and 'less fit for active life, and common conversation'.[29] In 1627 John Brinsley thought it enough for 'your ordinarie grammar scholler' to know the numbers in figures and letters. 'If you do require more for any, you must seek *Records Arithmetique* or other like authors, and set them to the cyphering school.'[30]

At the universities, arithmetic was part of the quadrivium and we know that much serious mathematics was practised at Oxford and Cambridge in this period.[31] But it did not follow that the numerical attainments of the average undergraduate were very high. Sir Thomas Smith appeared a reformer in 1573 when he prescribed that students at Queens' College, Cambridge, should not proceed to the B.A. until they could do addition, subtraction, multiplication, division and the extraction of roots. John Aubrey may not have been far wrong when he asserted that 'a Barre-boy at an Alehouse will reckon better and readier than a Master of Arts in the University'.[32]

---

[27] *Educational Writings of John Locke*, ed. Axtell, 290.

[28] Foster Watson, *The Beginnings of the Teaching of Modern Subjects in England* (1909), chap. viii; *id, The English Grammar Schools to 1660* (1968 reprint), 150–4; W. A. L. Vincent, *The Grammar Schools. Their Continuing Tradition 1660–1714* (1969), 73–4.

[29] Roger Ascham, *English Works*, ed. William Aldis Wright (Cambridge, 1904), 190; Obadiah Walker, *Of Education* (1673; Menston, 1970), 113; Richard Mulcaster, *Positions*, ed. Robert Herbert Quick (1888), 239. Cf. Edward Worsop, *A Discoverie of Sundrie Errours and Faults daily committed by Lande-Meaters, ignorant of Arithmetick and Geometrie* (1582), sig. F2ᵛ ('They which have no understanding in mathematicall arts, when they see a fellow with a running head, or light braine, especially if he be studious, and given to solitarines, say in way of scorning, he hath a mathematicall head.').

[30] John Brinsley, *Ludus Literarius or the Grammar Schoole*, ed. E. T. Campagnac (Liverpool, 1917), 26.

[31] Mordechai Feingold, *The Mathematicians' Apprenticeship. Science, Universities and Society in England, 1560–1640* (Cambridge, 1984); John Gascoigne, 'The Universities and the Scientific Revolution', *History of Science*, 23 (1985), 413–19.

[32] Feingold, *op. cit.*, 39–40; Bodleian Lib., MS Aubrey 10, f. 29.

Throughout the early modern period, most arithmetic teaching was provided outside the main educational system. It was taught, in separate schools for writing and accounts, by scriveners, surveyors, accountants and instrument-makers. John Wallis, for example, learned Latin, Greek and Hebrew at Felsted School. His taste for mathematics was acquired from a younger brother who was destined for trade and had therefore been learning to write, cipher and cast accounts; it was he who taught him 'the practical part of common arithmetic, numeration, addition, etc.' Many of the other mathematicians of the period seem to have been self-taught, picking up the subject in their spare time, often after leaving school.[33]

In the later seventeenth century there was a mounting demand that arithmetic should be part of everyone's education. The mathematical sciences, as Thomas Hobbes put it, were 'the foundations of navigatory and mechanick employments';[34] and the movement to establish special mathematical schools was explicitly related to the needs of 'a Trading People', particularly one concerned during the French wars to maintain its naval presence.[35] In response to this pressure, mathematics was added to the curriculum of some grammar schools, though not to all of them: arithmetic did not become compulsory at Eton until 1851.[36] There was a great increase in the number of private teachers or educational establishments offering a mathematical training, in response to commercial and industrial demand.[37] But, even in the eighteenth century, many people seem to have had to teach themselves the rudiments of arithmetic from Wingate, Cocker or one of the other textbooks.[38]

Part of the reason for the relative neglect of the subject in the schools

[33] 'Dr Wallis's Account of Some Passages of his Own Life', in *Peter Langtoft's Chronicle*, ed. Thomas Hearne (2 vols., Oxford, 1925), i. clxvi–clxvii. Cf. Jonas Moore, *Moores Arithmetick* (1650) sig. A4ᵛ; *The Journal of Richard Norwood* (New York, 1945), 16, 41; Francis Baily, *An Account of the Revd. John Flamsteed* (1835), 9–10; *Dictionary of National Biography*, s.n., 'James Ferguson, FRS'; 'Thomas Simpson, FRS'; Taylor, *Mathematical Practitioners of Tudor and Stuart England*, 81, 216, 232.

[34] Thomas Hobbes, *De Cive, The English Version*, ed. Howard Warrender (Oxford, 1983), 164–5 (XIII.xiv).

[35] L. Maidwell, *An Essay upon the Necessity and Excellency of Education* (1705), sig. b6.

[36] Geoffrey Holmes, *Augustan England. Professions, State and Society, 1680–1730* (1982), 48–50; Vincent, *The Grammar Schools. Their Continuing Tradition*, 74–5; Nicholas Hans, *New Trends in Education in the Eighteenth Century* (1951), 67; Sir H. C. Maxwell Lyte, *A History of Eton College (1440–1910)* (4th edn., 1911), 478.

[37] Diana Harding, 'Mathematics and Science Education in Eighteenth-century Northamptonshire', *History of Education*, i (1972), 140–6; Hans, *New Trends in Education*, chaps. v and vii; Ralph Davis, *The Rise of the English Shipping Industry* (Newton Abbot, 1972), 124–6; Taylor, *Mathematical Practitioners of Hanoverian England, passim*.

[38] E.g., *The Autobiography of William Stout of Lancaster, 1665–1752*, ed. J. D. Marshall (Manchester, 1967), 74; 'Χρονεχα seu Annales: Or Memoirs of the Birth Education

was the assumption that arithmetic was a practical form of expertise necessary for specific occupations rather than an essential form of mental training for everybody. Arithmetical textbooks which described themselves as 'peculiarly fitted for merchants and trades-men'[39] could hardly be expected to draw other readers. So long as arithmetic was thought of primarily as a piece of commercial technique, it was liable to be despised by those who thought themselves above such things and neglected by those who had no option but to be below. The founders of charity schools did not usually think arithmetic a necessary subject for those destined to a life of subor-dination. As Thomas Firmin asked in 1681, 'Why ... must a poor Boy that is destined for a Mason, Bricklayer, Shoemaker, or the like honest and necessary Trade, be taught ... so far in Arithmetic, as if he were destined for a Merchant?'[40]

Conversely, there were plenty of gentlemen who were 'so Brisk and Airy, as to think that the knowing how to cast Accompt is requisite only for such Underlings as Shop-keepers or Trades-men, but unneces-sary and below Persons of plentiful Estates'.[41] 'I am ill at Reck'ning,' declares the fop Armado in *Love's Labour Lost*, 'it fitteth the spirit of a tapster'; and in *Othello* Iago scornfully denigrates Cassio as 'a great arithmetician', 'this counter-caster'.[42] In a much quoted but still revealing passage, John Wallis recalled that in his boyhood (around 1630) mathematics 'were scarce looked upon as academical studies, but rather mechanical; as in the business of traders, merchants, seamen, carpenters, surveyors of land, or the like; and perhaps some almanack-makers in London.' John Aubrey knew young men of high birth who at the age of eighteen could not add up pounds, shillings and pence.[43]

For arithmetical help, the supposedly educated classes often had to turn to business people or artisans. The most notorious example is that of Samuel Pepys, sometime scholar of St Paul's and MA of Magdalene College, Cambridge, getting up early in the morning at the age of twenty-nine to learn his multiplication tables with the help

---

Life and Death of Mr. John Cannon' (MS in Somerset County Record Office), 59; J. Spence, 'An Account of the Author', in Stephen Duck, *Poems on Several Occasions* (1736), xvi–xvii; Taylor, *Mathematical Practitioners in Hanoverian England*, 207.

[39] Noah Bridges, *Vulgar Arithmetique* (1653), title-page.

[40] Thomas Firmin, *Some Proposals for the Imployment of the Poor* (1681), 5. Cf. M. G. Jones, *The Charity School Movement* (Cambridge, 1938), 80.

[41] Edward Wells, *The Young Gentleman's Course of Mathematicks* (3 vols., 1714), i. sig. (b3).

[42] *Love's Labour's Lost*, I.ii; *Othello*, I.i.

[43] 'Dr Wallis's Account of his Own Life', in *Peter Langtoft's Chronicle*, ed. Hearne, i, cxlvii–cxlvii, *Aubrey on Education*, ed. Stephens, 103.

of Richard Cooper, the one-eyed ship's mate of the *Royal Charles*.[44] There was also the Tudor martyrologist John Foxe, musing in bed about the duration of the time of persecution under the Beast and wondering what forty-two months of sabbaths of years came to; 'to have the matter more sure', he got up and 'repaired to certain merchants of mine acquaintance'.[45]

Lawyers might also be relatively innumerate. Robert Recorde, author of the first vernacular textbook of arithmetic, said that justice was 'often tymes' hindered in the courts because 'ignorance of Arithmetike' prevented the judge from fully understanding the point at issue. Others agreed: Masters of Chancery who lacked the art of accounts 'never understand [the] cause, but through ignorance they haze and perplex the cause more ... and then leave it, after a great deal of money spent, to be decided by the merchants.[46] One of the reforms intended by the first earl of Shaftesbury when Lord Chancellor was to have the issues in business cases stated exactly by the mathematician John Collins before they came to trial.[47]

Of course, many gentlemen soon realised that it could be very disadvantageous if their political and economic authority were at the mercy of some lowborn accountant or craftsman.[48] Stimulated no doubt by cautionary tales about the financial disasters which had overtaken those unable to read their own accounts, many well-born figures, Charles I included, took up mathematics.[49] From the Elizabethan period onwards, all the projects for gentlemen's academies included the subject in their curricula, partly for this reason, partly because of its importance for the military arts.[50] By the eighteenth century it was generally held that mathematics *was* an essential part of a gentleman's education.[51] A degree of numeracy was indispensable if the gentry were to retain their social position.

[44] *The Diary of Samuel Pepys*, ed. Robert Latham and William Matthews (11 vols., 1970–83), iii. 131, 134, 135.

[45] *The Acts and Monuments of John Foxe*, ed. Stephen Reed Cattley (8 vols., 1837–41), i. 290.

[46] Recorde, *Ground of Artes*, sig. Biii; *Aubrey on Education*, ed. Stephens, 104.

[47] John Collins, *An Introduction to Merchants-Accompts* (1674), sig. B^v.

[48] George Atwell, *The Faithfull Surveyour* (Cambridge, 1662), 4–5; *Educational Writings of John Locke*, ed. Axtell, 319–20; Arbuthnot, *Essay on the Usefulness of Mathematical Learning*, 50–1; 'A Person of Honour' (Roger North), *The Gentleman Accomptant* (1714), 102–3, 245 and *passim*.

[49] Feingold, *Mathematicians' Apprenticeship*, chap. vi.

[50] J. P. Cooper, *Land, Men and Beliefs. Studies in Early-Modern History*, ed. G. E. Aylmer and J. S. Morrill (1983), 61; Taylor *Mathematical Practitioners of Tudor and Stuart England*, 82.

[51] E.g., Archibald, late Marquis of Argyle, *Instructions to a Son* (1661), 101; John Clarke, *Bishop Gilbert Burnet as Educationist* (Aberdeen, 1914), 61–6; 'Dr. Wallis's Letter against Mr. Maidwell, 1700', in *Collectanea*, i, ed. C. R. L. Fletcher, (Oxford Hist. Soc., 1885), 320; James Grant, *History of the Burgh Schools of Scotland* (Glasgow, 1876), 399.

Arithmetic, however, was not a normal part of the education of a lady. Women lagged behind in numeracy, perhaps even more than they did in literacy. Mathematics was thought of as an essentially masculine affair, giving what John Arbuthnot revealingly called 'a manly vigour to the Mind.'[52] In 1695 Thomas Tryon declared that 'Females are naturally as fit for, and capable of, all excellent Learning as men, even the Mathematicke it self', but he had to admit that this, though 'a Great Truth', was very little believed'.[53] Arithmetic was for businessmen and technicians, not women. In the eighteenth century only a small fraction of girls at charity schools seem to have been taught any. An early statistical survey of numeracy, made in a Scottish parish in the early nineteenth century, revealed that, whereas the women were very slightly behind the men in their ability to read and write, they were only half as likely to be able to do simple arithmetic.[54] In 1678 an anonymous writer urged that the females of London should learn bookkeeping rather than needlework;[55] and many late seventeenth-century commentators thought it important that women should know arithmetic and accounts so that they could run their husband's businesses in their absence or after their deaths.[56] Of course, there were many such business women; the daughters of well-to-do families sometimes learned mathematics to great effect; and many women kept household accounts.[57] But overall it is true to say that access to numeracy for women was relatively restricted.

Those persons of either sex who had the opportunity and incentive to learn usually found arithmetic a very difficult subject. 'Most men despaire to attaine the knowledge thereof,' thought Edmund Wingate in 1630; and Thomas Hylles agreed that there was no skill 'more slippery or apter to be forgotten'.[58] This was partly because so many people came to it relatively late in life. Aubrey thought that if the rules of arithmetic did not become habitual in childhood the subject

---

[52] Arbuthnot, *Essay on the Usefulness of Mathematical Learning*, 7. Cf. *Vives and the Renascence Education of Women*, ed. Foster Watson (1912), 205.

[53] Thomas Tryon, *A New Method of Educating Children* (1695), 15–16.

[54] Neil Tranter, 'The Reverend Andrew Urquhart and the Social Structure of Portpatrick in 1832', *Scottish Studies*, 18 (1974), 55–6.

[55] *Advice to Women and Maidens of London* (1678) (probably by Stephen Monteage; see B. S. Yamey, 'Stephen Monteage. A Seventeenth Century Accountant', *Accountancy*, 70 (1959), 594n).

[56] Sir Josiah Child, *A New Discourse of Trade* (1693), 5; *The Petty–Southwell Correspondence, 1676–1687*, ed. Marquis of Lansdowne (1928), 131.

[57] Alice Clark, *Working Life of Women in the Seventeenth Century* (1919), chap. ii; Note by Alice Clark in *The Household Account Book of Sarah Fell of Swarthmoor Hall*, ed. Norman Penney (Cambridge, 1920), xxviii.

[58] Edmund Wingate, *Arithmetique made Easie* (1630), Preface; Thomas Hylles, *The Arte of Vulgar Arithmeticke* (1600), sig. B.ii.

made men 'almost mad ... for, not having the habit, they are apt to be out, and then infinitely running into mistakes, so confound themselves that many times they leave off', whereas 'boys will add, multiply and divide as fast as a dog will trot'.[5]

But arithmetic was also made difficult by its cumbersome procedures. The learner who mastered the first two rules, Addition and Subtraction, was still liable to come unstuck at the next ones, Multiplication and Division. Wingate thought that they 'so confound and perplex the new Practitioner that he takes them to be Hercules' Pillars, and writes upon them *Non plus ultra*'.[60] There were many different ways of doing multiplication, some, like the so-called 'sluggard's rule', designed to avoid having to learn anything beyond the five times table and therefore very slow. But most of them involved memorising longer multiplication tables; and it is clear that contemporaries did not find this new requirement easy: '9 tymes 9 is 82,' writes the Warwickshire antiquary, Henry Ferrers.[61]

As for division, this was universally agreed to be a formidable problem, requiring, as one textbook put it, 'a mynde not wandering, or setled uppon other matters'.[62] Until the mid seventeenth century the most common technique was the so-called 'galley' or 'scratch' method, which involved subtraction from the left, continual crossing-out, a heavy burden on the memory and (*experto crede*) a strong risk of ultimate confusion.[63] The instrument-maker John Smith remarked in 1673 that there were many 'ingenious persons' who had 'a competent readiness in the Rule of Multiplication', but were 'unskilful in Division'. When Pepys taught his wife arithmetic, she learned the first three rules very well, but he decided not to 'trouble her' for the time being with division.[64]

After division came the Rule of Three or Golden Rule, 'the chiefest most profitable, and the most excellent Rule of all the rules of Arithmeticke, as one authority called it.[65] It was a rule of proportion whose

[59] *Aubrey on Education*, ed. Stephens, 98, 99.
[60] Edm(und) Wingate, *Arithmetique made Easie, The Second Book* (2nd edn., 1652), sig. A1.
[61] Elizabeth K. Berry, *Henry Ferrers, an early Warwickshire Antiquary* (Dugdale Soc., Occl. Papers, Oxford, 1965), 30. The textbooks frequently apologised for the burden on the memory imposed by multiplication and proposed methods of avoiding it. On the ways of multiplying, see Smith, *History of Mathematics*, ii. 101–28.
[62] Hylles, *Art of Vulgar Arithmeticke*, f. 37ᵛ.
[63] On this and other methods of division see Smith, *History of Mathematics*, ii. 128–44. The scratch method began to be displaced in the mid-seventeenth century, but lingered on for another century; David Murray, *Chapters in the History of Bookkeeping, Accountancy and Commercial Arithmetic* (Glasgow, 1930), 280.
[64] John Smith, *Stereometrie: or, The Art of Practical Gauging* (1673), sig. A4; *Diary of Samuel Pepys*, ed. Latham and Matthews, iv. 406.
[65] Baker, *The Well-Spring of Sciences*, f. 41.

aim was to find a fourth number when three were known. Thus, if the wages of three carpenters are 24d, what would the wages of seven carpenters be? Today we divide 24d by three, producing 8d as the wages of one carpenter, and then multiply by seven to get the answer: 56d. But contemporaries were taught to multiply the second number (24) by the third (7) and divide the product (168) by the first number (3). Since the first stage of the operation produces a meaningless figure (168), learners seldom grasped the rationale of the procedure and they often became confused as to what order the numbers should be placed in. Their difficulties were compounded when it came to the Rule of Three Inverse (if the wages of three carpenters are 24d, how many carpenters would 56d employ?) or the Double Rule of Three (if the wages of three carpenters are 24d for one day, what will the wages of five carpenters be for ten days?) Every textbook struggled to make the Rule of Three intelligible: Thomas Hylles in 1600 even tried to explain it with twenty-four lines of verse.[66] But there must have been many learners like Jack Verney, who confessed that in the 1650s he had mastered the first five rules of arithmetic (presumably Numeration, Addition, Subtraction, Multiplication and Division) and 'begunne the 6th, which is called the Rule of 3, but I was never perfect in it'.[67] There were also so-called Rules of Practice, designed to simplify the calculations in the Rule of Three by the use of aliquot parts. It is easy to sympathise with the author of that child's rhyme which survives in many versions from the later sixteenth century onwards:

> Multiplication is mie vexation
> Division is quite as bad.
> The Golden Rule is mie stumbling-stool
> And Practice makes me mad.[68]

So long as arithmetic was badly taught, in ill-constructed textbooks, and with all the emphasis on learning so-called 'rules' by rote rather than understanding the processes involved, it was inevitable that many made slow progress. As an Elizabethan almanac-maker said, with a wealth of understatement, 'every man is not skilful to multiply and divide'.[69] From Thomas Wentworth, Earl of Strafford, downwards, many people continued to rely on addition and subtraction for all their operations, like the Indians of North America or many

[66] Hylles, *Arte of Vulgar Arithmeticke*, f. 121.

[67] Frances Parthenope Verney, *Memoirs of the Verney Family during the Civil War* (4 vols., 1971 reprint), iii. 368.

[68] Iona and Peter Opie, *The Lore and Language of Schoolchildren* (Oxford, 1959), 173.

[69] *A Blank and Perpetual Almanack* (1566), sig. B6, cit. Bernard Capp, *Astrology and the Popular Press. English Almanacs 1500–1800* (1979), 201.

African peoples of more recent times.[70] Oliver Cromwell himself was not ashamed to tell Parliament that he had 'as little skill in Arithmetic as ... in the Law'.[71]

Nowadays, in the era of the pocket-calculator, we can see how short-lived was the period when people were required to do long multiplication and division for themselves. We are not surprised that much of the energy of seventeenth-century mathematicians was devoted to finding techniques which would relieve contemporaries of this burden. John Napier devised his 'bones' or calculating rods to help with multiplication and division, and Henry Briggs followed these up with the spectacular invention of logarithms, which enabled most operations henceforth to be done by addition and subtraction alone. The new technique, we are told, was 'greedily-imbraced in all parts, as of unspeakable advantage'.[72] There was much experiment with slide-rules and calculating machines. In the 1670s Sir Samuel Morland's calculating machine was advertised as suitable for 'any Gentleman or other, especially Ladies, that desire to look into their disbursements, or layings out, and yet have not time to practise in Numbers'.[73] Algebra would ultimately make obsolete such formulae as the Rule of Three, while decimals were widely advocated because they simplified calculations and avoided 'the intricacie of fractions'.[74] Surveyors adopted a decimal chain; sailors, some administrators and a few astrologers used logs.[75] When Adam Martindale set up as a mathematics teacher in Manchester in 1666 he offered decimals, logarithms and algebra: his scholars, he claims, could in an hour answer questions which his rivals could not solve in a month.[76] But

[70] C. V. Wedgwood, 'The Scientists and the English Civil War', in *The Logic of Personal Knowledge. Essays presented to Michael Polanyi* (1961), 60; *The Field Book of Walsham-le-Willows 1577*, ed. Kenneth Melton Dodd (Suffolk Records Soc., 1974), 21; R. T. Gunther, *Early British Botanists and Their Gardens* (Oxford, 1922), 12. Cf. *The Correspondence of John Locke*, ed. E. S. de Beer (Oxford, 1976 –), iii. 24; Jack Goody, *The Domestication of the Savage Mind* (Cambridge, 1977), 12.

[71] Wilbur Cortez Abbott, *The Writings and Speeches of Oliver Cromwell* (4 vols., Cambridge, Mass., 1937–47), iv. 496.

[72] John Wallis, *A Treatise of Algebra* (1685), 56.

[73] Nicholas Stephenson, *A Mathematical Compendium ... collected out of the Notes and Papers of Sir Jonas Moore* (1674), 20. See D. J. Bryden, 'A Didactic Introduction to Arithmetic, Sir Charles Cotterell's "Instrument for Arithmeticke" of 1667', *History of Education*, 2 (1973).

[74] Henry Lyte, *The Art of Tens, or Decimall Arithmeticke* (1619), title-page.

[75] Taylor, *Mathematical Practitioners of Tudor and Stuart England*, 51; Waters, *Art of Navigation*, chap. 5; G. Herbert Fowler, 'The Civil War Papers of Sir Will. Boteler, 1642–1655', *Publications of the Beds. Hist. Rec. Soc.*, xviii (1936), 38; *The Collected Essays of Christopher Hill* (Brighton, 1985 –), iii. 276.

[76] *The Life of Adam Martindale written by himself*, ed. Richard Parkinson (Chetham Soc., 1845), 187.

these developments seem to have spread only slowly outside the world of professional mathematicians.

Meanwhile, mental arithmetic remained, in Commander Waters's words, 'a rare accomplishment'. Admittedly, one mid-seventeenth century witness tells us that 'we finde children, one with another, making it one of the first tryals of their abilities to pose each other in mental addition of numbers';[77] and there were many arithmetical puzzles designed for children's recreation: for example, if there are thirty people in a boat, fifteen Turks and fifteen Christians, and if, to save the boat from sinking, fifteen have to be thrown into the sea by counting round and ejecting every ninth person in succession, how should one arrange the seating so as to ensure that the choice always falls on a Turk?[78] But one need look no further than the scribbles on the end papers of many seventeenth-century books to see that many contemporaries needed a pen and paper before they could add, say, a shilling to one and sixpence. Most seventeenth-century tradesmen were heavily dependent on the tables and ready reckoners which poured out in profusion, enabling the user to look up rates of simple or compound interest or to work out the price of some commodity.[79]

Such devices were essential for people whose arithmetical skill was rudimentary. They also helped them to cope with the bewildering complexity of English weights and measures. The pound sterling gave rise to awkward and irreducible fractions, making English money difficult to add and subtract, while multiplication required 'a world of paines'.[80] This was particularly the case when pounds, shillings and pence co-existed with nobles and groats (still remembered in the mid seventeen 'among the common people'[81]), and when very small sums of money had a value; not just halfpennies and farthings, but eighths of a penny and sixteenths.[82] Matters were made worse by the inconstancy of many units of measurement. The size of the perch and the acre varied in different parts of the country, while that of the bushel varied both regionally and when applied to different commodities. It was said in 1656 that there was almost as many bushels as markets.[83]

---

[77] Waters, *Art of Navigation*, 345; John Hall of Richmond, *Of Government and Obedience, as they stand Directed and Determined by Scripture and Reason* (1654), 465.

[78] *Mr Wingate's Arithmetick* 5th edn., ed. John Kersey (1671), 498–9.

[79] *The Winter's Tale*, IV.iii. On ready reckoners, see Murray, *Chapters in the History of Bookkeeping, Accountancy and Commercial Arithmetic*, 296–308.

[80] Robert Wood, 'Ten to One' (1655), in Charles Webster, *The Great Instauration. Science, Medicine and Reform 1626–1660* (1975), 537.

[81] *Ibid.*

[82] Recorde, *Ground of Artes*, sig. a vi'; Hilary Jenkinson, 'The Use of Arabic and Roman Numerals in English Archives', *Antiquaries Journal*, vi (1926), 272–3.

[83] James Stansfield, 'A Coppy of a Letter to Mr. Hartlib' (1656), Hartlib Papers 53/20 (cited by courtesy of Sheffield University Library and Lord Delamere).

In the remoter shires a bushel contained two or three times as much as in the counties near London, and a perch was a good deal longer. There were twelve ounces in the pound troy (used by goldsmiths), sixteen in the pound avoirdupois and eighteen in a Cornish pound of wool or mutton. The stone varied from eight pounds in weight to twenty-four pounds according to the commodity concerned.[84]

Given such complications, it is hardly surprising that, even with the help of ready-reckoners, frequent arithmetical errors should have occurred in the accounts and calculations of the time. Every student of the period will have noticed them, for they can be found in muster rolls, in inventories, in subsidy rolls and in excise returns.[85] The recently-published building accounts of Combe Abbey (in the 1680s), for example, contain sundry errors in multiplication, sometimes to Lord Craven's disadvantage.[86] Even the great Dr. Busby, Headmaster of Westminster School, made several mistakes when adding up the value of his own silver plate.[87] When one recalls the accuracy of medieval bureaucrats or of some of the earlier business accounts kept in Roman numerals,[88] it is tempting to conclude that the transition to paper calculations in Arabic figures may have initially created as many problems as it solved.

Meanwhile there were people to whom the new arithmetic remained a closed book. The works of Robert Recorde, Thomas and Leonard Digges and other Tudor mathematicians were notoriously too difficult to be 'understoode of the common sorte',[89] while the commercial arithmetics had a necessarily limited readership. Thomas Masterson remarked in 1592 of the art of numbers that 'few men know it'; and Richard Witt agreed in 1613 that 'most men' had 'but small skill therein'.[90] In 1627 John Brinsley complained that some people were so ignorant of numeration, 'whether in figures or in

---

[84] *The Agrarian History of England and Wales*, v (1640–1750), ed. Joan Thirsk (Cambridge, 1985), ii, appendix 1; 'Select Tracts and Table Books relating to English Weights and Measures (1100–1742)', ed. Hubert Hall and Frieda J. Nicholas, *Camden Miscellany, XV* (Camden ser., 1929).

[85] E. E. Rich, 'The Population of Elizabethan England', *Economic Hist. Rev.*, 2nd ser., ii (1949–50), 249; W. K. Jordan, *Philanthropy in England, 1480–1660* (1959), 36; *Household and Farm Inventories in Oxfordshire, 1550–1590*, ed. M. A. Havinden (Oxon. Record Soc., 1965), 34; *Taxation in Salford Hundred, 1524–1802*, ed. James Tait (Chetham Soc., 1924), xxvi; Mathias, *Brewing Industry in England*, 371.

[86] 'Letters and Papers relating to the Rebuilding of Combe Abbey, Warwickshire, 1681–1688', ed. Howard Colvin (*The Walpole Soc.*, 1984).

[87] G. F. Russell Barker, *Memoir of Richard Busby, D. D. (1606–1695)* (1895), 125.

[88] *The Collected Papers of Thomas Frederick Tout* (3 vols., Manchester, 1932–34), iii. 212; G. F. Hammersley in *EHR*, xcii (1977), 195.

[89] Worsop, *Discoverie of Sundrie Errours* sig. A2ᵛ.

[90] *Thomas Masterson. His First Booke of Arithmeticke* (1592), sig. Aiiij; Richard Witt, *Arithmeticall Questions* (1613), sig. A3ᵛ.

letters, insomuch as when they heare the Chapters named in Church, many of them cannot turne to them, much less to the verse'. There were, he said, 'schollers, almost readie to go to the Universitie, who yet can hardly tell you the number of Pages, Sections, Chapters, or other divisions in their bookes, to finde what they should'.[91]

Victims of an exclusively literary education though Brinsley's scholars may have been, it is unlikely that they, or anyone else, were unable to count at all. There were several available alternatives to the use of written arabic figures. Some people counted on their fingers, a technique which could be used even for very large numbers and was said in the nineteenth century to be 'still in use among children and peasants'.[92] Others, like ale-house keepers, chalked scores on a board; the agricultural writer Gervase Markham declared in 1635 that there was 'more trust in an honest score chaulkt on a Trencher, then in a cunning written scrowle, how well so ever painted on the best Parchment' and 'more Benefit in simple and single Numeration in Chaulke, then in double Multiplication, though in never so faire an hand written'.[93] Shepherds counted sheep by making notches on a stick: an asterisk to represent twenty, a cross for ten and four notches crossed through for five.[94] In the early seventeenth century George Purefoy's servants kept a reckoning of the number of the poor who had been fed at his gates by bringing him two basins of birch twigs, each twig denoting a person who had received his alms.[95] In the eighteenth century many small traders were, like the King's Exchequer, still using tally-sticks as a record of their transactions: the tally, it was said in 1714, was 'of ordinary Use in keeping Accompts with illiterate People, and serves well enough for meer Tale'.[96] In fact, there was an infinity of tactile substitutes for abstract written numbers. The grandfather of the exciseman John Cannon was an 'unlearned' (i.e. illiterate) butcher; he kept his accounts with beans, which he carried to market for that purpose.[97] Daniel Defoe knew a country shopkeeper who had an elaborate (and infallible) system involving innumerable split sticks kept in separate drawers for each customer:

[91] Brinsley, *Ludus Literarius*, ed. Campagnac, 25.

[92] Edward B. Tylor, *Primitive Culture* (2 vols., 1871), i. 245. On finger reckoning, see, e.g., Recorde, *Ground of Artes*, sigs. Oviii–Piii^v; Sir Thomas Browne, *Pseudodoxia Epidemica*, ed. Robin Robbins (Oxford, 1981), 908; George Brown, *A Compendious, but a Compleat System of Decimal Arithmetick* (Edinburgh, 1701), 3–4.

[93] Iervis Markham, *The English Husband-Man* (1635), i. 9.

[94] *The Farming and Memorandum Books of Henry Best of Elmswell, 1642*, ed. Donald Woodward (British Academy, 1984), 87.

[95] *Purefoy Letters, 1735–1753*, ed. G. Eland (1931), 397.

[96] (North), *The Gentleman Accomptant*, sig. b4. On tallies, see Hilary Jenkinson, 'Medieval Tallies, Public and Private', *Archaeologia*, 2nd ser., xxiv (1925).

[97] 'Memoirs of John Cannon' (note 38 above), 11.

'every stick had notches on one side for single pounds, on the other side for tens of pounds ... and the length and breadth also had its signification, and the colour too ... and his way of casting up was very remarkable; for he knew nothing of figures, but he kept six spoons in a place on purpose, near his counter, which he took out when he had occasion to cast up any sum, and laying the spoons on a row before him, he counted them thus:

One, two, three and another; one odd spoon and t'other

/   /   /   /   /   /

By this he told up to six: if he had any occasion to tell any further he began again.'[98]

But the main alternative to written arabic figures was the old system of counters and roman numerals. Arabic figures had come relatively late to England; it was only between the mid-sixteenth and mid-seventeenth centuries that they established themselves in most forms of account-keeping. During this transitional period they were often used side by side with roman letters in the same document, with roman the language of record and grand totals, and arabic that of calculation.[99] Meanwhile, arabic figures had to be explained to those who found them strange and unfamiliar. In 1565, for example, Richard Grafton told the readers of his abridgement of the chronicles that he proposed to 'nomber the yeres of our Lorde, and of the Kynges in plaine nombers, and not in Figures, for the helpe of suche as are not acquainted with the use of Figures'.[100] The need for instruction in the new methods explains the otherwise baffling entry in the earl of Northumberland's accounts for 1607: 'to one that taught the account-ant, Mr. Fotherley, the art of arithmetic, 20s'.[101] Elizabeth I's treasurer Lord Burghley, we are told, was never really at home with arabic figures and neither, apparently, were many students at Elizabethan Oxford.[102] For people at large they may have remained a mystery even longer. The new 'cyphers' were distrusted by many early Stuart sailors. Indeed the very word 'cipher' had overtones of concealment and obscurity: ciphers, as Bailey's *Dictionary* (1721) explained, were 'certain odd Marks and Characters, in which Letters are Written,

[98] Defoe, *Complete English Tradesman*, i. 312–13.
[99] Jenkinson, 'The Use of Arabic and Roman Numerals in English Archives'; Eustace F. Bosanquet, 'An Early Printed Account Book', *The Library*, 4th ser., xi (1931), 206–10; Lawrence Stone, *The Crisis of the Aristocracy, 1558–1641* (Oxford, 1979), 278–9; J. M. Pullan, *The History of the Abacus* (1968), 39–41.
[100] *A Manuell of the Chronicles of Englande ... abridged and collected by Richard Grafton* (1565), sig. Aii.
[101] *Historical MSS Commission Reports*, vi. 229ᵃ.
[102] Stone, *Crisis of the Aristocracy*, 278; Mark H. Curtis, *Oxford and Cambridge in Transition 1558–1642* (Oxford, 1959), 245.

that they may not be understood'.[103] To the ignorant, arithmetic appeared a bizarre and mysterious art; small wonder, when 'mathematician' was a synonym for astrologer, and when a battered copy of some arithmetical textbook was part of the fortune-teller's stock-in-trade.[104]

Since counters and roman numerals were perfectly effective within their limits, they continued to retain devotees to whom written arithmetic did not appeal. The new system required access to paper and the ability to use a pen. Arabic figures could more easily be forged: hence the long-enduring practice of writing, say, one penny as 'oo.oo.oi'. Figures were all very well for calculations, but, as an adviser on the Cannock ironworks put it in 1590, 'Prises, for to avoide mistaking, are better written in letters.'[105] Above all, the new written arithmetic required a greater sense of abstract numeration than did the visible and tangible counters employed on the abacus.[106]

The old medieval battle between abacists and algorismists thus continued to be waged in early modern England. The textbooks made concessions to 'such as lacke the knowledge of Arithmetike by the Penne';[107] and it was assumed that bookkeepers would cast accounts by either method, pen or counters.[108] Thomas Willsford asserted in 1656 that arabic figures were much the speediest for computation, but he admitted that roman letters were 'in many things frequently continued to these dayes'.[109] Forty years later, however, Samuel Jeake declared flatly that, since arabic figures were the best for the art of numbers, his book on arithmetic would totally disregard the use of counters and letters.[110] By this time arabic numerals had come to be known as 'English figures' and the Roman numbers seemed archaic. To be able to calculate only with counters had become a badge of

[103] Waters, *Art of Navigation*, 498; N. Bailey, *An Universal Etymological English Dictionary* (1721).

[104] *Oxford English Dictionary, s.v.* 'mathematician'; Keith Thomas, *Religion and the Decline of Magic* (1971), 303, 362–3.

[105] Owens, *Plain Papers relating to the Excise Branch*, 132; A. C. Jones and C. J. Harrison, 'The Cannock Chase Ironworks, 1590', *EHR*, xciii (1978), 810 (kindly shown me by Dr C. J. Harrison).

[106] On the reasons for adherence to the roman system, see Menninger, *Number Words and Number Systems*, 298, 427–8; Murray, *Reason and Society in the Middle Ages*, 169–70; Pullan, *History of the Abacus*, 35.

[107] John Mellis, *A Briefe Intruction and Maner how to keepe bookes of Accompts* (1588), sig, A7ᵛ; Recorde, *Ground of Artes*, sig. Mviᵛ; Francis Pierrepont Barnard, *The Casting-Counter and the Counting-Board* (Oxford, 1916), 266.

[108] Yamey, Edey and Thompson, *Accounting in England and Scotland*, 48; James Peele, *The Maner and Fourme how to kepe a Perfecte Reconyng* (1553), sig. Aiiiᵛ; Joseph Chamberlaine, *A New Almanacke and Prognostication for ... 1631*, sig. Cl.

[109] Thomas Willsford, *Willsfords Arithmetick, Naturall, and Artificiall* (1656), 116.

[110] Samuel Jeake, *ΛΟΓΣΤΙΚΗΛΟΓΙΑ or Arithmetick Surveighed and Reviewed*, 1696, 4.

ignorance.[111] The 1699 reissue of Robert Recorde's Tudor textbook finally dropped the section on manual reckoning. In 1714 Roger North referred to counters as things of the past. They survived only in the scoring-system for cribbage and similar games.[112]

The gradual association of counters with the ignorant and illiterate illustrates how the common people were slower to move over to the new arithmetic than were some of their superiors, just as they were slower to abandon black-letter script.[113] They also continued to use numbers and quantities in a more subjective and qualitative way. The English standard measures had, after all, been based originally on real objects or activities: three barley-corns, the breadth of a thumbnail, a human foot, a thousand paces, a day's ploughing, the amount of land necessary to maintain a family. Units of trade and manufacture had been equally visible: the load, the barrel, the bundle, the sheaf, the bale. Only gradually did such items acquire numerical precision. But the survival of huge regional differences in their meaning was a reminder that they were still rooted in distinctive human actitivies and perceived accordingly. Different units were used for different commodities: one measured cloth in ells, height in feet, depth in fathoms. Two pheasants were a brace, two bullocks a yoke, two gloves a pair. Quantities, in short, were still apprehended in sensory or visual terms.

In ordinary speech, therefore, measurements were as likely to be expressed in terms of human experience as of number. A Parliamentary majority was heard rather than counted.[114] Distances were still 'a day's journey', a 'bow shot', or 'a stone's throw'. (It was ironic that in the very same letter of 1656 in which the reformer James Stansfield urged the adoption of 'one constant measure (Winchester) per Universam Angliam', he should also have remarked that one could see the damage done by rooks and crows to growing crops 'for a Coyt's cast on each side of the high-way'.)[115] Physicians and cooks used measures like 'a greate handfull' and 'a little handfull'.[116] Individuals reckoned time by relation to important social events, to seasons or

[111] The Reports of Sir Creswell Levinz (2nd edn., 3 vols., 1722), ii. 102; Smith, History of Mathematics, ii. 188.

[112] Barnard, The Casting-Counter and the Counting-Board, 87–8; North, The Gentleman Accomptant, sig. a3ᵛ.

[113] Thomas, 'The Meaning of Literacy in Early Modern England', 99; M. F. Roberts, 'Wages and Wage-Earners in England: the Evidence of the Wage Assessments' (Oxford Univ. D. Phil. thesis, 1981), 86–7.

[114] Sir Goronwy Edwards, 'The Emergence of Majority Rule in the Procedure of the House of Commons', T.R.H.S., 5th ser., xv (1965), 186–7.

[115] Stansfield, 'A Coppy of a Letter to Mr. Hartlib' (note 83 above).

[116] The Farming and Memorandum Books of Henry Best, 142; Gervase Markham, Markhams Maister-Peece (1610), 505; J. F. D. Shrewsbury, A History of Bubonic Plague in the British Isles (Cambridge, 1970), 146–7. Cf. Andrew Jones, 'Harvest Customs and Labourers'

saints' days, rather than to numerical dates. In the early eighteenth
century an observer commented on the difficulty of getting rural
witnesses in criminal cases to state the date of the crime: 'For all
Persons (especially ordinary labouring Men of the Country) don't
keep their Accounts of Time by the Names of the Calendar Months;
but some reckon from the Seasons of the Year, as Spring and Fall,
&c., others from the Seasons of Husbandry, as the different Seed-
times or Harvest-Times; and others by County-Wakes and Fairs, ...
If none were to be admitted for Witnesses, but such as speak to
particular Days in this or that Month, [a] great part of the labouring
people in the Countries would be rendered incapable of providing the
Truth.'[117]

Even when numbers were used, they did not always mean what
they seemed to mean. John Quincy Adams would later tell the US
Congress that 'in England ... numbers lose the definite character
which is essential to their nature'.[118] He was thinking of those stylised
quantities, like the baker's dozen, into which there entered an element
of gift exchange or 'complimentary excess', like the modern tradesman's discount. The most ubiquitous of these was the 'great' or
'long' hundred. Though originally six score, this now varied so much
according to the quantity concerned that all that can be said for
certain is that the one total it never indicated was a hundred. Citizens
of London claimed 'trett', whereby they received not 100 lbs of
groceries or drugs but 104 lbs. A hundred in tin or copper was 112
lbs, the modern hundredweight. In herrings or ells of canvas, a
hundred was 120. In codfish and ling it meant 124. For some other
fish it could mean 180.[119]

Such customary and local measures were deeply irritating to the
converts to the new arithmetic and the exponents of a rigorously
quantitative view of the world. For them, the failure of the Winchester
bushel to gain general acceptance outside the South East was a
tiresome piece of local obstruction. The lack of a decimal base for the
pound sterling was deplorable because it made calculation unnecess-
arily difficult. The absence of standard-size containers created math-

Perquisites in Southern England, 1150–1350: the Hay Harvest', *Agricultural Hist. Rev.*,
25 (1977), 106–7.
[117] John Ellis, *Instructions for Collectors of Excise* (1716), i. 39.
[118] John Quincy Adams, *Report upon Weights and Measures* (Washington, 1821), 87.
[119] *Oxford English Dictionary, s.v.* 'baker'; 'dozen'; 'hundred'; Murray, *Chapters in the
History of Bookkeeping, Accountancy and Commercial Arithmetic*, 256; 'Select Tracts and Table
Books', ed. Hall and Nicholas, 18, 29, 30; *Englands Golden Treasury: or, The True Vade
Mecum* (1694), 3; W. H. Stevenson 'The Long Hundred and its Use in England',
Archaeological Review, iv (1899–90). Cf. Monique Aubain, 'Par-Dessus les Marchés:
Gestes et Paroles de la Circulation des Biens d'après Savary des Bruslons', *Annales
(Économies, Sociétés, Civilisations)*, 39ᵉ année (1984), 823–4.

ematical nightmares for gaugers and excise collectors. The long hundred was an infuriating complication.

Yet there were good reasons for these apparently arbitrary and capricious units of measurement. The system seemed chaotic only to those rationalisers who were indifferent to all the local variations in soil fertility, ease of cultivation, mode of transport and form of social relationship which had generated different regional measures in the first place. A common standard was hardly necessary for commodities which, like land, were essentially local; a customary acre was a day's ploughing and it made better agricultural sense than a statute acre.[120] The notion of a standard weight conflicted with the deep-rooted preference for a standard price, as in the Assize of Bread, whereby a loaf always cost a penny (or a halfpenny), but varied in weight according to the price of wheat.[121] The introduction of metropolitan weights and measures could thus appear a threat to local interests. Discussing Sir William Petty's desire to have a standard unit for the whole of England, John Aubrey commented that 'the poor (who are ignorant) are against it; my great-grandfather Browne, my mother's grandfather in King James the First's time ... made an attempt to have brought the Winchester bushell in use all over England, or at least over the West: but the Country people mutinied and were like to have knock't him in the head at Salisbury'.[122] A belief in customary rights, an attachment to functionally significant units and a strong sense of local identity took priority over any commitment to an abstract conception of number. As a character in Elizabethan dialogue remarked, 'The worlde was merrier before measurings were used then it hath been since.'[123]

Meanwhile, at all levels of society, number remained as much a language of quality as of quantity. I do not need to rehearse the importance of numbers in religious symbolism and allegory or of numerology in poetry and philosophical speculation.[124] But it is worth observing that this qualitative view of number constantly threatened

[120] *Surveys of the Manors of Philip, First Earl of Pembroke and Montgomery, 1631–2,* ed. Eric Kerridge (Wilts. Archaeol. and Nat. Hist. Soc., 1953), xiii; *Agrarian History of England and Wales,* v (ii), 818. Cf. Witold Kula, *Measures and Men,* trans. R. Szreter (Princeton, N.J., 1986), 34–5.

[121] See, e.g., John Powel, *The Assize of Bread* (1615). On the ubiquity of this principle, see Kula, *op. cit.,* chap. 8.

[122] Bodleian Lib., MS Gen. Top. c. 25, f. 222.

[123] Worsop, *Discoverie of Sundrie Errours,* sig. I2^v. On the tendency of the economically weak to fear metrological change, see Kula, *Measures and Men,* 16, 70.

[124] See, e.g. William Ingpen, *The Secrets of Numbers; according to Theologicall, Arithmeticall, Geometricall and Harmonicall Computation* (1624); John Heydon, *The Holy Guide* (1622), bk. ii; Vincent Foster Hopper, *Medieval Number Symbolism* (New York, 1938); Christopher Butler, *Number Symbolism* (1970); John MacQueen, *Numerology* (Edinburgh, 1985), chap. 5.

to spill over from the study into the world of affairs. Francis Potter was a practical mathematician who made quadrants and dials. But he also expounded the meaning of the number 666 by using the latest technique to show that the approximate square root of 666 was 25, which, he claimed, was a Popish number, for there were originally twenty-five cardinals in the sacred college and twenty-five abbots in the English Parliament.[125]

In 1610, at the height of the negotiations over the Great Contract, Parliament offered James I nine score thousand pounds for the abolition of royal warship, after the King had demanded eleven score thousand. The Lord Treasurer informed Parliament of James's reaction: 'As concerning the Number nine-score thousand Pounds, which was our Number, he could not affect, because nine was the Number of the Poets, who were always Beggars ... and eleven was the Number of the Apostles when the traitor *Judas* was away, and therefore might best be affected by his Majesty; but there was a mean Number which might accord us both *and that was ten*; which, said my Lord Treasurer, is a sacred Number, for so many were God's commandments.'[126]

Such learned affectations were not typical of popular speech. But there is good evidence that numbers were generally perceived as uneven in value and connotation. Some figures were more prominent than others. They came more readily to the tongue and were more likely to be invoked when making estimates, striking bargains or devising practical arrangements. 'Country People and Farmers,' it was said, 'reckon or count their numbers more simply: by Pairs, half Scores or Tens, Dozens or Twelves, and Scores or Twentys.'[127] Scores were indeed very widely used for ordinary reckoning. Other figures were symbolically important. Seven, for example, was the number of the days of the week, the planets, the Catholic sacraments and the liberal arts. Ages involving multiples of seven were deemed climacteric years, dangerous and critical. Many Protestant clergy scoffed at that notion.[128] But they did not question the convention that apprenticeships should last seven years or the legal doctrine that the ages of special significance in a male child's growth to maturity were seven (the age of innocence), fourteen (puberty) and twenty-one (adulthood).[129]

A closer look suggests indeed that, far from drawing equally on the

[125] Francis Potter, *An Interpretation of the Number 666* (Oxford, 1642).

[126] *Memorials of Affairs of State in the Reign of Q. Elizabeth and K. James I collected (chiefly) from the Original Papers of the Right Honourable Sir Robert Winwood* (3 vols., 1725), iii. 193.

[127] Randle Holme, *The Academy of Armory* (Chester, 1688), iii. 141.

[128] Thomas, *Religion and the Decline of Magic*, 617 and n.1.

[129] Keith Thomas, 'Age and Authority in Early Modern England', *Proceedings of the British Academy*, lxii (1977), 222.

whole numerical system, most people used a limited and stylised repertoire. Their perceptions were shaped by a sort of mental template which inclined them to use some numbers rather than others. We can see this if we look at any list of reported ages during the period. For the demographer, such lists are unreliable because many adults either did not know their true age or chose to misrepresent them. But to the historian the errors are fascinating because they reveal people's unconscious digital preferences. In such lists we find that ages ending in nought will always predominate. There will be more people aged forty than thirty-nine or forty-one, for forty is a rounder number. In the 1597 list of Ipswich poor, for example, there were twenty-four people aged sixty, as against only eighteeen between 51 and 59, twenty-four aged fifty, as against only nineteen in their forties.[130] This is what we would expect, for the decimal thinking encouraged by finger-reckoning had been much strengthened by the use of the abacus, which was based on tens and hundreds.[131] Institutions like tithings, hundreds, tenths and tithes all reflected this bias; and totals were frequently given in multiples of ten: for example, the numbers of communicants in many of the chantry certificates in the reign of Edward VI.[132]

But what was the most popular final digit in the age-listings after nought? Today it would be five. In the early modern period it was six. In the lists of reported ages which I have examined for the period before 1700 the digits nought and six are over-represented; and all the others under-represented.[133] For the abacus had not obliterated the duodecimal thinking which had been so common in Anglo-Saxon England. There were still twelve pence in a shilling, twelve inches in a foot and twelve men in a jury. There were twelve great Livery Companies in London and twelve mysteries in Newcastle-upon-Tyne. Dozens and half-dozens were conventional units of sale. The long hundred of 120 was a duodecimal figure, very conveniently divisible and very useful for multiplying pennies into pounds. 'Of all the numbers,' wrote Rice Vaughan in 1675, 'Twelve ... is most proper for money.'[134] It may be that duodecimal reckoning was strongest in

---

[130] *Poor Relief in Elizabethan Ipswich*, ed. John Webb (Suffolk Records Soc., 1966), 119–40.

[131] R. L. Poole, *The Exchequer in the Twelfth Century* (Oxford, 1912), 45.

[132] Josiah Cox Russell, *British Medieval Population* (Albuquerque, New Mexico, 1948), 21.

[133] My analysis of these digital preferences is still in progress and further work may modify this conclusion. But my current findings suggest that only during the eighteenth century did five replace six as the most frequent terminal digit (after nought) in lists of reported ages.

[134] Rice Vaughan, *A Discourse of Coin and Coinage* (1675), 74.

the old Danelaw region,[135] but all over the country the names of the councils, select vestries and other local governing bodies reveal a similar preference: more often than not, the ruling body was known as the Twelve or the Twenty-Four. Twenty-four was also the minimum age for entry to the priesthood, a common age of inheritance and the age of final release from apprenticeship.[136]

This deeply-rooted habit of thinking in sixes, twelves, and twenty-fours may have been one element in the tacit resistance to the attempts of progressive reformers in the seventeenth century to introduce a decimalised coinage in England, along with decimalised weights and measures. Virtually all the leading mathematicians of the day supported such proposals, for they were interested only in ease of calculation and had no emotional attachment to one unit rather than another. In their view the old system caused 'distraction of the mind, and consequently pronenes to mistake'.[137] Proposals for decimalisation were advanced in the 1650s (the decade of the decimation tax) and again during the Recoinage of the 1690s. On each occasion they were unsuccessful.[138] It was said that the new monetary denominations would cause confusion, that the poor needed smaller coins than a hundredth of a pound and that the task of translation was too difficult (in decimals a farthing came out at the inconvenient figure of approximately £0.0010417).[139] But the real objection was what John Wallis contemptuously called 'a kind of tenaciousness of old Customs rather than any necessity (and even convenience)'.[140] Just as the Exchequer stuck to its tallies and roman numerals, so English traders had got used to conducting a complex economic life in the traditional units. It would be left to the Americans, with their dollars, and the French revolutionaries, with their metric system, to champion decimals as symbols of Enlightenment.[141]

---

[135] H. C. Darby, *Domesday England* (Cambridge, 1977), 10; Reginald Lennard, 'Statistics of Sheep in Medieval England', *Agricultural History Rev.*, vii (1959).

[136] J. H. Thomas, *Town Government in the Sixteenth Century* (1933), 18; Sidney and Beatrice Webb, *English Local Government from the Revolution to the Municipal Corporations Act: the Parish and the County* (1906), 178–81; Thomas, 'Age and Authority', 216, 227–8.

[137] Wood, 'Ten to One', in Webster, *The Great Instauration*, 537.

[138] Webster, *The Great Instauration*, 412–20.

[139] Robert Jager, *Artificial Arithmetick in Decimals* (1651), 4; 'Objections against the discourse of Decimal Coynes', Hartlib Papers, 27/20/9. Sir William Petty's retort to this was that 'if your old defective farthings were cryed down to five a Penny, you might keep all Accompts in a way of Decimal Arithmetick, which hath been long desired'; *Quantulumcunque* (1695), in *A Select Collection of Scarce and Valuable Tracts on Money* (1856), 166–7.

[140] Wallis, *A Treatise of Algebra*, 30.

[141] Kula, *Measures and Men*, chap. 23 and (on the reasons for English reluctance to adopt the metric system) p. 280.

There can be little doubt that numerical skills were more widely dispersed in 1700 than they had been two centuries earlier. The change cannot be quantified, but it is reflected in the spread of written account-keeping down the social scale and in a slight, but discernible, improvement in the accuracy of age-reporting during the period. The new written arithmetic had established itself as the dominant mode; and there was improved provision for arithmetical teaching, at school, in the universities, in the business world and among the instrument-makers and mathematical practitioners. The textbooks of the late seventeenth century envisaged a higher standard of attainment than did those published earlier; and there was no longer any suggestion that the very idea of arabic numeration would be unfamiliar to some readers. Of course, the adoption of the new arithmetical language did not in itself imply greater numerical proficiency. But improved education, the spread of a wider range of mathematically-demanding crafts and techniques and the greater involvement of most people in pecuniary transactions had their inevitable effect.

Nevertheless, popular numeracy remained pragmatic and limited in scope. The value of number depended entirely on its social relevance. Just as people resisted the pressure for universal weights and measures because it seemed to disregard local realities, so they were indifferent to precise calculation in contexts where it had no practical value. Time, for example, did not need to be reckoned with great precision by most of those engaged in agriculture or handicraft because their energies were determined more by the task than by the hours of the day. Few Elizabethans used units of time-reckoning smaller than a half-quarter or quarter of an hour.[142] At the beginning of the eighteenth century the 'common division' of the hour was still into quarters; only 'Astronomers and such as are more accurate in accounting time', it was said, regularly divided the hour into minutes and seconds.[143] Similarly, ages were reported with precision for people under twenty, because differences in age could be of considerable social and administrative importance for young persons. But when people reached adulthood their exact numerical age had much less social meaning; and it was much more vaguely reported.[144] Equally vague were people's estimates in court depositions of the number of years they had lived in some particular place.[145]

[142] William Harrison, *The Description of England*, ed. Georges Edelen (Ithaca, N.Y., 1968), 379.
[143] Edward Wells, *The Young Gentleman's Astronomy, Chronology and Dialling* (2nd edn., 1718), ii. 7.
[144] This is a strikingly consistent feature of all the listings I have analysed.
[145] Walter C. Renshaw, 'Witnesses from Ecclesiastical Deposition Books, 1580–1640', *Sussex Archaeological Collections*, lvi (1914).

What encouraged precision in measurement was scarcity. Exact figures had always been used in financial accounts and business transactions because everyone sought to look after his money. The needs of the state to raise taxes and fighting men encouraged more accurate estimates of the country's population and resources. Just as in the thirteenth century the spread of demense farming had created a demand for precise measurement, so in the sixteenth land hunger and inflation stimulated the development of more rigorous surveying techniques: 'seeing most Landlords covet to let their grounds to the uttermost and most tenants seeke to sell wares at the hyest prices, it is verie requisite for both sides that the land be truely measured.'[146] (No wonder that 'the common people' were said in 1582 to be 'for the most part ... in great fear when survey is made of their land'.)[147] In industry, the increasing scale of production made unacceptable those trivial errors in calculation which would have been tolerable in smaller enterprises where the mistake was not magnified many times over.[148]

So it came about that great numerical precision was expected in some areas while, in others, figures which were either vague or absurdly inaccurate continued to be tolerated. This had been the case in the Middle Ages and it was also true in the early modern period. As an example of what he called 'the absolute untrustworthiness of medieval figures', Bishop Stubbs cited the belief of members of Parliament in 1371 that there were 40,000 parishes in England.[149] Although this figure was over four times too large, it, or something similarly unrealistic, continued to be seriously advanced throughout the sixteenth century.[150] Yet the late medieval world which accepted that estimate was very far from innumerate, as we are reminded by

[146] Worsop, *Discoverie of Sundrie Errours*, sig. I2ᵛ; H. C. Darby, 'The Agrarian Contribution to Surveying in England', *Geographical Journ.*, lxxxii (1933); F. G. R. Taylor, 'The Surveyor', *Economic Hist. Rev.*, xvii (1947); *Local Maps and Plans from Medieval England*, eds. R. A. Skelton and P. D. A. Harvey (Oxford, 1986), 12–13, 18–19. I am grateful to Professor Harvey for letting me see a copy of his important forthcoming paper on 'Estate Surveyors and the Spread of the Scale-Map in England, 1550–80'.

[147] Worsop, *Discoverie of Sundrie Errours*, sig. I2ᵛ.

[148] Mathias, *The Brewing Industry in England*, 63.

[149] William Stubbs, *The Constitutional History of England* (3 vols., 4th edn., Oxford, 1883), ii. 442, n. 4.

[150] Simon Fish, *A Supplication for the Beggars* (1529), ed. Edward Arber (1878), 4 (repudiated as 'one plaine lye' by Sir Thomas More, *Supplycacyon of Soulys* (1529), sig. B1ᵛ); *Tudor Economic Documents*, ed. R. H. Tawney and Eileen Power (3 vols., 1924), iii. 323; *Tudor Treatises*, ed. A. G. Dickens (Yorks. Archaeol. Soc. 1959), 113, 36n. For other medieval exaggerations, see, e.g., J. H. Round, *Feudal England* (1909), 290–2; Sir James H. Ramsay, 'Chroniclers' Estimates of Numbers and Official Records', *EHR* lxxii (1903); Hastings Rashdall, *The Universities of Europe in the Middle Ages*, ed. F. M. Powicke and A. B. Emden (3 vols., 1936), iii. 327.

its trade, its financial administration, its navigation and its architecture. It has been justly remarked that none 'of the country's business, from that of the royal Exchequer to that of the manorial reeve,
could have been conducted by people with no sense of numbers'.[151]
The same was true in the early modern period. It was just that the
concern for exact measurement operated within a limited sphere.
Only gradually was the numerical precision which was shown daily
by accountants, craftsmen and techniques extended into other areas
of life. Sustained to a great extent by its own momentum, the quest
for mathematical exactitude penetrated areas where, in Professor
Hall's words, 'previously judgment, experience or taste alone had
prevailed'.[152] The sixteenth century saw a growing amount of statistical inquiry and the production of figures and measurements for
matters which had never been measured before.[153]

The spread of popular numeracy is bound to remain an elusive
subject and I cannot claim to chart its history with any exactness. To
do so would require a huge assault upon all the extant figures of the
period, checking accounts and calculations for their accuracy and
assessing all reported estimates of age, times, distances and dimensions
for their relative vagueness or precision. Meanwhile, I suggest that by
the end of the seventeenth century it is possible to detect in England
two conflicting attitudes to number. On the one hand were those for
whom figures made sense only when anchored in their own experience.
Like Locke's Red Indians, the vast mass of the population still used
a 'scanty' numerical language, 'accommodated only to the few necess-
aries of a needy, simple Life'.[154] Their vocabulary was limited and
stylised, making much greater use of some numbers than of others
because they were 'rounder', and seldom extending to very high

---

[151] Olive Coleman, 'What Figures? Some Thoughts on the Use of Information by
Medieval Governments', in *Trade, Government and Economy in Pre-Industrial England*, ed.
D. C. Coleman and A. H. John (1976), 105. Cf. the fifteenth-century antiquary William
Worcestre's almost obsessive interest in the measurements of the buildings he visited;
Itineraries, ed. John H. Harvey (Oxford, 1969), xii, xvii–xviii and *passim*.

[152] A. R. Hall, *Ballistics in the Seventeenth Century* (Cambridge, 1952), 72–3.

[153] John U. Nef, *Cultural Foundations of Industrial Civilization* (Cambridge, 1958), 12–
14, 16; G. N. Clark, *Guide to English Commercial Statistics, 1696–1782* (Royal Hist. Soc.
1938), xi; *Tudor Economic Documents*, ed. Tawney and Power, iii, 323; A. B. Ferguson,
The Articulate Citizen and the English Renaissance (Durham, N.C., 1965), 205–6; Lawrence
Stone 'Elizabethan Overseas Trade', *Economic Hist. Rev.* 2nd Ser. ii (1949–50), 31–3;
G. R. Elton, *Reform and Renewal. Thomas Cromwell and the Common Weal* (Cambridge,
1973), 14, 65; Paul Slack, *The Impact of Plague in Tudor and Stuart England* (1985), 113,
120. The statistical estimates with which Simon Fish buttressed his attack upon the
religious orders in his *Supplication for the Beggars* (1529) would subsequently earn him
the title of a 'Columbus' of calculation; Sir Peter Pett, *The Happy Future State of England*
(1688), 91.

[154] Locke, *Essay concerning Human Understanding*, ed. Nidditch, 207 (II. xvi. 6.).

figures, because large-scale calculations did not concern them. The rudiments of 'vulgar arithmetic', simple addition and subtraction, were widely known, but only if one's occupation required it were more advanced numerical techniques attempted. As a preacher remarked, it took only a little skill in arithmetic to number the days of man. One needed to know to use tens and units, but it was not necessary to go into hundreds.[155]

On the other hand were the proto-quantifiers, the scientists and political arithmeticians who were attempting to reduce all experience to 'number, weight and measure', the categories in which they believed God to have created the world. For them arithmetic and geometry offered the only prospect of intellectual certainty, of 'clear knowledge'.[156] In numerical calculation they saw a powerful solvent of custom, superstition and prejudice: 'it is wonderful', wrote William Leybourn, 'to see how Numbers will discover that to be erronious and absurd, which to common sense and man's apprehension appears reasonable'.[157] They stressed the moral value of a method which accustomed the mind to careful accounting and close demonstrative reasoning. For Sir Josiah Child, arithmetic did not merely improve the rational faculties; it also inclined those expert in it to 'thriftiness and good-husbandry'. For Sir William Petty, 'mathematical reasoning' afforded 'the best means of judging in all the concerns of human life'. 'He that has such a computing head,' agreed Charles Davenant, 'will seldom enter into ill measures.'[158]

As an example, almost the apotheosis, of what a computing head could do, I conclude with *Computatio Universalis*, a tract produced by an anonymous writer in 1697.[159] It was a sort of felicific calculus claiming to offer 'an universal standard whereby one may judge of the true value of everything in the world'. Allowing for an average expectation of life of sixty-four years, and deducting the time likely to be consumed by childhood, sleep, prayer and illness, its author calculated that there remained only thirty-two years of rational waking life. Assuming an annual income of £120 and making the necessary subtraction for unavoidable expenditure, he estimated that a total of £4940 remained to be freely spent. Dividing this sum by the

[155] Thomas Hardcastle, *Christian Geography and Arithmetick* (1674), 59.

[156] *Economic Writings of Sir William Petty*, ed. Hull, ii. 397. Cf. John Kersey, *The Elements of that Mathematical Art commonly called Algebra* (1673), sig. b2; Barbara J. Shapiro, *Probability and Certainty in Seventeenth-Century England* (Princeton, N.J., 1983), 32.

[157] Will[iam] Leybourn, *Arithmetical Recreations* (2nd edn., 1676), 140.

[158] Child, *New Discourses of Trade*, 4–5; *Philosophical Transactions*, xvi (for 1686 and 1687) (1688), 152; *The Political and Commercial Works of ... Charles D'Avenant*, ed. Sir Charles Whitworth (5 vols., 1771), i. 135.

[159] *Computatio Universalis seu Logica Rerum* (1697) (Wing C. 5675).

thirty-two years, he concluded that a year of one's life was worth £154 7s 6d, one hour 4 1/4d and one minute one fourteenth of a farthing. With these figures in mind, it would at last be possible to make rational decisions about what any form of expenditure of time or money really involved.

If Defoe's country shop-keeper, banging out his accounts with six spoons and innumerable wooden splinters, belongs to the world we have lost, then this relentless advocate of value for money was indubitably the shape of the future.

JOHN OF GAUNT: PARADIGM OF THE LATE FOURTEENTH-CENTURY CRISIS

By Anthony Goodman

READ 17 OCTOBER 1986

MARTIN I of Aragon, who was no friend to John of Gaunt, wrote respectfully on hearing news of his death.[1] The remarks of foreign writers such as Froissart and Wyntoun echo similar reactions in French and Scottish princely circles.[2] But English chroniclers tended to be perfunctory. Gower, for instance, despite his Lancastrian connection, was to say merely that death had resolved everything for the duke.[3] Another contrast with such indifference is provided by the hostility which Gaunt often encountered in England in his lifetime. The most fully informed native chroniclers of the later fourteenth century amply testify to this hostility which, they imply, was sometimes national in scale, sometimes regional (especially concentrated in London and south-east England) and which animated members of elite groups (magnates, courtiers, knights of the shire in parliament, London citizens) or embraced wide sections of the commons as well. The Anonimalle Chronicler reports these reactions in a matter-of-fact way, Henry Knighton sorrowfully, Thomas Walsingham for a number of years with righteous approval, the Westminster Chronicler sometimes approvingly, sometimes not. Their reports have some features in common. They are for the most part not concerned with the duke's local exercise of power and influence in his capacities as duke of Lancaster and as the holder of important royal commissions. The attacks on his rural properties during the Great Revolt of 1381 and the involvement of his tenants in its disturbances went unreported.[4] The rejection during the Revolt of his authority as royal lieutenant in the northern Marches by substantial number of Border gentlefolk is implicit in the accounts of his quarrel with the earl of Northumberland: this quarrel, as a matter of national importance,

---

[1] Archivo de la Corona de Aragón, reg. 2242, f. 104. I owe this reference to Mr Peter Rycraft.

[2] *Oeuvres de Froissart*, ed. K. de Lettenhove, xvi (Brussels, 1872), 138–9; *The Orygynale Cronykil of Scotland*, ed. D. Laing (Edinburgh, 1879), iii. 68–9.

[3] 'The Tripartite Chronicle', *The Major Latin Works of John Gower*, ed. E. W. Stockton (Seattle, 1962), 315.

[4] *John of Gaunt's Register, 1379–1383* (hereafter *JGR, 1379–83*), ed. E. C. Lodge and R. Somerville (Camden Third Series, lvi–ii, 1937), i. xv; J. A. Tuck, 'Nobles, Commons and the Great Revolt of 1381', *The English Rising of 1381*, ed. R. H. Hilton and T. H. Aston (Cambridge, 1984), 201–2.

brought regional tensions within chroniclers' purview.[5] Exceptionally, in the early 1390s the Westminster Chronicler and Walsingham were interested in the troubles on the ducal estates in Yorkshire, possibly because the fame of their main instigator, William Beckwith, had spread through a ballad or newsletter.[6]

But chroniclers were above all interested in reporting the impact of Gaunt's behaviour and policies on the 'common weal' of the realm, as viewed by a suspicious and sensitive public opinion. The critical ones inclined to believe that he was the sole author of his unpopularity, not the victim of evil counsel, and that his aims, when reprehensible, were for the satisfaction of his own appetites and ambitions rather than those of his followers. They did not suggest that factious and intimidating behaviour by his uniquely conspicuous body of retainers was a cause of his unpopularity. Walsingham accused those whom he had given livery collars only of inordinate pride in their possession of the collars.[7] Only once did he come near to insinuating that the duke made a corrupt political use of his followers: he alleged that Gaunt procured the choice of more amenable shire knights to sit in Edward III's last parliament, though he did not say whether these were ducal retainers. Except for his remarks about Sir Thomas Hungerford's conduct as Speaker of the Commons in that parliament,[8] Walsingham's references to the duke's retainers in the context of the political crisis of 1376–7 suggest that he believed that they either disapproved of his policies or did nothing of note to promote them. He certainly did not regard their habitual conduct as constituting one of the common grievances against the duke. He recounted at some length how a ducal esquire reproved his master for his contemptuous attitude towards the Commons in 1376: since the reproof was delivered supposedly when Gaunt was taking counsel 'cum suis privatis hominibus' and since he was chastened by it, the implication of the story is that the council sympathised with the esquire's viewpoint, not Gaunt's.[9] In 1377, Walsingham says, the Londoners attacked Gaunt's Scottish retainer Sir John Swinton because they were infuriated by his flaunting of the Lancastrian livery collar.[10] Walsingham passed up the opportunity to denounce Swinton as one of an alien coterie in

[5] The Anonimalle Chronicle 1333 to 1381 (hereafter AC), ed. V. H. Galbraith (Manchester, 1927), 152, 154–6. For defiance of Gaunt's authority by Border esquires in 1383, The Westminster Chronicle 1381–1394 (hereafter WC), ed. L. C. Hector and B. F. Harvey (Oxford, 1982), 40–3.
[6] WC, 442–5, 486–7, 516–17; 'Annales Ricardi Secundi et Henrici Quarti', Johannis de Trokelowe . . . Annales, ed. H. T. Riley (Rolls Series, 1866),160–1.
[7] Chronicon Angliae (hereafter CA), ed. E. M. Thompson (Rolls Series, 1874), 125–6.
[8] Ibid., 112.
[9] Ibid., 74–5.
[10] Ibid., 125.

what was probably the most foreign of English noble households—in fact Castilians associated with the Lancastrian household seem to have been welcome visitors at St Albans Abbey.[11] The Londoners whom the chronicler has rushing to attack the house of the Lancastrian councillor Sir John Ypres do so because they expect to find Gaunt and Lord Percy there: Walsingham failed to note anything sinister about Ypres and his tenure of the stewardship of the royal household.[12] The chronicler's indifference about the role of Gaunt's followers is weighty testimony to their collective lack of impact on national affairs, since he was ready to use any rumour to discredit Gaunt and had potential access to good sources of information about their roles and opinions. Hertford Castle, frequently a suburban residence of the ducal household, was not far from his convent[13] and Adam Rous, surgeon, and Juliane his wife, recipients of ducal annuities, were notable benefactors of the house.[14] Some of the main bodies of rebels in 1381 seem to have taken a view of the Lancastrian following similar to Walsingham's, punishing his men because of their association with the duke rather than any alleged participation in his misdeeds or committal of their own. The Kentishmen wanted to execute Thomas Haselden (controller of the household) and ransacked his property 'par envy qils avoient al dit duc'.[15] There is a hint of more personal animus against the duke's physician, William Appleton, executed on Tower Hill, in the Anonimalle Chronicler's reflection that he was 'graunt meistre' with the king and duke.[16] If after 1381 the duke had had a phalanx of followers pushing his interests in great councils and parliaments—e.g., the policy of the 'way of Portugal' in the early 1380s and the plans for peace with the French Crown in the 1390s—one might have expected that well-informed observer, the Westmins-

---

[11] Walsingham regarded the Duchess Constance as a victim of Gaunt (*ibid.*, 196). She and her company (including some Castilians) were received into the confraternity of St Alban in 1386 (B.l., 'Liber Benefactorum', MS. Cotton Nero D vii, ff. 132 v.–133 r.).

[12] *CA*, 123–4.

[13] A gift of oaks to the duke from the abbot of St Albans for the works at Hertford Castle rankled with Walsingham (*ibid.*, 163–4; cf *JGR, 1379–83*, i. no. 519).

[14] P.R.O., Receiver General's Account, 1376–77, DL 28/3/1, m. 5; *JGR, 1379–83*, i. nos. 140, 284; 'Liber Benefactorum', ff. 83 r., 104 v. A medical recipe attributed to Rous is in York Minister Library, MS. XVI.E.32, ff. 82 r.–82 v., lines 67–87. I owe this reference to Miss Antoinette Verveen.

[15] *AC*, 138, 194. Haselden had been considered at the papal court in 1374 as one of those influential with Gaunt (*Calendar of Entries in the Papal Registers relating to Great Britain and Ireland. Papal Letters*, ed. W. H. Bliss and J. A. Twemlow, iv (1902, 131–2, 136).

[16] *AC*, 145; *Chronicon Henrici Knighton*, ed. J. R. Lumby (Rolls Series, 1895), ii. 133 ('duci ... familiarissimus'). For gifts from Gaunt to Appleton in 1380–81, *JGR, 1379–83*, i. nos. 430, 557.

ter Chronicler, to have remarked on the fact. One might also have expected his policies to have been promoted more successfully. Therefore Gaunt did not recruit an affinity for use as a political force in national affairs and his affinity was not seen by his leading critics as an oppressive element contributing to his general bouts of unpopularity.

Why was the Lancastrian affinity not delineated as either a forceful or oppressive element in the affairs of the realm? On the whole, the nature and composition of the retinue probably militated against such a forceful use of it. It did possess some features likely to promote a sense of common political loyalties. There were considerable continuities in service to the House of Lancaster. Gaunt patronised some of the leading retainers of his ducal predecessor Henry of Grosmont, such as Simon Simeon esquire, a member of Duke Henry's household in 1344 and his chamberlain in 1358.[16] When about to go to Aquitaine in 1370, Gaunt appointed Sir Godfrey Foljambe and Simeon as his attorneys and in 1383 he appointed Simeon steward of Bolingbroke, Lincolnshire.[18] Simeon's will of 1386 displays a remarkable sense of personal identification with the Lancastrian House: it is remarkable too that this is largely unparalleled in the surviving wills of other Lancastrian servants of the period.[19] A similar example of continuity in Lancastrian service is provided by the career of John Neumarche esquire, executor of Duke Henry and appointed by Gaunt as his chamberlain in 1371.[20] Sir John Ypres had been made sheriff of Lancashire for life by Duke Henry: he was confirmed in office by Gaunt and in 1383 became chief of his council.[21] It was rare for the life contracts between Gaunt and the knights and esquires whom he retained to be prematurely terminated—the earl of Warwick's brother Sir William Beauchamp was exceptional in giving up a large ducal annuity.[22] The hereditary patronage which Gaunt disposed of provided rich incentives to stay in his service. Some retainers were appar-

---

[17] R. Somerville, *History of the Duchy of Lancaster* (1953), 358.

[18] Nottinghamshire Record Office, Foljambe of Osberton Collection, i. 700; Somerville, 376. In 1365 Simeon and three other leading servants of the duke were leasing property from the queen to Gaunt's use in Yorkshire (Foljambe of Osberton Collection, i. 650).

[19] Simeon willed his burial in the church of Duke Henry's collegiate foundation of St Mary in the Newarke at Leicester and endowed a chantry there in part for the souls of the two dukes of Lancaster and Henry of Bolingbroke (*Early Lincoln Wills*, ed. A. Gibbons, Lincoln, 1888, 78). Gaunt's councillor Sir Robert Swillington bequeathed a missal to the church in 1391 (*ibid.*, 77).

[20] Somerville, 363. Neumarche was probably also an executor of Gaunt in 1369 (*Calendar of Patent Rolls*, hereafter *CPR*, *1367–70*, 212–13).

[21] Somerville, 372. A Ralph Ypres was a valet of Duke Henry and an esquire of Gaunt (*ibid.*, 373–74).

[22] *John of Gaunt's Register 1372–1376* (hereafter *JGR*, *1372–76*,), ed. S. Armitage-Smith (Camden Third Series, xx, xxi, 1911) i. no. 832; ii. no. 1548).

ently successful in promoting kinsmen into it. Sir John Ypres' son Sir John became a ducal retainer in 1382.[23] The Yorkshire knight Richard Roucliffe and his son Sir Richard were both in receipt of ducal fees in 1379; a younger son, Sir David, was also to be retained.[24] Sometimes family continuities in Lancastrian service went back a long way. The Sir Hugh Hastings of Elsing (Norfolk) who went with Gaunt to Spain in 1386 was the son and heir of the Sir Hugh whom Gaunt had retained for life in 1366 and who had contracted to serve in some of Duke Henry's military retinues: that Sir Hugh's father (another Sir Hugh) had been an executor of Earl Henry of Lancaster.[25] Contractual obligations often meshed with feudal ties as well as family ones: the Sir John Marmion who resolved to share the duke's fate when it was at its nadir in 1381 was acting as a faithful vassal as well as a faithful retainer.[26] But perhaps the most important factor in his decision and the similar one of Sir Walter Urswick was that they belonged to the inner group of the duke's companions, knights and esquires frequently attendant on him, with whom he had long and close ties, and from among whom he selected his councillors.[27]

Continuities of vassalic and family service promoted the recruitment of retainers from families with concentrations of property in ducal lordships, especially those in northern England. In the West Riding of Yorkshire, for instance, Lancastrian service was part of the fabric of social relationships among gentlefolk. The retinue facilitated the making of networks of local and distant relationships which assisted property management and dynasticism and which provided opportunities for business such as were especially desirable for those of lower gentle status making their way by professional employment. In 1384 Sir Robert Swillington, Lancastrian councillor and leading Yorkshire landowner, had as feoffees a large number of local men, William Bayley, William Gascoigne, Hugh Wombwell and John Woderoue,[28] all of them employed at some time by Gaunt as lawyers and administrators,[29] and William Keteryng, esquire of the ducal household.[30]

---

[23] *JGR, 1379–83*, i. no. 49.

[24] *Ibid.*, i. no. 72; *Calendar of Close Rolls* (hereafter *CCR*), *1396–99*, 443–4. Sir David succeeded his father as steward of Pickering (Somerville, 378).

[25] A. Goodman, 'The military subcontracts of Sir Hugh Hastings, 1380', *EHR*, xcv (1980), 114. For the 1366 contract, Norfolk Record Office, MR 287. 242 X 4.

[26] *AC*, 152–3; *JGR, 1379–83*, i. no. 431.

[27] Groups of fifteen knights were attendant on Gaunt over periods of a month probably in 1381; among those who recurred were John Marmion, John Ypres, William Croyser, Richard Burley, Walter Urswick, Walter Blount, Maubruny de Linières and John Swinton (East Sussex Record Office, Glynde Place Archives, John of Gaunt's Household rolls, 3469, Rolls A.7, B.5, B.10).   [28] *CCR, 1381–85*, 607–8.

[29] For Bayley, Somerville, 378, 383; for Gascoigne, *ibid.*, 468; *CCR, 1396–99*, 471; for Wombwell, *JGR, 1372–76*, i. nos. 353, 447; Somerville, 458; for Woderoue, *ibid.*, 386.

[30] East Sussex R.O., 3469, Polls A.1, A.7, B.10.

Membership of the affinity opened up opportunities to augment or found inheritances with good assurance of sound titles. Swillington, involved in the duke's administration in Leicestershire, acquired property there from Sir Ralph Hastings, fellow Yorkshireman and retainer,[31] with the bonus of a quitclaim from the venerable steward of the honour of Leicester, Simon Pakeman.[32] For knightly families such as the Swillingtons and Hastings, long traditions of Lancastrian service had helped to create patterns of landholding in various shires parallel to ducal ones and to each other's, a parallelism which provided incentives to attempt to continue in Lancastrian service and to cultivate Lancastrian circles.

Gaunt was certainly aware of the importance of exploiting such traditions of service, in part a necessity to protect his properties from constant threats of encroachment and trespass posed by neighbouring gentlefolk. But the variety of needs which he had to meet led him to restrict the benefits given to 'Lancastrian' families in favour of 'outsiders'. There were no guarantees of hereditary favour. It was seventeen years after the death of Sir Godfrey Foljambe, councillor and chief steward, before another member of the family received an office, and then only a local stewardship.[33] Retainers whose main concentrations of property lay outside the Lancastrian orbit were not necessarily absorbed within it. Sir William Croyser associated with fellow retainers as steward of the household and councillor,[34] but his private interests and links as a property-holder lay mostly in different regions from theirs and the duke's, mainly in Bedfordshire.[35] The Yorkshireman Thomas Haselden used his position in Cambridgeshire as ducal steward as a means of establishing himself as a landowner there. His descendants dropped out of Lancastrian service, aspiring instead to roles in the elite of a shire where Lancastrian properties and retainers were scarce.[36]

Gaunt's affinity was distinguished by his recruitment of foreigners as knights and esquires, in addition to a few of the Castilian exiles

---

[31] Historical Manuscripts Commission. Report on the Manuscripts of the late Reginald Rawdon Hastings, I (1928), 21–2. For Hastings' career, The Parliamentary Representation of the County of York 1258–1832, i (Yorkshire Archaeological Society, 1935), 131–3.

[32] JGR, 1372–76, i. no. 730.

[33] Somerville, 382.

[34] Ibid., 364. In 1369 the Lancastrian retainer Sir Walter Blount granted a manor house to Sir Godfrey Foljambe and his wife. The witnesses were headed by Gaunt and included three of his knights (one of them Croyser) and one of his esquires (Nottinghamshire R.O., Foljambe of Osberton, 1/75/1).

[35] For some of Croyser's landed interests, Victoria County History of Bedfordshire, ii. 256, 354, iii.78.

[36] Victoria County History of Cambridgeshire, viii, 99.

who came in the wake of the Duchess Constance.[37] He brought some notable alien knights into the circle of his household attendants, such as Maubruny de Linières, retained in 1371 with the exceptionally large annuity of fifty marks.[38] The Savoyard knight Otes de Granson was granted a fee of the same amount.[39] His famed skills and virtues are reflected in his corpus of poetry, Philippe de Mézières' appointment of him as an evangelist for the proposed Order of the Passion and Christine de Pisan's lament for his death.[40] A more speculative investment than the retaining of these two knights was Gaunt's contract with John Swinton esquire, a Scotsman, in 1372.[41] This paid off: after the 1373–4 expedition to France Swinton was retained as a knight and was to attend the household.[42] These highly paid foreign retainers added nothing to Gaunt's regional influence in England, nor did many of his English esquires and some of his English knights. But either their courtly qualities, their diplomatic skills or their fighting reputations (or a combination of these) was vital to his standing in the realm and in Christendom.[43]

The knights and esquires who habitually surrounded the duke were recruited for their individual courtly and governmental skills, and sometimes too for their Lancastrian connections and their status within the duke's lordships. Sir Walter Urswick, recruited when Gaunt was a very young earl of Richmond, was his specialist in venery.[44] Sir John Marmion may have been specially valued because of his expertise in the law of arms.[45] Sir Thomas Percy and Sir Richard Burley, appointed respectively admiral and one of the marshals of the 1386 expedition, were distinguished soldiers long associated with Gaunt's military enterprises.[46] Percy was also an admired diplomat, in whom, according to Walsingham, the kings of France and Castile reposed exceptional trust: Gaunt used him as a principal in negotiating a

---

[37] Gaunt does not seem to have been eager to give his houshold a Castilian complexion. One of the few Castilians whom he admired was Juan Fernandez, retained by him as a knight (DL 28/3/1, m. 5; *JGR, 1379–83*, i. nos. 296, 463; East Sussex Record Office, 3469, Rolls A.7, B.5).

[38] *JGR, 1372–76*, i. no. 786; DL 28/3/1, m. 5.

[39] *Ibid.; JGR, 1379–83*, i. no. 68.

[40] H. Braddy, *Chaucer and the French Poet Graunson* (Port Washington, 1968), 3–4, 17–18, 45–8.

[41] *JGR, 1372–76*, i. no. 789.

[42] *Ibid.*, ii. no. 868.

[43] For a reference to jousts at Hertford, *JGR, 1379–83*, ii. no. 803.

[44] *JGR, 1372–76*, i. no. 260; Somerville, 374. For Gaunt's gift of a horn to Urswick, *JGR, 1372–76*, ii. no. 1431.

[45] *The Controversy between Sir Richard Scrope and Sir Robert Grosvenor in the Court of Chivalry*, ed. N. Harris Nicolas (1832), i. 45.

[46] P. E. Russell, *The English Intervention in Spain and Portugal in the Time of Edward III and Richard II* (Oxford, 1955), 406–7, 421.

settlement with Juan I.[47] Such exalted and highly rewarded retainers, on whom Gaunt relied for customary companionship, the maintenance of a pricely culture and the initiation of policies, are to be distinguished from others who, though contracted in precisely the same way, were primarily valued as administrators, protectors of local interests and as 'sleepers', summoned to attend occasionally to make up an imposing company for a state occasion, a tournament or campaign. 'Sleepers' might have a primarily local role. The Northumberland knights John Fenwick and William Heron were retainers of Gaunt, probably in the 1390s.[48] Their principal function is likely to have been to provide Gaunt with hospitality, supplies and an escort when he was passing through the shire on his way to and from international conferences on the Anglo-Scottish Border: they were to help uphold his honour in a shire which he might frequent, where he had little territorial interest, the scene of his great disgrace.

There was one domestic context, a politically sensitive and at times contentious one, in which Gaunt made systematic use of his affinity. They were to be appointed on commissions of the peace in the shires where Lancastrian territorial interests were concentrated, in larger numbers than had been the case under Duke Henry. For instance, in the commissions appointed in 1368, local landowners prominent as ducal retainers or ministers came to dominate the West Riding commission in Yorkshire and to be strongly represented on the Holand commission in Lincolnshire and on the Derbyshire and Leicestershire commissions. Sir Godfrey Foljambe, chief steward of the duke's lands, was in that year first appointed on the commission for his native Derbyshire.[49] When he died in 1376, his place on the commission was taken by another ducal retainer, Sir Avery Sulny, keeper of Gaunt's Needlewood Chace there since 1372.[50] The increase in the numbers of Lancastrian retainer on many peace commissions in the 1370s and early 1380s can be to some extent explained in terms of the general tendency of the commissions to grow in size and in terms of the duke's expansion of his retinue coincidentally. Some of the new appointments of his retainers probably had nothing to do with him and did not affect his interests. The appearance of Sir Thomas Hungerford (steward of the south parts) on the Somerset bench is to be related to his property

[47] 'Annales Ricardi Secundi et Henrici Quarti', 365–6. For Gaunt's use of Percy in the negotiations of 1387, see J.J.N. Palmer and B.J. Powell, 'El Tratado de Bayona (1388) y los Tratados de Trancoso (1387)' (forthcoming). I owe thanks to the authors for allowing me to consult their typescript.

[48] Northumberland County Record Office, Swinburne of Capheaton Collection, 1/105 (letter to earl of Derby n.d.).

[49] CPR, 1367–70, 191–5; Somerville, 366.

[50] CPR, 1374–77, 323; Somerville, 381. Sulny had been appointed on the Derbyshire commission in 1368 (CPR, 1367–70, 418).

acquisitions in the shire.[51] But appointments of justices whose main local interest was the management of the duke's property rights are likely to have been made on his recommendation. Examples are the appointment of the northerner Foljambe on the Norfolk commission in 1370 and of the southerner Hungerford on a Lincolnshire commission in 1377.[52] Gaunt's recognition of the growing prestige and power of the peace commissions may have led him to grant fees and stewardships to existing justices of the peace: Edmund Gournay, appointed on the Norfolk bench in 1370, was keeper of ducal fees there and in Suffolk in 1372.[53] Appointment on the bench was probably becoming a favour which retainers hoped that Gaunt would procure for them: the addition of Sir Edmund Appleby to the Leicestershire commission in 1371 is a possible example of this.[54]

Notable ducal retainers were appointed for the first time on the commissions of peace issued in May 1380, which were empowered to judge the misdeeds of criminal bands, extortions and the abuse of liveries: these appointments were in shires where Gaunt's property interests were concentrated.[55] But his influence on this aspect of local government was spread more widely afield in the aftermath of the Great Revolt. Use was made as commissioners of his knightly companions such as Richard Burley, John Dabridgecourt, Walter Urswick and John Marmion, who were not usually appointed on local commissions. They were among the ducal retainers on the commissions of November 1381 and March and December 1382 for the suppression and punishment of the rebels.[56] Such appointments suggest that the Crown placed a high degree of reliance on the Lancastrian affinity for the purpose of restoring order generally. Some of the appointments perhaps reflect doubt about the ability of local gentlefolk to cope with the situation after the Revolt. The Lancashireman Sir John Ypres, for instance, was assigned to the Berkshire commission. Marmion and Urswick respectively were placed on the Nottinghamshire and Derbyshire commissions, in shires where the duke had a concentration of lordships, but not their native shires. In Norfolk a prominent landowner who was one of the duke's leading military men, Sir Hugh Hastings, was appointed: so was another local man whom Gaunt had recently retained, Thomas Erpingham.[57] Some of the retainers also

[51] CPR, 1377–81, 46; J. S. Roskell, 'Three Wiltshire Speakers', Wiltshire Archaeological and Natural History Magazine (1955–56), 276.
[52] CPR, 1367–70, 419; CPR, 1377–81, 46.
[53] CPR, 1367–70, 419; Somerville, 377.
[54] CPR, 1370–74, 107; CPR, 1367–70, 243, 405; JGR, 1372–76, ii. no. 1220.
[55] CPR, 1377–81, 512–15. Sir Robert Swillington was appointed on the Derbyshire commission and Sir Henry Grene on the Northamptonshire in 1380.
[56] CPR, 1381–85, 84–6, 138–42, 244–9.
[57] JGR, 1379–83, i. no. 29.

appeared for the first time on the commissions of peace issued in December 1382, giving the Lancastrian affinity a high profile on the commissions of many shires which was to last till 1389.[58]

The marked rise in the number of Lancastrian retainers on the commissions of peace in the two decades after Gaunt gained control of the duchy in 1361–2 was paralleled by the rising number of appointments of the duke himself to head the commissions, principally in the shires where his lordships were concentrated. By 1380 he headed far more than any other peer.[59] The domination of the commissions by peers had increased generally in this period, the office usually being performed by deputy. Control by peers had not decreased as a result of the criticism by the Commons in 1378 that the 'Seigneurs du pays' appointed on the commissions did not attend them in person but sent deputies who were 'plus povres et nientz suffisantz'. Their concern over the functioning of the commissions and desire to strengthen their powers to deal with disorders were shown in their petitions in 1380, which evoked some favourable responses, reflected in the powers granted to the commissions in May. But their suggestion that justices of the peace be elected in parliament was turned down.[60] That would have undermined the basis of magnates' control of the commissions. In 1380 Gaunt was appointed for the first time to head the commissions in Staffordshire, Nottinghamshire, Norfolk and Warwickshire, an indication of his confidence that he and his deputies could deal with social problems—a confidence perhaps not always welcome to other magnates when it resulted in ducal intrusion on their patch, nor entirely shared by gentlefolk suspicious that magnates' followers were among the perpetrators of the abuses which they complained of.[61] Professor R. L. Storey has shown that the continuing concern of gentlefolk over the issues of magnate domination of the commissions and the abuse of liveries led to the exclusion of peers from the commissions in 1389 and the promulgation of the ordinance of 1390 restricting the right to grant liveries.[62] It was Gaunt's influence which was worst hit by the exclusions of 1389, which extended to many of his retainers: the position in local government which he had built up

[58] CPR, 1381–85, 251–4. Swillington appeared on the Leicestershire commission and Urswick on the Nottinghamshire commission.

[59] In 1380 Gaunt headed the commissions in Yorkshire, Lincolnshire, Derbyshire, Nottinghamshire, Staffordshire, Warwickshire, Leicestershire, Norfolk and Hertfordshire (CPR, 1377–81, 512 ff, 571). Henry Duke of Lancaster headed the commissions in the West Riding of Yorkshire, Derbyshire and Northamptonshire in 1361 (CPR, 1361–64, 63 ff).

[60] Rotuli Parliamentorum, iii. 44, 83–4.

[61] CPR, 1377–81, 512–15.

[62] 'Liveries and Commissions of Peace 1388–90', The Reign of Richard II, ed. F. R. H. Du Boulay and C. M. Barron (1971), 131 ff.

in Richard II's early years was in this respect largely, if temporarily, undermined during his absence abroad.[63]

The Commons could not but have been aware that some of the remedies which they proposed for the alleged ineffectiveness of the peace commissions in 1378 and 1380 and for the abuses of livery in the Salisbury parliament of 1384 especially threatened Gaunt's exercise of power: they may well have seen him as one of the biggest stumbling-blocks to their proposed reforms. Certainly his public opposition at Salisbury to the petition from the Commons for a new measure to curb the excesses of livery-holders was determined and, for the moment, decisive.[64] He commented that 'illud nimis generaliter fuisse locutum': there is no evidence that the Commons agitation was aimed specifically at abuses committed by him and his men. But in view of the size of his affinity, it is not surprising that some of its members can be found engaged in intimidation and chicanery, for which their liveries would have helped as cover.

In 1380 Sir William Burcestre and his wife complained that they could not get justice against Sir Thomas Hungerford in Wiltshire 'a cause de grant maintenance de dit Thomas en le dit la Countee'. They alleged that he would not allow his fellow justices of the peace to enquire into their complaint and prayed for a remedy for the great maintenance of Hungerford and those of his affinity, which caused murmuring among the people.[65] Just before the Salisbury parliament Sir Edmund Appleby and a fellow commissioner were removed from an inquisition concerning property acquisitions by the abbot of Burton and his predecessors 'upon particular information that they are of evil will to the abbot and convent, and are scheming themselves to oppress the abbey to the utmost of their power'.[66] In 1381 Gaunt, on receiving a complaint that his retainer Sir Thomas Fichet and his wife had no livery of seisin in a Cornish manor which they had granted to him, procured the agreement of the parties at issue to abide his award in the matter: this went against his retainer.[67] Gaunt was ready to arbitrate in the disputes of his retainers. In June 1386, on the eve of his departure to Spain, and of Sir Hugh Hastings' departure in his company, he issued letters patent recording a treaty and accord made in his presence by Hastings and John Churchman, citizen of London, parties to a suit.[68] Gaunt's undertaking in parliament at Salisbury to

[63] Not all Lancastrian retainers were swept from the commission in 1389; among those appointed were William Chetewynd (Staffordshire), Sir John Thornbury (Hertfordshire) and Thomas Fog (Kent), (CPR, 1388–92, 135 ff).

[64] WC, 80–4.   [65] Rotuli Parliamentorum, iii. 109–10.

[66] CCR, 1381–85, 381.   [67] Ibid., 78; JGR, 1379–83, i. no. 499.

[68] Norfolk R.O., NA 44 (Le Strange). For a reference to an accord made by the duke between Sir John Boseville, on the one hand, and the parson of Badsworth and his friends, on the other, JGR, 1372–76, ii. no. 1378.

mete out exemplary punishment to any of his men who committed abuses under cover of his livery deserves to be taken seriously as an expression of his policy. His determination to curb the tendency was the principal reason why his affinity was not viewed as the main element in the abuse of liveries. Even so, his establishment of a large following and the promotion of many of his retainers to the magisterial bench were policies which were liable to set him at odds with a powerful current of aristocratic opinion. He had strong motives to retain knights and esquires whose qualities and skills were symbolised in the honourable nature of the livery collar which they wore. His fellow magnates to some extent had similar incentives. The development of a parliamentary peerage and Edward III's policies of inventing dukedoms and conferring and creating earldoms (policies continued under Richard II) renovated the aristocratic *cursus honorum*. When the duchy of Lancaster was conferred on Henry of Grosmont in 1351, the grant of palatine powers in the duchy was justified on the grounds that addition of profit and honour should accompany exaltation of name.[69] The deep involvement of the higher nobility in the Hundred Years War led to a high valuation of the chivalrous aspect of honour. Froissart tells the story approvingly of how, in the Black Prince's household at Bordeaux, Sir John Chandos drank from the prince's cup before the earl of Oxford did, successfully claiming precedence over the holder of an ancient comital title on the grounds that he was constable of Aquitaine, and that Oxford had failed in his obligations to Edward III and the prince. This episode was recalled years later, according to the chronicler, as a reason why Oxford's son, the duke of Ireland, ought not to have been so bold as to challenge the precedence of Richard's uncles.[70] The anecdote is characteristic of the heyday of secular orders of knights, with their high degree of chivalrous egalitarianism. In this social milieu those with new dignities required a variety of means to gain and display honour as well as to preserve profit. Those of ancient noble lineage and title needed to demonstrate and emphasise their honour anew. One means was the elaboration of ceremony and dress, as in Edward III's novelty of crowning Gaunt with a fur cap and coronet when he conferred the duchy of Lancaster on him in 1362.[71] It may not have been entirely coincidental that nobles newly elevated in title founded some of the most impressive collegiate churches in the period, material as well as spiritual commemorations of dynastic advancement. They also

[69] J. Enoch Powell and K. Wallis, *The House of Lords in the Middle Ages* (1968), 356.
[70] *Oeuvres*, ed. K. de Lettenhove, xii (Brussels, 1871), 235–8.
[71] Powell and Wallis, 363–4.

founded some of the few new monasteries. One long-established comital family emphasised the nobility of its blood by highlighting a famous ancestor. Thomas Beauchamp, earl of Warwick, in his will of 1369, was the first earl to bequeath specifically the sword and coat of mail sometime belonging to the worthy Guy of Warwick and at the end of the century there was a much admired set of tapestries in Warwick Castle depicting Guy's exploits.[72]

The household and retinue were also a means of projecting honour for this reconstructed higher nobility. Gaunt's way was to form a chivalrous company of annuitants with a core of highly rewarded knights conspicuous for their courtly and chivalrous skills. Their deeds added to his honour and the distinction of his service. The adventures of the duke and his retinue in Castile in 1367 were considered worthy of celebration in verses addressed to a member of his household.[73] Twenty years later a number of his long-serving *familiares*, middle-aged men, some of them veterans of that campaign, died in his service in Spain.[74] In the 1390s the jousting and military skills of his knights and esquires were the launching pad for Henry of Bolingbroke's career in international chivalry. But Gaunt's recruitment on courtly and chivalrous principles, though not incompatible with the strengthening of his traditional Lancastrian ties with knightly families, did not always increase the social coherence of his affinity or add to his political weight. Some of his annuitants had no useful local standing. His distribution of fees in new directions could cause upsets in local communities. The Northumbrian retainers Fenwick and Heron were prepared to invoke his lordship in local disputes, ostentatiously seeking to eschew conflict and violence, in accordance with his policy.

This element of Lancastrian patronage is not likely to have been uniformly welcomed by their neighbours. Institutional developments from the 1360s onwards gave Gaunt a strong incentive to assert his authority in regional affairs. This was the period in which the judicial

---

[72] *Testamenta Vetusta*, ed. N. Harris Nicolas (1826), i. 52–4, 79–80, 153–5. In 1398 Richard II granted this set of tapestries to the duke of Surrey, an appropriate decorative possession for one of the newly elevated dukes whom, according to Walsingham, 'vulgares derisorie vocabant, non "Duces" sed "Dukettos" a diminutivo' (*CPR, 1396–99*, 315; *Calendar of Inquisitions Miscellaneous*, vi, 1392–1399, no. 307, p. 171; 'Annales Ricardi Secundi et Henrici Quarti', 223). The earl of Warwick seems to have recovered the tapestries (*Testamenta Vetusta*, i. 154).

[73] *Political Poems and Songs*, ed. T. Wright (Rolls Series, 1859), i. 97 ff. The author, Walter of Peterborough, mentions the wounding of Sir Richard Burley and the capture of Sir Ralph Hastings.

[74] Pedro López de Ayala lists principal captains who died in Gaunt's service in Spain in 1386–87, mostly through illness, including some of his retainers (*Biblioteca de Autores Españoles. Cronicas de los reyes de Castilla*, ed. Cayetano Rosell, ii (Madrid, 1914), 115. Among those who died were John Marmion, Richard Burley and Hugh Hastings.

authority of the justices of the peace was consolidated.[75] The composition of the peace commissions had often reflected the will of lords to uphold their influence and prestige: now the commissions became a more vital means of providing protection for property and servants and of marking status. After the humiliations which Gaunt endured in the Great Revolt of 1381, his honour and interest were restored in a variety of ways. The king's council arranged for him to be escorted southwards to court from Scotland in a sort of regal progress, accompanied by notables who were augmented in each shire by a guard of honour which received him 'cum honoris tripudio'.[76] Gaunt was placed at the head of many of the commissions appointed to punish the rebels, including those in Northumberland, Cumberland, Westmorland and Yorkshire, embracing regions where gentlefolk had flouted his authority and shown the Duchess Constance scant respect during the Revolt. But it was his many appointments and those of his retainers in 1382 on commissions of peace which lastingly imprinted his restored pre-eminence. For the previous two decades Gaunt had set the pace with such appointments, a policy which in the 1380s does not seem to have impressed the lesser aristocracy agitating for the more effective suppression of crime. The fact that they did not agitate specifically against his annuitants and other livery-holders suggests that his affinity was not a model for those of the 'overmighty subjects' with which abuses of livery and maintenance were often linked in the fifteenth century. In trying to realise the ideal of a chivalrous company of knights and esquires, Gaunt was perhaps imitating (as his father had been fond of doing) the noble society projected in Arthurian romance. This was an attractive ideal for other magnates to copy as a means of exalting their 'profit and honour'. But they could not afford Gaunt's luxurious priority of retaining large numbers of knights and esquires for life. They had to concentrate their resources on maintaining influence and prestige in the regions where their properties were concentrated. According to Dr Cherry, the affinity of Edward Courtenay, earl of Devon, 'was designed to consolidate his position in the area where his landed and political power was greatest'. To this end he was the 'major patron of members of Devonshire political society'; his affinity extended beyond a core of knights, esquires and lawyers 'to embrace most of the senior members of Devon political society, along with many others of varying importance'.[77] The affinity of Richard Beauchamp, earl of Warwick, according to

[75] *Proceedings before the Justices of the Peace in the Fourteenth and Fifteenth Centuries*, ed. B. H. Putnam (1938), xxii ff.

[76] Knighton, ii. 149.

[77] M. Cherry, 'The Courtenay Earls of Devon: The Formation and Disintegration of a Late Medieval Aristocratic Affinity', *Southern History*, i (1979), 74–6.

Dr Carpenter, 'in common with those of other noblemen, consisted primarily of the gentry resident in the areas where his estates lay'.[78] Other magnates such as these lacked the stunning array of resources at Gaunt's disposal to keep the ambitions of his affinity concentrated on winning the prizes in his gift. When he appointed Thomas Hungerford a member of his council in 1375, and was considering knighting him, for these reasons he granted Hungerford the constableship of Monmouth Castle with the stewardship of the lordship and the Three Castles for life.[79] Magnates unable to offer such munificent rewards when they chose councillors and dubbed knights, or a large number of permanent fees, were vulnerable to the competitive patronage of other nobles,[80] and lacked the degree of control over the conduct of a large group of leading clients which these rewards and the hope of increased fees and more keeperships and wardships gave to Gaunt. The competitive aspirations of their followers could not be contained to the same extent as Gaunt could contain his within the enclosed system of paid offices presented by the duchy of Lancaster.[81] Other magnates had to offer extraneous incentives for service—incentives tending in some circumstances to politicise their affinities and to the abuse by them and their clients of livery and maintenance. They were under greater pressure to seek rewards for their followers by lobbying for favours at court. Like Gaunt they were concerned to secure the appointment of their clients on peace commissions and the clientage of magisterial gentlefolk. Less able than him to buy an interest in a shire, they were more inclined to sustain traditional influence or create a new power-centre by condoning illegal maintenance.

Gaunt's policies in regard to his affinity, like those of other contemporary magnates, were strongly influenced by the characteristic problems which they faced in the period in maintaining 'profit and honour to accompany exaltation of name'. In some respects Gaunt's policies were brilliantly successful. It is a tribute to his ability and perhaps to a degree of what might be termed public-spiritedness, as well as to his advantages of birth and wealth, that his affinity's conduct did not become one of the items in the catalogues of general grievances raised against him: the worst that Walsingham accused them of was a stiff-necked pride. But the options he chose in selecting and funding retainers were not open on a commensurate scale for the higher

[78] C. Carpenter, 'The Beauchamp affinity: a study of bastard feudalism at work', *EHR*, xcv (1980), 514–15.

[79] *JGR, 1372–76*, i. no. 358.

[80] For multiple retaining, N. Saul, *Knights and Esquires: The Gloucestershire Gentry in the Fourteenth Century* (Oxford, 1981), 92–4.

[81] Competition for duchy offices could be intense: it was at issue in the revolt of William Bekwith. For a struggle over the constableship of Pevensey Castle, see Somerville, 380.

nobility in general. For the most part, they had to rely on the offer of less certainly binding and often more contentious favours and rewards. Fifteenth-century affinities often appear more in the guise of political caucuses, in national as well as regional affairs, than Gaunt's had done, but sometimes lacking in the stable habits of Lancastrian service which sustained the power of Gaunt and Henry of Bolingbroke through their political vicissitudes. Yet, however old-fashioned and irrelevant the ducal model appears in a later perspective, it may have been an influential factor in the development of the noble affinity, by encouraging the higher nobility to solve their problems of status and influence through the maintenance of impressive followings and to intensify their competition in using them to try to dominate the peace commissions.

POLITICS AS THEATRE: METAPHORS OF THE STAGE IN GERMAN HISTORY, 1848–1933

By David Blackbourn

READ 12 DECEMBER 1986

ALL the world's a stage, as we know, and the concept of a *theatrum mundi* is a venerable one. So too is the specific idea of politics as theatre. As an idea it may not seem very remarkable. Politics lives off metaphor, after all, and theatrical metaphor might seem especially appropriate to describe political activity. Do we not refer naturally to the political stage, to politicians assuming roles, to dramatic political scenes? This very naturalness, derived from repeated usage, presents a challenge. For one of the tasks of the historian is to show how what has come to seem natural came to seem so: to restore the novelty of artefacts and institutions we take for granted, to recover the impact of ideas and metaphors worn smooth by repetition. I want to argue below that metaphors of politics as theatre can be more than just a figure of speech: that they had specific and revealing meanings in the period of German history from the revolutions of 1848 to the advent of National Socialism.

The idea of politics as a form of theatre appeared as an important motif in European history generally in 1848. Few who have written on the events of that year have failed to note in passing the self-consciousness of the revolutionaries, their verbal, gestural and sartorial theatricality. We know that Alphonse de Lamartine rehearsed his speeches—as he rehearsed much of his life—in front of a mirror, just as his public appearances as an orator owed a debt to the virtuoso performances of his good friend Franz Liszt. We know that the radical leader Ledru-Rollin had paid close attention to the impact made on his audiences by the celebrated actor Frédéric Lemaître.[1] And of course those two sharp-eyed observers, de Tocqueville and Marx, have helped to fix 1848 in our minds as a time when politics was a matter of performance. De Tocqueville described events in France on the 24th February in the following terms: 'I was never able to take the actors very seriously and the whole seemed to me like a bad tragedy performed by provincial actors'.[2] Marx's contemporary writing is

---

[1] R. Sennett, *The Fall of Public Man* (Cambridge, 1974), 227–31, 236–7. W. Fortescue, *Alphonse de Lamartine* (1983) has details on Lamartine's friendship with Liszt.

[2] A. de Tocqueville, *Recollections* (New York, 1970), 53.

littered with metaphors depicting political developments as theatre: on and off the stage, upstage and downstage, role playing and dramatic effect, chorus and solo performance, tragedy and farce. In a characteristic passage from *The Class Struggles in France*, Marx wrote: 'The official scene was transformed in a trice: scenery, costumes, language, actors, dummies, prompters, the themes of the play, the content of the conflict, the whole situation.'[3]

These are all French examples, and France might be thought of as the classic modern case of a national politics conceived as theatre. Was it not the revolutionary tradition that condemned French politicians to restage the same scenes and repeat the old lines? Many of the same themes can nevertheless be found in the German events of 1848–49. The would-be poet-revolutionary Georg Herwegh, for example, modelled himself very much on Lamartine.[4] And the critique of French events by the patrician de Tocqueville and the revolutionary Marx found echoes in the German case. Friedrich Wilhelm IV of Prussia attacked 'the sinful burlesques and the hateful play-acting of modern constitutions',[5] while Friedrich Engels' writings on Germany offer many parallels to those of Marx on France. When the Prussian Constituent Assembly was threatened by General Wrangel's troops it began, for Engels, its 'grand comedy' of passive and legal resistance. The Frankfurt Assembly was likewise 'nothing but a stage where old and worn-out political characters exhibited their involuntary ludicrousness and their impotence of thought, as well as action'. These parliamentary puppets, he went on, served only to amuse and divert the shopkeepers and petty tradesmen, before the parliament came to its 'tragi-comical' end. And when renewed insurrection broke out in south-west Germany during the summer of 1849, the National Assembly simply 'disappeared from the political theatre without any notice being taken of its exit'.[6]

Patricians and revolutionaries therefore found much to agree about in 1848. Both used metaphors of the theatre to imply criticism and scorn, because they believed the political actors were not serious. They reached this conclusion for opposite reasons. Patricians assumed that the people was conservative and had been misled by men playing the role of demagogue. Marx and Engels assumed the people was

---

[3] There is an outstanding discussion of this theme in S. S. Prawer, *Karl Marx and World Literature* (Oxford, 1976), where the passage from *The Class Struggles in France* is also quoted (p. 167). *The Eighteenth Brumaire of Louis Napoleon* (1852) is the other contemporary work of Marx where theatrical metaphors are widely used.

[4] W. J. Brazill, 'Georg Herwegh and the Aesthetics of German Unification', *Central European History*, V (1972), 99–126.

[5] E. Kaeber, *Berlin 1848* (Berlin, 1948), 28.

[6] F. Engels, *Germany: Revolution and Counter-Revolution*, in *The German Revolutions*, ed. L. Krieger (Chicago, 1967), 169, 205–14, 235.

revolutionary and had been misled by men who merely assumed the role of revolutionaries. Right and left agreed once again in associating the theatricality of 1848 with the existence of popular politics—with the presence of a 'public'. But here they drew opposite conclusions from the same premise. For a critic such as Friedrich Wilhelm IV the very entry of the people into public affairs created a dangerously theatrical politics; for Engels it was the diversion of the people that made the politics theatrical. This fundamental difference has persisted in attitudes towards the course of modern German history. The patrician view has been echoed by conservative historians, down to the connection they have drawn between the success of Hitler and the revolt of the star-struck masses. For them, the roots of National Socialism are to be found in the dangerous political mobilisation of the nineteenth century, typified by 1848, in which prudence and statesmanship came to be replaced by the meretricious appeal of the political actor or showman.[7] For historians of a more liberal or radical persuasion, it is not the revolt of the masses but their diversion which provides the link in the period from 1848 to the advent of fascism. On this reading, statesmen did not yield the political stage to showmen; they became showmen themselves.[8]

This provides a suggestive background against which to take a fresh look at some of the changes and continuities in German history between 1848 and the rise of Hitler. This essay is an attempt to explore a series of themes and arguments that arise out of the idea that politics was a form of theatre. Partly I want to examine the way in which contemporaries themselves used such terms; partly I want to see how metaphors of this kind have come to assume a significant place in accounts of modern German history, although this has seldom been explicitly recognised. In the first three parts of this paper I shall be concerned with Germany before the First World War. The fourth and final part tries to bring together the themes that have been raised in considering the advent of that most theatrical of political movements, National Socialism.

Political Drama as Distraction

The idea that bold political acts, especially of foreign policy, can serve as a drama to distract public attention, is a fairly familiar one. It is also at least as old as the Roman emperors' provision of 'bread and

[7] This approach is well represented by the 'dean of German historians', Gerhard Ritter, who died in 1967. It can also be seen in the influential American historian, Carlton J. Hayes. For a recent example, see Noël O'Sullivan's *Fascism* (1983).

[8] See the quotation from Adorno and Horkheimer that concludes this essay, and more generally the writers on Bonapartism mentioned below. There are interesting pointers in the same direction in Sir Lewis Namier's essay on Napoleon III, 'The First Mountebank Dictator', in *Vanished Supremacies* (1958).

circuses'. In our period the key concept is indeed Caesarism, or
Bonapartism as it is more usually called. The modern idea of Caesarism, or Bonapartism owes much to Marx, who developed it as a way
of describing the regime of Napoleon III that followed the revolution
of 1848 in France.[9] Of the many features of Bonapartist rule about
which historians continue to argue, two are especially relevant here.
One is the use of foreign policy success to divert opinion at home, the
other the use of plebiscitary techniques to appeal direct to the people
over the heads of political opponents. In recent years many German
historians have looked at Bismarck's form of rule in this way. They
have argued that his foreign policy can be interpreted as an attempt
to deflect attention from pressing economic, social and political problems at home, whether the liberal-constitutionalist challenge of the
1860s, or the crises and uncertainties generated by the Great
Depression. The stage-managing of the 1864 war against Denmark
for domestic consumption, the playing up of the war-in-sight crisis of
1875, and the political uses to which colonial issues were put in the
1880s have all been cited as examples.[10] Bismarck's encouragement of
Sedan Day as a new celebratory ritual could be viewed in the same
light.[11] But this argument does not apply to foreign policy alone.
Michael Stürmer has argued that Bismarck used domestic incidents
during the 1870s in similar Caesarist fashion. He exploited the 'dramatic effects' of the attempt on his life by a Catholic journeyman in
1874, just as he 'dramatised the branding of a pistol into a murder
attempt' when a similar experience befell the Kaiser in 1878. The first
incident served to strengthen support for Bismarck's anti-Catholic
Kulturkampf measures; the second provided the pretext for introducing
the anti-socialist law. Similarly, when the Reichstag complained in
1874 about the arrest on press charges of the Catholic deputy Majunke
during a parliamentary session, Bismarck 'staged a crisis' and 'dramatised the situation' by threatening to resign and warning of turmoil.[12]
  It is possible to argue that historians such as Stürmer and Hans-
Ulrich Wehler have exaggerated Bismarck's Caesarist intentions, that
the Bonapartist technique of rule weighs less heavily in the balance
than a more straightforwardly opportunist (but also fatalistic) conservatism.[13] But the more far-sighted and flexible German con-

---

[9] In *The Eighteenth Brumaire of Louis Napoleon* (footnote 3).

[10] See, especially, the works of Hans-Ulrich Wehler: *Bismarck und der Imperialismus* (Cologne and Berlin, 1969), and *The German Empire 1871–1918* (Leamington Spa, 1985).

[11] On the new cult of *Sedanstag* and its operation in Bavaria, see W. Blessing, *Staat und Kirche in der Gesellschaft* (Göttingen, 1982), 181, 190–1, 198, 236.

[12] M. Stürmer, *Regierung und Reichstag im Bismarckstaat 1871–1880: Cäsarismus oder Parlamentarismus* (Düsseldorf, 1974), 128–33.

[13] Critics of the Bonapartist concept as applied to Bismarck made a wide range of points that cannot be dealt with here. The critics include Lothar Gall, 'Bismarck

servatives of the period, among whom Bismarck was certainly the most prominent, undoubtedly paid close attention to the form of regime developed by Napoleon III in France. Constantin Frantz in the 1850s, and Bismarck's close political ally Hermann Wagener in the 1860s, wrote appreciatively of Bonapartism.[14] And Bismarck himself argued against that dyed-in-the-wool Prussian conservative Ludwig von Gerlach that Bonapartism as practised in France, far from being revolutionary, put revolutionary principles at the service of social order.[15] There was at the very least a Bonapartist strain in Bismarck's policies, and the motif of a deliberately dramatised politics is certainly not just a construct of later historians. Nothing illustrates this better than the well-known incident when the new German Reichstag had read out to it a letter from Ludwig II of Bavaria, inviting Wilhelm I of Prussia to assume the German imperial crown. The scene was carefully prepared, and after a planted question Bismarck's deputy Delbrück rose to announce that he happened to have Ludwig's letter with him. He then had unfortunate difficulty finding it, causing widespread laughter as he fumbled about his person. When he finally read the letter out his dry diction further undermined the occasion. Bismarck's reaction was telling. The event, he remarked, 'needed a more skilful stage-manager, there should have been an effective *mise en scène*'.[16]

There can be little doubt, however, that under Kaiser Wilhelm II and his ministers, and particularly under Bülow, the dramatisation of politics in this sense assumed a new dimension. At the end of the 1890s, commenting on the passage of the first navy bill through the Reichstag, the Social Democrat Bruno Schoenlank observed sardonically that all that was missing was a navy theatre and a navy opera.[17] Many would argue that these were still to come: that the public launching of ships and the official encouragement of sailor

---

und der Bonapartismus', *Historische Zeitschrift*, 223 (1976), 618–37, and A. Mitchell, 'Bonapartism as a Model of Bismarckian Politics', *Journal of Modern History*, 49 (1977). This issue of the JMH also includes comments by O. Pflanze, C. Fohlen and M. Stürmer. See, most recently, O. Pflanze, 'Bismarcks Herrschaftstechnik als Problem der gegenwärtigen Historiographie', *Historische Zeitschrift*, 234 (1982), 562–99.

[14] G. Grünthal, *Parlamentarismus in Preußen 1848/49–1857/58* (Düsseldorf, 1982), 261–95; Stürmer, *Regierung und Reichstag*, 89, 96 ff; H. Gollwitzer, 'Der Cäsarismus Napoleons III. im Widerhall der öffentlichen Meinung Deutschlands', *Historische Zeitschrift*, 173 (1952), 23–75.

[15] On the major exchange of letters between the two men in 1857, see the works cited in footnote 14, and L. Gall, *Bismarck: Der weiße Revolutionär* (Frankfurt/M, Berlin and Vienna, 1980), 173–84.

[16] R. W. Dill, *Der Parlamentarier Eduard Lasker und die parlamentarische Stilentwicklung der Jahre 1867–1884*, Dissertation (Erlangen, 1958), 64–5.

[17] J. Steinberg, *Yesterday's Deterrent. Tirpitz and the Birth of the German Battle Fleet* (1965), 167–8.

suits, together with the rallies and slide shows funded by the Information Bureau of Tirpitz's Navy Office and mounted by the Navy League, marked a conscious effort to rally support behind an old governing elite by tapping popular enthusiasm for spectacle.[18] As a result, projects such as battleship building took on the aura of a public drama. Indeed General von Einem and Friedrich von Holstein both talked of the Kaiser's operetta politics.

This approach has undeniable appeal. It forms part of a more general rediscovery by historians of the part played in popular consciousness during this period by ceremonial, monuments, national symbols and other 'invented traditions'.[19] The way in which such arguments have often been advanced in the German case has not, however, lacked its critics. One of them has argued with a good deal of plausibility that the picture of Imperial Germany thus painted resembles too closely a 'puppet-theatre': the puppet masters pulled the strings and the people danced.[20] The criticism here applies not so much to the intentions of the would-be puppet masters, more to the effects of their actions. In following up this point I want to suggest two respects at least in which the idea of a theatrical politics of this sort is for historians (as it was for contemporaries) considerably richer and more ambiguous than this straightforwardly 'diversionary' reading would allow.

First, there were many who remained singularly unimpressed by the spectacle being presented. They were unimpressed, not least, because an extravaganza carries with it the idea of extravagance. The more elaborate the spectacle, the broader the flank left open to charges of this kind. This was important in a country where indirect taxes on consumption formed such a major part of government revenue. In other words: where bread was particularly expensive, as a result of tariffs, the cost of the circuses was likely to have opponents.[21] This point applies with particular force to the Social Democrats, and the

[18] V. R. Berghahn, Der Tirpitz-Plan. Genesis und Verfall einer innenpolitischen Krisenstrategie unter Wilhelm II (Düsseldorf, 1971); idem, Germany and the Approach of War in 1914 (1973); W. Deist, Flottenpolitik und Flottenpropaganda. Das Nachrichtenbureau des Reichsmarineamtes 1897–1914 (Stuttgart, 1976).

[19] On this subject generally, see E. Hobsbawm and T. Ranger, eds., The Invention of Tradition (Cambridge, 1983), esp. chs. 1 and 7 by Hobsbawm. On Germany specifically, there are very valuable pointers in T. Nipperdey, 'Nationalidee und Nationaldenkmal in Deutschland im 19. Jahrhundert', in Nipperdey, Gesellschaft, Kultur, Theorie (Göttingen, 1976), 133–73, and E. Fehrenbach, Wandlungen des Kaisergedankens 1871–1918 (Munich and Vienna, 1969).

[20] H.-G. Zmarzlik, in his review of the German edition of Hans-Ulrich Wehler's The German Empire, 'Das Kaiserreich in neuer Sicht?', Historische Zeitschrift, 222 (1976), 105–26.

[21] It is worth noting in passing, that the high price of bread in Imperial Germany also points to a divergence from the classic Bonapartist model. Hitler, to whose regime

organised labour movement more generally, for whom opposition to dear food and hostility to military parades and naval razzmatazz went hand-in-hand. But it is also relevant to a group such as the peasantry, as the history of opposition to naval construction in rural areas demonstrates. The point applies even to a social group like the petite bourgeoisie, whose susceptibility to the mass emotion of nationalist issues is often, but wrongly, taken as axiomatic. Many craftsmen and shopkeepers seem to have begrudged the costs of the 'navy theatre' as much as they begrudged the financing of any other kinds of theatre.[22]

Secondly, there were those who were critical of the theatricality that surrounded the government's foreign policy from the 1890s for a different, although not entirely unrelated, reason: not because of its cost, but because they thought it—and this is their own language— *merely* theatrical, in the pejorative sense. Sometimes this criticism came from within the elite itself. One thinks of the younger Moltke's exasperation that the Kaiser's mania for colourful uniforms and the external symbols of great-power status had, among other things, reduced military drill to 'nothing but a theatrical entertainment'.[23] It also came from outside critics. Max Weber was typical of many intelligent imperialists when he perceived a gap between rhetoric and deeds. Hence his scorn for the 'noisy intermezzi' of German foreign policy and his dismissal of the government's 'theatrical Moroccan policy' in 1911.[24] Doubts of this kind were by no means confined to liberal imperialists like Weber. They were expressed outspokenly on the radical right, by the nationalists of the Pan-German and Navy Leagues. Thus the Pan-German leader Heinrich Claß criticised 'stage pageants and celebrations, parades and the unveiling of statues',[25] for he argued that these merely disguised the failure of true national will at the top. Paradoxically, therefore, attempts by Imperial governments to stage-manage politics could provoke criticism precisely because of their 'theatricality', in the sense that they were perceived as frivolous, concealing the true state of affairs. The charge was levelled with particular venom and frequency against that soft-shoe shuffler, Bülow. Bülow may not, like his French contemporary Viviani, have taken lessons at the *Comédie Française*; but it often sounded as if he had.[26]

---

the model has also been applied, was—by contrast—always very concerned to try and keep down the cost of living for reasons of social stability.

[22] Details in D. Blackbourn, *Populists and Patricians* (London, 1987), chs. 5, 6.

[23] E. Ludwig, *Kaiser Wilhelm II* (1926), 277.

[24] W. J. Mommsen, *Max Weber and German Politics* (Chicago, 1985), 144, 154.

[25] H. Claß, *Führergedanken, Aus Reden und Schriften von Justizrat Claß 1903–1913* (Berlin, n.d.), 6.

[26] On Viviani, see T. Zeldin, *France 1848–1945*, vol. 1; *Ambition, Love and Politics* (Oxford, 1973), 760.

It was a favourite rhetorical device of the radical nationalists that the onstage presentation did not accord with the offstage reality. But this was not a figure that was unique to this section of opinion on this particular issue. To understand why this was so, we must turn to another important and widespread usage of theatrical metaphor in German political debate. That was the preoccupation with what went on 'behind the scenes'.

Behind the Scenes
Radical nationalists talked a lot about hidden enemies. As one of the Pan-German leaders put it in 1908, 'a broadly based conspiracy has developed with the aim of harming Germandom'.[27] The League's publications argued that the covert enemies were more dangerous than the overt ones: those who posed 'behind the mask of harmlessness', those who remained 'behind the scenes'.[28] They included, among these, three familiar conspirators: the Red International of Socialism, the Gold International of Jewish finance capital and the Black International of ultramontanism. They also included those officials in high places whom Pan-Germans, like other radical nationalists, believed to be sacrificing true national interests. Yet this was a game that more than one could play. If those great anti-Polish Germanisers, the Hakatisten, talked darkly of 'sabotage' in high places, the writer Fritz Krysiak in turn offered a revelatory glimpse 'behind the scenes of the *Ostmarkenverein*, from the secret documents of the Prussian parallel government for the extermination of the Poles'.[29]

It is easy to be lofty about the conspiracy view of history, and to forget (as the original Caesar knew) that there are conspiracies in history, just as paranoids do have enemies. My concern is to take the talk of men behind the scenes seriously, and to ask why it should have been so common in Imperial Germany. The preoccupation with hidden wire-pullers was not, of course, a peculiarity of German politics. The most cursory of glances at contemporary France shows similar concerns on both left and right. The latter saw Freemasons and Jews as the hidden influences; the former tended to focus on the 'two hundred families'. Each put its own gloss on the scandals that ran from Wilson and Panama through to Dreyfus. Parallel examples could certainly be found elsewhere in Europe. It is nevertheless true that suspicions of this kind were probably more extensive in Imperial

[27] A writer in the *Alldeutsche Blätter*, cited in Roger Chickering, *We Men Who Feel Most German. A Cultural Study of the Pan-German League 1886–1914* (1984), 123.
[28] Ibid.
[29] F. Krysiak, *Hinter den Kulissen des Ostmarkenvereins: Aus den Geheimakten der preussischen Nebenregierung für die Polenausrottung* (Posen, 1919). On the Hakatisten themselves, see A. Galos, F.-H. Gentzen, W. Jacóbczyk, *Die Hakatisten. Der Deutsche Ostmarkenverein (1894–1934)* (Berlin, 1966).

Germany, not least because the political system itself offered so many grounds for them.

Take, at the most obvious level, the way in which the Reichstag and other German parliaments worked. The third quarter of the nineteenth century had been the great age of the parliamentary orators: Lasker, Bennigsen, Windthorst and Bismarck himself. But the last years of the century saw a change. The great formal debaters departed and the balance shifted to committee men, especially lawyers. In the Reichstag, as in the state parliaments, considerably longer hours were worked; but the additional work now went on outside plenary sessions and set-piece debates, in committee.[30] Journalists and pamphlet writers who offered a glance behind the scenes reflected public recognition that a significant part of politics had disappeared from open view. This phenomenon had its counterparts elsewhere; but it was compounded in Germany by the general working of the complex political structure established by Bismarck. The open-ended, plastic constitution of the Reich required a high level of activity in the interstices of the formal system. The legacy of constitutional dualism, which strictly separated ministers from party leaders, also encouraged intense, behind-the-scenes consultations and short-term agreements, in which politics often became a matter of brokering. Parliamentary arithmetic intensified this tendency from the 1880s onwards, as Bismarck and his successors lived an increasingly hand-to-mouth existence in trying to keep government business running. All of this naturally excited suspicion of shabby deals and horse-trading behind the scenes—*Kuhhandel*, as it was generally called. Nowhere was this more true than in the case of the Catholic Centre Party, the spokesman of a minority, whose pivotal position in German politics united much of the rest of the nation in the belief that German government policy was being determined by whispered arrangements between Centre leaders and ministers.[31] Centre relations with successive governments after 1890 undoubtedly lent some credence to this view, and the leaders of the party appear sometimes to have played the part with a certain conspiratorial relish. Ernst Lieber, for example, discussing the logistics of a series of meetings with state secretary Posadowsky in 1894, used highly cloak-and-dagger language. On one occasion he suggested a visit to the Wilhelmstrasse late at

[30] This change in the balance of parliamentary work in the Reichstag is noted in memoirs of the period. Information can also be found in P. Molt, *Der Reichstag vor der improvisierten Revolution* (Cologne and Opladen, 1963), and in the work of Manfred Rauh: *Föderalismus und Parlamentarismus im Wilhelminischen Reich* (Düsseldorf, 1972), and *Die Parlamentarisierung des Deutschen Reiches* (Düsseldorf, 1977).
[31] See D. Blackbourn, *Class, Religion and Local Politics in Wilhelmine Germany* (1980), esp. ch. 1.

night, and—in order to throw the 'pack of snoopers' off the scent—minus top hat.[32]

But chancellors and ministers did not just have to deal in this way with party leaders and experts. They also had to mediate between interests in the Reich, Prussia and the other individual states represented in the Bundesrat, as well as with the Kaiser. The Kaiser's particular form of attempted personal rule served to multiply the number of individuals from certain groups—the army, the bureaucracy, the courtiers of the entourage—who had personal access to the All-Highest.[33] Contemporaries asked the question: 'Who rules in Berlin?' Historians have answered, accurately if inelegantly, that the system was a polycratic but uncoordinated authoritarianism, a pseudo-constitutional semi-absolutism.[34] This system positively invited the emergence of what Hans-Ulrich Wehler has called 'secretive key figures, like Admiral von Tirpitz', and of courtiers like Philipp Eulenburg, of whom Fritz Hartung remarked that 'he preferred to remain behind the scenes in semi-darkness and from here exerted his influence'.[35] This system naturally also encouraged suspicion and rumour about the role played behind the scenes by these men, and by others such as Friedrich von Holstein, General Waldersee and the so-called Camarilla. It was not only Social Democrats and left liberals who talked in this context of backstairs intrigues and cover-ups: the growing radical right also habitually attacked the 'Byzantine' politics of the Kaiser's Germany, and increasingly did not exempt the All-Highest himself from their strictures.[36]

One of the most obvious objects of suspicion was the role supposedly played behind the scenes by economic interests. State and economy were interlocked to an exceptional degree in Imperial Germany, and these links were becoming closer in the years before the First World War. This much, at least, is generally agreed by historians who differ on whether to describe the result as state monopoly capitalism, organised capitalism or state corporatism.[37] The political parties were also notable for the way in which they served as the vehicles of

[32] Pfälzische Landesbibliothek Speyer, Ernst Lieber Papers, L. 39, Lieber to Posadowsky, 10 July 1894. For similar conspiratorial communications, see ibid, L. 36–38, Lieber to Posadowsky, 24 June, 29 June and 3 July 1894.

[33] See, now, the contributions to J. C. G. Röhl and N. Sombart (eds), *Kaiser Wilhelm II: New Interpretations* (Cambridge, 1982), esp. those by Röhl himself, Paul Kennedy, Wilhelm Deist, Isabel Hull, Kathy Lerman and Terence Cole.

[34] See Wehler, *The German Empire*, esp. 52–71.

[35] Ibid, 63; Fritz Hartung quoted in E.-T. P. W. Wilke, *Political Decadence in Imperial Germany, Personnel-Political Aspects of the German Government Crisis 1894–97* (Urbana/Illinois, 1976), 228.

[36] See D. Blackbourn, 'The Politics of Demagogy in Imperial Germany', *Past and Present*, 113 (1986), 163–4, 167–8.

[37] See the contributions to H. A. Winkler (ed), *Organisierter Kapitalismus* (Göttingen,

major economic interests.[38] The political system devised by Bismarck encouraged them to become the brokers of particular interests by depriving the parties of positive responsibility in parliament. The rising costs of political organisation and campaigning further increased the dependence of the parties on their various paymasters. Hence the growing political role exercised in the background, especially from the 1890s, by a wide spectrum of interest groups: the Agrarian League and the CVDI, representing perhaps the most influential interests of large-scale agriculture and heavy industry respectively, the BdI of smaller manufacturing industry, the Hansabund of bankers, shippers, insurers and exporters, the myriad organisations of craftsmen, shop-keepers and white-collar workers, and the trade unions and co-operatives of the working class. Hence, too, the mounting importance assumed by economic affairs in German political life. It has been calculated that they accounted, directly or indirectly, for 90 per cent of Reichstag business by 1914.[39]

Much of this business was dealt with in committee. In the legislative period 1890–93 alone, Reichstag committees considered the following: trade treaties, patents, the telegraph, railway freight, the protection of goods and trade-marks, working hours, the hire-purchase system, limited company law, the accountancy system, the taxation of distilled spirits, internal trade regulations, the bankruptcy code, trade descriptions, and labour statistics.[40] As the language of business entered political life—political speculator and broker, political nicknames based on popular advertisements[41]—so economic interests themselves retreated into the committee room, or outside parliament altogether. The number of businessmen in German parliaments dropped sharply towards the end of the century.[42] Increasingly it was not industrialists,

1974), and for general discussion of these debates: G. Eley, 'Capitalism and the Wilhelmine State: Industrial Growth and Political Backwardness in German Historiography, 1890–1918', *Historical Journal*, 21 (1978), 737–50; and U. Nocken, 'Corporatism and Pluralism in Modern German History', in D. Stegmann, B.-J. Wendt, P.-C. Witt (eds), *Industrielle Gesellschaft und Politisches System* (Bonn, 1978), 37–56.

[38] For an overview of the very large literature on this subject, see H.-J. Puhle, 'Parlament, Parteien und Interessenverbände 1890–1914', in M. Stürmer (ed), *Das kaiserliche Deutschland. Politik und Gesellschaft 1870–1918* (Düsseldorf, 1970), 340–77. The German literature is extensively drawn on in M. Kitchen, *The Political Economy of Germany 1815–1914* (1978).

[39] H. Jaeger, *Unternehmer in der deutschen Politik (1890–1913)* (Bonn, 1967), 95.

[40] Ibid, 97.

[41] The left liberal Georg Gothein, an extremely dull speaker, was referred to by the political wags as 'Gothë-in', after a popular sleeping draft. See Karl von Einem, *Erinnerungen eines Soldaten* (Leipzig, 1933), 69.

[42] The decline of businessmen in parliaments, both local and national, is detailed by Jaeger, *Unternehmer*, 25–106. For a good analysis of a particular group and region, which comes to the same conclusion, see T. Pierenkemper, *Die westfälischen Schwerindustriellen 1852–1913* (Göttingen, 1979), 61–70.

bankers and landowners themselves who represented their interests in
the political forum, but pressure-group spokesmen and other inter-
mediaries. Gustav Stresemann, whose first political experience was to
organise the Saxon chocolate manufacturers against the sugar cartel,
provides only one of many instances.[43]

There is plenty to be said against a certain kind of muck-raking
history à la Charles Beard, which reduces politics to the crude elaboration of material interests. But the interests were real enough, indeed
ubiquitous, in the Imperial political system; and they prompted frequent comment on the discrepancy between the public face of politics
and the reality of what went on behind the scenes. This criticism came
quite literally from left, right and centre. As early as the 1860s the
National Liberal von Twesten noted gloomily that 'the landed interest
calls itself conservative, the money interest liberal, the labour interest
democratic'.[44] That continued to be the lament from a party that
liked to see itself as universal rather than sectional, and tended to
blame the rise of interest-politics for its own decline. Socialists and left
liberals pointed, with some reason, to the hidden influence of the
large Junker landowners, the heavy industrialists and the armaments
manufacturers. Fritz Krupp was a classic target: a member of the
Kaiser's entourage and his frequent host at Villa Hügel, a man who
carefully cultivated key officials and employed many ex-officers on his
own payroll, Krupp enjoyed a reputation as a malevolent influence on
government policy. It was, for example, widely rumoured—plausibly,
although probably wrongly—that the Kaiser owned a substantial
block of shares in the Krupp business.[45] With less warrant the political
right claimed to detect the hidden power of Jewish capital operating
behind the scenes. Bismarck's banker Bleichröder was one target, but
the charge was more general. The *Kulturkampf* had been widely viewed
on the right as a cloak behind which the 'swindlers' of *laissez-faire*
capitalism in general, and Jewish interests in particular, prospered.
During the stock exchange and commodity exchange scandals of the
1890s the charge of hidden Jewish political influence surfaced again
on the agrarian, anti-semitic and Catholic right.

[43] G. Eley, *Reshaping the German Right* (1980), 311, and for further details on Stresemann, D. Warren, *The Red Kingdom of Saxony, Lobbying Grounds for Gustav Stresemann
1901–1909* (The Hague, 1964).

[44] Cited in M. Gugel, *Industrieller Aufstieg und bürgerliche Herrschaft* (Cologne, 1975), 171.

[45] R. Owen, 'Military-Industrial Relations: Krupp and the Imperial Navy Office',
in R. J. Evans, ed., *Society and Politics in Wilhelmine Germany* (1978), 71–89. On Krupp's
role in the Kaiser's entourage, see I. V. Hull, *The entourage of Kaiser Wilhelm II 1888–
1918* (Cambridge, 1982), 146–74; and on the movement of government officials into
large private concerns, J. Kocka, *Die Angestellten in der deutschen Geschichte 1850–1980*
(Göttingen, 1981), 80–1. This was something that engaged the interest of the Reichstag
in 1912.

Parliament as Theatre

The presence, real or imagined, of powerful offstage interests did much to discredit the Imperial political 'system'. At the same time, there is also an undeniable sense in which politics in Wilhelmine Germany became a form of popular spectacle in a way that had not been true earlier. In the third quarter of the nineteenth century political indifference was still widespread, election turn-out was low and results often followed the lines of deference. Even in the 1870s, when universal manhood suffrage existed for Reichstag elections, electoral participation remained around the 55% mark and there was little campaigning. The National Liberal leader Rudolf von Bennigsen wrote in December 1873 to a clergyman in his Reichstag constituency, explaining why he would be unable to visit the constituency at all before the election in the new year—and expressing the hope that he would be able to visit his Prussian Landtag constituency by the following summer.[46] His attitude was typical. Public life remained largely the preserve of a handful of notables (*Honoratioren*), who constituted the true political nation. In these circumstances, the Reichstag and state parliaments did indeed—as Rudolf Dill has noted—resemble theatres.[47] But they were theatres in which the narrow political class itself formed the public. When parliamentarians referred to themselves as 'actors' on the 'parliamentary stage', when deputies acted out entire scenes from Shakespeare in the course of their speeches, or when Bismarck reminded Lasker that 'the masks we wear are temporary', it is this lack of a broader audience that we should remember.[48] In fact those who spoke for 'out of doors', who 'played to the gallery', were often censured—especially Social Democrats, as the incidence of calls to order shows. A large number of parliamentarians in the 1870s would have echoed the National Liberal Jungermann when he stated: 'I have not come here for the sake of my constituents'.[49]

This genteel mode of politics crumbled towards the end of the century. Popular economic and social aspirations found a new level of political expression, a process helped by the spread of education, improved communications and a greatly expanded press. A much enlarged political nation emerged, signalled by the mobilisation of new social strata, a markedly increased level of electoral participation and more intensive forms of campaigning. Turn-out reached 85 per

---

[46] Bennigsen to Pastor Pfaff, 30 December 1873, cited in H. Oncken, *Rudolf von Bennigsen*, 2 vols. (Stuttgart and Leipzig, 1910), ii. 242–3.

[47] Dill, *Parlamentarische Stilentwicklung*.

[48] Ibid., pp. 45–6; L. Pastor, *August Reichensperger*, 2 vols. (Freiburg i. B., 1899), i. 424–6; ii. 179, 201.

[49] Dill, *Parlamentarische Stilentwicklung*, 14.

cent in Reichstag elections and even higher in some keenly fought local contests. Patrician politicians like Georg von Hertling, who had been a member of the Reichstag in more leisurely times and rejoined it in the turbulent 1890s after a gap of some years, remarked on the great differences.[50] The changes all pointed to a new form of popular identification with politics. In rural areas such as Brandenburg or Upper Swabia politicians were now seen frequently in the flesh, and voters could read parliamentary speeches reported at length in the burgeoning local newspapers, alongside barley prices and advertisements for corsets. A thriving black market developed for tickets to the visitor's gallery of the Reichstag.[51] In short, in the age of the ubiquitous local paper and politicians on the stump, politics assumed a new dimension as popular drama.

There is no contradiction between this political leavening, and the importance of behind-the-scenes decision making. The two were mutually reinforcing. Bureaucrats and business leaders were more inclined to retreat from public view as the everyday surface of politics became more brash and noisy. As Krupp wrote to his managing director Jencke, on the subject of the navy: 'I should like to urge you strongly to confine your activity to that of an advisor—*as much as possible behind the scenes*'.[52] Newly mobilised political forces, in turn, saw in the drama of public life an opportunity to 'unmask' the powerful and influential. The new popular politics at the end of the nineteenth century contained a powerful rhetoric dedicated to the idea of disclosing and unmasking. Alex Hall has reminded us of the preoccupation in the SPD press with 'scandal and sensation'; the new organisations of the peasantry and lower middle class, like the antisemitic political parties and the radical nationalists, employed similar terms.[53] The identity of those who were unmasked varied, from the Junkers to the Jesuits to the Jews, and the credence that we can give to the disclosures varies too; but the common metaphor of unmasking testifies to the explosive gap that existed generally in Germany between oligarchic, bureaucratic and corporate power wielded behind the scenes, and a vigorous (and often vindictive) popular politics that drew its energy from a thwarted, suspicious public.

Once again there are naturally analogues elsewhere, from American

[50] G. von Hertling, *Erinnerungen aus meinem Leben*, 2 vols. (Munich, 1919–20), ii. 175–6.

[51] R. S. Levy, *The Downfall of the Anti-Semitic Political Parties in Imperial Germany* (New Haven, Conn. 1975), 39; K. Wernecke, *Der Wille zur Weltgeltung* (Dusseldorf, 1970), 115.

[52] Owen, 'Military-Industrial Relations', 74 (emphasis in the original).

[53] On the SPD, see A. Hall, *Scandal, Sensation and Social Democracy. The SPD Press in Wilhelmine Germany 1890–1914* (Cambridge, 1977). On the other movements, see Blackbourn, 'The Politics of Demagogy', 166–8.

muckraking to the French concern with scandal. There are also, of course, non-German examples of politicians using the whistle-stop tour as a means of encouraging popular identification with the political drama. Gladstone's Midlothian campaign and Gambetta's great Republican sweep through France in 1871–2 come to mind. The difference in Germany lay in the overall political context. The German political system, combining constitutional but not parliamentary government on the one hand, with the possibilities offered by universal manhood suffrage on the other, invited a meretriciously theatrical politics. The non-responsibility of parliamentary politicians nurtured an irresponsible politics of posture. It was not only parliamentary mavericks who indulged in this game, men such as the anti-semite Hermann Ahlwardt, who used the floor of the Reichstag to accuse the government of buying defective rifles from the Jews.[54] Party leaders and established politicans could also play to the gallery without running the danger of having to take responsibility for their words.

In the 1860s von Twesten, true to form, had warned that universal manhood suffrage would lead to political 'charlatanry'[55] His doubts were echoed in the years before the war by many conservatives, concerned by what Bethmann Hollweg called 'currying favour with the voters'.[56] We should remember here that it was often other conservatives who were the worst offenders. The crucial point, however, is that it was not universal suffrage coupled with parliamentarism, but universal suffrage coupled with sham-parliamentarism, that explains why German politicians played to the gallery so brazenly in the years before 1914. The Reichstag became a 'theatre of opinions'—in Hermann Baumgarten's dismissive phrase[57] for the same reason that it became a clearing-house for economic interests: because it could not become the seat of political power and responsibility. Popular and parliamentary politics thus became a form of 'acting out' of aspirations and resentments. In this it only paralleled the conduct of those at the top. We are already familiar with the Kaiser's 'operetta politics', and we have often been told that he sought a political stage on which to act out his dreams. Ekkehard-Teja Wilke is only one of many historians whose language conveys a sense that Wilhelmine high politics was, as he puts it, 'second-rate tragi-comedy'. But his conclusion about the many crises, scandals and affairs in the highest circles could reasonably be applied to German politics more generally in the years before 1914: they were 'an expression of political decadence—when

[54] On Ahlwardt, see Blackbourn, 'The Politics of Demagogy', 162 ff.
[55] Gugel, *Industrieller Aufstieg*, 184–8.
[56] H. Pogge v. Strandmann and I. Geiss, *Die Erforderlichkeit des Unmöglichen* (Frankfurt/M, 1965), 20.
[57] S. Zucker, *Ludwig Bamberger* (Pittsburgh Pa, 1975), 86.

politics disintegrates into mere role-playing and mere theatrical performance'.[58]

The Weimar Republic: Fascism as Theatre, Hitler as Puppet

Both decadence and theatricality have an obvious place in our understanding of Weimar Germany. Here, for example, is Peter Sloterdijk, talking about the idea we gain of Weimar when we approach it through the memoir literature and the oral recollections of contemporaries: these, argues Sloterdijk, suggest 'a time when politics and culture proceeded in a dramatic, vital and tumultuous way, full of upswings and downswings—as if theatricality had been the common denominator of all social expressions of life—from Expressionism to Marlene Dietrich's spectacular legs in the *Blue Angel*, from the bloody comedy of the 1923 Hitler putsch to the *Threepenny Opera*, from the imposing burial of Rathenau in 1923 to the *Schurkenstück* of the Reichstag fire in 1933. The permanent crisis, of which everyone spoke, proved itself a good director, able to produce impressive effects'.[59] This is a thoughtful and recognisable account of a certain Weimar atmosphere; but—like much similar writing—it remains very impressionistic. I think we can go further in following through the central theme of this paper by isolating two specific metaphors of the theatre that run through the literature on Weimar and the rise of Hitler. One is the idea of Nazism as a theatrical kind of political movement, the other the idea of Hitler himself as the puppet of hidden manipulators. Neither on its own convinces. When combined, however, the two approaches tell us a good deal about National Socialism. They also suggest links with what has already been discussed and thus underline some of the continuities between nineteenth- and twentieth-century German history.

The idea of Nationalist Socialist theatricality, indeed of fascist theatricality generally, is commonly encountered. A recent writer on the subject actually has a chapter headed 'fascism as theatrical politics',[60] and this has been a standard theme among those concerned with the outward political forms and the projected image of the Nazis. We are familiar with the concept of National Socialism as spectacle, the carefully lit rallies and the crowd scenes contributing to a very conscious *mise en scène*. Beno von Arent, who staged the Nuremberg rallies and received the title of *Reichsbühnenbildner*—Designer of Reich Stage Sets—had actually been a theatre director.[61] The idea of German fascism as theatre finds plenty of support in contemporary

[58] Wilke, *Political Decadence*, 20.
[59] P. Sloterdijk, *Kritik der zynischen Vernunft*, 2 vols. (Frankfurt/M, 1983), ii. 705.
[60] O'Sullivan, *Fascism*, ch. 3.
[61] Z. A. B. Zeman, *Nazi Propaganda* (Oxford, 1964), 8–9.

accounts, including fictional works like Thomas Mann's *Mario the Magician*, and there are certainly many who testified to the spellbinding quality of the Nazi performance.[62] George Mosse and others have reminded us that this strand of Nazism had nineteenth-century antecedents, from the choral societies to Wagner.[63]

Hard-headed historians are often sceptical about the large claims made by those who view National Socialism in this way, particularly because of what is omitted. Certainly, the glittering Nazi self-presentation tells us little about many important reasons for Nazi success, even their success specifically as a mass movement. If one focuses on the seductive drama it is, for example, easy to underestimate the real failures of the Weimar Republic, both as a structurally flawed democracy in the 1920s, and as an authoritarian political system lubricated by intrigue after autumn 1930. Nor do we generally learn from those who favour this approach why the spectacle proved so much more popular among some parts of the public than others, or whether the enthusiasm for National Socialism even among its supporters might not have had causes that were more prosaic than dramatic: the appeal, for example, to the material resentments of the small man, to the thwarted careerism of ambitious professionals, to provincial philistinism. We must therefore recognise limits to what can be exlained in terms of Nazi success with a theatrical form of politics. Party rallies and Hitler's rhetoric hardly seduced the German people into rejecting a going political concern; and the Nazi spectacle often worked to reinforce the allegiance of those who had adequate reason to support the party anyway.

These qualifications made, we should not be too hard headed to acknowledge the value of this approach. In many respects the Nazis only carried further a development that began before 1914, whereby politics became the acting out of aspirations and resentments. Just as Weimar's Communists continued this SPD tradition on the left, so the Nazis continued it for that mass public of peasants, petite bourgeoisie and middle class that had been attracted before the war by agrarian populism, political anti-semitism and radical nationalism. As we have seen, Nazi criticism of the Weimar 'system' and its offstage machinations, like the rhetorical Nazi promise to unmask the offstage manipulators, had clear precedents in pre-war politics. And these

---

[62] Thus, as one convert put it: 'On April 20 1932, in Kassel, for the first time I heard the Führer Adolf Hitler speak in person. After this, there was only one thing for me, either to win with Adolf Hitler or to die for him. The personality of the Führer had me totally in its spell.' Cited in I. Kershaw, 'Ideology, Propaganda, and the Rise of the Nazi Party', in P. D. Stachura, ed. *The Nazi Machtergreifung* (1983), 176. Kershaw provides an exemplary introduction to the subject.

[63] G. L. Mosse, *The Nationalization of the Masses. Political Symbolism and Mass Movements in Germany from the Napoleonic Wars through the Third Reich* (New York, 1975).

were genuinely important aspects of the Nazi appeal. Playing to the gallery in this way succeeded because it spoke to the concerns of those same social groups, heightened as they had been by revolution, inflation and depression. It was all the more effective because the efforts of the established centre-right parties to use the same methods (as they had done before 1914) were undermined by the degree of political responsibility they now had to accept for their policies, however reluctantly, under Weimar's formal political democracy. In this respect, as in others, National Socialism enjoyed the best of both worlds. It promised a dramatic resolution of Germany's problems by transcending the parliamentary 'farce' for which it was itself partly responsible, just as it promised law and order in response to a lawlessness to which it had itself made a major contribution.

In this sense National Socialism did indeed 'aestheticise politics', as one of its victims, Walter Benjamin, remarked of fascism generally.[64] This undoubtedly contributes to our understanding of Nazism as a mass movement. But what of that other central question, the function performed by the Nazi mass movement? What of the silent beneficiaries? Here we must turn to another motif that recurs in accounts of the period: that of the puppet. The figure of the puppet seems to be a common one in discourse on German politics. Thomas Mann's Adrian Leverkühn avails himself of a familiar idea when he suggests at one point in *Doctor Faustus* that German revolutions 'are the puppet-shows of world history': a point that both revolutionary left and reactionary right made about the 1918 revolution, just as their predecessors had about 1848. The metaphor clearly reflects both scorn, and a broad comment on the inability of the 'land of poets and thinkers' to produce a serious politics. But the puppet also carries the more specific connotation of a creature manipulated by unseen hands. That is the implication of Engels' 'parliamentary puppets' in 1848; and that is how his followers in the early 1930s depicted Hitler. 'Millions are behind me' reads the ironic text of John Heartfield's famous photomontage, as Hitler's hand, stretched back in the 'German greeting', receives millions of Reichsmarks. Here we have Hitler as the puppet of German capital. The relationship between the Nazi seizure of power and German capitalism is an important one, but it is by no means exhausted as a theme by narrowing the range of enquiry to active Nazi supporters and paymasters in big business. That is precisely the problem with the view of Hitler as capitalist puppet.[65] It is, in fact, the least plausible way of presenting the part played by capitalist interests in Nazi success, especially when support

[64] Walter Benjamin, *Das Kunstwerk im Zeitalter seiner technischen Reproduzierbarkeit* (Frankfurt/M, 1963), 48, 51.
[65] A good guide to the very large literature on this subject is D. Geary, 'The Industrial

for Hitler is identified (as in Dimitrov's notorious Third International definition) with one exceptionally narrow section of capital. On this reading it is difficult to make much sense of how (or why) the puppet sometimes turned on his puppet-master.

If the metaphor is ultimately unsatisfactory, it is nevertheless easy to see why it enjoyed such wide currency. And some comparable idea of Hitler as the player of a role is still needed, to balance and complement the way the Nazis presented themselves. For it remains true that what the Nazis alleged of their political opponents was even more true of themselves: appearances were deceptive, unseen hands were at work behind the scenes. The Nazis had the popular non-proletarian votes. And Hitler found support from important parts of the ruling elite because he did what they themselves were neither able nor willing to do: to take the centre of the political stage. For businessmen, generals, Junkers and high officials, the Nazi movement was attractive because it promised to square the circle: to maintain their own interests in dangerous, potentially revolutionary times, without requiring them to appear themselves to be playing an overt political role.[66] Just as their Wilhelmine predecessors had shunned the political spotlight, so the Reichswehr generals and the industrialists left Hitler to get on with the politics while this in turn left them free to get on with their own interests. The fact that Hitler came to demand a larger role than the one for which he had been cast does not invalidate this view.

Hitler was not a puppet. But he was, in this sense, an actor playing a role. In 1848, as we have seen, de Tocqueville had talked disdainfully of 'a bad tragedy performed by provincial actors'. The sentiment was echoed by Marx and Engels. Almost a century later, as the period of European fascism approached its end in 1944, Theodor Adorno and Max Horkheimer took up the same theme. Intellectually indebted to Marx, but sharing more than a little of de Tocqueville's patrician *hauteur*, they also talked of the modern *Führer* figures who resembled 'provincial actors'. They continued: 'The "leaders" have become what they already were in a less developed form throughout the bourgeois era: actors playing the part of leaders.'[67]

Elite and the Nazis in the Weimar Republic', in Stachura (ed), *Nazi Machtergreifung*, 85–100.

[66] Michael Geyer makes a good case for this reading of the Reichswehr, in 'Études in Political History: Reichswehr, NSDAP, and the Seizure of Power', in Stachura, ed., *Nazi Machtergreifung*, 101–23.

[67] T. Adorno and M. Horkheimer, *Dialectic of Enlightenment* (1979), 236–7 (first published 1944).

THE ROYAL HISTORICAL SOCIETY
REPORT OF COUNCIL, SESSION 1986 1987

THE Council of the Royal Historical Society has the honour to present the following report to the Anniversary Meeting.

Although this has been a comparatively uneventful year, Council has remained very conscious of the continuing threats to, and deterioration in the available facilities and support for, historical education and research at all levels. It has therefore acted where possible to prevent further damage and to assist new initiatives.

At the request of the Chairman of the ESRC Committee on Electoral Studies, Council submitted comments on the future importance for modern historians of the ESRC Data Archive: these were warmly received. However, the general level of support from the Economic and Social Research Council for economic history, and the success rate of applications for ESRC studentships has continued to cause concern. Representations were therefore made to the committee, chaired by Professor J. G. Edwards, which reviewed the future work and priorities of the ESRC, urging the importance of its continued support for research in economic and social history undertaken by trained historians. Sadly, the earliest signs are that Council's views have had little or no impact on the committee's recommendations.

An approach was made to the Chairman of the UGC, supporting the case made by the Bibliographical Society for urgent consideration of the need for special funding in the national and university libraries, the protection and maintenance of whose manuscript and rare book collections is a matter of international concern.

Representations have also been made to the Bodleian Library, Oxford, and the University Library, Cambridge, protesting at the policy of charging for admission to copyright libraries and urging its reconsideration.

Council has not only continued to support the History at the Universities Defence Group, but has extended financial support to the Campaign for Public Sector History, and is currently watching with sympathy the recent initiatives of the Historical Association, particularly the Young Historian Scheme. Council also expressed its concern to the UGC at the damaging effect on the teaching of history to mature students likely to result from the short-funding of Birkbeck College, and received assurances from the Chairman of additional financial support.

To encourage the work of younger historians, Council has revised the terms of the Society's Alexander Prize, restricting it to candidates under the age of 30. The President also wrote to chairmen and heads of history departments drawing attention to both the Alexander and Whitfield prizes, and encouraging submissions.

A loan and grant have been made to assist in the establishment of the newly-formed United Kingdom branch of the Association for History and Computing.

Members of Council have in the course of the year attended meetings on behalf of the Society, including those arranged by the Royal Society to consider Copyright legislation, and by the Historical Manuscripts Commission on national archival policy.

Council has also set up working parties both to consider revision of the Bibliographies of British History, and to examine a proposal for a parallel series of Bibliographies of European History.

For the Society itself, the outstanding event of the year has been its move to new accommodation within University College. An addendum to the original agreement between the Society and the College was signed on 21 November 1986, guaranteeing the Society its own distinct rooms within the College for a further one hundred years. Following refurbishment of the new Council Room and offices by the College, the Society took over the accommodation during April. The Society met for the first time to hear a paper in the Gustave Tuck Lecture Theatre on 24 April 1987. The move has involved not only new offices and a new venue for meetings, but also the reorganisation of the Society's Library. The greater part of its holdings, while remaining the property of the Society, have now been physically incorporated in the Library of University College. Fellows and Associates of the Society have been granted in return full use of the College Library, the history sections of which occupy rooms immediately adjacent to those of the Society. The Society's rare books have been retained as a Special Collection in the new Council Room.

The progress of the *Studies in History Monograph Series* continues to be encouraging. Council has therefore approved the extension of a portion of the Society's existing loan to the publisher, Boydell and Brewer. Two volumes are to be published this autumn, and a large number are scheduled for next year. The Society's own publications, after surmounting the production difficulties referred to in last year's *Report,* have continued to appear as planned.

Council was delighted to note the conferment of knighthood upon Professor Michael Howard, and the award to Dr G. H. Martin of the CBE, in the Birthday Honours.

A conference to mark the 900th Anniversary of the Domesday Book was held at King Alfred's College, Winchester, from 14–18 July 1986. 130 members and guests attended, including 25 from overseas. 17 papers were read and these have been published as a volume entitled national d'Histoire Ecclésiastique Comparée and Dr A. I. Doyle on the Anthony Panizzi Foundation.

The Vice-Presidents retiring under By-law XVI were Professor R. Ashton and Professor H. R. Loyn, FBA. Miss Barbara Harvey, FBA and Professor W. R. Ward were elected to replace them. The members of Council retiring under By-law XIX were Dr J. H. Baker, FBA, Professor A. Harding, Dr K. O. Morgan, FBA, and Professor W. R. Ward. Professor Olive Anderson, Professor H. T. Dickinson, Professor N. McCord and Professor D. M. Palliser were elected to fill the vacancies. Mr J. Campbell, FBA, having resigned from Council on account of his absence in the USA, Professor W. Doyle was elected to serve for the remainder of the term of Mr Campbell.

Council reports with great regret the sudden death on 11 December 1986 of Professor J. K. Hyde, a member of Council. Professor B. S. Pullan accepted Council's invitation to fill the vacancy created by this sad event.

Professor J. H. Burns was elected an Honorary Vice-President.

Messrs Beeby, Harmar and Co. were appointed auditors for the year 1986–7 under By-law XXVIII.

Publications and Papers read

Transactions, Fifth Series, volume 37, *Camden Miscellany XXIX* (Camden Fourth Series, volume 34), and the *Supplement* to Ker's *Medieval Libraries of Great Britain* (Guides and Handbooks, no. 15), edited by A. G. Watson went to press during the session and are due to be published in November 1987. The following works were published during the session: *Reading Abbey Cartularies* II (Camden Fourth Series, volume 33), edited by B. R. Kemp; *Handbook of British Chronology* (Third and revised edition, Guides and Handbooks no. 2); *Medieval Exchange,* edited by P. Spufford (Guides and Handbooks no. 13); *Scottish Texts and Calendars,* edited by D. and W. B. Stevenson (Guides and Handbooks no. 14); the *Annual Bibliography of British and Irish History* (1985 publications); and five volumes in the STUDIES IN HISTORY series: *James Gordon Bennett and the New York Herald,* by Douglas Fermer (volume 46); *Reform and Revival: English Government in Ireland, 1470–1534,* by Steven G. Ellis (volume 47); *The d'Aligres de la Rivière: Servants of the Bourbon State in the 17th Century,* by D. J. Sturdy (volume 48); *Victorian Shipping, Business and Imperial Policy: Donald Currie, the Castle Line and Southern Africa,* by Andrew Porter (volume 49); *Representatives of the Lower Clergy in Parliament, 1295–1340,* by Jeffrey H. Denton and John P. Dooley (volume 50).

Domesday Studies: Novocentenary Conference, Winchester 1986, edited by J. C. Holt.

An evening party was held for members and guests at University College London on Wednesday, 2 July 1986. 184 acceptances to invitations were received, and it was as usual well-attended.

At the Anniversary Meeting on 21 November 1986, Dr M. T. Clanchy, Dr D. E. Greenway and Professor M. H. Port retired from their respective posts as Honorary Treasurer, co-Literary Director and Honorary Secretary. Council wishes to record its warmest appreciation of the services rendered to the Society by Dr Clanchy during his period of office, and by Dr Greenway not only as co-Literary Director but for some years previously as assistant Literary Director. Council also wishes to record its very real gratitude to Professor Port, and its deep appreciation of his many and considerable services to the Society during five strenuous years. Dr M. J. Daunton accepted Council's invitation to become Honorary Treasurer, Dr A. B. Worden that to become co-Literary Director, and Dr A. N. Porter to become Honorary Secretary.

The representation of the Society upon various bodies was as follows: Professor F. M. L. Thompson and Mr A. T. Milne on the Joint Anglo-American Committee exercising a general supervision over the production of the *Bibliographies of British History*; Professor G. W. S. Barrow, Dr P. Chaplais, Mr M. Roper and Professor P. H. Sawyer on the Joint Committee of the Society and the British Academy established to prepare an edition of Anglo-Saxon charters; Professor E. B. Fryde on a committee to regulate British co-operation in the preparation of a new repertory of medieval sources to replace Potthast's *Bibliotheca Historica Medii Aevi*; Professor H. R. Loyn on a committee to promote the publication of photographic records of the more significant collections of British coins; Professor P. Lasko on the Advisory Council of the Reviewing Committee on the Export of Works of Art; Professor R. C. Floud and Professor W. A. Speck on the British National Committee of the International Historical Congress; Dr G. H. Martin on the Council of the British Records Association; Mr M. R. D. Foot on the Committee to advise the publishers of *The Annual Register*; Professor K. Cameron on the Trust for Lincolnshire Archaeology; Professor C. J. Holdsworth on the History at the Universities Defence Group. Council received reports from its representatives.

Professor W. N. Medlicott represents the Society on the Court of the University of Exeter, Professor Glanmor Williams on the Court of the University College of Swansea, Professor A. L. Brown on the University Conference of Stirling University; Professor C. N. L. Brooke on the British Sub-Commission of the Commission Inter-

At the ordinary meetings of the Society the following papers were read:

'John of Gaunt: paradigm of the late fourteenth-century crisis', by Mr A. Goodman (17 October 1986).
'Politics as Theatre: metaphors of the stage in German history, 1848–1933', by Dr D. Blackbourn (12 December 1986).
'Conspicuous consumption and working-class culture in late Victorian and Edwardian Britain', by Dr P. Johnson (30 January 1987).
'Power, status and precedence: rivalries among the provincial élites of Louis XIV's France', by Dr R. Mettam (6 March 1987).
'The "Mother Gin" controversy in early eighteenth-century England', by P. A. Clark (24 April 1987).
'The First Army Plot of 1641', by Professor C. S. R. Russell (29 May 1987). (In place of the Alexander Prize Essay, which was not awarded this year).
'The Empress Matilda and Church Reform', by Dr Marjorie Chibnall (1 July 1987: Prothero lecture).

At the Anniversary Meeting on 21 November 1986, the President, Dr G. E. Aylmer delivered an address on 'Collective mentalities in mid-seventeenth-century England: II: Royalist attitudes'.

The Whitfield Prize for 1986 was awarded to Dr Diarmaid Mac-Culloch for his book *Suffolk and the Tudors: Politics and Religion in an English County 1500–1600* (OUP).

The Alexander Prize for 1987 was not awarded.

Membership

Council records with regret the deaths of Dr Ricardo Donoso and Professor José Honório Rodrigues, Corresponding Fellows, and of 18 Fellows and 4 Associates. Among these Council would mention especially Sir David Evans, a former Vice-President, Professor J. K. Hyde, a serving member of Council, Professor W. P. Morrell and Professor E. L. G. Stones, former members of Council. The resignations of 4 Fellows, 6 Associates and 11 Subscribing Libraries were received. 4 Fellows, 4 Associates and 10 Libraries were removed from the roll for non-payment of subscription. Professor B. Guenée and Professor Wang Juefei were elected Corresponding Fellows. 117 Fellows and 8 Associates were elected and 7 Libraries were admitted. The membership of the Society on 30 June 1987 comprised 1,649 Fellows (including 69 Life Fellows and 116 Retired Fellows), 39 Corresponding Fellows, 147 Associates and 707 Subscribing Libraries (1,558, 39, 153, 721 respectively on 30 June 1986). The Society exchanged publications with 12 Societies, British and foreign.

Finance

The accounts for the year ending 30 June 1987 differ in one important respect from the previous year. Council decided to merge the General and Sinking Funds now that the purpose for which the Sinking Fund was originally created – the acquisition of new premises – no longer applies. The merger necessitated a reassessment of the structure of the portfolio in order to provide a better balance of investments. The merged funds showed a surplus for the year of £8,335, exceeding that from both Funds during the previous year (£5,489). The level of subscriptions may be held for a further year, although the net publishing costs after receipt of royalties considerably exceeded the income from subscriptions. The removal of the need to make financial provision for new premises has led Council to consider the possibility of new calls upon the Society's finances for the support of historical work, which may lead to an increase in expenditure in the next financial year.

ROYAL HISTORICAL SOCIETY

BALANCE SHEET AS AT 30 JUNE 1987

	1987 £	£	£	1986 £	£	£
ACCUMULATED FUNDS						
GENERAL FUNDS						
As at 1 July 1986	143,729			131,687		
Add SIR GEORGE PROTHERO BEQUEST	15,894			15,894		
REDDAWAY FUND	5,000			5,000		
ANDREW BROWNING FUND	80,162			80,162		
	244,785			232,743		
Add Transfer of Sinking Fund	157,066	401,851		—	232,743	
Add Surplus on Sale of Investments	49,159			5,795		
Excess of Income over Expenditure						
General Funds	8,335			6,247		
Miss E. M. Robinson Bequest	2,395	59,889	461,740		12,042	244,785
SINKING FUND						
As at 1 July 1986		157,066			154,432	
Add Surplus on Sale of Investments		—			3,392	
		157,066			157,824	
		—			758	
		157,066			157,066	
Transfer to General Funds		157,066	—		—	157,066
MISS E. M. ROBINSON BEQUEST						
As at 1 July 1986		21,463			21,463	
Add Surplus on Sale of Investments		3,057	24,520		—	21,463
A. S. WHITFIELD PRIZE FUND						
As at 1 July 1986		12,344			10,679	
Add Surplus on Sale of Investments		—			1,061	
Excess of Income over Expenditure		720	13,064		604	12,344
STUDIES IN HISTORY ACCOUNT						
As at 1 July 1986		9,504			11,791	
Add Excess of Income over Expenditure		401	9,905		(2,287)	9,504
TOTAL ACCUMULATED FUNDS			509,229			445,162

	1987 £	£	£	£	1986 £	£
REPRESENTED BY:						
INVESTMENTS						
Quoted Securities at Cost		447,410			394,276	
(Market Values)						
30 June 1986 £915,262						
30 June 1987 £1,270,452						
Money at Call		41,578			42,500	
Short Term Deposit		20,000			30,000	
Due from Stockbrokers		—	508,988		614	467,390
CURRENT ASSETS						
Stocks of paper for Publications, at cost	947			5,053		
Sundry Debtors	5,185			5,185		
Income Tax Recoverable on Dividends	5,135			8,563		
Payments and Accruals in advance	1,350			3,984		
Balances at Bank:						
Deposit Accounts	43,659			29,934		
Current Accounts	7,570			4,232		
Cash in Hand	16	63,862		24	56,975	
LESS CURRENT LIABILITIES						
Sundry Creditors and Accruals	1,726			1,476		
Provision for Publications	55,246			61,839		
Conference fees received in advance	—			9,234		
Subscriptions received in advance	6,649	63,621		6,654	79,203	
NET CURRENT ASSETS/(LIABILITIES)			241			(22,228)
TOTAL NET ASSETS			509,229			445,162

The Society's Library and Archives and its Furniture, Fittings and Equipment are written off in the respective years of purchase.

ROYAL HISTORICAL SOCIETY

INCOME AND EXPENDITURE ACCOUNT FOR THE YEAR ENDED 30 JUNE 1987

GENERAL FUND

		1987			1986	
INCOME	£	£	£	£	£	£
Subscriptions for 1986/87: Fellows	21,169			20,002		
Associates	839			858		
Libraries	14,508	36,516		14,290	35,150	
Note The Society had 69 Life Fellows at 30 June 1987						
Income Tax recovered on Covenanted subscriptions		1,831			1,697	
Subscriptions arrears received		1,910	40,257		2,598	39
Interest, Dividends and Income Tax recoverable			45,584			36
Royalties and Reproduction fees			279			
Donations and sundry receipts			1,514			2
TOTAL INCOME			87,634			77

EXPENDITURE						
SECRETARIAL AND ADMINISTRATIVE						
Salaries, Pensions and National Insurance		17,618			16,583	
Printing and Stationery		3,704			1,943	
Postage, Telephone and sundry expenses		2,337			1,648	
Accountancy and Audit		1,265			1,093	
Insurance		301			262	
Meetings and Travel		2,335			2,282	
Fixtures and Fittings		2,500	30,060		—	23
PUBLICATIONS						
Literary Directors' expenses		240			533	
Publishing costs for the year:						
Transactions, Fifth Series, Vol. 36	12,132					
Camden, Fourth Series, Vol. 32	8,629					
Camden, Fourth Series Vol. 33	15,834					
Guides and Handbooks No. 2						
British Chronology	13,094					
Guides and Handbooks No. 13						
Medieval Exchange	8,640					
	58,329					
Less Provision made 30 June 1986	41,788	16,541			21,693	
		16,781	30,060		22,226	25
Provision for Publications in progress:						
Transactions, Fifth Series, Vol. 37	14,000					
Camden, Fourth Series, Vol. 34	14,100					
Guides and Handbooks No. 15	21,250					
Domesday Book Conference	2,000					
	51,350					
Less Provision made 30 June 1986	20,050	31,300			24,850	
Other Publication Costs		—				
Preparation of *Annual Bibliography*	2,157			1,957		
Less Royalties received in the year	1,926	231		1,309	648	
Scottish Texts and Calendars		8,977			—	
Storage and Insurance of books		—			475	
		57,289			48,199	
Less Sales of Publications received in the year		11,286	46,003		2,209	4
LIBRARY AND ARCHIVES						
Purchase of Books and Publications		733			714	
Binding		792			352	
Library Assistance		62	1,587		—	1
C/Fwd			77,650			70

ROYAL HISTORICAL SOCIETY

INCOME AND EXPENDITURE ACCOUNT FOR THE YEAR ENDED 30 JUNE 1987

B/Fwd		77,650	70,867
OTHER CHARGES			
Alexander Prize, Medal and Expenses . . .	132		335
Prothero Lecture Fee	100		100
Grant—Sutton Hoo	200		200
Subscriptions and Donations to Other Bodies . .	134		166
Grant—Oxford Revolution Conference. . . .	500		—
Mrs W. M. Frampton Bequest—A Level Prizes .	500	1,566	—	801
CONFERENCE			
Domesday Conference Expenditure	10,250		—
Less Income received	10,167	83		—
TOTAL EXPENDITURE		79,299	71,668
TOTAL INCOME		87,634	77,915
EXCESS OF INCOME OVER EXPENDITURE FOR THE YEAR .		8,335	6,247

SINKING FUND (From 1 July 1986 the Sinking Fund has been combined with the General Funds)

INCOME			
Interest, Dividends and Income Tax recoverable. .		10,997	
Transfer of Income for the year, Miss E. M. Robinson Bequest	—	1,887	12,884
Less EXPENDITURE			
Office Equipment		3,142	
MRS W. M. FRAMPTON BEQUEST			
A Level Prizes		500	
		3,642	
CONTRIBUTIONS TO GENERAL FUNDS			
Publications Account:			
British Chronology		5,000	
Medieval Exchange . . . , . . .	—	5,000	13,642
Excess of Expenditure over Income for the year . .	—		(758)

MISS E. M. ROBINSON BEQUEST

INCOME			
Interest, Dividends and Income Tax recoverable .	2,395		1,887
Less Transfer to Sinking Fund			1,887
Less Transfer to General Funds	2,395		—

D. WHITFIELD PRIZE FUND

INCOME			
Interest, Dividends and Income Tax recoverable .		1,452	1,327
Less EXPENDITURE			
Prize Awarded	600		600
Advertisement	132	732	123	723
Excess of Income over Expenditure for the year . .		720	604

STUDIES IN HISTORY ACCOUNT

INCOME			
Royalties received	3,226		—
Interest	887	4,113	1,176	1,176
Less EXPENDITURE			
Honorarium to Executive Editor . . .	2,750		2,750
Expenses of Executive Editor . . .	574		712
Review Copies.	188		—
Ex Gratia Payments.	200	3,712	—	3,462
Excess of Income/ (Expenditure) for the year . .		401	(2,286)

G. E. AYLMER, *President.*
M. J. DAUNTON, *Treasurer.*

We have prepared the foregoing Balance Sheet, Source and Application of Funds, and Income and Expenditure Account, under the Historical Cost Convention, from the books, vouchers, records and information available to us.
We have verified the Investments and Bank Balances appearing in the Balance Sheet.
In our opinion the financial statements give a true and fair view of the state of the Society's affairs as at 30 June 1987.

6 SOUTH STREET, DORKING
4 August 1987

BEEBY, HARMAR & CO.,
Chartered Accountants

THE DAVID BERRY TRUST

BALANCE SHEET AS AT 30 JUNE 1987

	1987 £	£	1986 £	£
ACCUMULATED FUND				
As at 1 July 1986		2,263		
Add Excess of Income over Expenditure . . .		321		
		2,584		
REPRESENTED BY:				
INVESTMENTS				
483.63 shares in the Charities Official Investment Fund (Market Value 30.06.87 £2,450—30.06.86 £1,842)		530		
CURRENT ASSETS				
Cash at Bank:				
Deposit Account	2,053		1,732	
Current Account	1	2,054	1	
TOTAL ASSETS		2,584		

INCOME AND EXPENDITURE ACCOUNT FOR THE YEAR ENDED 30 JUNE 198'

INCOME				
Dividends on shares held in the Charities Official Investment Fund		223		
Deposit Interest.		98		
		321		
Less EXPENDITURE				
Prize		—	100	
Examiner's Fee		—	40	
Sundry Expenses		— —	3	
Excess of Income over Expenditure for the year . .		321		

We have prepared the above balance sheet and account from the records and information available to u
In our opinion they give a true and fair view of the Trust's affairs as at 30 June 1987 and of the Income
Expenditure for the year ended on that date.

118 SOUTH STREET, DORKING
17th August 1987

BEEBY, HARMAR & «
Chartered Accour

The late David Berry, by his Will dated 23 April 1926, left £1,000 to provide in every three years a
medal and prize money for the best essay on the Earl of Bothwell or, at the discretion of the Trustees, on Sco
History of the James Stuarts I to VI, in memory of his father, the late Rev. David Berry.

The Trust is regulated by a scheme sanctioned by the Chancery Division of the High Court of Justice d
23 January 1930, and made in an action 1927 A 1233 David Anderson Berry deceased, Hunter and Anot
Robertson and Another and since modified by an order of the Charity Commissioners made on 11 Jan
1978, removing the necessity to provide a medal.

The Royal Historical Society is now the Trustee. The Investment held on Capital Account consists o
Charities Official Investment Fund Shares (Market Value £3,213).

The Trustee will in every second year of the three-year period advertise inviting essays.

ALEXANDER PRIZE

The Alexander Prize was established in 1897 by L. C. Alexander, F.R.Hist.S. It consists of a silver medal and £100 awarded annually for an essay upon some historical subject. Candidates may select their own subject provided such subject has been previously submitted to and approved by the Literary Director. The essay must be a genuine work of original research, not hitherto published, and one which has not been awarded any other prize. It must not exceed 6,000 words in length and must be sent in on or before 1 November of any year. The detailed regulations should be obtained in advance from the Secretary. Candidates must be under the age of 30.

LIST OF ALEXANDER PRIZE ESSAYISTS (1898–1986)[1]

1898. F. Hermia Durham ('The relations of the Crown to trade under James 1').
1899. W. F. Lord, BA ('The development of political parties during the reign of Queen Anne').
1901. Laura M. Roberts ('The Peace of Lunéville').
1902. V. B. Redstone ('The social condition of England during the Wars of the Roses').
1903. Rose Graham ('The intellectual influence of English monasticism between the tenth and the twelfth centuries').
1904. Enid W. G. Routh ('The balance of power in the seventeenth century').
1905. W. A. P. Mason, MA ('The beginnings of the Cistercian Order').
1906. Rachel R. Reid, MA ('The Rebellion of the Earls, 1569').
1908. Kate Hotblack ('The Peace of Paris, 1763').
1909. Nellie Nield, MA ('The social and economic condition of the unfree classes in England in the twelfth and thirteenth centuries').
1912. H. G. Richardson ('The parish clergy of the thirteenth and fourteenth centuries').
1917. Isobel D. Thornely, BA ('The treason legislation of 1531–1534').
1918. T. F. T. Plucknett, BA ('The place of the Council in the fifteenth century').
1919. Edna F. White, MA ('The jurisdiction of the Privy Council under the Tudors').
1920. J. E. Neale, MA ('The Commons Journals of the Tudor Period').
1922. Eveline C. Martin ('The English establishments on the Gold Coast in the second half of the eighteenth century').
1923. E. W. Hensman, MA ('The Civil War of 1648 in the east midlands').
1924. Grace Stretton, BA ('Some aspects of mediæval travel').
1925. F. A. Mace, MA ('Devonshire ports in the fourteenth and fifteenth centuries').

[1] No award was made in 1900, 1907, 1910, 1911, 1913, 1914, 1921, 1946, 1948, 1956, 1969, 1975, 1977, and 1987. The Prize Essays for 1909 and 1919 were not published in the *Transactions*. No Essays were submitted in 1915, 1916 and 1943.

1926. Marian J. Tooley, MA ('The authorship of the *Defensor Pacis*').
1927. W. A. Pantin, BA ('Chapters of the English Black Monks, 1215–1540').
1928. Gladys A. Thornton, BA, PhD ('A study in the history of Clare, Suffolk, with special reference to its development as a borough').
1929. F. S. Rodkey, AM, PhD ('Lord Palmerston's policy for the rejuvenation of Turkey, 1839–47').
1930. A. A. Ettinger, DPhil ('The proposed Anglo-Franco-American Treaty of 1852 to guarantee Cuba to Spain').
1931. Kathleen A. Walpole, MA ('The humanitarian movement of the early nineteenth century to remedy abuses on emigrant vessels to America').
1932. Dorothy M. Brodie, BA ('Edmund Dudley, minister of Henry VII').
1933. R. W. Southern, BA ('Ranulf Flambard and early Anglo-Norman administration').
1934. S. B. Chrimes, MA, PhD ('Sir John Fortescue and his theory of dominion').
1935. S. T. Bindoff, MA ('The unreformed diplomatic service, 1812–60').
1936. Rosamund J. Mitchell, MA, BLitt ('English students at Padua, 1460–1475').
1937. C. H. Philips, BA ('The East India Company "Interest", and the English Government, 1783–4').
1938. H. E. I. Philips, BA ('The last years of the Court of Star Chamber, 1630–41').
1939. Hilda P. Grieve, BA ('The deprived married clergy in Essex, 1553–61').
1940. R. Somerville, MA ('The Duchy of Lancaster Council and Court of Duchy Chamber').
1941. R. A. L. Smith, MA, PhD ('The *Regimen Scaccarii* in English monasteries').
1942. F. L. Carsten, DPhil ('Medieval democracy in the Brandenburg towns and its defeat in the fifteenth century').
1944. Rev. E. W. Kemp, BD ('Pope Alexander III and the canonization of saints').
1945. Helen Suggett, BLitt ('The use of French in England in the later middle ages').
1947. June Milne, BA ('The diplomacy of John Robinson at the court of Charles XII of Sweden, 1697–1709').
1949. Ethel Drus, MA ('The attitude of the Colonial Office to the annexation of Fiji').
1950. Doreen J. Milne, MA, PhD ('The results of the Rye House Plot, and their influence upon the Revolution of 1688').
1951. R. G. Davies, BA ('The origins of the commission system in the West India trade').
1952. G. W. S. Barrow, BLitt ('Scottish rulers and the religious orders, 1070–1153').
1953. W. E. Minchinton, BSc(Econ) ('Bristol—metropolis of the west in the eighteenth century').
1954. Rev. L. Boyle, OP ('The *Oculus Sacerdotis* and some other works of William of Pagula').
1955. G. F. E. Rudé, MA, PhD ('The Gordon riots: a study of the rioters and their victims').
1957. R. F. Hunnisett, MA, DPhil ('The origins of the office of Coroner').

1958. Thomas G. Barnes, AB, DPhil ('County politics and a puritan *cause célèbre*: Somerset churchales, 1633').

1959. Alan Harding, BLitt ('The origins and early history of the Keeper of the Peace').

1960. Gwyn A. Williams, MA, PhD ('London and Edward I').

1961. M. H. Keen, BA ('Treason trials under the law of arms').

1962. G. W. Monger, MA, PhD ('The end of isolation: Britain, Germany and Japan, 1900-1902').

1963. J. S. Moore, BA ('The Domesday teamland: a reconsideration').

1964. M. Kelly, PhD ('The submission of the clergy').

1965. J. J. N. Palmer, BLitt ('Anglo-French negotiations, 1390-1396').

1966. M. T. Clanchy, MA, PhD ('The Franchise of Return of Writs').

1967. R. Lovatt, MA, DPhil, PhD ('The *Imitation of Christ* in late medieval England').

1968. M. G. A. Vale, MA, DPhil ('The last years of English Gascony, 1451-1453').

1970. Mrs Margaret Bowker, MA, BLitt ('The Commons Supplication against the Ordinaries in the light of some Archidiaconal Acta').

1971. C. Thompson, MA ('The origins of the politics of the Parliamentary middle groups, 1625-1629').

1972. I. d'Alton, BA ('Southern Irish Unionism: A study of Cork City and County Unionists, 1884-1914').

1973. C. J. Kitching, BA, PhD ('The quest for concealed lands in the reign of Elizabeth I').

1974. H. Tomlinson, BA ('Place and Profit: an Examination of the Ordnance Office, 1660-1714').

1976. B. Bradshaw, MA, BD ('Cromwellian reform and the origins of the Kildare rebellion, 1533-34').

1978. C. J. Ford, BA ('Piracy or Policy: The Crisis in the Channel, 1400-1403').

1979. P. Dewey, BA, PhD ('Food Production and Policy in the United Kingdom, 1914-1918').

1980. Ann L. Hughes, BA, PhD ('Militancy and Localism: Warwickshire Politics and Westminster Politics, 1643-1647)'.

1981. C. J. Tyerman, MA ('Marino Sanudo Torsello and the Lost Crusade. Lobbying in the Fourteenth Century').

1982. E. Powell, BA, DPhil ('Arbitration and the Law in England in the Late Middle Ages').

1983. A. G. Rosser, MA ('The essence of medieval urban communities: the vill of Westminster 1200-1540').

1984. N. L. Ramsay, MA, LLB ('Retained Legal Counsel, c. 1275-1475').

1985. George S. Garnett, MA ('Coronation and Propaganda: Some Implications of the Norman Claim to the Throne of England in 1066').

1986. C. J. Given-Wilson ('The King and the Gentry in Fourteenth-Century England').

DAVID BERRY PRIZE

The David Berry Prize was established in 1929 by David Anderson-Berry in memory of his father, the Reverend David Berry. It consists of a money prize awarded every three years for Scottish history. Candidates may select any subject dealing with Scottish history within the reigns of James I to James VI inclusive, provided such subject has been previously submitted to and approved by the Council of the Royal Historical Society. The essay must be a genuine work of original research not hitherto published, and one which has not been awarded any other prize. The essay should be between 6,000 and 10,000 words, excluding footnotes and appendices. It must be sent in on or before 31 October 1988.

LIST OF DAVID BERRY PRIZE ESSAYISTS (1937–85)[1]

1937. G. Donaldson, MA ('The polity of the Scottish Reformed Church c. 1460–1580, and the rise of the Presbyterian movement').
1943. Rev. Prof. A. F. Scott Pearson, DTh, DLitt ('Anglo-Scottish religious relations, 1400–1600').
1949. T. Bedford Franklin, MA, FRSE ('Monastic agriculture in Scotland, 1440–1600').
1955. W. A. McNeill, MA (' "Estaytt" of the king's rents and pensions, 1621').
1958. Prof. Maurice Lee, PhD ('Maitland of Thirlestane and the foundation of the Stewart despotism in Scotland').
1964. M. H. Merriman ('Scottish collaborators with England during the Anglo-Scottish war, 1543–1550').
1967. Miss M. H. B. Sanderson ('Catholic recusancy in Scotland in the sixteenth century').
1970. Athol Murray, MA, LLB, PhD ('The Comptroller, 1425–1610').
1973. J. Kirk, MA, PhD ('Who were the Melvillians: A study in the Personnel and Background of the Presbyterian Movement in late Sixteenth-century Scotland').
1976. A. Grant, BA, DPhil ('The Development of the Scottish Peerage').
1985. Rev. G. Mark Dilworth ('The Commendator System in Scotland').

[1] No essays were submitted in 1940 and 1979. No award was made in 1946, 1952, 1961 and 1982.

WHITFIELD PRIZE

The Whitfield Prize was established by Council in 1976 as a money prize of £400 out of the bequest of the late Professor Archibald Stenton Whitfield: in May 1981 Council increased the prize to £600. Until 1982 the prize was awarded annually to the STUDIES IN HISTORY series. From 1983 the prize, value £600, will be awarded annually to the best work of English or Welsh history by an author under 40 years of age, published in the United Kingdom. The award will be made by Council in the Spring of each year in respect of works published in the preceding calendar year. Authors or publishers should send two copies (non-returnable) of a book eligible for the competition to the Society to arrive not later than 31 December of the year of publication.

LIST OF WHITFIELD PRIZE WINNERS (1977-1986)

1977. K. D. Brown, MA, PhD (*John Burns*).
1978. Marie Axton, MA, PhD (*The Queen's Two Bodies: Drama and the Elizabethan Succession*).
1979. Patricia Crawford, MA, PhD (*Denzil Holles, 1598-1680: A study of his Political Career*).
1980. D. L. Rydz (*The Parliamentary Agents: A History*).
1981. Scott M. Harrison (*The Pilgrimage of Grace in the Lake Counties 1536-7*).
1982. Norman L. Jones (*Faith by Statute: Parliament and the Settlement of Religion 1559*).
1983. Peter Clark (*The English Alehouse: A social history 1200-1830*).
1984. David Hempton, BA, PhD (*Methodism and Politics in British Society 1750-1850*).
1985. K. D. M. Snell, MA, PhD (*Annals of the Labouring Poor*).
1986. Diarmaid MacCulloch, MA, PhD, FSA (*Suffolk and the Tudors: Politics and Religion in an English County 1500-1600*).

THE ROYAL HISTORICAL SOCIETY

(INCORPORATED BY ROYAL CHARTER)

OFFICERS AND COUNCIL—1987

Patron
HER MAJESTY THE QUEEN

President
G. E. AYLMER, MA, DPhil, FBA

Honorary Vice-Presidents
Professor J. H. Burns, MA, PhD
Professor A. G. Dickens, CMG, MA, DLit, DLitt, LittD, FBA, FSA
Professor G. Donaldson MA, PhD, DLitt, DLitt, FRSE, FBA
Sir Geoffrey Elton, MA, PhD, LittD, DLitt, DLitt, DLit, FBA
Professor P. Grierson, MA, LittD, FBA, FSA
Sir John Habakkuk, MA, FBA
Professor Sir Keith Hancock, KBE, MA, DLitt, FBA
Professor D. Hay, MA, DLitt, FBA, FRSE, Dr h.c. Tours
Professor J. C. Holt, MA, DPhil, DLitt, FBA, FSA
Professor R. A. Humphreys, OBE, MA, PhD, DLitt, LittD, DLitt, DUniv
Miss K. Major, MA, BLitt, LittD, FBA, FSA
Professor D. B. Quinn, MA, PhD, DLit, DLitt, DLitt, DLitt, LLD, DHL,
    Hon FBA
The Hon. Sir Steven Runciman, CH, MA, DPhil, LLD, LittD, DLitt, LitD,
    DD, DHL, FBA, FSA
Sir Richard Southern, MA, DLitt, LittD, DLitt, FBA
Professor C. H. Wilson, CBE, MA, LittD, DLitt, DLitt, DLitt, FBA

Vice-Presidents
Professor P. Collinson, MA, PhD, FBA
Professor P. Smith, MA, DPhil
G. H. Martin, CBE, MA, DPhil
Professor K. G. Robbins, MA, DPhil, DLitt
Professor R. B. Dobson, MA, DPhil
Professor G. S. Holmes, MA, DLitt, FBA
Miss B. Harvey, MA, BLitt, FBA
Professor W. R. Ward, DPhil

LIST OF FELLOWS OF THE
ROYAL HISTORICAL SOCIETY

Names of Officers and Honorary Vice-Presidents are printed in capitals.
Those marked* have compounded for their annual subscriptions.

Abramsky, Professor Chimen A., MA, Dept of Hebrew and Jewish Studies, University College London, Gower Street, London WC1E 6BT.
Abulafia, D. S. H., MA, PhD, Gonville and Caius College, Cambridge CB2 1TA.
Acton, E. D. J., PhD, School of History, The University, P.O. Box 147, Liverpool L69 3BX.
Adair, Professor J. E., MA, PhD, Newlands Cottage, 41 Pewley Hill, Guildford, Surrey.
Adam, Professor R. J., MA, Easter Wayside, Hepburn Gardens, St Andrews KY16 9LP.
Adams, Professor Ralph J. Q., PhD, Dept of History, Texas A & M University, College Station, Texas 77843-4236, U.S.A.
Adams, S. L., MA, DPhil, 4 North East Circus Place, Edinburgh EH3 6SP.
Adamthwaite, Professor A.P., BA, PhD, Dept of History, The University, Loughborough LE11 3TU.
Addison, P., MA, DPhil, Dept of History, The University, William Robertson Building, George Square, Edinburgh EH8 9JY.
Ailes, A., MA, 24 Donnington Gardens, Reading, Berkshire RG1 5LY.
Akrigg, Professor G. P. V., BA, PhD, FRSC, 8-2575 Tolmie Street, Vancouver, B.C., V6R 4M1, Canada.
Alcock, Professor L., MA, FSA, 29 Hamilton Drive, Glasgow G12 8DN.
Alder, G. J., BA, PhD, Dept of History, The University, Whiteknights, Reading RG6 2AA.
Alderman, G., MA, DPhil, 172 Colindeep Lane, London NW9 6EA.
Allan, D. G. C., MSc(Econ), PhD, c/o Royal Society of Arts, John Adam Street, London WC2N 6EZ.
Allen, D. F., BA, PhD, School of History, The University, P.O. Box 363, Birmingham B15 2TT.
Allen, D. H., BA, PhD, 105 Tuddenham Avenue, Ipswich, Suffolk IP4 2HG.
Allmand, C. T., MA, DPhil, FSA, 111 Menlove Avenue, Liverpool L18 3HP.
Alsop, J. D., MA, PhD, Dept of History, McMaster University, 1280 Main Street West, Hamilton, Ontario, Canada L8S 4L9.
Altholz, Professor J., PhD, Dept of History, University of Minnesota, 614 Social Sciences Building, Minneapolis, Minn. 55455, U.S.A.
Altschul, Professor M., PhD, Case Western Reserve University, Cleveland, Ohio 44106, U.S.A.
Ambler, R. W., PhD, 37 Cumberland Avenue, Grimsby, South Humberside DN32 0BT.
Anderson, Professor M. S., MA, PhD, 45 Cholmeley Crescent, London N6 5EX.

Anderson, Professor Olive, MA, BLitt, Dept of History, Westfield College, London NW3 7ST.

Anderson, R. D., MA, DPhil, 7 North West Circus Place, Edinburgh EH3 6ST.

Anderson, Miss S. P., MA, BLitt, 17-19 Chilworth Street, London W2 3QU.

Andrew, C. M., MA, PhD, Corpus Christi College, Cambridge CB2 1RH.

Anglesey, The Most Hon., The Marquess of, FSA, FRSL, Plas-Newydd, Llanfairpwll, Anglesey LL61 6DZ.

Anglo, Professor S., BA, PhD, FSA, 59 Green Ridge, Withdean, Brighton BN1 5LU.

Annan, Lord, OBE, MA, DLitt, DUniv, 16 St John's Wood Road, London NW8 8RE.

Annis, P. G. W., BA, 65 Longlands Road, Sidcup, Kent DA15 7LQ.

Appleby, J. S., Little Pitchbury, Brick Kiln Lane, Great Horkesley, Colchester, Essex CO6 4EU.

Armstrong, Miss A. M., BA, 7 Vale Court, Mallord Street, London SW3.

Armstrong, C. A. J., MA, FSA, Gayhurst, Lincombe Lane, Boars Hill, Oxford OX1 5DZ.

Armstrong, Professor F. H., PhD, Dept of History, University of Western Ontario, London, Ontario, Canada N6A 3K7.

Armstrong, W. A., BA, PhD, Eliot College, The University, Canterbury, Kent CT2 7NS.

Arnstein, Professor W. L., PhD, Dept of History, University of Illinois at Urbana-Champaign, 309 Gregory Hall, Urbana, Ill. 61801, U.S.A.

Artibise, Professor Alan F. J., PhD, Inst. of Urban Studies, University of Winnipeg, 515 Portage Avenue, Winnipeg, Canada R3B 2E9.

Ash, Marinell, BA, MA, PhD, 42 Woodburn Terrace, Edinburgh EH10 4ST.

Ashton, Professor R., PhD, The Manor House, Brundall, near Norwich NOR 86Z.

Ashworth, J., BA, MLitt, DPhil, School of English and American Studies, University of East Anglia, Norwich NR4 7TJ.

Ashworth, Professor W., BSc(Econ), PhD, Flat 14, Wells Court, Wells Road, Ilkley, W. Yorks. LS29 9LG.

Asquith, Ivon, BA, PhD, 19 Vicarage Lane, New Hinksey, Oxford OX1 4RQ.

Aston, Margaret, MA, DPhil, Castle House, Chipping Ongar, Essex.

Austin, The Rev. Canon, M. R. BD, MA, PhD, 22 Marlock Close, Fiskerton, Nr Southwell, Notts. NG25 0UB.

Axelson, Professor E. V., DLitt, Box 15, Constantia, 7848, S. Africa.

*Aydelotte, Professor W. O., PhD, State University of Iowa, Iowa City, U.S.A.

AYLMER, G. E., MA, DPhil, FBA, (President), St Peter's College, Oxford OX1 2DL.

Bahlman, Professor Dudley W. R., MA, PhD, Dept of History, Williams College, Williamstown, Mass. 01267, U.S.A.

Bailie, The Rev. W. D., MA, BD, PhD, DD, Kilmore Manse, 100 Ballynahinch Road, Crossgar, Downpatrick, N. Ireland BT30 9HT.

Bailyn, Professor B., MA, PhD, LittD, LHD, Widener J., Harvard University, Cambridge, Mass. 02138, U.S.A.

Baines, A. H. J., PhD, MA, LLB, FSA, FRSA, FSS, Finmere, 90 Eskdale Avenue, Chesham, Bucks. HP5 3AY.

Baker, D., BSc, PhD, MA, BLitt, 21 Valenciennes Road, Sittingbourne, Kent, ME10 1EN.

Baker, J. H., LLD, FBA, St Catharine's College, Cambridge CB2 1RL.

Baker, L. G. D., MA, BLitt, 5 Allendale, Southwater, Horsham, West Sussex RH13 7UE.

Baker, T. F. T., BA, Camden Lodge, 50 Hastings Road, Pembury, Kent.

Ball, A. W., BA, 71 Cassiobury Park Avenue, Watford, Herts. WD1 7LD.

Ballhatchet, Professor K. A., MA, PhD, 11 The Mead, Ealing, London W13.

Banks, Professor J. A., MA, Dept of Sociology, The University, Leicester LE1 7RH.

Barber, M. C., BA, PhD, Dept of History, The University, Whiteknights, Reading, Berks. RG6 2AA.

Barber, R. W., MA, PhD, FSA, Stangrove Hall, Alderton, near Woodbridge, Suffolk IP12 3BL.

Barker, E. E., MA, PhD, FSA, 9 Abbeystead, Little Digmoor, Skelmersdale, Lancs. WN8 9LP.

Barker, Professor T. C., MA, PhD, Minsen Dane, Brogdale Road, Faversham, Kent.

Barkley, Professor the Rev. J. M., MA, DD, 2 College Park, Belfast, N. Ireland.

*Barlow, Professor F., MA, DPhil, FBA, Middle Court Hall, Kenton, Exeter.

Barnard, T. C., MA, DPhil, Hertford College, Oxford OX1 3BW.

Barnes, Miss P. M., PhD, 6 Kings Yard, Kings Ride, Ascot, Berks. SL5 8AH.

Barnett, Correlli, MA, Churchill College, Cambridge CB3 0DS.

Barratt, Miss D. M., DPhil, The Corner House, Hampton Poyle, Kidlington, Oxford.

Barratt, Professor G. R. de V., PhD, 197 Belmont Avenue, Ottawa, Canada K1S 0V7.

Barron, Mrs C. M., MA, PhD, 35 Rochester Road, London NW1.

Barrow, Professor G. W. S., MA, BLitt, DLitt, FBA, FRSE, 12a Lauder Road, Edinburgh EH9 2EL.

Bartlett, Professor C. J., PhD, Dept of Modern History, The University, Dundee DD1 4HN.

Bartlett, Professor R. J. MA, DPhil, Dept of History, University of Chicago, 1126 East 59th Street, Chicago, Illinois 60637, U.S.A.

Bates, D., PhD, Dept of History, University College, P.O. Box 78, Cardiff CF1 1XL.

Batho, Professor G. R., MA, Fivestones, 3 Archery Rise, Durham DH1 4LA.

Baugh, Professor Daniel A., PhD, Dept of History, McGraw Hall, Cornell University, Ithaca, N.Y. 14853, U.S.A.

Baxter, Professor S. B., PhD, 608 Morgan Creek Road, Chapel Hill, N.C. 27514, U.S.A.

Baylen, Professor J. O., MA, PhD, 38 Dean Court Road, Brighton, E. Sussex BN2 7DJ.

Beachey, Professor R. W., BA, PhD, 1 Rookwood, De La Warr Road, Milford-on-Sea, Hampshire.

Beales, Professor D. E. D., MA, PhD, Sidney Sussex College, Cambridge CB2 3HU.

Bealey, Professor F., BSc(Econ), Dept of Politics, The University, Taylor Building, Old Aberdeen AB9 2UB.

Bean, Professor J. M. W., MA, DPhil, 622 Fayerweather Hall, Columbia University, New York, N.Y. 10027, U.S.A.

Beardwood, Miss Alice, BA, BLitt, DPhil, 415 Miller's Lane, Wynnewood, Pa, U.S.A.

Beasley, Professor W. G., PhD, FBA, 172 Hampton Road, Twickenham, Middlesex TW2 5NJ.

Beattie, Professor J. M., PhD, Dept of History, University of Toronto, Toronto M5S 1A1, Canada.

Beauroy, Dr Jacques M., 15 Avenue Marie-Amélie, Chantilly, France 60500.

Bebbington, D. W., MA, PhD, 5 Pullar Avenue, Bridge of Allan, Stirling FK9 4TB.

Beckerman, John S., PhD, 225 Washington Avenue, Hamden, Ct. 06518, U.S.A.

Beckett, I. F. W., BA, PhD, 11 Tolpuddle Way, Yateley, Camberley, Surrey GU17 7BH.

Beckett, Professor J. C., MA, 19 Wellington Park Terrace, Belfast 9, N. Ireland.

Beckett, J. V., BA, PhD, Dept of History, The University, Nottingham NG7 2RD.

Bedarida, Professor F., 13 rue Jacob, 75006 Paris, France.

Beddard, R. A., MA, DPhil, Oriel College, Oxford OX1 4EW.

*Beer, E. S. de, CBE, MA, DLitt, FBA, FSA, Stoke House, Stoke Hammond MK17 9BN.

Beer, Professor Samuel H., PhD, Faculty of Arts & Sciences, Harvard University, Littauer Center G-15, Cambridge, Mass. 02138, U.S.A.

Bell, A., Rhodes House Library, Oxford OX2 7RU.

Bell, P. M. H., BA, BLitt, School of History, The University, P.O. Box 147, Liverpool L69 3BX.

Bellenger, Dominic T. J. A., MA, PhD, Downside Abbey, Stratton-on-the-Fosse, Bath BA3 4RH.

Beloff, Lord, DLitt, FBA, Flat No. 9, 22 Lewes Crescent, Brighton BN2 1GB.

Benedikz, B. S., MA, PhD, Main Library, University of Birmingham, P.O. Box 363, Birmingham B15 2TT.

Bennett, Rev. Canon G. V., MA, DPhil, FSA, New College, Oxford OX1 3BN.

Bennett, M. J., BA, PhD, History Dept, University of Tasmania, Box 252C, G.P.O., Hobart, Tasmania 7001, Australia.

Benson, J., BA, MA, PhD, The Polytechnic, Wolverhampton WV1 1LY.

Bentley, M., BA, PhD, Dept of History, The University, Sheffield S10 2TN.

Berghahn, Professor V. R., MA, PhD, Dept of History, University of Warwick, Coventry CV4 7AL.

Bernard, G. W., MA, DPhil, 92 Bassett Green Village, Southampton.

Bhila, Professor H. H. K., BA, MA, PhD, Dept of History, University of Zimbabwe, P.O. Box MP 167, Mount Pleasant, Harare, Zimbabwe.

Biddiss, Professor M. D., MA, PhD, Dept of History, The University, Whiteknights, Reading RG6 2AA.

Biddle, M., MA, FBA, FSA, Christ Church, Oxford OX1 1DP.

Bidwell, Brigadier R. G. S., OBE, 8 Chapel Lane, Wickham Market, Woodbridge, Suffolk IP13 0SD.

Bill, E. G. W., MA, DLitt, Lambeth Palace Library, London SE1.

Biller, P. P. A., MA, DPhil, Dept of History, The University, Heslington, York Yo1 5DD.

Binfield, J. C. G., MA, PhD, 22 Whiteley Wood Road, Sheffield S11 7FE.

Birch, A., MA, PhD, University of Hong Kong, Hong Kong.
Bishop, A. S., BA, PhD, 44 North Acre, Banstead, Surrey SM7 2EG.
Bishop, T. A. M., MA, 16 Highbury Road, London SW19 7PR.
Black, Professor Eugene C., PhD, Dept of History, Brandeis University, Waltham, Mass. 02154, U.S.A.
Black, J. M. PhD, 3 Roseworth Crescent, Gosforth, Newcastle NE3 1NR
Black, R. D., BA PhD, School of History, The University, Leeds LS2 9JT.
Blackbourn, D., MA, PhD, Dept of History, Birkbeck College, Malet Street, London WC1E 7HX.
Blackwood, B. G., MA, BLitt, DPhil, 4 Knights Close, Felixstowe, Suffolk IP11 9NU.
Blake, E. O., MA, PhD, Roselands, Moorhill Road, Westend, Southampton SO3 3AW.
Blake, Lord, MA, FBA, The Queen's College, Oxford OX1 4AW.
Blakemore, H., PhD, 43 Fitzjohn Avenue, Barnet, Herts.
*Blakey, Professor R. G., PhD, c/o Mr Raymond Shove, Order Dept, Library, University of Minnesota, Minneapolis, Minn., U.S.A.
Blanning, T. W. C., MA, PhD, Sidney Sussex College, Cambridge CB2 3HU.
Blewett, Hon Dr N., BA, DipEd, MA, DPhil, 68 Barnard Street, North Adelaide, South Australia 5006.
Blinkhorn, RM., BA, AM, DPhil, Dept of History, The University, Bailrigg, Lancaster LA1 4YG.
Blomfield, Mrs K., 8 Elmdene Court, Constitution Hill, Woking, Surrey GU22 7SA.
Blunt, C. E., OBE, FBA, FSA, Ramsbury Hill, Ramsbury, Marlborough, Wilts.
Board, Mrs Beryl A., The Old School House, Stow Maries, Chelmsford, Essex CM3 6SL.
*Bolsover, G. H., OBE, MA, PhD, 7 Devonshire Road, Hatch End, Middlesex HA5 4LY.
Bolton, Miss Brenda, BA, Dept of History, Westfield College, London NW3 7ST.
Bolton, Professor G. C., MA, DPhil, Dept of History, Murdoch University, Murdoch, S. Australia 6150.
Bolton, J. L. BA, BLitt, Dept of History, Queen Mary College, Mile End Road, London E1 4NS.
Bond, B. J., BA, MA, Dept of War Studies, King's College, London WC2R 2LS.
Bonney, Professor R. J., MA. DPhil, Dept of History, The University, Leicester LE1 7RH.
Booker, J. M. L., BA, MLitt, DPhil, Braxted Place, Little Braxted, Witham, Essex CM8 3LD.
Boon, G. C., BA, FSA, FRNS, National Museum of Wales, Cardiff CF1 3NP.
Borrie, M. A. F., BA, 142 Culford Road, London N1.
Bossy, Professor J. A., MA, PhD, Dept of History, University of York, York YO1 5DD.
Bottigheimer, Professor Karl S., Dept of History, State University of New York at Stony Brook, Long Island, N.Y., U.S.A.
Bourne, Professor K., BA, PhD, FBA, London School of Economics, Houghton Street, London WC2A 2AE.
Bowker, Mrs M., MA, BLitt, 14 Bowers Croft, Cambridge CB1 4RP.
Bowyer, M. J. F., 32 Netherhall Way, Cambridge.

*Boxer, Professor C. R., DLitt, FBA, Ringshall End, Little Gaddesden, Berkhamsted, Herts.

Boyce, D. G., BA, PhD, Dept of Political Theory and Government, University College of Swansea, Swansea SA2 8PP.

Boyle, T., Cert.Ed, BA, MPhil, Jersey Cottage, Mark Beech, Edenbridge, Kent TN8 5NS.

Boynton, L. O. J., MA, DPhil, FSA, Dept of History, Westfield College, London NW3 7ST.

Brading, D. A., MA, PhD, 28 Storey Way, Cambridge.

Bradshaw, Rev. B., MA, BD, PhD, Queens' College, Cambridge CB3 9ET.

Brake, Rev. G. Thompson, 19 Bethell Avenue, Ilford, Essex IG1 4UX.

Brand, P. A., MA, DPhil, 155 Kennington Road, London SE11.

Brandon, P. F., BA, PhD, Greensleeves, 8 St Julian's Lane, Shoreham-by-Sea, Sussex BN4 6YS.

Bray, Jennifer R., MA, PhD, 99 Benthall Road, London N16.

Breck, Professor A. D., MA, PhD, LHD, DLitt, University of Denver, Denver, Colorado 80210, U.S.A.

Brentano, Professor R., DPhil, University of California, Berkeley 4, Calif., U.S.A.

Brett, M., MA, DPhil, Robinson College, Cambridge CB3 9AN.

Breuilly, J. J., BA, DPhil, Dept of History, The University, Manchester M13 9PL.

Bridge, F. R., PhD, The Poplars, Rodley Lane, Rodley, Leeds.

Bridges, R. C., BA, PhD, Dept of History, University of Aberdeen, King's College, Aberdeen AB9 2UB.

Brigden, Susan, BA, PhD, MA, Lincoln College Oxford, OX1 3DR.

Briggs, Lord, BSc(Econ), MA, DLitt, FBA, Worcester College, Oxford OX1 2HB.

Briggs, J. H. Y., MA, Dept of History, University of Keele, Staffs. ST5 5BG.

Briggs, R., MA, All Souls College, Oxford OX1 4AL.

Broad, J., BA, DPhil, Dept of History, Polytechnic of North London, Prince of Wales Road, London NW5 3LB.

Broadhead, P. J., BA, PhD, Dept of History Goldsmiths' College, London SE14 6NW.

Brock, M. G., MA, Nuffield College, Oxford OX1 1NF.

Brock, Professor W. R., MA, PhD, 49 Barton Road, Cambridge CB3 9LG.

Brocklesby, R., BA, The Elms, North Eastern Road, Thorne, Doncaster, S. Yorks. DN8 4AS.

Brogan, D. H. V., MA, Dept of History, University of Essex, Colchester CO4 3SQ.

*Brooke, Professor C. N. L., MA, LittD, FBA, FSA, Faculty of History, West Road, Cambridge CB3 9EF.

Brooke, Mrs R. B., MA, PhD, c/o Faculty of History, West Road, Cambridge CB3 9EF.

Brooks, Professor N. P., MA, DPhil, Dept of Medieval History, The University, Birmingham B15 2TT.

Brown, Mrs Alison M., MA, 25 Rosemont Road, Richmond, Surrey TW10 6QN.

Brown, Professor A. L., MA, DPhil, Dept of History, The University, Glasgow G12 8QQ.

Brown, The Rev. A. W. G., BA, BD, PhD, The Manse, 28 Quay Road, Ballycastle, Co. Antrin BT54 6BH.

Brown, G. S., PhD, 1720 Hanover Road, Ann Arbor, Mich. 48103, U.S.A.

Brown, Judith M., MA, PhD, 8 The Downs, Cheadle, Cheshire SK8 1JL.

Brown, K. D., BA, MA, PhD, Dept of Economic and Social History, The Queen's University, Belfast BT7 1NN, N. Ireland.

Brown, Professor M. J., MA, PhD, 350 South Candler Street, Decatur, Georgia 30030, U.S.A.

Brown, P. D., MA, 18 Davenant Road, Oxford OX2 8BX.

Brown, P. R. L., MA, FBA, Hillslope, Pullen's Lane, Oxford.

Brown, R. A., MA, DPhil, DLitt, FSA, King's College, London WC2R 2LS.

Brown, Professor Wallace, PhD, Dept of History, University of New Brunswick, P.O. Box 4400, Fredericton, NB., Canada E3B 5AE.

Bruce, J. M., ISO, MA, FRAeS, 51 Chiltern Drive, Barton-on-Sea, New Milton, Hants. BH25 7JZ.

Brundage, Professor J. A., Dept of History, University of Wisconsin at Milwaukee, Milwaukee, Wisconsin, U.S.A.

Bryson, Professor W. Hamilton, School of Law, University of Richmond, Richmond, Va. 23173, U.S.A.

Buchanan, R. A., MA, PhD, School of Humanities and Social Sciences, The University, Claverton Down, Bath BA2 7AY.

Buckland, P. J., MA, PhD, 6 Rosefield Road, Liverpool L25 8TF.

Bueno de Mesquita, D. M., MA, PhD, 283 Woodstock Road, Oxford OX2 7NY.

Buisseret, Professor D. J., MA, PhD, The Newberry Library, 60 West Walton Street, Chicago, Ill. 60610, U.S.A.

Bullock, Lord, MA, DLitt, FBA, St Catherine's College, Oxford OX1 3UJ.

Bullock-Davies, Constance, BA, PhD, Dept of Classics, University College of North Wales, Bangor, Gwynedd LL57 2DG.

Bullough, Professor D. A., MA, FSA, Dept of Mediaeval History, 71 South Street, St Andrews, Fife KY16 9AJ.

Burke, U. P., MA, Emmanuel College, Cambridge CB2 3AP.

BURNS, Professor J. H., MA, PhD, 6 Chiltern House, Hillcrest Road, London W5 1HL.

Burroughs, P., PhD, Dalhousie University, Halifax, Nova Scotia, Canada B3H 3J5.

Burrow, Professor J. W., MA., PhD, Sussex University, Falmer, Brighton BN1 9QX.

Butler, R. D'O., CMG, MA, DLitt, All Souls College, Oxford OX1 4AL.

Byerly, Professor B. F., BA, MA, PhD, Dept of History, University of Northern Colorado, Greeley, Colorado 80631, U.S.A.

Bythell, D., MA, DPhil, Dept of Economic History, University of Durham, 23–26 Old Elvet, Durham City DH1 3HY.

Cabaniss, Professor J. A., PhD, University of Mississippi, Box No. 253, University, Mississippi 38677, U.S.A.

Callahan, Professor Raymond, PhD, Dept of History, University of Delaware, Newark, Delaware 19716, U.S.A.

Callahan, Professor Thomas, Jr., PhD, Dept of History, Rider College, Lawrenceville, N.J. 08648, U.S.A.

Calvert, Brigadier J. M. (ret.), DSO, MA, MICE, 33a Mill Hill Close, Haywards Heath, Sussex.

Calvert, Professor P. A. R., MA, PhD, AM, Dept of Politics, University of Southampton, Highfield, Southampton SO9 5NH.

Cameron, A., BA, 6 Braid Crescent, Morningside, Edinburgh EH10 6AU.

Cameron, Professor J. K., MA, BD, PhD, St Mary's College, University of St Andrews, Fife KY16 9JU.

Cameron, Professor K., PhD, FBA, Dept of English, The University, Nottingham NG7 2RD.

Campbell, Professor A. E., MA, PhD, School of History, University of Birmingham, P.O. Box 363, Birmingham B15 2TT.

Campbell, J., MA, FBA, Worcester College, Oxford OX1 2HB.

*Campbell, Professor Mildred L., PhD, Vassar College, Poughkeepsie, N.Y., U.S.A.

Campbell, Professor R. H., MA, PhD, Craig, Glenluce, Newton Stewart, Wigtownshire DG8 0NR.

Cannadine, D. N., BA, DPhil, Christ's College, Cambridge CB2 3BU.

Canning, J. P., MA, PhD, Dept of History, University College of North Wales, Bangor, Gwynedd LL57 2DG.

Cannon, Professor J. A., CBE, MA, PhD, Dept of History, The University, Newcastle upon Tyne NE1 7RU.

Canny, Professor N. P., MA, PhD, Dept of History, University College, Galway, Ireland.

Cant, R. G., MA, DLitt, 2 Kinburn Place, St Andrews, Fife KY16 9DT.

Cantor, Professor N. F., PhD, New York University, Dept of History, 19 University Place, New York, N.Y. 10003, U.S.A.

Capp, B. S., MA, DPhil, Dept of History, University of Warwick, Coventry, Warwickshire CV4 7AL.

Carey, P. B. R., DPhil, Trinity College, Oxford OX1 3BH.

*Carlson, Leland H., PhD, Huntington Library, San Marino, California 91108, U.S.A.

Carlton, Professor Charles, Dept of History, North Carolina State University, Raleigh, N.C. 27607, U.S.A.

Carman, W. Y., FSA, 94 Mulgrave Road, Sutton, Surrey.

Carpenter, D. A., MA, DPhil, Dept of History, Queen Mary College, Mile End Road, London E1 4NS.

Carpenter, M. Christine, MA, PhD, New Hall, Cambridge CB3 0DF.

Carr, A. D., MA, PhD, Dept of Welsh History, University College of North Wales, Bangor, Gwynedd LL57 2DG.

Carr, A. R. M., MA, FBA, St Antony's College, Oxford OX2 6JF.

Carr, W., PhD, 22 Southbourne Road, Sheffield S10 2QN.

Carrington, Miss Dorothy, 3 Rue Emmanuel Arene, 20 Ajaccio, Corsica.

Carter, Jennifer J., BA, PhD, The Old Schoolhouse, Glenbuchat, Strathdon, Aberdeenshire AB3 8TT.

Carwardine, R. J., MA, DPhil, Dept of History, The University, Sheffield S10 2TN.

Casey, J., BA, PhD, School of Modern Languages and European History, University of East Anglia, Norwich NR4 7TJ.

Cassels, Professor Alan, Dept of History, McMaster University, Hamilton, Ontario L8S 4L9.

Catto, R. J. A. I., MA, Oriel College, Oxford OX1 4EW.

Cazel, Professor Fred A., Jr., Dept of History, University of Connecticut, Storrs, Conn. 06268, U.S.A.

Chadwick, Professor W. O., OM, KBE, DD, DLitt, FBA, Selwyn Lodge, Cambridge CB3 9DQ.

Challis, C. E., MA, PhD, 14 Ashwood Villas, Headingley, Leeds 6.

Chalmers, C. D., Public Record Office, Kew, Richmond, Surrey TW9 4DU.

Chamberlain, Muriel E., MA. DPhil, Dept of History, University College of Swansea, Singleton Park, Swansea SA2 7BR.
Chambers, D. S., MA, DPhil, Warburg Institute, Woburn Square, London WC1H oAB.
Chandaman, Professor C. D., BA, PhD, 23 Bellamy Close, Ickenham, Uxbridge UB10 8SJ.
Chandler, D. G., MA, Hindford, Monteagle Lane, Yateley, Camberley, Surrey.
Chaplais, P., PhD, FBA, FSA, Lew Lodge, Lew, Oxford OX8 2BE.
Charles-Edwards, T. M., DPhil, Corpus Christi College, Oxford OX1 4JF.
Charmley, J., MA, DPhil, School of English and American Studies, University of East Anglia, Norwich NR4 7TJ.
Chaudhuri, Professor Kirti Narayan, BA, PhD, History Department, S.O.A.S., University of London, Malet Street, London WC1E 7HD.
Cheney, Mrs Mary, MA, 17 Westberry Court, Grange Road, Cambridge CB3 9BG.
Cherry, John, MA, 58 Lancaster Road, London N4.
Chibnall, Mrs Marjorie, MA, DPhil, FBA, 6 Millington Road, Cambridge CB3 9HP.
Child, C. J., OBE, MA, PhD, 94 Westhall Road, Warlingham, Surrey CR3 9HB.
Childs, J. C. R., BA, PhD, School of History, The University, Leeds LS2 9JT.
Childs, Wendy R., MA, PhD, School of History, The University, Leeds LS2 9JT.
Chitnis, Anand Chidamber, BA, MA, PhD, Dept of History, The University, Stirling FK9 4LA.
Christiansen, E., New College, Oxford OX1 3BN.
Christianson, Assoc. Professor P. K., PhD, Dept of History, Queen's University, Kingston, Ontario K7L 3N6, Canada.
Christie, Professor I. R., MA, FBA, 10 Green Lane, Croxley Green, Herts. WD3 3HR.
Church, Professor R. A., BA, PhD, School of Social Studies, University of East Anglia, Norwich NOR 88C.
Cirket, A. F., 71 Curlew Crescent, Bedford.
Clanchy, M. T., MA, PhD, FSA, 28 Hillfield Road, London NW6 1PZ.
Clark, A. E., MA, 32 Durham Avenue, Thornton Cleveleys, Blackpool FY5 2DP.
Clark, D. S. T., BA, PhD, History Dept, University College of Swansea, Swansea SA2 8PP.
Clark, Professor Dora Mae, PhD, Menno Village, 510d, Chambersburg, Pa. 17201, U.S.A.
Clark, J. C. D., MA, PhD, All Souls College, Oxford OX1 4AL.
Clark, P. A., MA, Dept of Economic and Social History, The University, Leicester LE1 7RH.
Clarke, Howard B., BA, PhD, Room K104, Arts-Commerce-Law Building, University College, Dublin 4, Ireland.
Clarke, P. F., MA, PhD, St John's College, Cambridge CB2 1TP.
Clementi, Miss D., MA, DPhil, Flat 7, 43 Rutland Gate, London SW7 1BP.
Clemoes, Professor P. A. M., BA, PhD, Emmanuel College, Cambridge CB2 3AP.
Cliffe, J. T., BA, PhD, 263 Staines Road, Twickenham, Middx. TW2 5AY.

Clive, Professor J. L., PhD, 38 Fernald Drive, Cambridge, Mass. 02138, U.S.A.
Clough, C. H., MA, DPhil, FSA, School of History, The University, P.O. Box 147, Liverpool L69 3BX.
Cobb, H. S., MA, FSA, 1 Child's Way, London NW11.
Cobban, A. B., MA, PhD, School of History, The University, P.O. Box 147, Liverpool L69 3BX.
Cockburn, Professor J. S., LLB, LLM, PhD, History Dept, University of Maryland, College Park, Maryland 20742, U.S.A.
Cocks, E. J., MA, Middle Lodge, Ardingly, Haywards Heath, Sussex RH17 6TS.
Cohn, H. J., MA, DPhil, University of Warwick, Coventry CV4 7AL.
Cohn, Professor N., MA, DLitt, FBA, Orchard Cottage, Wood End, Ardeley, Herts. SG2 7AZ.
Cole, Maija J., MA, PhD, 117 Glen Parkway, Hamden, Conn. 06517, U.S.A.
Coleman, B. I., MA, PhD, Dept of History, The University, Exeter EX4 4QH.
Coleman, C. H. D., MA, Dept of History, University College London, Gower Street, London WC1E 6BT.
Coleman, Professor D. C., BSc(Econ.), PhD, LittD, FBA, Over Hall, Cavendish, Sudbury, Suffolk.
Coleman, Professor F. L., MA, PhD, Dept of Economics & Economic History, Rhodes University, P.O. Box 94, Grahamstown 6140, S. Africa.
Collier, W. O., MA, FSA, 34 Berwyn Road, Richmond, Surrey.
Collinge, J. M., BA, Institute of Historical Research, Senate House, Malet Street, London WC1E 7HU.
Collini, S. A., MA, PhD, Dept of History, The University, Falmer, Brighton, Sussex BN1 9QX.
Collins, B. W., MA, PhD, Dept of Modern History, The University, Glasgow G12 8QQ.
Collins, Mrs I., MA, BLitt, School of History, The University, P.O. Box 147, Liverpool L69 3BX.
Collinson, Professor P., MA, PhD, FBA, Dept of History, The University, Sheffield ST10 2TN.
Colvin, H. M., CBE, MA, FBA, St John's College, Oxford OX1 3JP.
Colyer, R. J., BSc, PhD, Inst. of Rural Sciences, University College of Wales, Aberystwyth, Dyfed.
Congreve, A. L., MA, FSA, Galleons Lap, Sissinghurst, Kent TN17 2JG.
Connell-Smith, Professor G. E., PhD, 7 Braids Walk, Kirkella, Hull, Yorks. HU10 7PA.
Connolly, Sean J., BA, DPhil, Dept of History, University of Ulster, Coleraine, Northern Ireland BT52 1SA.
Constantine, S., BA, DPhil, Dept of History, The University, Bailrigg, Lancaster LA1 4YG.
Contamine, Professor P., DèsL., 12 Villa Croix-Nivert, 75015 Paris, France.
Conway, Professor A. A., MA, University of Canterbury, Christchurch 1, New Zealand.
Cook, C. P., MA, DPhil, Dept of History, The Polytechnic of North London, Prince of Wales Road, London NW5 3LB.
Cooke, Professor, J. J., PhD., Dept of History, College of Liberal Arts, University of Mississippi, University, Miss. 38677, U.S.A.
Coolidge, Professor R. T., MA, BLitt, History Dept, Loyola Campus, Con-

cordia University, 7141 Sherbrooke Street West, Montreal, Quebec H4B 1R6, Canada.

Cooper, Janet M., MA, PhD, 7 Stonepath Drive, Hatfield Peverel, Chelmsford CM3 2LG.

Cope, Professor Esther S., PhD, Dept of History, Univ. of Nebraska, Lincoln, Neb. 68508, U.S.A.

Copley, A. R.H., MA, MPhil, Rutherford College, The University, Canterbury, Kent CT2 7NX.

Corfield, Penelope J., MA, PhD, Dept of History, Royal Holloway and Bedford New College, Egham, Surrey TW20 0EX.

Cornell, Professor Paul G., PhD, 202 Laurier Place, Waterloo, Ontario, Canada N2L 1K8.

Corner, D. J., BA, Dept of History, St Salvator's College, The University, St Andrews, Fife KY16 9AJ.

Cornford, Professor J. P., MA, The Brick House, Wicken Bonhunt, Saffron Walden, Essex CB11 3UG.

Cornwall, J. C. K., MA, 1 Orchard Close, Copford Green, Colchester, Essex.

Corson, J. C., MA, PhD, Mossrig, Lilliesleaf, Melrose, Roxburghshire.

Cosgrove, A. J., BA, PhD, Dept of Medieval History, University College, Dublin 4, Ireland.

Coss, P. R., BA, PhD, 20 Whitebridge Close, Whitebridge Grove, Gosforth, Newcastle upon Tyne NE3 2DN.

Costeloe, Professor M. P., BA, PhD, Dept of Hispanic and Latin American Studies, The University, 83 Woodland Road, Bristol BS8 1RJ.

Cowan, I. B., MA, PhD, Dept of History, University of Glasgow, Glasgow G12 8QQ.

Coward, B., BA, PhD, Dept of History, Birkbeck College, Malet Street, London WC1E 7HX.

Cowdrey, Rev. H. E. J., MA, St Edmund Hall, Oxford OX1 4AR.

Cowie, Rev. L. W., MA, PhD, 38 Stratton Road, Merton Park, London SW19 3JG.

Cowley, F. G., PhD, 17 Brookvale Road, West Cross, Swansea, W. Glam.

Cox, D. C., BA, PhD, 12 Oakfield Road, Copthorne, Shrewsbury SY3 8AA.

Craig, R. S., BSc(Econ), The Anchorage, Bay Hill, St Margarets Bay, nr Dover, Kent CT15 6DU.

Cramp, Professor Rosemary, MA, BLitt, FSA, Department of Archaeology, The Old Fulling Mill, The Banks, Durham.

Crampton, R. J., BA, PhD, Rutherford College, The University, Canterbury, Kent CT2 7NP.

Cranfield, L. R., Lot 2, Selby Avenue, Warrandyte, Victoria, Australia 3113.

Craton, Professor M. J., BA, MA, PhD, Dept of History, University of Waterloo, Waterloo, Ontario, Canada N2L 3G1.

Crawford, Patricia M., BA, MA, PhD, Dept of History, University of Western Australia, Nedlands, Western Australia 6009.

*Crawley, C. W., MA, 1 Madingley Road, Cambridge.

Cremona, His Hon Chief Justice Professor J. J., KM, DLitt, PhD, LLD, DrJur, 5 Victoria Gardens, Sliema, Malta.

Cressy, D. A., 231 West Sixth Street, Claremont, Calif. 91711, U.S.A.

Crimmin, Patricia K., MPhil, BA, Dept of History, Royal Holloway and Bedford New College, Egham, Surrey TW20 0EX.

Crisp, Professor Olga, BA, PhD, 'Zarya', 1 Millbrook, Esher, Surrey.

Croft, Pauline, MA, DPhil, Dept of History, Royal Holloway and Bedford New College, Egham, Surrey TW20 0EX.

Crombie, A. C., BSc, MA, PhD, Trinity College, Oxford OX1 3BH.
Cromwell, Miss V., MA, University of Sussex, Falmer, Brighton, Sussex BN1 9QX.
Crook, D., MA, PhD, Public Record Office, Chancery Lane, London WC2A 1LR.
Cross, Professor Claire, MA, PhD, Dept of History, University of York, York YO1 5DD.
Crossick, G. J., MA, PhD, Dept of History, University of Essex, Wivenhoe Park, Colchester CO4 3SQ.
Crouch, D. B., PhD, 17c St Johns Grove, London N19 5RW.
Crowder, Professor C. M. D., DPhil, Queen's University, Kingston, Ontario, Canada K7L 3N6.
Crowder, Professor M., MA, Dept of History, University of Botswana, P.B. 0022, Gaborone, Botswana.
Crowe, Miss S. E., MA, PhD, 112 Staunton Road, Headington, Oxford.
Cruickshank, C. G., MA, DPhil, 15 McKay Road, Wimbledon Common, London SW20.
Cruickshanks, Eveline G., PhD, 46 Goodwood Court, Devonshire Street, London W1N 1SL.
Cumming, Professor A., MA, DipMA, PGCE, PhD, Centre for Education Studies, University of New England, Armidale, Australia 2351.
Cumming, I., MEd, PhD, 672a South Titirangi Road, Titirangi, Auckland, New Zealand.
Cummins, Professor J. S., PhD, University College London, Gower Street, London WC1E 6BT.
Cumpston, Miss I. M., MA, DPhil, Birkbeck College, Malet Street, London WC1E 7HX.
Cunliffe, Professor M. F., MA, BLitt, DHL, Room 102, T Building, George Washington University, 2110 G. Street N.W., Washington, D.C., 20052, U.S.A.
Cunningham, Professor A. B., MA, PhD, Simon Fraser University, Burnaby 2, B.C., Canada.
Currie, C. R. J., MA, DPhil, Institute of Historical Research, Senate House, Malet Street, London WC1E 7HU.
Currie, R., MA, DPhil, Wadham College, Oxford OX1 3PN.
Curry, Anne E., BA, MA, PhD, 12 Melrose Avenue, Reading, Berkshire RG6 2BN.
Curtis, Professor L. Perry, Jr, PhD, Dept of History, Brown University, Providence, R.I. 02912, U.S.A.
*Cúttino, G. P., DPhil, FBA, FSA, 1270 University Dr. N. E., Atlanta, Ga. 30306, U.S.A.
Cuttler, S. H., BPhil, DPhil, 5051 Clanranald #302, Montreal, Quebec, Canada H3X 2S3.

*Dacre, Lord, MA, FBA, Peterhouse, Cambridge CB2 1RD.
Dakin, Professor D., MA, PhD, 20 School Road, Apperley, Gloucester GL19 4DJ.
DAUNTON, M. J., BA, PhD (*Hon. Treasurer*), Dept of History, University College London, Gower Street, London WC1E 6BT.
Davenport, Professor T. R. H., MA, PhD, Dept of History, Rhodes University, P.O. Box 94, Grahamstown 6140, South Africa.
Davenport-Hines, R. P. T., PhD, BA, 51 Elsham Road, London W14 8HD.
Davidson, R., MA, PhD, Dept of Economic and Social History, The University, 50 George Square, Edinburgh EH8 9JY.

Davies, C. S. L., MA, DPhil, Wadham College, Oxford OX1 3PN.
Davies, Canon E. T., BA, MA, 11 Tŷ Brith Gardens, Usk, Gwent.
Davies, I. N. R., MA, DPhil, 22 Rowland Close, Wolvercote, Oxford.
Davies, P. N., MA, PhD, Cmar, Croft Drive, Caldy, Wirral, Merseyside.
Davies, R. G., MA, PhD, Dept of History, The University, Manchester M13 9PL.
Davies, Professor R. R., BA, DPhil, University College of Wales, Dept of History, 1 Laura Place, Aberystwyth SY23 2AU.
Davies, Professor Wendy, BA, Dept of History, University College London, Gower Street, London WC1E 6BT.
*Davis, G. R. C., CBE, MA, DPhil, FSA, 214 Somerset Road, London SW19 5JE.
Davis, Professor J. C., Dept of History, Massey University, Palmerston North, New Zealand.
Davis, Professor R. H. C., MA, FBA, FSA, 349 Banbury Road, Oxford OX2 7PL.
Davis, Professor Richard W., Dept of History, Washington University, St Louis, Missouri 63130, U.S.A.
*Dawe, D. A., 46 Green Lane, Purley, Surrey.
Deane, Professor Phyllis M., MA, 4 Stukeley Close, Cambridge CB3 9LT.
*Deeley, Miss A. P., MA, 41 Linden Road, Bicester, Oxford.
de Hamel, C. F. R., BA, DPhil, FSA, Chase House, Perry's Chase, Greenstead Road, Ongar, Essex CM5 9LA.
de la Mare, Miss A. C., MA, PhD, Bodleian Library, Oxford.
Denham, E. W., MA, 27 The Drive, Northwood, Middx. HA6 1HW.
Dennis, P. J., MA, PhD, Dept of History, Royal Military College, Duntroon, A.C.T. 2600, Australia.
Denton, J. H., BA, PhD, Dept of History, The University, Manchester M13 9PL.
Devine, T. M., BA, Viewfield Cottage, 55 Burnbank Road, Hamilton, Strathclyde Region.
Dewey, P. E., BA, PhD, Dept of History, Royal Holloway and Bedford New College, Egham Hill, Egham, Surrey TW20 0EX.
DICKENS, Professor A. G., CMG, MA, DLit, DLitt, LittD, FBA, FSA, Institute of Historical Research, University of London, Senate House, London WC1E 7HU.
Dickinson, Professor H. T., MA, PhD, Dept of Modern History, The University, Edinburgh EH8 9YL.
Dickinson, Rev. J. C., MA, DLitt, FSA, Yew Tree Cottage, Barngarth, Cartmel, South Cumbria.
Dickson, P. G. M., MA, DPhil, St Catherine's College, Oxford, OX1 3UJ.
Dilks, Professor D. N., BA, Dept of International History, The University, Leeds LS2 9JT.
Dilworth, Rev. G. M., OSB, MA, PhD, Columba House, 16 Drummond Place, Edinburgh EH3 6PL.
Dinwiddy, J. R., PhD, Dept of History, Royal Holloway and Bedford New College, Egham Hill, Egham, Surrey TW20 0EX.
Ditchfield, G. McC, BA, PhD, Darwin College, University of Kent, Canterbury, Kent CT2 7NY.
Dobson, Professor R. B., MA, DPhil, Dept of History, The University, York YO1 5DD.
Dockrill, M. L., MA, BSc(Econ), PhD, King's College London, Strand, London WC2R 2LS.

*Dodwell, Miss B., MA, The University, Reading RG6 2AH.
Dodwell, Professor C. R., MA, PhD, FSA, History of Art Department, The University, Manchester M13 9PL.
Don Peter, The Rt Revd Monsignor W. L. A., MA, PhD, Aquinas University College, Colombo 8, Sri Lanka.
Donahue, Professor Charles, Jr, AB, LLB, Dept of Law, Harvard University, Cambridge, Mass. 02138, U.S.A.
*DONALDSON, Professor G., MA, PhD, DLitt, DLitt, FRSE, FBA, 6 Pan Ha', Dysart, Fife KY1 2TL.
Donaldson, Professor P. S., MA, PhD, Dept of Humanities, 14n-422, Massachusetts Institute of Technology, Cambridge, Mass. 02139, U.S.A.
*Donaldson-Hudson, Miss R., BA, (address unknown).
Donoughue, Lord, MA, DPhil, 7 Brookfield Park, London NW5 1ES.
Dore, R. N., MA, Holmrook, 19 Chapel Lane, Hale Barns, Altrincham, Cheshire WA15 0AB.
Dow, Frances D., MA, DPhil, Dept of History, University of Edinburgh, George Square, Edinburgh EH8 9JY.
Downer, L. J., MA, LLB, 29 Roebuck Street, Red Hill, Canberra, Australia 2601.
Doyle, A. I., MA, PhD, University College, The Castle, Durham.
Doyle, Professor W., MA, DPhil, Dept of History, The University, 13-15 Woodland Road, Bristol BS8 1TB.
Driver, J. T., MA, BLitt, PhD, 25 Abbot's Grange, Chester CH2 1AJ.
*Drus, Miss E., MA, 18 Brampton Tower, Bassett Avenue, Southampton SO1 7FB.
Duckham, Professor B. F., MA, Dept of History, St David's University College, Lampeter, Dyfed SA48 7ED.
Duffy, Michael, MA, DPhil, Dept of History and Archaeology, The University, Exeter EX4 4QH.
Duggan, Anne J., BA, PhD, Dept of History, Queen Mary College, Mile End Road, London E1 4NS.
Duggan, C., PhD, King's College London, Strand, London WC2R 2LS.
Dugmore, The Rev. Professor C. W., DD, Thame Cottage, The Street, Puttenham, Guildford, Surrey GU3 1AT.
Duke, A. C., MA, Dept of History, The University, Southampton SO9 5NH.
Dumville, D. N., MA, PhD, Dept of Anglo-Saxon, Norse and Celtic, 9 West Road, Cambridge CB3 9DP.
Dunbabin, Jean H., MA, DPhil, St Anne's College, Oxford OX2 6HS.
Dunbabin, J. P. D., MA, St Edmund Hall, Oxford OX1 4AR.
Duncan, Professor A. A. M., MA, The University, Dept of History, Glasgow G12 8QQ.
Dunn, Professor R. S., PhD, Dept of History, The College, University of Pennsylvania, Philadelphia, Pa. 19104, U.S.A.
Dunning, R. W., BA, PhD, FSA, Musgrove Manor East, Barton Close, Taunton TA1 4RU.
Durack, Mrs I. A., MA, PhD, University of Western Australia, Nedlands, Western Australia 6009.
Durey, M. J., BA, DPhil, School of Social Inquiry, Murdoch University, Perth 6150, Western Australia.
Durie, A. J., MA, PhD, Dept of Economic History, Edward Wright Building, The University, Aberdeen AB9 2TY.
Durkan, J., MA, PhD, Dept of Scottish History, The University, Glasgow G12 8QH.

Durston, C. G., MA, PhD, 49 Percy Street, Oxford.
Dutton, D. J., BA, PhD, School of History, The University, P.O. Box 147, Liverpool L69 3BX.
Dyer, C. C., BA, PhD, School of History, The University, P.O. Box 363, Birmingham B15 2TT.
Dykes, D. W., MA, Cherry Grove, Welsh St Donats, nr Cowbridge, Glam. CF7 7SS.
Dyson, Professor K. H. F., BSc(Econ), MSc(Econ), PhD, Undergraduate School of European Studies, The University, Bradford BD7 1DP.

Earle, P., BSc(Econ), PhD, Dept of Economic History, London School of Economics, Houghton Street, London WC2A 2AE.
Eastwood, Rev. C. C., PhD, Heathview, Monks Lane, Audlem, Cheshire CW3 0HP.
Eckles, Professor R. B., PhD, Apt 2, 251 Brahan Blvd., San Antonio, Texas 78215, U.S.A.
Edbury, P. W., MA, PhD, Dept of History, University College, P.O. Box 78, Cardiff CF1 1XL.
Ede, J. R., CB, MA, Palfreys, East Street, Drayton, Langport, Somerset TA10 0JZ.
Edmonds, Professor E. L., MA, PhD, University of Prince Edward Island, Charlottetown, Prince Edward Island, Canada.
Edwards, F. O., SJ, BA, FSA, 114 Mount Street, London W1Y 6AH.
Edwards, J. H., MA, DPhil, School of History, The University, P.O. Box 363, Birmingham B15 2TT.
Edwards, O. D., BA, Dept of History, William Robertson Building, The University, George Square, Edinburgh EH8 9YL.
Edwards, Professor R. W. D., MA, PhD, DLitt, 21 Brendan Road, Donnybrook, Dublin 4, Ireland.
Ehrman, J. P. W., MA, FBA, FSA, The Mead Barns, Taynton, Nr Burford, Oxfordshire OX8 5UH.
Eisenstein, Professor Elizabeth L., PhD, 82 Kalorama Circle N.W., Washington D.C. 20008, U.S.A.
Eldridge, C. C., PhD, Dept of History, Saint David's University College, Lampeter, Dyfed SA48 7ED.
Eley, G. H., BA, DPhil, MA, Dept of History, University of Michigan, Ann Arbor, Michigan 48109, U.S.A.
Elliott, Professor J. H., MA, PhD, FBA, The Institute for Advanced Studies, Princeton, New Jersey 08540, U.S.A.
Elliott, Marianne, BA, DPhil, Dept of History, The University, P.O. Box 147, Liverpool L69 3BX.
Ellis, G. J., MA, DPhil, Hertford College, Oxford OX1 3BW.
Ellis, R. H., MA, FSA, Cloth Hill, 6 The Mount, London NW3.
Ellis, S. G., BA, MA, PhD, Dept of History, University College, Galway, Ireland.
Ellsworth, Professor Edward W., AB, AM, PhD, 27 Englewood Avenue, Brookline, Mass. 02146, U.S.A.
Ellul, M., BArch, DipArch, 'Pauline', 55 Old Railway Road, Birkirkara, Malta.
Elrington, C. R., MA, FSA, Institute of Historical Research, Senate House, London WC1E 7HU.
ELTON, Sir Geoffrey, MA, PhD, LittD, DLitt, DLitt, DLit, FBA, 30 Millington Road, Cambridge CB3 9HP.
Elvin, L., FSA, FRSA, 10 Almond Avenue, Swanpool, Lincoln LN6 0HB.

*Emmison, F. G., MBE, PhD, DUniv, FSA, 8 Coppins Close, Chelmsford, Essex CM2 6AY.

Emsley, C., BA, MLitt, Arts Faculty, The Open University, Walton Hall, Milton Keynes MK7 6AA.

Erickson, Charlotte, J., PhD, 8 High Street, Chesterton, Cambridge CB4 1NG.

*Erith, E. J., Shurlock House, Shurlock Row, Berkshire.

Erskine, Mrs A. M., MA, BLitt, FSA, 44 Birchy Barton Hill, Exeter EX1 3EX.

Evans, Mrs A. K. B., PhD, FSA, White Lodge, 25 Knighton Grange Road, Leicester LE2 2LF.

Evans, E. J., MA, PhD, Dept of History, Furness College, University of Lancaster, Bailrigg, Lancaster LA1 4YG.

Evans, Gillian R., PhD, Sidney Sussex College, Cambridge CB2 3HU.

Evans, R. J., MA, DPhil, School of European Studies, University of East Anglia, Norwich NR4 7TJ.

Evans, R. J. W., MA, PhD, Brasenose College, Oxford OX1 4AJ.

Everitt, Professor A. M., MA, PhD, The University, Leicester LE1 7RH.

Eyck, Professor U. F. J., MA, BLitt, Dept of History, University of Calgary, Alberta T2N IN4, Canada.

Fage, Professor J. D., MA, PhD, Centre of West African Studies, The University, Birmingham B15 2TT.

Fairs, G. L., MA, Thornton House, Bear Street, Hay-on-Wye, Hereford HR3 5AN.

Falkus, M. E., BSc(Econ), Dept of History, London School of Economics, Houghton Street, London WC2A 2AE.

Farmer, D. F. H., BLitt, FSA, The University, Reading RG6 2AH.

Farr, M. W., MA, FSA, 12 Emscote Road, Warwick.

Fell, Professor C. E., MA, Dept of English, The University, Nottingham NG7 2RD.

Fellows-Jensen, Gillian M., BA, PhD, Københavns Universitets, Institut For Navneforskning, Njalsgade 80, DK-2300 København S, Denmark.

Fenlon, Revd D. B., BA, PhD, St Edmunds, 21 Westgate Street, Bury St Edmunds, Suffolk IP33 1QG.

Fenn, Rev. R. W. D., MA, BD, FSAScot, The Ditch, Bradnor View, Kington, Herefordshire.

Fennell, Professor J., MA, PhD, 8 Canterbury Road, Oxford OX2 6LU.

Ferguson, Professor A. B., PhD, Dept of History, 6727 College Station, Duke University, Durham, N.C. 27708, U.S.A.

Fernandez-Armesto, F. F. R., DPhil, River View, Headington Hill, Oxford.

Feuchtwanger, E. J., MA, PhD, Highfield House, Dean Sparsholt, nr Winchester, Hants.

Fieldhouse, Professor D. K., MA, Jesus College, Cambridge CB5 8BL.

Finer, Professor S. E., MA, All Souls College, Oxford OX1 4AL.

Fines, J., MA, PhD, 119 Parklands Road, Chichester.

Finlayson, G. B. A. M., MA, BLitt, 11 Burnhead Road, Glasgow G43 2SU.

Fisher, Professor Alan W., PhD, Dept of History, Michigan State University, East Lansing, Michigan 48824, U.S.A.

Fisher, D. J. V., MA, Jesus College, Cambridge CB3 9AD.

Fisher, Professor F. J., MA, London School of Economics, Houghton Street, London WC2A 2AE.

Fisher, F. N., Holmelea, Cromford Road, Wirksworth, Derby DE4 4FR.

Fisher, H. E. Stephen, BSc, PhD, Dept of History, The University, Exeter EX4 4RJ.

Fisher, J. R., BA, MPhil, PhD, School of History, The University, P.O. Box 147, Liverpool L69 3BX.

Fisher, R. M., MA, PhD, Dept of History, University of Queensland, St Lucia, Queensland, Australia 4067.

Fisher, Professor S. N., PhD, 6000 Riverside Drive, B333, Dublin, Ohio 43017-1494, U.S.A.

Fishwick, Professor D., MA, DLitt, Dept of Classics, Humanities Centre, University of Alberta, Edmonton, Alberta, Canada T6G 2E6.

Fitch, Dr M. F. B., FSA, 37 Avenue de Montoie, 1007 Lausanne, Switzerland.

Fitzpatrick, M. H., PhD, 'Garreg-Wen', Bronant, Aberystwyth, Dyfed SY23 4TQ.

Fletcher, A. J., MA, 16 Southbourne Road, Sheffield S10 2QN.

*Fletcher, The Rt Hon. The Lord, PC, BA, LLD, FSA, 51 Charlbury Road, North Oxford OX2 6UX.

Fletcher, R. A., MA, Dept of History, The University, York YO1 5DD.

Flint, Professor J. E., MA, PhD, Dalhousie University, Halifax, Nova Scotia B3H 3J5, Canada.

Flint, Valerie I. J., MA, DPhil, Dept of History, The University, Private Bag, Auckland, New Zealand.

Floud, Professor R. C., MA, DPhil, Dept of History, Birkbeck College, Malet Street, London WC1E 7HX.

Fogel, Professor Robert W., PhD, Center for Population Economics, University of Chicago, 1101 East 58th Street, Chicago, Illinois 60637, U.S.A.

Foot, M. R. D., MA, BLitt, 45 Countess Road, London NW5 2XH.

Forbes, D., MA, 89 Gilbert Road, Cambridge.

Forbes, Thomas R., BA, PhD, FSA, 86 Ford Street, Hamden, Conn. 06517, U.S.A.

Ford, W. K., BA, 48 Harlands Road, Haywards Heath, West Sussex RH16 1LS.

Forster, G. C. F., BA, FSA, School of History, The University, Leeds LS2 9JT.

Foster, Professor Elizabeth R., AM, PhD, 205 Strafford Avenue, Wayne, Pa. 19087, U.S.A.

Foster, R. F., MA, PhD, Dept of History, Birkbeck College, Malet Street, London WC1E 7HX.

Fowler, Professor K. A., BA, PhD, 2 Nelson Street, Edinburgh 3.

Fowler, Professor P. J., MA, PhD, Dept of Archaeology, The University, Newcastle upon Tyne NE1 7RU.

Fox, J. P., BSc(Econ), MSc(Econ), PhD, 98 Baring Road, London SE12 0PT.

Fox, L., OBE, DL, LHD, MA, FSA, FRSL, Silver Birches, 27 Welcombe Road, Stratford-upon-Avon, Warwickshire.

Fox, R., MA, DPhil, The University, Bailrigg, Lancaster LA1 4YG.

Frame, R. F., MA, PhD, Dept of History, The University, 43 North Bailey, Durham DH1 3HP.

Franklin, M. J., MA, PhD, Wolfson College, Cambridge CB3 9BB.

Franklin, R. M., The Corner House, Eton College, Windsor, Berkshire SL4 6DB.

Fraser, Lady Antonia, 52 Campden Hill Square, London W8.

*Fraser, Miss C. M., PhD, 39 King Edward Road, Tynemouth, Tyne and Wear NE30 2RW.

Fraser, D., BA, MA, PhD, 117 Alwoodley Lane, Leeds, LS17 7PN.
Fraser, Professor Peter, MA, PhD, The Priory, Old Mill Lane, Marnhull, Dorset DT10 1JX.
Freeden, M. S., DPhil, Mansfield College, Oxford OX1 3TF.
French, D. W., BA, PhD, Dept of History, University College London, Gower Street, London WC1E 6BT.
Frend, Professor W. H. C., MA, DPhil, DD, FBA, FRSE, FSA, The Rectory, Barnwell, nr Peterborough, Northants. PE8 5PG.
Fritz, Professor Paul S., BA, MA, PhD, Dept of History, McMaster University, Hamilton, Ontario, Canada.
Fryde, Professor E. B., DPhil, Preswylfa, Trinity Road, Aberystwyth, Dyfed.
Fryde, Natalie M., BA, DrPhil, Schloss Grünsberg, D-8503 Altdorf, Germany.
*Fryer, Professor C. E., MA, PhD (address unknown).
Fryer, Professor W. R., BLitt, MA, 68 Grove Avenue, Chilwell, Beeston, Notts. NG9 4DX.
Frykenberg, Professor R. E., MA, PhD, 1840 Chadbourne Avenue, Madison, Wis. 53705, U.S.A.
Fuidge, Miss N. M., 13 Havercourt, Haverstock Hill, London NW3.
*Furber, Professor H., MA, PhD, c/o History Department, University of Pennsylvania, Philadelphia, Pa., U.S.A.
Fussell, G. E., DLitt, 3 Nightingale Road, Horsham, West Sussex RH12 2NW.
Fyrth, H. J., BSc(Econ), 72 College Road, Dulwich, London SE21.

Gabriel, Professor A. L., PhD, FMAA, CFIF, CFBA, P.O. Box 578, University of Notre Dame, Notre Dame, Indiana 46556, U.S.A.
*Galbraith, Professor J. S., BS, MA, PhD, University of California, Los Angeles, Calif. 90024, U.S.A.
Gale, Professor H. P. P., OBE, PhD, 38 Brookwood Avenue, London SW13.
Gale, W. K. V., 19 Ednam Road, Goldthorn Park, Wolverhampton WV4 5BL.
Gann, L. H., MA, BLitt, DPhil, Hoover Institution, Stanford University, Stanford, Calif. 94305, U.S.A.
Garnett, G., MA, St John's College, Cambridge CB2 1TP.
Gash, Professor N., MA, BLitt, FBA, Old Gatehouse, Portway, Langport, Somerset TA10 0NQ.
Gee, E. A., MA, DPhil, FSA, 28 Trentholme Drive, The Mount, York YO2 2DG.
Geggus, D. P., MA, DPhil, Dept of History, University of Florida, Gainesville, Florida 32611, U.S.A.
Genet, J.-Ph., Agrégé d'Histoire, 147 Avenue Parmentier, Paris 75010, France.
Gentles, Professor I., BA, MA, PhD, Dept of History, Glendon College, 2275 Bayview Avenue, Toronto M4N 3M6, Canada.
Gerlach, Professor D. R., MA, PhD, University of Akron, Akron, Ohio 44325, U.S.A.
Gibbs, G. C., MA, Birkbeck College, Malet Street, London WC1E 7HX.
Gibbs, Professor N. H., MA, DPhil, All Souls College, Oxford OX1 4AL.
Gibson, J. S. W., FSA, Harts Cottage, Church Hanborough, Oxford OX7 2AB.
Gibson, Margaret T., MA, DPhil, School of History, The University, P.O. Box 147, Liverpool L69 3 BX.
Gifford, Miss D. H., PhD, FSA, 1 Pondtail Road, Fleet, nr Aldershot, Hants. GU13 9JW.
Gilbert, Professor Bentley B., PhD, Dept of History, University of Illinois at Chicago Circle, Box 4348, Chicago, Ill. 60680, U.S.A.

Gildea, R. N., MA, DPhil, Merton College, Oxford OX1 4JD.
Gilkes, R. K., MA, 75 Fouracre Road, Downend, Bristol.
Gilley, S. W., BA, DPhil, Dept of Theology, University of Durham, Abbey House, Palace Green, Durham DH1 3RS.
Gillingham, J. B., MA, London School of Economics, Houghton Street, London WC2A 2AE.
Ginter, Professor D. E., AM, PhD, Dept of History, Sir George Williams University, Montreal 107, Canada.
de Giorgi, Roger, Development House, Floriana, Malta.
Girtin, T., MA, Butter Field House, Church Street, Old Isleworth, Middx.
Gleave, Group Capt. T. P., CBE, RAF (ret.), Willow Bank, River Gardens. Bray-on-Thames, Berks.
*Glover, Professor R. G., MA, PhD, 2937 Tudor Avenue, Victoria, B.C. V8N IM2 Canada.
*Godber, Miss A. J., MA, FSA, Mill Lane Cottage, Willington, Bedford.
*Godfrey, Professor J. L., MA, PhD, 231 Hillcrest Circle, Chapel Hill, N.C., U.S.A.
Goldie, Mark, MA, PhD, Churchill College, Cambridge CB3 0DS.
Golding, B. J., MA, DPhil, Dept of History, The University, Southampton SO9 5NH.
Goldsmith, Professor M. M., PhD, Dept of Politics, University of Exeter, Exeter EX4 4RJ.
Gollin, Professor A., DLitt, University of California, Dept of History, Santa Barbara, Calif. 93106, U.S.A.
Gooch, John, BA, PhD, Dept of History, The University, Bailrigg, Lancaster LA1 4YG.
Goodman, A. E., MA, BLitt, Dept of Medieval History, The University, Edinburgh EH8 9YL.
Goodspeed, Professor D. J., BA, 164 Victoria Street, Niagara-on-the-Lake, Ontario, Canada.
*Gopal, Professor S., MA, DPhil, 30 Edward Elliot Road, Mylapore, Madras, India.
Gordon, Professor P., BSc(Econ), MSc(Econ), PhD, 241 Kenton Road, Kenton, Harrow HA3 0HJ.
Goring, J. J., MA, PhD, 31 Houndean Rise, Lewes, East Sussex BN7 1EQ.
Gorton, L. J., MA, 41 West Hill Avenue, Epsom, Surrey.
Gosden, Professor P. H. J. H. MA, PhD, School of Education, The University, Leeds LS2 9JT.
Gough, Professor Barry M., PhD, History Dept, Wilfrid Laurier University, Waterloo, Ontario, Canada N2L 3C5.
Gowing, Professor Margaret, CBE, MA, DLitt, BSc(Econ), FBA, Linacre College, Oxford OX1 1SY.
*Graham, Professor G.S., MA, PhD, DLitt, LLD, Hobbs Cottage, Beckley, Rye, Sussex.
Graham-Campbell, J. A., MA, PhD, FSA, Dept of History, University College London, Gower Street, London WC1E 6BT.
Gransden, Antonia, MA, PhD, DLitt, FSA, Dept of History, The University, Nottingham NG7 2RD.
Grant, A., BA, DPhil, Dept of History, The University, Bailrigg, Lancaster LA1 4YG.
Grattan-Kane, P., 12 St John's Close, Helston, Cornwall.
Graves, Professor Edgar B., PhD, LLD, LHD, 318 College Hill Road, Clinton, New York 13323, USA.

Gray, Professor J. R., MA, PhD, School of Oriental and African Studies, University of London, London WC1E 7HP.

Gray, J. W., MA, Dept of Modern History, The Queen's University of Belfast, Belfast BT7 1NN, N. Ireland.

Gray, Miss M., MA, BLitt, 68 Dorchester Road, Garstang, Preston PR3 1HH.

Greaves, Professor Richard L., PhD, 910 Shadowlawn Drive, Tallahassee, Florida 32312, U.S.A.

Greaves, Mrs R. L., PhD, 1920 Hillview Road, Lawrence, Kansas 66044, U.S.A.

Green, I. M., MA, DPhil, Dept of Modern History, The Queen's University of Belfast, Belfast BT7 1NN, N. Ireland.

Green, Judith A., BA, DPhil, Dept of Modern History, The Queen's University of Belfast, Belfast BT7 1NN, N. Ireland.

Green, Professor Thomas A., BA, PhD, JD, Legal Research Building, University of Michigan Law School, Ann Arbor, Michigan 48109, U.S.A.

Green, Rev. V. H. H., MA, DD, Lincoln College, Oxford OX1 3DR.

Greene, Professor Jack P., Dept of History, Johns Hopkins University, Baltimore, Md. 21218, U.S.A.

Greengrass, M., MA, DPhil, Dept of History, The University, Sheffield S10 2TN.

Greenhill, B. J., CB, CMG, DPh, FSA, West Boetheric Farmhouse, St Dominic, Saltash, Cornwall PL12 6SZ.

Greenslade, M. W., JP, MA, FSA, 20 Garth Road, Stafford ST17 9JD.

Greenway, D. E., MA, PhD, Institute of Historical Research, Senate House, Malet Street, London WC1E 7HU.

Gregg, E., MA, PhD, Dept of History, University of South Carolina, Columbia, S.C. 29208, U.S.A.

Grenville, Professor J. A. S., PhD, University of Birmingham, P.O. Box 363, Birmingham B15 2TT.

Gresham, C. A., BA, DLitt, FSA, Bryn-y-deryn, Criccieth, Gwynedd, LL52 0HR.

GRIERSON, Professor P., MA, LittD, FBA, FSA, Gonville and Caius College, Cambridge CB2 1TA.

Grieve, Miss H. E. P., BA, 153 New London Road, Chelmsford, Essex.

Griffiths, Professor R. A., PhD, University College, Singleton Park, Swansea SA2 8PP.

Grimble, I., MA, PhD, 10 Cumberland Road, London SW13.

Grisbrooke, W. J., MA, Jokers, Bailey Street, Castle Acre, King's Lynn, Norfolk PE32 2AG.

*Griscom, Rev. Acton, MA (address unknown).

Gruner, Professor Wolf D., DrPhil, DrPhil. Habil, Pralleweg 7, 2000 Hamburg 67 (Volksdorf), West Germany.

Guth, Professor D. J., Faculty of Law, University of British Columbia, Vancouver, B.C., Canada V6T 1Y1.

Guy, J. A., PhD, Dept of History, The University, Wills Memorial Building, Queens Road, Bristol BS8 1RJ.

HABAKKUK, Sir John (H.), MA, FBA, Jesus College, Oxford OX1, 3DW.

Haber, Professor F. C., PhD, 3110 Wisconsin Avenue NW, #904, Washington, D.C. 20016, U.S.A.

Hackett, Rev. M. B., OSA, BA, PhD, Curia Generalizia Agostiniana, Via del S. Uffizio 25, 00193 Rome, Italy.

Hackmann, Willem D., DPhil, Museum of the History of Science, University of Oxford, Broad Street, Oxford OX1 3AZ.

Haffenden, P. S., PhD, 4 Upper Dukes Drive, Meads, Eastbourne, East Sussex BN20 7XT.

Haigh, C. A., MA, PhD, Christ Church, Oxford OX1 1DP.

Haight, Mrs M. Jackson, PhD, 3 Wolger Road, Mosman, N.S.W. 2088, Australia.

Haines, R. M., MA, MLitt, DPhil, FSA, 20 Luttrell Avenue, London SW15 6PF.

Hainsworth, D. R., MA, PhD, University of Adelaide, Dept of History, North Terrace, Adelaide, South Australia 5001.

Hair, Professor P. E. H., MA, DPhil, School of History, The University, P.O. Box 147, Liverpool L69 3BX.

Hale, Professor J. R., MA, FBA, FSA, University College London, Gower Street, London WC1E 6BT.

Haley, Professor K. H. D., MA, BLitt, 15 Haugh Lane, Sheffield S11 9SA.

Hall, Professor A. R., MA, PhD, DLitt, FBA, 14 Ball Lane, Tackley, Oxford OX5 3AG.

Hall, B., MA, PhD, FSA, DD, 2 Newton House, Newton St Cyres, Devon EX5 5BL.

Hallam, Elizabeth M., BA, PhD, Public Record Office, Chancery Lane, London WC2A 1LR.

Hallam, Professor H. E., MA, PhD, University of Western Australia, Nedlands 6009, Western Australia.

Hamer, Professor D. A., MA, DPhil, History Dept, Victoria University of Wellington, Private Bag, Wellington, New Zealand.

Hamilton, B., BA, PhD, The University, Nottingham NG7 2RD.

Hammersley, G. F., BA, PhD, University of Edinburgh, William Robertson Building, George Square, Edinburgh EH8 9JY.

Hamnett, B. R., BA, MA, PhD, Dept of History, University of Strathclyde, McLance Building, 16 Richmond Street, Glasgow G1 1QX.

Hampson, Professor N., MA, Ddel'U, 305 Hull Road, York YO1 3LB.

Hand, Professor G. J., MA, DPhil, Faculty of Law, University of Birmingham, P.O. Box 363, Birmingham B15 2TT.

Handford, M. A., MA, MSc, 6 Spa Lane, Hinckley, Leicester LE10 1JB.

Hanham, H. J., MA, PhD, The Croft, Bailrigg Lane, Bailrigg, Lancaster LA1 4XP.

Harcourt, Freda, PhD, Dept of History, Queen Mary College, Mile End Road, London E1 4NS.

Harding, Professor A., MA, BLitt, School of History, The University, P.O. Box 147, Liverpool L69 3BX.

Harding, The Hon. Mr Justice H. W., BA, LLD, FSA, 39 Annunciation Street, Sliema, Malta.

Haren, M. J., DPhil, 5 Marley Lawn, Dublin 16, Ireland.

Harfield, Major A. G., BEM, 19 Grove Road, Barton-on-Sea, Hampshire BH25 7DJ.

Hargreaves, Professor J. D., MA, 'Balcluain', Raemoir Road, Banchory, Kincardineshire.

Harkness, Professor D. W., MA, PhD, Dept of Irish History, The Queen's University, Belfast BT7 1NN, N. Ireland.

Harman, Rev. L. W., 72 Westmount Road, London SE9.

Harper Marjory-Ann D., MA, PhD, Silverdale, Disblair, Newmachar, Aberdeen AB5 0RN.

Harper-Bill, C., BA, PhD, 15 Cusack Close, Strawberry Hill, Twickenham, Middlesex.

Harris, B. E., MA, PhD, 25 Platts Lane, Tarvin, Chester CH3 8LH.

Harris, G., MA, 4 Lancaster Drive, London NW3.
Harris, Mrs J. F., BA, PhD, 30 Charlbury Road, Oxford OX1 3UJ.
Harris, Professor J. R., MA, PhD, The University, P.O. Box 363, Birmingham B15 2TT.
Harrison, B. H., MA, DPhil, Corpus Christi College, Oxford OX1 4JF.
Harrison, C. J., BA, PhD, The University, Keele, Staffs. ST5 5BG.
Harrison, Professor Royden, MA, DPhil, 4 Wilton Place, Sheffield S10 2BT.
Harriss, G. L., MA, DPhil, FSA, Magdalen College, Oxford OX1 4AU.
Hart, C. J. R., MA, MB, DLitt, Goldthorns, Stilton, Cambs. PE7 3RH.
Harte, N. B., BSc(Econ), Dept of History, University College London, Gower Street, London WC1E 6BT.
Hartley, T. E., BA, PhD, Dept of History, The University, Leicester LE1 7RH.
Harvey, Miss B. F., MA, BLitt, FBA, Somerville College, Oxford OX2 6HD.
Harvey, Margaret M., MA, DPhil, St Aidan's College, Durham DH1 3LJ.
Harvey, Professor P. D. A., MA, DPhil, FSA, Dept of History, The University, Durham DH1 3EX.
Harvey, Sally P. J., MA, PhD, Sint Hubertuslaan 7, 1980 Tervuren, Brussels, Belgium.
Haskell, Professor F. J., MA, FBA, Trinity College, Oxford OX1 3BH.
Haskins, Professor G. L., AB, LLB, JD, MA, University of Pennsylvania, The Law School, 3400 Chestnut Street, Philadelphia, Pa. 19104 U.S.A.
Haslam, Group Captain E. B., MA, RAF (retd), 27 Denton Road, Wokingham, Berks. RG11 2DX.
Haslam, Jonathan G., BSc(Econ), MLitt, PhD, 1610c Beekman Place NW, Washington, D.C., 20009, U.S.A.
Hasler, Peter W., BA, MA, History of Parliament Trust, Institute of Historical Research, 34 Tavistock Square, London WC1H 9EZ.
Hassall, W. O., MA, DPhil, FSA, The Manor House, 26 High Street, Wheatley, Oxford OX9 1XX.
Hast, Adele, PhD, NORC, University of Chicago, 6030 South Ellis, Chicago, Illinois 60637, U.S.A.
Hatcher, M. J., BSc(Econ), PhD, Corpus Christi College, Cambridge CB2 1RH.
Hatley, V. A., BA, ALA, 6 The Crescent, Northampton NN1 4SB.
Hatton, Professor Ragnhild M., PhD, Cand.Mag(Oslo), Dr.h.c., 49 Campden Street, London W8.
Havighurst, Professor A. F., MA, PhD, 11 Blake Field, Amherst, Mass. 01002, U.S.A.
Havinden, M. A., MA, BLitt, Dept of Economic History, Amory Building, The University, Exeter EX4 4QH.
Havran, Professor M. J., MA, PhD, Corcoran Dept of History, Randall Hall, University of Virginia, Charlottesville, Va. 22903, U.S.A.
HAY, Professor D., MA, DLitt, FBA, FRSE, Dr. h.c. Tours, 31 Fountainville Road, Edinburgh EH9 2LN.
Hayes, P. M., MA, DPhil, Keble College, Oxford OX1 3PG.
Hayter, A. J., BA, PhD, Chase House, Mursley, N. Bucks. MK17 0RT.
Hayton, D. W., BA, DPhil, 8 Baker Street, Ampthill, Bedford MK45 2QE.
Hazlehurst, Cameron, BA, DPhil, FRSL, 8 Hunter Street, Yarralumla, A.C.T. 2600, Australia.
Heal, Mrs Felicity, PhD, Jesus College, Oxford OX1 3DW.
Hearder, Professor H., BA, PhD, University College, P.O. Box 78, Cardiff CF1 1XL.

Heath, P., MA, Dept of History, The University Hull HU6 7RX.
Heathcote, T. A., BA, PhD, Cheyne Cottage, Birch Drive, Hawley, Camberley, Surrey.
Heesom, A. J., MA, Dept of History, The University, 43 North Bailey, Durham DH1 3HP.
Hellmuth, Eckhart H., PhD, German Historical Institute, 17 Bloomsbury Square, London WC1A 2LP.
Helmholz, R. H., PhD, LLB, The Law School, University of Chicago, 1111 East 60th Street, Chicago, Ill. 60637, U.S.A.
Hembry, Mrs P. M., BA, PhD, Pleasant Cottage, Crockerton, Warminster, Wilts. BA12 8AJ.
Hempton, D. N., BA, PhD, 57 Gilnahirk Park, Belfast, N. Ireland BT5 7DY.
Hendy, M. F., MA, Dept of History, The University, P.O. Box 363, Birmingham B15 2TT.
Hennessy, Professor C. A. M., MA, DPhil, Dept of History, University of Warwick, Coventry CV4 7AL.
Henning, Professor B. D., PhD, History of Parliament, 34 Tavistock Square, London WC1H 9EZ.
Hennock, Professor E. P., MA, PhD, School of History, University of Liverpool, P.O. Box 147, Liverpool L69 3BX.
Henstock, A. J. M., BA, Nottinghamshire Record Office, County House, Nottingham NG1 1HR.
Heppell, Muriel, BA, MA, PhD, 97 Eton Place, Eton College Road, London NW3 2DB.
Herde, Professor Peter, PhD, Cranachstr. 7, 8755 Alzenau, F.R. of Germany.
Herrup, Cynthia B., PhD, MA, BSJ, Dept of History, 6727 College Station, Duke University, Durham, N.C. 27708, U.S.A.
Hexter, Professor J. H., PhD, Dept of History, Washington University, St Louis, Missouri, U.S.A.
Hey, D. G., MA, PhD, Division of Continuing Education, The University, Sheffield S10 2TN.
Hicks, M. A., BA, MA, DPhil, King Alfred's College, Winchester SO22 4NR.
Higham, R. A., BA, PhD, Dept of History and Archaeology, University of Exeter, Queen's Drive, Exeter.
Highfield, J. R. L., MA, DPhil, Merton College, Oxford OX1 4JD.
Hill, B. W., BA, PhD, School of English and American Studies, University of East Anglia, Norwich NR4 7TJ.
Hill, J. E. C., MA, DLitt, FBA, Woodway, Sibford Ferris, nr Banbury, Oxfordshire OX15 5RA.
Hill, Professor L. M., AB, MA, PhD, 5066 Berean Lane, Irvine, Calif. 92664, U.S.A.
*Hill, Miss M. C., MA, Crab End, Brevel Terrace, Charlton Kings, Cheltenham, Glos.
*Hill, Professor Rosalind M. T., MA, BLitt, FSA, Westfield College, Kidderpore Avenue, London NW3 7ST.
Hilton, A. J. Boyd, MA, DPhil, 1 Carlyle Road, Cambridge CB4 3DN.
Hilton, Professor R. H., DPhil, FBA, University of Birmingham, P.O. Box 363, Birmingham B15 2TT.
Himmelfarb, Professor Gertrude, PhD, The City University of New York, Graduate Center, 33 West 42 St, New York, N.Y. 10036, U.S.A.

Hind, R. J., BA, PhD, Dept of History, University of Sydney, Sydney, N.S.W. 2006, Australia.
*Hinsley, Professor F. H., OBE, MA, St John's College, Cambridge CB2 1TP.
Hirst, Professor D. M., PhD, Dept of History, Washington University, St Louis, Missouri, U.S.A.
Hoak, Professor Dale E., PhD, Dept of History, College of William and Mary, Williamsburg, Virginia 23185, U.S.A.
Hockey, The Rev. S. F., BA, Quarr Abbey, Ryde, Isle of Wight PO33 4ES.
*Hodgett, G. A. J., MA, FSA, King's College London, Strand, London WC2R 2LS.
Holderness, B. A., MA, PhD, School of Economic and Social Studies, University of East Anglia, Norwich NR4 7TJ.
Holdsworth, Professor C. J., MA, PhD, FSA, 5 Pennsylvania Park, Exeter EX4 6HD.
Hollaender, A. E. J., PhD, FSA, 119 Narbonne Avenue, South Side, Clapham Common, London SW4 9LQ.
Hollis, Patricia, MA. DPhil, 30 Park Lane, Norwich NOR 4TF.
Hollister, Professor C. Warren, MA, PhD, University of California, Santa Barbara, Calif. 93106, U.S.A.
Holmes, Professor Clive A., MA, PhD, Dept of History, McGraw Hall, Cornell University, N.Y. 14853, U.S.A.
Holmes, G. A., MA, PhD, Highmoor House, Weald, Bampton, Oxon. OX8 2HY.
Holmes, Professor G. S., MA, DLitt, FBA, Tatham House, Burton-in-Lonsdale, Carnforth, Lancs.
Holroyd, M. de C. F., 85 St Mark's Road, London W10.
HOLT, Professor J. C., MA, DPhil, DLitt, FBA, FSA, Fitzwilliam College, Cambridge CB3 0DG.
Holt, Professor P. M., MA, DLitt, FBA, Dryden Spinney, South End, Kirtlington, Oxford OX5 3HG.
Holt, The Rev. T. G., SJ, MA, FSA, 114 Mount Street, London W1Y 6AH.
Honey, Professor, J. R. de S., MA, DPhil, 5 Woods Close, Oadby, Leicester LE2 4FJ.
Hopkin, D. R., BA, PhD, Maesgwyn, Llangawsai, Aberystwyth, Dyfed.
Hopkins, E., MA, PhD, 77 Stevens Road, Stourbridge, West Midlands DY9 0XW.
Hoppen, K. T., MA, PhD, Dept of History, The University, Hull HU6 7RX.
Horrox, Rosemary E., MA, PhD, 61–3 High Street, Cottenham, Cambridge CB4 3SA.
Horton, A.V.M., MA, PhD, 4 Birch Lea, East Leake, Loughborough LE12 6LA.
Horwitz, Professor H. G., BA, DPhil, Dept of History, University of Iowa, Iowa City, Iowa 52242, U.S.A.
Houlbrooke, R. A., MA, DPhil, Faculty of Letters and Social Sciences, The University, Reading RG6 2AH.
Housley, N. J., MA, PhD, Dept of History, The University, Leicester, LE1 7RH.
*Howard, C. H. D., MA, 15 Sunnydale Gardens, London NW7 3PD.
*Howard, Sir Michael, CBE, MC, DLitt, FBA, Oriel College, Oxford OX1 4EW.
Howarth, Mrs J. H., MA, St Hilda's College, Oxford OX4 1DY.

Howat, G. M. D., MA, MLitt, Old School House, North Moreton, Didcot, Oxfordshire OX11 9BA.

Howell, Miss M. E., MA, PhD, 10 Blenheim Drive, Oxford OX2 8DG.

Howell, P. A., MA., PhD, School of Social Sciences, The Flinders University of South Australia, Bedford Park, South Australia 5042.

Howell, Professor R., MA, DPhil, Dept of History, Bowdoin College, Brunswick, Maine 04011, U.S.A.

Howells, B. F., MA, Whitehill, Cwm Ann, Lampeter, Dyfed.

Hudson, Miss A., MA, DPhil, Lady Margaret Hall, Oxford OX2 6QA.

Hufton, Professor Olwen H., BA, PhD, 40 Shinfield Road, Reading, Berks.

Hughes, J. Q., MC, MA, BArch, PhD, Dip. Civic Design, 10a Fulwood Park, Liverpool L17 5AH.

Hull, F., BA, PhD, 135 Ashford Road, Bearsted, Maidstone ME14 4BT.

HUMPHREYS, Professor R. A., OBE, MA, PhD, DLitt, LittD, DLitt, DUniv, 5 St James's Close, Prince Albert Road, London NW8 7LG.

Hunnisett, R. F., MA, DPhil, 23 Byron Gardens, Sutton, Surrey SM1 3QG.

Hunt, K. S., PhD, MA, Rhodes University Grahamstown 6140, South Africa.

Hurst, M. C., MA, St John's College, Oxford OX1 3JP.

Hurt, J. S., BA, BSc(Econ), PhD, 66 Oxford Road, Moseley, Birmingham B13 9SQ.

*Hussey, Professor Joan M., MA, BLitt, PhD, FSA, Royal Holloway and Bedford New College, Egham Hill, Egham, Surrey TW20 0EX.

Hutchinson, J. H., 182 Burton Stone Lane, York YO3 6DF.

Hutton, R. E., BA, DPhil, Dept of History, The University, Queen's Road, Bristol BS8 1RJ.

Hyams, P. R., MA, DPhil, Pembroke College, Oxford OX1 1DW.

*Hyde, H. Montgomery, MA, DLit, Westwell House, Tenterden, Kent.

Ingham, Professor K., OBE, MA, DPhil, The Woodlands, 94 West Town Lane, Bristol BS4 5DZ.

Ingram Ellis, Professor E. R., MA, PhD, Dept of History, Simon Fraser University, Burnaby, B.C., VSA 1S6, Canada.

Inkster, Ian, PhD, Dept of Economic History, University of New South Wales, P.O. Box 1, Kensington, N.S.W., Australia 2033.

Israel, Professor J. I., MA, DPhil, Dept of History, University College London, Gower Street, London WC1E 6BT.

Ives, E. W., PhD, 214 Myton Road, Warwick.

Jack, Professor R. I., MA, PhD, University of Sydney, Sydney, N.S.W., Australia.

Jack, Mrs S. M., MA, BLitt, University of Sydney, Sydney, N.S.W., Australia.

Jackman, Professor S. W., PhD, FSA, 1065 Deal Street, Victoria, British Columbia, Canada.

Jackson, J. T., PhD, Dept of History, University College of Swansea, Swansea SA2 7BR.

Jackson, P., MA, PhD, Dept of History, The University, Keele, Staffs. ST5 5BG.

Jacob, Professor Margaret C., Eugene Lang College, New School for Social Research, 66 West 12th Street, New York, N.Y. 10011, U.S.A.

Jagger, Rev. P. J., MA, MPhil, St Deiniol's Library, Hawarden, Deeside, Clwyd CH5 3DF.

Jalland, Patricia, PhD, MA, BA, Dept of History, School of Social Sciences, Western Australian Institute of Technology, South Bentley, Western Australia 6102.

James, Edward, MA, DPhil, FSA, Dept of History, The University, York YO1 5DD.

James, M. E., MA, Middlecote, Stonesfield, Oxon. OX7 2PU.

James, R. Rhodes, MP, MA, FRSL, The Stone House, Great Gransden, nr Sandy, Beds.

James, Thomas B., MA, PhD, 35 Alresford Road, Winchester SO23 8HG.

Jarrett, J. D., 58 Beaconsfield Road, London SE3 7LG.

Jeffery, K. J., MA, PhD, Dept of History, University of Ulster, Shore Road, Newtownabbey, Co. Antrim, N. Ireland BT37 0QB.

Jenkins, Professor B. A., PhD, 133 Lorne, Lennoxville, Quebec, Canada.

Jenkins, Professor D., MA, LLM, LittD, Adeilad Hugh Owen, Penglais, Aberystwyth SY23 3DY.

Jeremy, D. J., BA, MLitt, PhD, 16 Britannia Gardens, Westcliff-on-Sea, Essex SS0 8BN.

Jewell, Miss H. M., MA, PhD, School of History, The University, P.O. Box 147, Liverpool L69 3BX.

Johnson, D. J., BA, 41 Cranes Park Avenue, Surbiton, Surrey.

Johnson, Professor D. W. J., BA, BLitt, Dept of History, University College London, Gower Street, London WC1E 6BT.

*Johnson, J. H., MA, Whitehorns, Cedar Avenue, Chelmsford, Essex.

Johnston, Professor Edith M., MA, PhD, Dept of History, Macquarie Univ., North Ryde, N.S.W. 2113, Australia.

Johnston, Professor S. H. F., MA, Fronhyfryd, Llanbadarn Road, Aberystwyth, Dyfed.

Jones, C. D. H., BA, DPhil, Dept of History and Archaeology, The University, Exeter EX4 4QH.

Jones, Clyve, MA, MLitt, 41 St Catherines Court, London W4 1LB.

Jones, D. J. V., BA, PhD, Dept of History, University College of Swansea, Singleton Park, Swansea SA2 8PP.

Jones, Dwyryd W., MA, DPhil, Dept of History, The University, York YO1 5DD.

Jones, Revd F., BA, MSc, PhD, 4a Castlemain Avenue, Southbourne, Bournemouth BH6 5EH.

Jones, G. A., MA, PhD, Monks Court, Deddington, Oxford OX5 4TE.

Jones, G. E., MA, PhD, MEd, 130 Pennard Drive, Pennard, Gower, West Glamorgan.

Jones, Professor G. Hilton, PhD, Dept of History, Eastern Illinois University, Charleston, Ill. 61920, U.S.A.

Jones, Professor G. W., BA, MA, DPhil, Dept of Government, London School of Economics, Houghton Street, London WC2A 2AE.

Jones, H. E., MA, DPhil, Flat 3, 115-117 Highlever Road, London W10 6PW.

Jones, Professor I.G., MA, DLitt, 12 Laura Place, Aberystwyth, Dyfed SY23 3DY.

Jones, J. D., MA, PhD, Woodlands Cottage, Marvel Lane, Newport, Isle of Wight PO30 3DT.

Jones, Professor J. R., MA, PhD, School of English and American Studies, University of East Anglia, Norwich NOR 30A.

Jones, Professor M. A., MA, DPhil, Dept of History, University College London, Gower Street, London WC1E 6BT.

Jones, Mrs Marian H., MA, Glwysgoed, Caradog Road, Aberystwyth, Dyfed.

Jones, M. C. E., MA, DPhil, FSA, Dept of History, The University, Nottingham NG7 2 RD.
Jones, The Venerable O. W., MA, 10 Camden Crescent, Brecon, Powys LD3 7BY.
Jones, P. J., DPhil, FBA, Brasenose College, Oxford OX1 4AJ.
Jones, Professor W. J., PhD, DLitt, FRSC, Dept of History, The University of Alberta, Edmonton T6G 2H4, Canada.
Jones-Parry, Sir Ernest, MA, PhD, Flat 3, 34 Sussex Square, Brighton, Sussex BN2 5AD.
Judd, D., BA, PhD, Dept of History and Philosophy, Polytechnic of North London, Prince of Wales Road, London NW6.
Judson, Professor Margaret A., PhD, 8 Redcliffe Avenue, Highland Park, N.J. 08904, U.S.A.
Judt, T. R., St Anne's College, Oxford OX2 6HS.
Jukes, Rev. H. A. Ll., MA, STh, 1 St Mary's Court, Ely, Cambs. CB7 4HQ.
Jupp, P. J., BA, PhD, 42 Osborne Park, Belfast, N. Ireland BT9 6JN.

Kaeuper, Professor R. W., MA, PhD, 151 Village Lane, Rochester, New York 14610, U.S.A.
Kamen, H. A. F., MA, DPhil, The University of Warwick, Coventry CV4 7AL.
Kanya-Forstner, A. S., PhD, Dept of History, York University, 4700 Keele Street, Downsview, Ontario M3J 1P3, Canada.
Kapelle, Asst. Professor, William E., History Department, Brandeis University, Waltham, Mass. 02254, U.S.A.
*Kay, H., MA, c/o 4a Hawthorne Road, Cherry Willingham, Lincoln LN3 4JT.
Kealey, Professor Gregory S., Dept of History, Memorial University of Newfoundland, St John's, Newfoundland. A1C 5S7, Canada.
Kedward, H. R., MA, MPhil, 137 Waldegrave Road, Brighton BN1 6GJ.
Keefe, Professor Thomas K., BA, PhD, Dept of History, Appalachian State University, Boone, N.C. 28608, U.S.A.
Keeler, Mrs Mary F., PhD, 302 West 12th Street, Frederick, Maryland 21701, U.S.A.
Keen, L. J., MPhil, Dip Archaeol, FSA, 7 Church Street, Dorchester, Dorset.
Keen, M. H. MA, Balliol College, Oxford OX1 3BJ.
Keene, D. J., MA, DPhil, 162 Erlanger Road, Telegraph Hill, London SE14 5TJ.
Kellas, J. G., MA, PhD, Dept of Politics, Glasgow University, Adam Smith Building, Glasgow G12 8RT.
Kellaway, C. W., MA, FSA, 18 Canonbury Square, London N1.
Kelly, Professor T., MA, PhD, FLA, Oak Leaf House, Ambleside Road, Keswick, Cumbria CA12 4DL.
Kemp, Miss B., MA, FSA, St Hugh's College, Oxford OX2 6LE.
Kemp, B. R., BA, PhD, 12 Redhatch Drive, Earley, Reading, Berks.
Kemp, The Right Rev. E. W., DD, The Lord Bishop of Chichester, The Palace, Chichester, Sussex PO19 1PY.
Kemp, Lt-Commander P. K., RN, Malcolm's, 51 Market Hill, Maldon, Essex.
Kennedy, J., MA, 14 Poolfield Avenue, Newcastle-under-Lyme, Staffs. ST5 2NL.
Kennedy, Professor P. M., BA, DPhil, Dept of History, Yale University, Hall of Graduate Studies, New Haven, Conn. 06520, U.S.A.

Kent, Professor C. A., DPhil, Dept of History, University of Saskatchewan, Saskatoon, Sask. S7N oWO, Canada.
Kent, Professor J. H. S., MA, PhD, Dept of Theology, University of Bristol, Senate House, Bristol BS8 1TH.
Kent, Miss M. R., PhD, BA, School of Social Sciences, Deakin University, Geelong, Victoria, Australia 3217.
Kenyon, Professor J. P., PhD, Dept of History, University of Kansas, 300 Wescol Hall, Lawrence, Kansas 66045-2130, U.S.A.
Kerridge, Professor E. W. J., PhD, 2 Bishops Court, off Church Road, Broughton, Chester CH4 OQ2.
Kettle, Miss A. J., MA, FSA, Dept of Mediaeval History, 71 South Street, St Andrews, Fife KY16 9AL.
Keynes, S. D., MA, PhD, Trinity College, Cambridge CB2 1TQ.
Kiernan, Professor V. G., MA, 'Woodcroft', Lauder Road, Stow, Galashiels, Scotland TD1 2QW.
*Kimball, Miss E. G., BLitt, PhD, 200 Leeder Hill Drive, Apt 640, Hamden, Conn. 06517, U.S.A.
King, Professor E. B., PhD, Dept of History, The University of the South, Box 1234, Sewanee, Tennessee 37375, U.S.A.
King, E. J., MA, PhD, Dept of History, The University, Sheffield S10 2TN.
King, P. D., BA, PhD, Dept of History, Furness College, The University, Bailrigg, Lancaster LA1 4YG.
Kirby, D. P., MA, PhD, Manoraven, Llanon, Dyfed.
Kirby, J. L., MA, FSA, 209 Covington Way, Streatham, London SW16 3BY.
Kirby, M. W., BA, PhD, Dept of Economics, Gillow House, The University, Lancaster LA1 4YX.
Kirk, J., MA, PhD, DLitt, Dept of Scottish History, University of Glasgow, Glasgow G12 8QQ.
Kirk-Greene, A. H. M., MBE, MA, St Antony's College, Oxford OX2 6JF.
Kishlansky, Professor Mark, Dept of History, University of Chicago, 1126 East 59th Street, Chicago, Illinois 60637, U.S.A.
Kitchen, Professor Martin, BA, PhD, Dept of History, Simon Fraser University, Burnaby, B.C. V5A 1S6, Canada.
Kitching, C. J., BA, PhD, FSA, 11 Creighton Road, London NW6 6EE.
Klibansky, Professor R., MA, PhD, DPhil, FRSC, 608 Leacock Building, McGill University, P.O. Box 6070, Station A, Montreal H3C 3G1, Canada.
Knafla, Professor L. A., BA, MA, PhD, Dept of History, University of Calgary, Alberta, Canada.
Knecht, R. J., MA, DLitt, 79 Reddings Road, Moseley, Birmingham B13 8LP.
Knowles, C. H., PhD, University College, P.O. Box 78, Cardiff CF1 1XL.
Koch, Hannsjoachim W., BA, DPhil, Dept of History, The University, Heslington, York YO1 5DD.
Kochan, L. E., MA, PhD, 237 Woodstock Road, Oxford OX2 7AD.
Koenigsberger, Dorothy M. M., BA, PhD, 41a Lancaster Grove, London NW3.
Koenigsberger, Professor H. G., MA, PhD, 41a Lancaster Grove, London NW3.
Kohl, Professor Benjamin G., AB, MA, PhD, Dept of History, Vassar College, Poughkeepsie, New York, 12601, U.S.A.
Kollar, Professor Rene M., BA, MDiv, MA, PhD, St Vincent Archabbey, Latrobe, Pa. 15650, U.S.A.

Korr, Charles P., MA, PhD, College of Arts and Sciences, Dept of History, University of Missouri, 8001 Natural Bridge Road, St Louis, Missouri 63121, U.S.A.
Kossmann, Professor E. H., DLitt, Rijksuniversiteit te Groningen, Groningen, The Netherlands.
Kouri, E. I., PhD, Clare Hall, Cambridge CB3 9AL.

Lake, P., BA, PhD, Dept of History, Royal Holloway and Bedford New College, Egham Hill, Surrey TW20 0EX.
Lambert, The Hon. Margaret, CMG, PhD. 39 Thornhill Road, Barnsbury Square, London N1 1JS.
Lambert, W. R., BA, PhD, 36 Five Mile Drive, Oxford OX2 8HR.
Lamont, W. M., PhD, Manor House, Keighton Road, Denton, Newhaven, Sussex BN9 0AB.
Lander, J. R., MA, MLitt, FRSC, 5 Canonbury Place, London, N1 2NQ.
Landes, Professor D. S., PhD, Widener U, Harvard University, Cambridge, Mass. 02138, U.S.A.
Landon, Professor M. de L., MA, PhD, Dept of History, The University, Mississippi 38677 U.S.A.
Langford, P., MA, DPhil, Lincoln College, Oxford OX1 3DR.
Langhorne, R. T. B., MA, 15 Madingley Road, Cambridge.
Lannon, Frances, MA, DPhil, Lady Margaret Hall, Oxford OX2 6QA.
Lapidge, M., BA, MA, PhD, Dept of Anglo-Saxon, Norse and Celtic, 9 West Road, Cambridge CB3 9DP.
Larkin, Professor M. J. M., MA, PhD, Dept of History, The University, George Square, Edinburgh EH8 9JY.
Larner, J. P., MA, The University, Glasgow G12 8QQ.
Lasko, Professor P. E., BA, FSA, 53 Montagu Square, London W1H 1TH.
Latham, R. C., CBE, MA, FBA, Magdalene College, Cambridge CB3 0AG.
Law, J. F., MA, DPhil, Dept of History, University College of Swansea, Swansea SA2 8PP.
Lawrence, Professor C. H., MA, DPhil, Royal Holloway and Bedford New College, Egham Hill, Surrey TW20 0EX.
Laws, Captain W. F., BA, MLitt, 23 Marlborough Road, St. Leonards, Exeter EX2 4TJ.
Lead, P., MA, 11 Morland Close, Stone, Staffs. ST15 0DA.
Le Cordeur, Professor Basil A., MA, PhD, Dept of History, University of Cape Town, Rondebosch 7700, Republic of South Africa.
Leddy, J. F., MA, BLitt, DPhil, University of Windsor, Windsor, Ontario, Canada.
Lee, Professor J. M., MA, BLitt, Dept of Politics, University of Bristol, 12 Priory Road, Bristol BS8 1TU.
Lehmann, Professor J. H., PhD, De Paul University, 25e Jackson Blvd., Chicago, Illinois 60604, U.S.A.
Lehmberg, Professor S. E., PhD, Dept of History, University of Minnesota, Minneapolis, Minn. 55455, U.S.A.
Leinster-Mackay, D. P., MA, MEd, PhD, Dept of Education, University of Western Australia, Nedlands, Western Australia 6009.
Lenman, B. P., MA, LittD, Dept of Modern History, University of St Andrews, St Andrews, Fife KY16 9AL.
Lentin, A., MA, PhD, 57 Maids Causeway, Cambridge CB5 8DE.
Leslie, Professor R. F., BA, PhD, Market House, Church Street, Charlbury, Oxford OX7 3PP.

216

LIST OF FELLOWS
Lester, Professor M., PhD, Dept of History, Davidson College, Davidson, N.C. 28036, U.S.A.

Levine, Professor Joseph M., Dept of History, Syracuse University, Syracuse, New York 13210, U.S.A.

Levine, Professor Mortimer, PhD, 529 Woodhaven Drive, Morgantown, West Va. 26505, U.S.A.

Levy, Professor F. J., PhD, University of Washington, Seattle, Wash. 98195, U.S.A.

Lewis, Professor A. R., MA, PhD, History Dept, University of Massachusetts, Amherst, Mass. 01003, U.S.A.

Lewis, Professor B., PhD, FBA, Near Eastern Studies Dept, Jones Hall, The University, Princeton, N.J. 08540, U.S.A.

Lewis, C. W., BA, FSA, University College, P.O. Box 78, Cardiff CF1 1XL.

Lewis, Professor G., MA, DPhil, Dept of History, University of Warwick, Coventry CV4 7AL.

Lewis, P. S., MA, All Souls College, Oxford OX1 4AL.

Lewis, R. A., PhD, Y Berth Glyd, Siliwen Road Bangor, Gwynedd LL57 2BS.

Lewis, R. Gillian, St Anne's College, Oxford OX2 6HS.

Leyser, Professor K., TD, MA, FBA, FSA, All Souls College, Oxford OX1 4AL.

Liddell, W. H., MA, Dept of Extra-Mural Studies, University of London, 26 Russell Square London WC1B 5DG.

Liddle, Peter H., BA, MLitt, 'Dipity Cottage', 20 Lime Street, Waldridge Fell, nr Chester-le-Street, Co. Durham.

Lieu, Samuel N. C., BA, MA, DPhil, 2a Dickinson Square, Croxley Green, Rickmansworth, Herts. WD3 3EZ.

Lindley, K. J., MA, PhD, Dept of History, New University of Ulster, Coleraine, N. Ireland BT52 1SA.

*Lindsay, Mrs H., MA, PhD (address unknown).

Lindsay, Colonel Oliver, MBIM, Brookwood House, Brookwood, nr Woking, Surrey.

Linehan, P. A., MA, PhD, St John's College, Cambridge CB2 1TP.

Lipman, V. D., CVO, MA, DPhil, FSA, 9 Rotherwick Road, London NW11 9DG.

Livermore, Professor H. V., MA, Sandycombe Lodge, Sandycombe Road, St Margarets, Twickenham, Middx.

Lloyd, Professor H. A., BA, DPhil, The University, Cottingham Road, Hull HU6 7RX.

Loach, Mrs J., MA, Somerville College, Oxford OX2 6HD.

Loades, Professor D. M., MA, PhD, University College of North Wales, Bangor, Gwynedd LL57 2DG.

Lobel, Mrs M. D., BA, FSA, 16 Merton Street, Oxford.

Lockie, D. McN., MA, 25 Chemin de la Panouche, Saint-Anne, 06130 Grasse, France.

Lockyer, R. W., MA, Dept of History, Royal Holloway and Bedford New College, Egham Hill, Egham, Surrey TW20 0EX.

Logan, F. D., MA, MSD, Emmanuel College, 400 The Fenway, Boston, Mass. 02115, U.S.A.

Logan, O. M. T., MA, PhD, 18 Clarendon Road, Norwich NR2 2PW.

London, Miss Vera C. M., MA, 55 Churchill Road, Church Stretton, Shropshire SY6 6EP.

Longley, D. A., MA, PhD, Dept of History, King's College, The University, Old Aberdeen AB9 2UB.

Longmate, N. R., MA, 30 Clydesdale Gardens, Richmond, Surrey.
Loomie, Rev. A. J., SJ, MA, PhD, Fordham University, New York, N.Y. 10458, U.S.A.
Loud, G. A., MA, DPhil, School of History, The University, Leeds LS2 9JT.
Louis, Professor William R., BA, MA, DPhil, Dept of History, University of Texas, Austin, Texas 78712, U.S.A.
Lourie, Elena, MA, DPhil, Dept of History, Ben Gurion University of The Negev, P.O. Box 653, Beer Sheva 84105, Israel.
Lovatt, R. W., MA, DPhil, Peterhouse, Cambridge CB2 1RD.
Lovegrove, D. W., MA, BD, PhD, Dept of Ecclesiastical History, St Mary's College, The University, St Andrews, Fife KY16 9JU.
Lovell, J. C., BA, PhD, Eliot College, University of Kent, Canterbury CT2 7NS.
Lovett, A. W., MA, PhD, 26 Coney Hill Road, West Wickham, Kent BR4 9BX.
Lowe, P. C., BA, PhD, The University, Manchester M13 9PL.
Lowe, R, BA, PhD, Dept of Economic and Social History, The University, 13-15 Woodland Road, Bristol BS8 2TJ.
Lowerson, J. R., BA, MA, Centre for Continuing Education, University of Sussex, Brighton.
Loyn, Professor H. R., MA, FBA, FSA, Westfield College, Kidderpore Avenue, London NW3 7ST.
Lucas, C. R., MA, DPhil, Balliol College, Oxford OX1 3BJ.
Lucas, P. J., MA, PhD, Dept of English, University College, Belfield, Dublin 4, Ireland.
*Lumb, Miss S. V., MA, Torr-Colin House, 106 Ridgway, Wimbledon, London SW19.
Lunn, D. C., STL, MA, PhD, 25 Cornwallis Avenue, Clifton, Bristol BS8 4PP.
Lunt, Major-General J. D., MA, Hilltop House, Little Milton, Oxfordshire OX9 7PU.
Luscombe, Professor D. E., MA, PhD, FSA, 4 Caxton Road, Broomhill, Sheffield S10 3DE.
Luttrell, A. T., MA, DPhil, 14 Perfect View, Bath BA1 5JY.
Lyman, Professor Richard W., PhD, 350 East 57th Street, Apt 14-B, New York, N.Y. 10022, U.S.A.
Lynch, Professor J., MA, PhD, Inst. of Latin American Studies, 31 Tavistock Square, London WC1H 9HA.
Lynch, M., MA, PhD, Dept of Scottish History, The University, 50 George Square, Edinburgh EH8 9YW.
Lyttelton, The Hon. N. A. O., BA, 30 Paulton's Square, London SW3.

Mabbs, A. W., 32 The Street, Wallington, Herts. SG7 6SW.
Macaulay, J. H., MA, PhD, 11 Kirklee Circus, Glasgow G12 0TW.
McBriar, Professor A. M., BA, DPhil, FASSA, Dept of History, Monash University, Clayton, Victoria 3168, Australia.
McCaffrey, J. F., MA, PhD, Dept of Scottish History, The University, Glasgow G12 8QH.
MacCaffrey, Professor W. T., PhD, 745 Hollyoke Center, Harvard University, Cambridge, Mass. 02138, U.S.A.
McCann, W. P., BA, PhD, 41 Stanhope Gardens, Highgate, London N6.
McCaughan, Professor R. E. M., MA, BArch, Hon. DSc, FSA, FRAnthI, FRIBA, FRSA, 'Rowan Bank', Kingsley Green, Fernhurst, West Sussex GU27 3LL.

McConica, Professor J. K., CSB, MA, DPhil, University of St Michael's College, 81 St Mary's Street, Toronto, Ontario, M5S 1J4, Canada.

McCord, Professor N., PhD, 7 Hatherton Avenue, Cullercoats, North Shields, Tyne and Wear NE30 3LG.

McCracken, Professor J. L., MA, PhD, 196 Tenth Street, Morningside, Durban 4001, South Africa.

MacCulloch, D. N. J., MA, PhD, FSA, Wesley College, Henbury Road, Westbury-on-Trym, Bristol BS10 7QD.

MacCurtain, Margaret B., MA, PhD, Dept of History, University College, Belfield, Dublin 4, Ireland.

McCusker, J. J., MA, PhD, Dept of History, University of Maryland, College Park, Maryland 20742, U.S.A.

MacDonagh, Professor O., MA, PhD, Research School of Social Sciences, Institute of Advanced Studies, Australian National University, P.O. Box 4, Canberra, A.C.T. 2600, Australia.

Macdonald, Professor D. F., MA, DPhil, 11 Arnhall Drive, Dundee.

McDowell, Professor R. B., PhD, LittD, Trinity College, Dublin, Ireland.

Macfarlane, A. D. J., MA, DPhil, PhD, King's College, Cambridge CB2 1ST.

Macfarlane, L. J., PhD, FSA, King's College, University of Aberdeen, Aberdeen AB9 1FX.

McGrath, Professor P. V., MA, Dept of History, University of Bristol, Bristol BS8 1RJ.

MacGregor, D. R., MA, ARIBA, FSA, 99 Lonsdale Road, London SW13 9DA.

McGurk, J. J. N., BA, MPhil, PhD, Conway House, 10 Stanley Avenue, Birkdale, Southport, Merseyside PR8 4RU.

McGurk, P. M., PhD, Dept of History, Birkbeck College, Malet Street, London WC1E 7HX.

McHardy, Alison K., MA, DPhil, Dept of History, Taylor Building, King's College, Aberdeen AB9 1FX.

Machin, G. I. T., MA, DPhil, Dept of Modern History, University of Dundee, Dundee DD1 4HN.

MacIntyre, A. D., MA, DPhil, Magdalen College, Oxford OX1 4AU.

MacKay, A. I. K., MA, PhD, Dept of History, The University, Edinburgh EH8 9YL.

McKendrick, N., MA, Gonville and Caius College, Cambridge CB2 1TA.

McKenna, Professor J. W., MA, PhD, Orchard Hill Farm, Sandown Road, P.O. Box 343, N. Danville, N.H. 03819, U.S.A.

MacKenzie, J. MacD., MA, PhD, Dept of History, The University, Bailrigg, Lancaster LA1 4YG.

Mackesy, P. G., MA, DPhil, DLitt, Pembroke College, Oxford OX1 1DW.

McKibbin, R. I., MA, DPhil, St John's College, Oxford OX1 3JP.

McKinley, R. A., MA, 42 Boyers Walk, Leicester Forest East, Leicester LE3 3LN.

McKitterick, Rosamond D., MA, PhD, Newnham College, Cambridge CB3 9DF.

Maclagan, M., MA, FSA, Trinity College, Oxford OX1 3BH.

MacLeod, Professor R. M., AB, PhD, Dept of History, The University of Sydney, Sydney, N.S.W., Australia 2006.

*McManners, Professor J., MA, DLitt, FBA, Christ Church, Oxford OX1 1DP.

McMillan, J. F., MA, DPhil, Dept of History, The University, York YO1 5DD.

MacNiocaill, Professor G., PhD, DLitt, Dept of History, University College, Galway, Ireland.

McNulty, Miss P. A., BA, 84b Eastern Avenue, Reading RG1 5SF.

Macpherson, Professor C. B., BA, MSc(Econ), DSc(Econ), DLitt, LLD, FRSC, 32 Boswell Avenue, Toronto M5R 1M4, Canada.

Madariaga, Professor Isabel de, PhD, 25 Southwood Lawn Road, London N6.

Madden, A. F., DPhil, Nuffield College, Oxford OX1 1NF.

Maddicott, J. R., MA, DPhil, Exeter College, Oxford OX1 3DP.

Maehl, Professor W. H., PhD, College of Liberal Studies, Office of the Dean, 1700 Asp Avenue, Suite 226, Norman, Oklahoma 73037, U.S.A.

Maffei, Professor Domenico, MLL, DrJur, Via delle Cerchia 19, 53100 Siena, Italy.

Magnus-Allcroft, Sir Phillip, Bt., CBE, FRSL, Stokesay Court, Craven Arms, Shropshire SY7 9BD.

Maguire, W. A., MA, PhD, 18 Harberton Park, Belfast, N. Ireland BT9 6TS.

Mahoney, Professor T. H. D., AM, PhD, MPA, 130 Mt. Auburn Street, #410, Cambridge, Mass. 02138, U.S.A.

*MAJOR, Miss K., MA, BLitt, LittD, FBA, FSA, 21 Queensway, Lincoln LN2 4AJ.

Malcolm, Joyce L., 1264 Beacon Street, Brookline, Mass. 02146, U.S.A.

Mallett, Professor M. E., MA, DPhil, Dept of History, University of Warwick, Coventry CV4 7AL.

Mallia-Milanes, V., BA, MA, PhD, 135 Zabbar Road, Paola, Malta.

Mangan, James A., BA, PhD, PGCE, DLC, 39 Abercorn Drive, Hamilton, Scotland.

Manning, Professor A. F., Bosweg 27, Berg en Dal, The Netherlands.

Manning, Professor B. S., MA, DPhil, New University of Ulster, Coleraine, Co. Londonderry, Northern Ireland BT52 1SA.

Manning, Professor R. B., PhD, 2848 Coleridge Road, Cleveland Heights, Ohio 44118, U.S.A.

Mansergh, Professor P. N. S., OBE, MA, DPhil, DLitt, LittD, FBA, St John's College, Cambridge CB2 1TP.

Maprayil, C., BD, LD, DD, MA, PhD, c/o Institute of Historical Research, Senate House, London WC1E 7HU.

Marchant, The Rev. Canon R. A., PhD, BD, Laxfield Vicarage, Woodbridge, Suffolk IP13 8DT.

Marett, W. P., MA, PhD, BSc(Econ), BCom, 20 Barrington Road, Stoneygate, Leicester LE2 2RA.

Margetts, J., MA, DipEd, DrPhil, 5 Glenluce Road, Liverpool L19 9BX.

Markus, Professor R. A., MA, PhD, The University, Nottingham NG7 2RD.

Marquand, Professor D., MA, Dept of Politics and Contemporary History, The University, Salford M5 4WT.

Marriner, Sheila, MA, PhD, Dept of Economic History, P.O. Box 147, Liverpool L69 3BX.

Marsh, Professor Peter T., PhD, Dept of History, Syracuse University, Syracuse, New York 13210, U.S.A.

Marshall, J. D., PhD, Brynthwaite, Charney Road, Grange-over-Sands, Cumbria LA11 6BP.

Marshall, Professor P. J., MA, DPhil, King's College London, Strand, London WC2R 2LS.

Martel, Professor André G., PhD, Dept of History, Royal Roads Military College, Victoria, B.C., Canada V0S 1B0.

Martin, E. W., Crossways, Editha Cottage, Black Torrington, Beaworthy, Devon EX21 5QF.
Martin, G. H., CBE, MA, DPhil, Public Record Office, Chancery Lane, London WC2A 1LR.
Martin, Professor Miguel, P.O. Box 1696, Zone 1, Panama, Republic of Panama.
Martindale, Jane M., MA, DPhil, School of English and American Studies, University of East Anglia, Norwich NR4 7TJ.
Marwick, Professor A. J. B., MA, BLitt, Dept of History, The Open University, Walton Hall, Milton Keynes, Bucks MK7 6AA.
Mason, A., BA, PhD, 1 Siddeley Avenue, Kenilworth, Warwickshire CV8 1EW.
Mason, E. Emma, BA, PhD, Dept of History, Birkbeck College, Malet Street, London WC1E 7HX.
Mason, F. K., Beechwood, Watton, Norfolk IP25 6AB.
Mason, J. F. A., MA, DPhil, FSA, Christ Church, Oxford OX1 1DP.
Mather, Professor F. C., MA, 69 Ethelburt Avenue, Swaythling, Southampton.
Mathew, W. M., MA, PhD, School of English and American Studies, University of East Anglia, University Plain, Norwich NR4 7TJ.
Mathias, Professor P., CBE, MA, FBA, All Souls College, Oxford OX1 4AL.
*Mathur-Sherry, Tikait Narain, BA, LLB, 3/193 4 Prem-Nagar, Dayalbagh, Agra-282005 (U.P.), India.
Matthew, Professor D. J. A., MA, DPhil, Dept of History, The University, Reading RG6 2AA.
MATTHEW, H. C. G., MA, DPhil, (*Literary Director*), St Hugh's College, Oxford OX2 6LE.
Matthews, J. F., MA, DPhil, Queen's College, Oxford OX1 4AW.
Mattingly, Professor H. B., MA, Dept of Ancient History, The University, Leeds LS2 9JT.
Le May, G. H. L., MA, Worcester College, Oxford OX1 2HB.
Mayhew, N. J. MA, 101 Marlborough Road, Oxford OX1 4LX.
Mayr-Harting, H. M. R. E., MA, DPhil, St Peter's College, Oxford OX1 2DL.
Mbaeyi, P. M., BA, DPhil, Alvan Ikoku College of Education, Dept of History, PMB 1033, Owerri, Imo State, Nigeria.
Medlicott, Professor W. N., CBE, MA, DLit, DLitt, LittD, 172 Watchfield Court, Sutton Court Road, Chiswick, London W4 4NE.
Meek, Christine E., MA, DPhil, 3145 Arts Building, Trinity College, Dublin 2, Ireland.
Meek, D. E., MA, BA, Dept of Celtic, University of Edinburgh, George Square, Edinburgh EH8 9JX.
Meller, Miss Helen E., BA, PhD, 2 Copenhagen Court, Denmark Grove, Alexandra Park, Nottingham NG3 4LF.
Merson, A. L., MA, Flat 12, Northerwood House, Swan Green, Lyndhurst, Southampton SO4 17DT.
Mettam, R. C., BA, MA, PhD, Dept of History, Queen Mary College, Mile End Road, London E1 4NS.
Mews, Stuart, PhD, Dept of Religious Studies, Cartmel College, Bailrigg, Lancaster.
Micklewright, F. H. A., MA, PhD, 4 Lansdowne Court, 1 Lansdowne Road, Ridgway, Wimbledon, London SW20.
Middlebrook, Norman M., 48 Linden Way, Boston, Lincs. PE21 9DS.

Midgley, Miss L. M., MA, 84 Wolverhampton Road, Stafford ST17 4AW.
Miller, Professor A., BA, MA, PhD, Dept of History, University of Texas, Houston, Texas, U.S.A.
Miller, E., MA, LittD, 36 Almoners Avenue, Cambridge CB1 4PA.
Miller, Miss H., MA, University College of North Wales, Bangor, Gwynedd LL57 2DG.
Miller, J., MA, PhD, Dept of History, Queen Mary College, Mile End Road, London E1 4NS.
Milne, A. T., MA, 9 Frank Dixon Close, London SE21 7BD.
Milne, Miss D. J., MA, PhD, King's College, Aberdeen, AB9 1FX.
Milsom, Professor S. F. C., MA, FBA, 113 Grantchester Meadows, Cambridge CB3 9JN.
Minchinton, Professor W. E., BSc(Econ), The University, Exeter EX4 4PU.
Mingay, Professor G. E., PhD, Mill Field House, Selling Court, Selling, nr Faversham, Kent.
Mitchell, C., MA, BLitt, LittD, Woodhouse Farmhouse, Fyfield, Abingdon, Berks.
Mitchell, L. G., MA, DPhil, University College, Oxford OX1 4BH.
Mitchison, Professor Rosalind, MA, Great Yew, Ormiston, East Lothian EH35 5NJ.
Miyoshi, Professor Yoko, 1-29-2 Okayama, Meguro, Tokyo 152, Japan.
Moloney, Thomas M., PhD, 33 Malvern Drive, Woodford Green, Essex IG8 0JR.
Momigliano, Professor A. D., DLitt, FBA, University College London, Gower Street, London WC1E 6BT.
Mommsen, Professor Dr W. J., German Historical Institute, 17 Bloomsbury Square, London WC1.
Mondey, D. C., 175 Raeburn Avenue, Surbiton, Surrey KT5 9DE.
Money, Professor J., PhD, 912 St Patrick Street, Victoria, B.C., Canada V8S 4X5.
Moody, Professor Michael E., PhD, 2713 Third Street, La Verne, Calif. 91750, U.S.A.
Moore, B. J. S., BA, University of Bristol, 67 Woodland Road, Bristol BS8 1UL.
Moore, Professor Cresap, 935 Memorial Drive, Cambridge, Mass. 02138, U.S.A.
Moore, R. I., MA, Dept of History, The University, Sheffield S10 2TN.
*Moorman, Mrs M., MA, 22 Springwell Road, Durham DH1 4LR.
Morey, Rev. Dom R. Adrian, OSB, MA, DPhil, LittD, Benet House, Mount Pleasant, Cambridge CB3 0BL.
Morgan, B. G., BArch, PhD, Tan-y-Fron, 43 Church Walks, Llandudno, Gwynedd.
Morgan, D. A. L., Dept of History, University College London, Gower Street, London WC1E 6BT.
Morgan, David R., MA, PhD, Dept of Politics, The University, P.O. Box 147, Liverpool L69 3BX.
Morgan, K. O., MA, DPhil, FBA, The Queen's College, Oxford OX1 4AW.
Morgan, Miss P. E., 1a The Cloisters, Hereford HR1 2NG.
Morgan, P. T. J., MA, DPhil, Dept of History, University College of Swansea, Swansea SA2 7BR.
Morgan, Victor, BA, School of English and American Studies, University of East Anglia, Norwich NR4 7TJ.
Morioka, Professor K., BA, 3-12 Sanno 4 Chome, Ota-Ku, Tokyo 143, Japan.

Morrell, J. B., BSc., MA, Dept of Social Sciences, The University, Richmond Road, Bradford BD7 1DP.

Morrill, J. S., MA, DPhil, Selwyn College, Cambridge CB3 9DQ.

Morris, The Rev. Professor C., MA, 53 Cobbett Road, Bitterne Park, Southampton SO2 4HJ.

Morris, G. C., MA, King's College, Cambridge CB2 1ST.

Morris, L. P., BA, PhD, Dept of History and Archaeology, The University, Exeter EX4 4QH.

Mortimer, R., PhD, 370 Mill Road, Cambridge, CB1 3NN.

Morton, Miss C. E., MA, MLS, FSA, An Tigh Béag, Glenteenassig, Castlegregory, Co. Kerry, Ireland.

Mosse, Professor W. E. E., MA, PhD, Dawn Cottage, Ashwellthorpe, Norwich, Norfolk.

Mullins, E. L. C., OBE, MA, Institute of Historical Research, University of London, Senate House, London WC1E 7HU.

Munro, D. J., MA, 65 Meadowcroft, St Albans, Herts. AL1 1UF.

Murdoch, D. H., MA, School of History, The University, Leeds LS2 9JT.

Murray, A., MA, BA, BPhil, University College, Oxford OX1 4BH.

Murray, Athol L., MA, LLB, PhD, 33 Inverleith Gardens, Edinburgh EH3 5PR.

Myatt-Price, Miss E. M., BA, MA, 20 Highfield Drive, Epsom, Surrey KT19 0AS.

Myerscough, J., MA, 39 Campden Street, London W8 7ET.

Myres, J. N. L., CBE, MA, LLD, DLitt, Dlit, FBA, FSA, The Manor House, Kennington, Oxford OX1 5PH.

Nef, Professor J. U., PhD, 2726 N Street NW, Washington, D.C. 20007, U.S.A.

Nelson, Janet L., BA, PhD, Dept of History, King's College, London WC2R 2LS.

Neveu, Dr Bruno, 30 rue Jacob, Paris VIᵉ, France.

New, Professor J. F. H., Dept of History, Waterloo University, Waterloo, Ontario, Canada.

Newbury, C. W., MA, PhD, Linacre College, Oxford OX1 3JA.

Newitt, M. D. D., BA, PhD, Queen's Building, University of Exeter, EX4 4QH.

Newman, A. N., MA, DPhil, 33 Stanley Road, Leicester.

Newman, P. R., BA, DPhil, 1 Ainsty Farm Cottage, Bilton in Ainsty, York YO5 8NN.

Newsome, D. H., MA, LittD, Master's Lodge, Wellington College, Crowthorne, Berks. RG11 7PU.

Nicholas, Professor David, PhD, Dept of History, University of Nebraska, Lincoln, Nebraska 68588, U.S.A.

Nicholas, Professor H. G., MA, FBA, New College, Oxford OX1 3BN.

Nicholls, A. J., MA, BPhil, St Antony's College, Oxford OX2 6JF.

Nicol, Mrs A., MA, BLitt, Public Record Office, Chancery Lane, London WC2A 1LR.

Nicol, Professor D. M., MA, PhD, King's College London, London WC2R 2LS.

Nightingale, Pamela, MA, PhD, 20 Beaumont Buildings, Oxford OX1 2LL.

Noakes, J. D., MA, DPhil, Queen's Bldg., The University, Exeter EX4 4QH.

Norman, E. R., MA, PhD, Peterhouse, Cambridge CB2 1RD.

Obolensky, Professor Sir Dimitri, MA, PhD, DLitt, FBA, FSA, Christ Church, Oxford OX1 1DP.
O'Brien, P. K., MA, DPhil, BSc(Econ), St Antony's College, Oxford OX2 6JF.
O'Day, A., MA, PhD, Polytechnic of North London, Prince of Wales Road, London NW5.
O'Day (Englander), Mrs M. R., BA, PhD, 14 Marshworth, Tinkers Bridge, Milton Keynes MK6 3DA.
*Offler, Professor H. S., MA, 28 Old Elvet, Durham DH1 3HN.
O'Gorman, F., BA, PhD, The University, Manchester M13 9PL.
O'Higgins, The Rev. J., SJ, MA, DPhil, Campion Hall, Oxford.
Olney, R. J., MA, DPhil, Historical Manuscripts Commission, Quality Court, Chancery Lane, London WC2A 1HP.
Orde, Miss A., MA, PhD, Dept of History, University of Durham, 43 North Bailey, Durham DH1 3EX.
Orme, N. I., MA, DPhil, The University, Exeter EX4 4QH.
*Orr, J. E., MA, ThD, DPhil, 11451 Berwick Street, Los Angeles, Calif. 90049, U.S.A.
Ó Tuathaigh, M. A. G., MA, Dept of History, University College, Galway, Ireland.
Otway-Ruthven, Professor A. J., MA, PhD, 7 Trinity College, Dublin, Ireland.
Outhwaite, R. B., MA, PhD, Gonville and Caius College, Cambridge CB2 1TA.
Ovendale, R., MA, DPhil, Dept of International Politics, University College of Wales, Aberystwyth SY23 3DB.
Owen, A. E. B., MA, 35 Whitwell Way, Coton, Cambridge CB3 7PW.
Owen, Mrs D. M., MA, LittD, FSA, 35 Whitwell Way, Coton, Cambridge CB3 7PW.
Owen, G. D., MA, PhD, 21 Clifton Terrace, Brighton, Sussex BN1 3HA.
Owen, J. B., BSc, MA, DPhil, Lincoln College, Oxford OX1 3DR.

Pagden, A. R. D., BA, Girton College, Cambridge CB9 0JG.
Palgrave, D. A., MA, CChem, FRSC, FSG, 210 Bawtry Road, Doncaster, S. Yorkshire DN4 7BZ.
Palliser, Professor D. M., MA, DPhil, FSA, Dept of History, The University, Hull HU6 7RX.
Palmer, J. G. MA, MSc(Econ), MPhil, 78 Norroy Road, London SW15 1PG.
Palmer, J. J. N., BA, BLitt, PhD, 59 Marlborough Avenue, Hull.
Palmer, Sarah, PhD, MA, Dept of History, Queen Mary College, Mile End Road, London E1 4NS.
Paret, Professor P., Inst. for Advanced Study, School of Historical Studies, Princeton, N.J. 08540, U.S.A.
Parish, Professor P. J., BA, Institute of U.S. Studies, 31 Tavistock Square, London WC1H 9EZ.
Parker, Professor N. G., MA, PhD, LittD, FBA, Dept of History, University of Illinois, 810 South Wright Street, Urbana, Ill. 61801, U.S.A.
Parker, R. A. C., MA, DPhil, The Queen's College, Oxford OX1 4AW.
Parkes, M. B., BLitt, MA, FSA, Keble College, Oxford OX1 3PG.
*Parkinson, Professor C. N., MA, PhD, Anneville Manor, Rue Anneville, Vale, Guernsey, C.I.
Parris, H. W., MA, PhD, Warwick House, 47 Guildhall Street, Bury St Edmunds, Suffolk IP33 1QF.

Parry, G. J. R., History Dept, University of Queensland, St Lucia, Australia 4067.
Patrick, Rev. J. G., MA, PhD, DLitt, 8 North Street, Braunton, N. Devon EX33 1AJ.
Pavlowitch, Stevan K., MA, LesL, Dept of History, The University, Southampton SO9 5NH.
Payne, Professor Peter L., BA, PhD, 68 Hamilton Place, Aberdeen AB2 4BA.
Paz, Denis G., PhD, Dept of History, Clemson University, Clemson, South Carolina 29634-1507, U.S.A.
Peake, Rev. F. A., DD, DSLitt, 310 Dalehurst Drive, Nepean, Ontario, K2G 4E4, Canada.
Pearl, Mrs Valerie, MA, DPhil, FSA, New Hall, Cambridge CB3 oDF.
Peck, Professor Linda L., PhD, Dept of History, Purdue University, University Hall, West Lafayette, Indiana 47907, U.S.A.
Peek, Miss H. E., MA, FSA, FSAScot, Taintona, Moretonhampstead, Newton Abbot, Devon TQ13 8LG.
Peel, Lynnette J., BAgrSc, MAgrSc, PhD, 49 Oaklands, Hamilton Road, Reading RG1 5RN.
Peele, Miss Gillian R., BA, BPhil, Lady Margaret Hall, Oxford OX2 6QA.
Pelling, Margaret, BA, MLitt, Wellcome Unit for the History of Medicine, 45-47 Banbury Road, Oxford OX2 6PE.
Pennington, D. H., MA, Balliol College, Oxford OX1 3BJ.
Perkin, Professor H. J., MA, Dept of History, Northwestern University, Evanston, Illinois 60201, U.S.A.
Perry, Norma, BA, PhD, Dept of French and Italian, The University, Exeter EX4 4QH.
Peters, Professor E. M., PhD, Dept of History, University of Pennsylvania, Philadelphia 19174, U.S.A.
Pfaff, Professor Richard W., MA, DPhil, Dept of History, Hamilton Hall 070A, University of North Carolina, Chapel Hill, N.C. 27514, U.S.A.
Phillips, Sir Henry (E. I.), CMG, MBE, MA, 34 Ross Court, Putney Hill, London SW15.
Phillips, Assoc. Professor John A., PhD, Dept of History, University of California, Riverside, Calif. 92521, U.S.A.
Phillips, J. R. S., BA, PhD, FSA, Dept of Medieval History, University College, Dublin 4, Ireland.
Phillipson, N.T., MA, PhD, Dept of History, The University George Square, Edinburgh EH8 9JY.
Phythian-Adams, C. V., MA, Dept of English Local History, The University, Leicester LE1 7RH.
Pierce, Professor G. O., MA, Dept of History, University College, P.O. Box 95, Cardiff CF1 1XA.
Pitt, H. G., MA, Worcester College, Oxford OX1 2HB.
Platt, Professor C. P. S., MA, PhD, FSA, Dept of History, The University, Southampton SO9 5NH.
Platt, Professor D. C. St M., MA, DPhil, St Antony's College, Oxford OX2 6JF.
Plumb, Sir John, PhD, LittD, FBA, FSA, Christ's College, Cambridge CB2 3BU.
Pocock, Professor J. G. A., PhD, Johns Hopkins University, Baltimore, Md. 21218, U.S.A.

Pogge von Strandmann, H. J. O., MA, DPhil, University College, Oxford OX1 4BH.
Pole, Professor J. R., MA, PhD, St Catherine's College, Oxford OX1 3UJ.
Pollard, A. J., BA, PhD, 22 The Green, Hurworth-on-Tees, Darlington, Co. Durham DL2 2AA.
Pollard, Professor S., BSc(Econ), PhD, Abteilung Geschichte, Fakultät für Geschichtswissenschaft und Philosophie, Univer. Bielefeld, 4800 Bielefeld 1.
Polonsky, A. B., BA, DPhil, Dept of International History, London School of Economics, Houghton Street, London WC2A 2AE.
Port, Professor M. H., MA, BLitt, FSA, Queen Mary College, Mile End Road, London E1 4NS.
PORTER, A. N., MA, PhD (*Hon. Secretary*), Dept of History, King's College London, London WC2R 2LS.
Porter, B. E., BSc(Econ), PhD, Merville, Allan Road, Seasalter, Whitstable, Kent CT5 4AH.
Porter, H. C., MA, PhD, Faculty of History, West Road, Cambridge CB3 9EF.
Porter, S., BA, MLitt, PhD, Royal Commission on Historical Monuments, 37-40 Berners Street, London W1P 4BP.
Post, J., MA, PhD, Public Record Office, Chancery Lane, London WC2A 1LR.
Potter, J., BA, MA(Econ), London School of Economics, Houghton Street, London WC2A 2AE.
Powell, W. R., BLitt, MA, FSA, 2 Glanmead, Shenfield Road, Brentwood, Essex CM15 8ER.
Power, M. J., BA, PhD, School of History, The University, P.O. Box 147, Liverpool L69 3BX.
Powicke, Professor M. R., MA. 67 Lee Avenue, Toronto, Ontario M43 2P1, Canada.
Powis, J. K. MA, DPhil, Balliol College, Oxford OX1 3BJ.
Prall, Professor Stuart E., MA, PhD, Dept of History, Queens College, C.U.N.Y., Flushing, N.Y. 11367, U.S.A.
Prentis, Malcolm D., MA, PhD, 3 Marina Place, Belrose, New South Wales 2085, Australia.
Prest, W. R., MA, DPhil, Dept of History, University of Adelaide, North Terrace, Adelaide 5001, S. Australia.
Preston, Professor P., MA, DPhil, Dept of History, Queen Mary College, Mile End Road, London E1 4NS.
*Preston, Professor R. A., MA, PhD, Duke University, Durham, N.C., U.S.A.
Prestwich, J. O., MA, 18 Dunstan Road, Old Headington, Oxford OX3 9BY.
Prestwich, Mrs M., MA, St Hilda's College, Oxford OX4 1DY.
Prestwich, Professor M. C., MA, DPhil, Dept of History, 43/46 North Bailey, Durham DH1 3EX.
Price, A. W., 19 Bayley Close, Uppingham, Leicestershire LE15 9TG.
Price, Rev. D. T. W., MA, St David's University College, Lampeter, Dyfed SA48 7ED.
Price, F. D., MA, BLitt, FSA, Keble College, Oxford OX1 3PG.
Price, Professor Jacob M., AM, PhD, University of Michigan, Ann Arbor, Michigan 48104, U.S.A.
Price, R. D., BA, DLitt, School of Modern Languages & European History, University of East Anglia, Norwich NR4 7TJ.

Prichard, Canon T. J., MA, PhD, Tros-yr-Afon, Llangwnnadl, Pwllheli, Gwynedd LL53 8NS.
Prins, G. I. T., MA, PhD, Emmanuel College, Cambridge CB2 3AP.
Pritchard, Professor D. G., PhD, 11 Coed Mor, Sketty, Swansea, W. Glam. SA2 8BQ.
Prochaska, Alice M. S., MA, DPhil, 9 Addison Bridge Place, London W14 8XP.
Pronay, N., BA, School of History, The University, Leeds LS2 9JT.
Prothero, I. J., BA, PhD, The University, Manchester M13 9PL.
Pugh, T. B., MA, BLitt, 28 Bassett Wood Drive, Southampton SO2 3PS.
Pullan, Professor B. S., MA, PhD, Dept of History, The University, Manchester M13 9PL.
Pulman, M. B., MA, PhD, AB, History Dept, University of Denver, Colorado 80210, U.S.A.
Pulzer, Professor P. G. J., MA, PhD, All Souls College, Oxford OX1 4AL.

Quested, Rosemary K. I., MA, PhD, 30 Woodford Court, Birchington, Kent CT7 9DR.
Quinault, R. E., MA, DPhil, 21 Tytherton Road, London N19.
QUINN, Professor D. B., MA, PhD, DLit, DLitt, DLitt, DLitt, LLD, DHL, Hon. FBA, 9 Knowsley Road, Liverpool L19 0PF.
Quintrell, B. W., MA, PhD, School of History, The University, P.O. Box 147, Liverpool L69 3BX.

Raban, Mrs S. G., MA, PhD, Trinity Hall, Cambridge CB2 1TJ.
Rabb, Professor T. K., MA, PhD, Princeton University, Princeton, N.J. 08540, U.S.A.
Radford, C. A. Ralegh, MA, DLitt, FBA, FSA, Culmcott, Uffculme, Cullompton, Devon EX15 3AT.
*Ramm, Miss A., MA, DLitt, Metton Road, Roughton, Norfolk NR11 8QT.
*Ramsay, G. D., MA, DPhil, 15 Charlbury Road, Oxford OX2 6UT.
Ramsden, J. A., MA, DPhil, Dept of History, Queen Mary College, Mile End Road, London E1 4NS.
Ramsey, Professor P. H., MA, DPhil, Taylor Building, King's College, Old Aberdeen AB9 1FX.
Ranft, Professor B. McL., MA, DPhil. 32 Parkgate, London SE3 9XF.
Ransome, D. R., MA, PhD, 10 New Street, Woodbridge, Suffolk.
Ratcliffe, D. J., MA, BPhil, PhD, Dept of History, The University, 43 North Bailey, Durham DH1 3EX.
Rawcliffe, Carole, BA, PhD, 24 Villiers Road, London NW2.
Rawley, Professor J. A., PhD, University of Nebraska, Lincoln, Nebraska 68508, U.S.A.
Ray, Professor R. D., BA, BD, PhD, University of Toledo, 2801, W. Bancroft Street, Toledo, Ohio 43606, U.S.A.
Read, Professor D., BLitt, MA, PhD, Darwin College, University of Kent at Canterbury, Kent CT2 7NY.
Reader, W. J., BA, PhD, 46 Gough Way, Cambridge CB3 9LN.
Reed, Michael A., MA, LLB, PhD, 1 Paddock Close, Quorn, Leicester LE12 8BJ.
Reeves, Professor A. C., MA, PhD, Dept of History, Ohio University, Athens, Ohio 45701, U.S.A.
Reeves, Miss M. E., MA, PhD, 38 Norham Road, Oxford OX2 6SQ.

Reid, B. H., MA, PhD, Dept of War Studies, Kings College London, Strand, London WC2R 2LS.
Reid, Professor L. D., MA, PhD, 200 E. Brandon Road, Columbia, Mo. 65201, U.S.A.
Reid, Professor W. S., MA, PhD, University of Guelph, Guelph, Ontario, Canada.
Renold, Miss P., MA, 51 Woodstock Close, Oxford OX2 8DD.
Renshaw, P. R. G., MA, Dept of History, The University, Sheffield S10 2TN.
Reuter, T. A., MA, DPhil, Monumenta Germaniae Historica, Ludwigstrasse 16, 8 München 34, West Germany.
Reynolds, D. J., MA, PhD, Christ's College, Cambridge CB2 3BU.
Reynolds, Miss S. M. G., MA, 26 Lennox Gardens, London SW1.
Richards, J. M., MA, Dept of History, The University, Bailrigg, Lancaster LA1 4YG.
Richards, Rev. J. M., MA, BLitt, STL, St Mary's, Cadogan Street, London SW3 2QR.
Richardson, R. C., BA, PhD, King Alfred's College, Winchester.
Richter, Professor M., DrPhil, habil, Universität Konstanz, Postfach 5560, D-7750 Konstanz 1, Germany.
Riden, Philip J., MA, MLitt, Dept of Extramural Studies, University College, P.O. Box 78, Cardiff CF1 1XL.
Ridgard, J. M., PhD, Dennington Place, Dennington, Woodbridge, Suffolk IP13 9AN.
Riley, P. W. J., BA, PhD, The University, Manchester M13 9PL.
Riley-Smith, Professor J. S. C., MA, PhD, Royal Holloway and Bedford New College, Egham Hill, Surrey TW20 0EX.
Rimmer, Professor W. G., MA, PhD, University of N.S.W., P.O. Box 1, Kensington, N.S.W. 2033, Australia.
Ritcheson, Professor C. R., DPhil, Dept of History, University of Southern California, Los Angeles 90007, U.S.A.
Rizvi, S. A. G., MA, DPhil, 7 Portland Road, Summertown, Oxford.
Roach, Professor J. P. C., MA, PhD, 1 Park Crescent, Sheffield S10 2DY.
Robbins, Professor Caroline, PhD, 815 The Chetwynd, Rosemount, Pa. 19010, U.S.A.
Robbins, Professor K. G., MA, DPhil, DLitt, Dept of History, The University, Glasgow G12 8QQ.
Roberts, J. M., MA, DPhil, Merton College, Oxford OX1 4JD.
Roberts, Professor M., MA, DPhil, DLit, FilDr, FBA, 1 Allen Street, Grahamstown 6140, C.P., South Africa.
Roberts, P. R., MA, PhD, FSA, Keynes College, The University, Canterbury, Kent CT2 7NP.
Roberts, Professor R. C., PhD, 284 Blenheim Road, Columbus, Ohio 43214, U.S.A.
Roberts, Professor R. S., PhD, History Dept, University of Zimbabwe, P.O. Box MP 167, Harare, Zimbabwe.
Roberts, Stephen K., BA, PhD, East View, Iron Cross, Salford Priors, Evesham, Worcs. WR11 5SH.
Robertson, J. C., MA, DPhil, St Hugh's College, Oxford OX2 6LE.
Robinson, F. C. R., MA, PhD, Alderside, Egham Hill, Egham, Surrey TW20 0BD.
Robinson, K. E., CBE, MA, DLitt, LLD, The Old Rectory, Church Westcote, Kingham, Oxford OX7 6SF.

Robinson, R. A. H., BA, PhD, School of History, The University, Birmingham B15 2TT.

Robinton, Professor Madeline R., MA, PhD, 210 Columbia Heights, Brooklyn 1, New York, U.S.A.

Rodger, N. A. M., MA, DPhil, 40 Grafton Road, Acton, London W3.

*Rodkey, F. S., AM, PhD, 152 Bradley Drive, Santa Cruz, Calif., U.S.A.

Rodney, Professor W., MA, PhD, Royal Roads Military College, FMO, Victoria, B.C., VoS 1Bo, Canada.

Roebuck, Peter, BA, PhD, Dept of History, New University of Ulster, Coleraine, N. Ireland BT48 7JL.

Rogers, Professor A., MA, PhD, FSA, Ulph Cottage, Church Plain, Burnham Market, Kings Lynn, Norfolk PE31 8EL.

Rogister, J. M. J., MA, DPhil, 4 The Peth, Durham DH1 4PZ.

Rolo, Professor P. J. V., MA, The University, Keele, Staffordshire ST5 5BG.

Rompkey, R. G., MA, BEd, PhD, Dept of English, Memorial University, St John's, Newfoundland A1C 5S7, Canada.

Roots, Professor I. A., MA, FSA, Dept of History, University of Exeter, Exeter EX4 4QH.

Roper, M., MA, Public Record Office, Ruskin Avenue, Kew, Richmond, Surrey TW9 4DU.

Rose, Margaret A., BA, PhD, c/o H.P.S. Faculty of Arts University of Melbourne, Parkville, Victoria 3052, Australia.

Rose, Professor P. L., MA, D.enHist (Sorbonne), Dept of General History, University of Haifa, Haifa, Israel.

Rosenthal, Professor Joel T., PhD, State University, Stony Brook, New York 11794, U.S.A.

Roseveare, Professor H. G., PhD, King's College London, Strand, London WC2R 2LS.

Roskell, Professor J. S., MA, DPhil, FBA, The University, Manchester M13 9PL.

Rothblatt, Professor Sheldon, PhD, Dept of History, University of California, Berkeley, Calif. 94720, U.S.A.

Rothney, Professor G. O., PhD, MA, LLD, St John's College, University of Manitoba, Winnipeg R3T 2MS, Canada.

Rothrock, Professor G. A., MA, PhD, Dept of History, University of Alberta, Edmonton, Alberta T6G 2H4, Canada.

Rousseau, P. H., MA, DPhil, Dept of History, University of Auckland, Private Bag, Auckland, New Zealand.

*Rowe, Miss B. J. H., MA, BLitt, St Anne's Cottage, Winkton, Christchurch, Hants.

Rowe, W. J., DPhil, Rock Mill, Par, Cornwall PL25 2SS.

Rowse, A. L., MA, DLitt, DCL, FBA, Trenarren House, St Austell, Cornwall.

Roy, I., MA, DPhil, Dept of History, King's College London, Strand, London WC2R 2LS.

Roy, Professor R. H., MA, PhD, 2841 Tudor Avenue, Victoria, B.C., Canada V8N 1L6.

Royle, E., MA, PhD, Dept of History, The University, York YO1 5DD.

Rubens, A., FRICS, FSA, 16 Grosvenor Place, London SW1.

Rubini, D. A., DPhil, Temple University, Philadelphia 19122, Penn., U.S.A.

Rubinstein, Professor N., PhD, Westfield College, London NW3 7ST.

Rubinstein, Assoc. Professor W. D., BA, PhD, School of Social Sciences, Deakin University, Victoria 3217, Australia.

Ruddock, Miss A. A., PhD, FSA, Wren Cottage, Heatherwood, Midhurst, W. Sussex GU29 9LH.

Rudé, Professor G. F. E., MA, PhD, The Oast House, Hope Farm, Beckley, nr Rye, E. Sussex.

Rule, Professor John C., MA, PhD, Ohio State University, 230 West 17th Avenue, Colombus, Ohio 43210, U.S.A.

Rule, J. G., MA, PhD, Dept of History, The University, Southampton SO9 5NH.

Rumble, A. R., BA, PhD, Dip Arch Admin., Dept of Palaeography, University of Manchester, Oxford Road, Manchester M13 8PL.

*RUNCIMAN, The Hon. Sir Steven, CH, MA, DPhil, LLD, LittD, DLitt, LitD, DD, DHL, FBA, FSA, Elshieshields, Lockerbie, Dumfriesshire.

Runyan, Professor Timothy J., Cleveland State University, Cleveland, Ohio 44115, U.S.A.

Rupke, N. A., MA, PhD, Wolfson College, Oxford OX2 6UD.

Russell, Professor C. S. R., MA, Dept of History, University College London, Gower Street, London WC1E 6BT.

Russell, Mrs J. G., MA, DPhil, St Hugh's College, Oxford OX2 6LE.

Russell, Professor P. E., MA, FBA, 23 Belsyre Court, Woodstock Road, Oxford OX2 6HU.

Ryan, A. N., MA, School of History, University of Liverpool, P.O. Box 147, Liverpool L69 3BX.

Rycraft, P., BA, Dept of History, The University, York YO1 5DD.

Ryder, A. F. C., MA, DPhil, Dept of History, Wills Memorial Building, Queen's Road, Bristol BS8 1RJ.

Sachse, Professor W. L., PhD, 4066 Whitney Avenue, Mt Carmel, Conn. 06518, U.S.A.

Sainty, Sir John, KCB, MA, 22 Kelso Place, London W8.

*Salmon, Professor E. T., MA, PhD, 36 Auchmar Road, Hamilton, Ontario LPC 1C5, Canada.

Salmon, Professor J. H. M., MA, MLitt, DLit, Bryn Mawr College, Bryn Mawr, Pa. 19101, U.S.A.

*Saltman, Professor A., MA, PhD, Bar Ilan University, Ramat Gan, Israel

Salvadori, Max W., Dr Sc, LittD, 36 Ward Avenue, Northampton, Mass. 01060, U.S.A.

Samuel, E. R., BA, MPhil, 8 Steynings Way, London N12 7LN.

Sanderson, Professor G. N., MA, PhD, 2 Alder Close, Englefield Green, Surrey TW20 0LU.

Sar Desai, Professor Damodar R., MA, PhD, Dept of History, University of California, Los Angeles, Calif. 90024, U.S.A.

Saunders, A. D., MA, FSA, 12 Ashburnham Grove, London SE10 8UH.

Saul, N. E., MA, DPhil, Dept of History, Royal Holloway and Bedford New College, Egham Hill, Egham, Surrey TW20 0EX.

Saville, Professor J., BSc(Econ), Dept of Economic and Social History, The University, Hull HU6 7RX.

Sawyer, Professor P. H., MA, Viktoriagatan 18, 441 33 Alingsas, Sweden.

Sayers, Miss J. E., MA, BLitt, PhD, FSA, University College London, Gower Street, London WC1 6BT.

Scammell, G. V., MA, Pembroke College, Cambridge CB2 1RF.

Scammell, Mrs Jean, MA, Clare Hall, Cambridge.

Scarisbrick, Professor J. J., MA, PhD, 35 Kenilworth Road, Leamington Spa, Warwickshire.

Schofield, A. N. E. D., PhD, 57 West Way, Rickmansworth, Herts. WD3 2EH.

Schofield, R. S., MA, PhD, 27 Trumpington Street, Cambridge CB2 1QA.

Schreiber, Professor Roy E., PhD, Dept of History, Indiana University, P.O.B. 7111, South Bend, Indiana 46634, U.S.A.

Schweizer, Karl W., MA, PhD, 4 Harrold Drive, Bishop's University, Lennoxville, Quebec, Canada.

Schwoerer, Professor Lois G., PhD, 7213 Rollingwood Drive, Chevy Chase, Maryland 20015, U.S.A.

Scott, Dom Geoffrey, MA, PhD, Dip Theol, Douai Abbey, Upper Woolhampton, Reading RG7 5TH.

Scott, H. M., MA, PhD, Dept of Modern History, The University, St Salvator's College, St Andrews, Fife.

Scott, Tom, MA, PhD, School of History, The University, P.O. Box 147, Liverpool L69 3BX.

Scouloudi, Miss I., MSc(Econ), FSA, 67 Victoria Road, London W8 5RH.

Scribner, R. W., MA, PhD, Clare College, Cambridge CB2 1TL.

Seaborne, M. V. J., MA, Chester College, Cheyney Road, Chester CH1 4BJ.

Searle, A., BA, MPhil, Dept of Manuscripts, British Library, London WC1B 3DG.

Searle, Professor Eleanor, AB, PhD, 431 S. Parkwood Avenue, Pasadena, Calif. 91107, U.S.A.

Searle, G. R., MA, PhD, School of English and American Studies, University of East Anglia, Norwich NR4 7TJ.

Seaver, Professor Paul S., MA, PhD, Dept of History, Stanford University, Stanford, Calif. 94305, U.S.A.

Seddon, P. R., BA, PhD, Dept of History, The University, Nottingham NG7 2RD.

Sell, Rev. A. P. F., BA, BD, MA, PhD, Rue de la Golette 11B, 1217 Meyrin, Geneva, Switzerland.

Sellar, W. D. H., BA, LLB, 6 Eildon Street, Edinburgh EH3 5JU.

Semmell, Professor Bernard, PhD, Dept of History, State University of New York at Stony Brook, N.Y. 11790, U.S.A.

Serjeant, W. R., BA, 51 Derwent Road, Ipswich IP3 0QR.

Seton-Watson, C. I. W., MC, MA, Oriel College, Oxford OX1 4EW.

Shannon, Professor R. T., MA, PhD, Dept of History, University College of Swansea, Swansea SA2 8PP.

Sharp, Mrs M., MA, PhD, c/o 96 London Road, Guildford, Surrey GU1 1TH.

Sharpe, J. A., MA, DPhil, Dept of History, The University, York YO1 5DD.

Sharpe, K. M., MA, DPhil, Dept of History, University of Southampton, Southampton SO9 5NH.

Shaw, I. P., MA, 3 Oaks Lane, Shirley, Croydon, Surrey CR0 5HP.

Shead, N. F., MA, BLitt, 8 Whittliemuir Avenue, Muirend, Glasgow G44 3HU.

Sheils, W. J., PhD, Goodricke Lodge, Heslington Lane, York YO1 5DD.

Shennan, Professor J. H., PhD, Dept of History, University of Lancaster, Bailrigg, Lancaster LA1 4YG.

Sheppard, F. H. W., MA, PhD, FSA, 10 West Street, Henley-on-Thames, Oxon RG9 2DT.

Sherborne, J. W., MA, 26 Hanbury Road, Bristol BS8 2EP.

Sherwood, R. E., 22 Schole Road, Willingham, Cambridge CB4 5JD.
Short, K. R. MacD., MA, BD, EdD, DPhil, 89 Bicester Road, Kidlington, Oxford OX5 2LD.
Shukman, H., BA, DPhil, MA, St Antony's College, Oxford OX2 6JF.
Simpson, D. H., MA, Royal Commonwealth Society, 18 Northumberland Avenue, London WC2.
Simpson, G. G., MA, PhD, FSA, Taylor Building, King's College, Old Aberdeen AB9 2UB.
Sinar, Miss J. C., MA, 60 Wellington Street, Matlock, Derbyshire DE4 3GS.
Siney, Professor Marion C., MA, PhD, 1890 East 107th Street, Apt 534, Cleveland, Ohio 44106, U.S.A.
Sked, A., MA, DPhil, Flat 3, Aberdeen Court, 68 Aberdeen Park, London N5 2BH.
Skidelsky, Professor R. J. A., BA, PhD, Tilton House, Selmerston, Firle, Sussex.
Skinner, Professor Q. R. D., MA, FBA, Christ's College, Cambridge CB2 3BU.
Slack, P. A., MA, DPhil, Exeter College, Oxford OX1 3DP.
Slade, C. F., PhD, FSA, 28 Holmes Road, Reading, Berks.
Slater, A. W., MSc(Econ), 146 Castelnau, London SW13 9ET.
Slatter, Miss M. D., MA, 2 Tuscan Close, Tilehurst, Reading, Berks. RG3 6DF.
Slavin, Professor A. J., PhD, College of Arts & Letters, University of Louisville, Louisville, Kentucky 40268, U.S.A.
Slee, P. R. H., PhD, BA, Dept of History, The University, Durham DH1 3EX.
Smith, A. G. R., MA, PhD, 5 Cargil Avenue, Kilmacolm, Renfrewshire.
Smith, A. Hassell, BA, PhD, School of English and American Studies, University of East Anglia, Norwich NR4 7TJ.
Smith, B. S., MA, FSA, Historical Manuscripts Commission, Quality Court, Chancery Lane, London WC2A 1HP.
Smith, D. M., MA, PhD, FSA, Borthwick Institute of Historical Research, St Anthony's Hall, York YO1 2PW.
Smith, E. A., MA, Dept of History, Faculty of Letters, The University, Whiteknights, Reading RG6 2AH.
Smith, F. B., MA, PhD, Research School of Social Sciences, Institute of Advanced Studies, Australian National University, G.P.O. Box 4, Canberra, A.C.T. 2601, Australia.
Smith, Professor Goldwin A., MA, PhD, DLitt, Wayne State University, Detroit, Michigan 48202, U.S.A.
Smith, J. Beverley, MA, University College, Aberystwyth SY23 2AX.
Smith, Joseph, BA, PhD, Dept of History, The University, Exeter EX4 4QH.
Smith, Julia M. H., MA, DPhil, Dept of History, Trinity College, Hartford, Conn. 06106, U.S.A.
Smith, Professor L. Baldwin, PhD, Northwestern University, Evanston, Ill. 60201, U.S.A.
Smith, Professor P., MA, DPhil, Dept of History, The University, Southampton SO9 5NH.
Smith, Professor R. E. F., MA, Dept of Russian, The University, P.O. Box 363, Birmingham B15 2TT.
Smith, Richard M., BA, PhD, All Souls College, Oxford OX1 4AL.
Smith, R. S., MA, BA, 7 Capel Lodge, 244 Kew Road, Kew, TW9 3JU.

Smith, S., BA, PhD, Les Haies, 40 Oatlands Road, Shinfield, Reading, Berks.
Smith, Professor T. A., BSc(Econ), Queen Mary College, Mile End Road, London E1 4NS.
Smith, W. H. C., BA, PhD, Erin Lodge, Symons Hill, Falmouth TR11 2SX.
Smith, W. J., MA, 5 Gravel Hill, Emmer Green, Reading, Berks. RG4 8QN.
Smyth, A. P., MA, DPhil, FSA, Keynes College, The University, Canterbury CT2 7NP.
*Smyth, Rev. Canon C. H. E., MA, 12 Manor Court, Pinehurst, Cambridge.
Snell, L. S., MA, FSA, FRSA, 27 Weoley Hill, Selly Oak, Birmingham B29 4AA.
Snow, Professor V. F., MA, PhD, Dept of History, Syracuse University, 311 Maxwell Hall, Syracuse, New York 13244, U.S.A.
Snyder, Professor H. L., MA, PhD, 5577 Majestic Court, Riverside, Calif. 92506, U.S.A.
Soden, G. I., MA, DD, Buck Brigg, Hanworth, Norwich, Norfolk.
Somers, Rev. H. J., JCB, MA, PhD, St Francis Xavier University, Antigonish, Nova Scotia, Canada.
Somerville, Sir Robert, KCVO, MA, FSA, 3 Hunt's close, Morden Road, London SE3 0AH.
Sommerville, Johann P., MA, PhD, 201 High Street, Chesterton, Cambridge CB4 1NL.
SOUTHERN, Sir Richard (W.), MA, DLitt, LittD, DLitt, FBA, 40 St John Street, Oxford OX1 2LH.
Southgate, D. G., BA, DPhil, The Old Harriers, Bridford, nr Exeter, Devon EX6 7HS.
Spalding, Miss R., MA, 34 Reynards Road, Welwyn, Herts.
Speck, Professor W. A., MA, DPhil, School of History, The University, Leeds LS2 9JT.
Spencer, B. W., BA, FSA, 6 Carpenters Wood Drive, Chorleywood, Herts.
Spiers, E. M., MA, PhD, 170 Alwoodley Lane, Leeds, West Yorkshire LS17 7PF.
Spinks, Revd B. D., BA, MTh, BD, Churchill College, Cambridge CB3 0DS.
Spooner, Professor F. C., MA, PhD, LittD, FSA, 31 Chatsworth Avenue, Bromley, Kent BR1 5DP.
Spring, Professor D., PhD, Dept of History, Johns Hopkins University, Baltimore, Md. 21218, U.S.A.
Spufford, Mrs H. M., MA, PhD, Newnham College, Cambridge CB3 9DF.
Spufford, P., MA, PhD, Queens' College, Cambridge CB3 9ET.
Squibb, G. D., QC, FSA, The Old House, Cerne Abbas, Dorset DT2 7JQ.
Stachura, P. D., MA, PhD, Dept of History, The University, Stirling FK9 4LA.
Stacpoole, Dom Alberic J., OSB, MA, Saint Benet's Hall, Oxford OX1 3LN.
Stafford, Pauline A., BA, DPhil, Athill Lodge, St Helen's Lane, Adel, Leeds LS16 8BS.
Stanley, The Hon. G. F. G., MA, BLitt, DPhil, The Office of Lieutenant-Governor, Fredericton, New Brunswick, Canada.
Stansky, Professor Peter, PhD, Dept of History, Stanford University, Stanford, Calif. 94305, U.S.A.

Starkey, D. R., MA, PhD, 49 Hamilton Park West, London N5 1AE.
Steele, E. D., MA, PhD, School of History, The University, Leeds LS2 9JT.
Steinberg, J., MA, PhD, Trinity Hall, Cambridge CB2 1TJ.
Steiner, Mrs Zara S., MA, PhD, New Hall, Cambridge CB3 0DF.
Stephens, J. N., MA, DPhil, Dept of History, University of Edinburgh, George Square, Edinburgh EH8 9JY.
Stephens, W. B., MA, PhD, FSA, 37 Batcliffe Drive, Leeds 6.
Stephenson, Mrs Jill, MA, PhD, Dept of History, University of Edinburgh, George Square, Edinburgh EH8 9JY.
Steven, Miss M. J. E., PhD, 3 Bonwick Place, Garran, A.C.T. 2605, Australia.
Stevenson, David, MA, PhD, Dept of International History, London School of Economics, Houghton Street, London WC2A 2AE.
Stevenson, D., BA, PhD, Dept of History, Taylor Buildings, King's College, Old Aberdeen AB1 0EE.
Stevenson, Miss J. H., BA, c/o Institute of Historical Research, Senate House, Malet Street, London, WC1E 7HU.
Stevenson, J., MA, DPhil, Dept of History, The University, Sheffield S10 2TN.
Stewart, A. T. Q., MA PhD, Dept of Modern History, The Queen's University, Belfast BT7 1NN.
Stitt, F. B., BA, BLitt, William Salt Library, Stafford.
Stockwell, A. J., MA, PhD, Dept of History, Royal Holloway and Bedford New College, Egham Hill, Egham, Surrey TW20 0EX.
Stone, E., MA, DPhil, FSA, Keble College, Oxford OX1 3PG.
Stone, Professor L., MA, Princeton University, Princeton, N.J. 08540, U.S.A.
Storey, Professor R. L., MA, PhD, 19 Elm Avenue, Beeston, Nottingham NG9 1BU.
Storry, J. G., Woodland View, Huntercombe End, Nettlebed, nr Henley-on-Thames, Oxon. RG9 5RR.
Story, Professor G. M., BA, DPhil, 335 Southside Road, St John's Newfoundland, Canada.
*Stoye, J. W., MA, DPhil, Magdalen College, Oxford OX1 4AU.
Street, J., MA, PhD, Badgers' Wood, Cleveley, Forton, Garstang, Preston PR3 1BY.
Stringer, K. J., BA, MA, PhD, Dept of History, Furness College, The University, Lancaster LA1 4YG.
Strong, Mrs F., MA, Traigh Gate, Arisaig, Inverness-shire PH39 4N1.
Strong, Sir Roy, BA, PhD, FSA, Victoria & Albert Museum, London SW7.
Stuart, C. H., MA, Christ Church, Oxford OX1 1DP.
Studd, J. R., PhD, Dept of History, The University, Keele, Staffs. ST5 5BG.
Sturdy, D. J., BA, PhD, Dept of History, New University of Ulster, Coleraine, N. Ireland BT52 1SA.
Supple, Professor B. E., BSc(Econ), PhD, MA, St Catharines College, Cambridge CB2 1RL.
Sutcliffe, Professor A. R., MA, DU, Dept of Economic and Social History, The University, 21 Slayleigh Avenue, Sheffield S10 3RA.
Sutherland, Professor D. W., DPhil, State University of Iowa, Iowa City, Iowa 52240, U.S.A.
Sutherland, Gillian, MA, DPhil, MA, PhD, Newnham College, Cambridge CB3 9DF.

Sutherland, N. M., MA, PhD, 15 Milton Manor Drive, Little Milton, Oxon. OX9 7PT.
Swanson, R. N., MA, PhD, School of History, The University, P.O. Box 363, Birmingham B15 2TT.
Swanton, Professor M. J., BA, PhD, FSA, Queen's Building, The University, Exeter EX4 4QH.
Swart, Professor K. W., PhD, LittD, University College London, Gower Street, London WC1 6BT.
Sweet, D. W., MA, PhD, Dept of History, The University, 43 North Bailey, Durham.
Sweetman, J., MA, PhD, 98 Kings Ride, Camberley, Surrey GU15 4LN.
Swenarton, M. C., BA, PhD, 10d Barnsbury Terrace, London N1 1JH.
Swift, R. E., PhD, MA, 14 Holly Drive, Penyfford, nr Chester, Clwyd.
Swinfen, D. B., MA, DPhil, 14 Cedar Road, Broughty Ferry, Dundee.
Sydenham, M. J., PhD, Carleton University, Ottawa, Canada K1S 5B6.
Syrett, Professor D., PhD, 46 Hawthorne Terrace, Leonia, N.J., 07605, U.S.A.
Szechi, D., BA, DPhil, 19 Henry Road, Oxford OX2 0DG.

Taft, Barbara, PhD, 3101 35th Street, Washington, D.C. 20016, U.S.A.
Talbot, C. H., PhD, BD, FSA, 47 Hazlewell Road, London SW15.
Tamse, Coenraad Arnold, DLitt, De Krom, 12 Potgieterlaan, 9752 Ex Haren (Groningen), The Netherlands.
Tanner, J. I., CBE, MA, PhD, DLitt, Flat One, 57 Drayton Gardens, London SW10 9RU.
Tarling, Professor P. N., MA, PhD, LittD, University of Auckland, Private Bag, Auckland, New Zealand.
Tarn, Professor J. N., B.Arch, PhD, FRIBA, Dept of Architecture, The University, P.O. Box 147, Liverpool L69 3BX.
Taylor, Arnold J., CBE, MA, DLitt, FBA, FSA, Rose Cottage, Lincoln's Hill, Chiddingfold, Surrey GU8 4UN.
Taylor, Professor Arthur J., MA, The University, Leeds LS2 9JT.
Taylor, Rev. Brian, MA, FSA, The Rectory, The Flower Walk, Guildford GU2 5EP.
Taylor, J., MA, School of History, The University, Leeds LS2 9JT.
Taylor, J. W. R., 36 Alexandra Drive, Surbiton, Surrey KT5 9AF.
Taylor, P. M., BA, PhD, School of History, The University, Leeds LS2 9JT.
Taylor, R. T., MA, PhD, Dept of Political Theory and Government, University College of Swansea, Swansea SA2 8PP.
Taylor, W., MA, PhD, FSAScot, 25 Bingham Terrace, Dundee.
Teichova, Professor Alice, BA, PhD, University of East Anglia, University Plain, Norwich NR4 7TJ.
Temperley, H., BA, MA, PhD, School of English and American Studies, University of East Anglia, Norwich NR4 7TJ.
Temple, Nora C., BA, PhD, University College, P.O. Box 78, Cardiff CF1 1XL.
Templeman, G., CBE, MA, DCL, DL, FSA, Barton Corner, 2a St Augustine's Road, Canterbury, Kent.
Terraine, J. A., 74 Kensington Park Road, London W11 2PL.
Thacker, A. T., MA, DPhil, Flat 1, 6 Liverpool Road, Chester, Cheshire.
Thackray, Professor Arnold W., PhD, E. F. Smith Hall D-6, University of Pennsylvania, Philadelphia 19104, U.S.A.
Thane, Patricia M., BA, PhD, 5 Twisden Road, London NW5 1DL.

Thirsk, Mrs I. Joan, PhD, FBA, 1 Hadlow Castle, Hadlow, Tonbridge, Kent TN11 0EG.
Thistlethwaite, Professor F., CBE, DCL, LHD, 15 Park Parade, Cambridge CB5 8AL.
Thomas, Professor A. C., MA, DipArch, FSA, MRIA, Lambessow, St Clement, Truro, Cornwall.
Thomas, D. O., MA, PhD, Orlandon, 31 North Parade, Aberystwyth, Dyfed SY23 2JN.
Thomas of Swynnerton, Lord, MA, 29 Ladbroke Grove, London W11 3BB.
Thomas, J. H., BA, PhD, School of Social and Historical Studies, Portsmouth Polytechnic, Southsea, Portsmouth PO5 3AT.
Thomas, K. V., MA, DLitt, FBA, Corpus Christi College, Oxford OX1 4JF.
Thomas, Professor P. D. G., MA, PhD, Dept of History, University College of Wales, Aberystwyth SY23 2AU.
Thomas, W. E. S., MA, Christ Church, Oxford OX1 1DP.
Thomis, Professor M. I., MA, PhD, University of Queensland, St Lucia, Brisbane 4067, Australia.
Thompson, A. F., MA, Wadham College, Oxford OX1 3PN.
Thompson, C. L. F., BA, Colne View, 69 Chaney Road, Wivenhoe, Essex.
Thompson, Mrs D. K. G., MA, School of History, The University, P.O. Box 363, Birmingham B15 2TT.
Thompson, D. M., MA, PhD, Fitzwilliam College, Cambridge CB3 0DG.
Thompson, E. P., MA, Wick Episcopi, Upper Wick, Worcester.
Thompson, Professor F. M. L., MA, DPhil, FBA, Institute of Historical Research, Senate House, London WC1E 7HU.
Thompson, I. A. A., MA, PhD, Dept of History, The University, Keele, Staffs. ST5 5BG.
Thompson, R. F., MA, School of English and American Studies, University of East Anglia, Norwich NR4 7TJ.
Thomson, J. A. F., MA, DPhil, The University, Glasgow G12 8QQ.
Thomson, R. M., MA, PhD, Dept of History, University of Tasmania, Box 252C, GPO, Hobart, Tasmania 7001, Australia.
Thorne, C., MA, DLitt, FBA, School of European Studies, University of Sussex, Brighton BN1 9QN.
Thornton, Professor A. P., MA, DPhil, University College, University of Toronto, Toronto M5S 1A1, Canada.
*Thrupp, Professor S. L., MA, PhD, 57 Balsam Lane, Princeton, New Jersey 08540, U.S.A.
Thurlow, The Very Rev. A. G. G., MA, FSA, 2 East Pallant, Chichester, West Sussex PO19 1TR.
Tomizawa, Professor Reigan, MA, DLitt, Dept of History, Kansai University, 3-10-12 Hiyoshidai, Taksukishi, Osaka 569, Japan.
Tomkeieff, Mrs O. G., MA, LLB, 88 Moorside North, Newcastle upon Tyne NE4 9DU.
Tomlinson, H. C., BA, DPhil, 'Upcott', Wellington College, Crowthorne, Berkshire RG11 7PU.
Tonkin, J. M., BA, BD, PhD, Dept of History, University of Western Australia, Nedlands, Western Australia 6009.
Townshend, C. J. N., MA, DPhil, 62 The Covert, Keele, Staffs.
Toynbee, Miss M. R., MA, PhD, FSA, 22 Park Town, Oxford OX2 6SH.
Trebilcock, R. C., MA, Pembroke College, Cambridge CB2 1RF.

Tsitsonis, S. E., PhD, 31 Samara Street, Paleo Psyhico, (15452), Athens, Greece.

Tuck, J. A., PhD, MA, The Master's House, Collingwood College, Durham DH1 3LT.

Turner, Mrs Barbara D. M., BA, 27 St Swithuns Street, Winchester, Hampshire.

Turner, G. L'E., FSA, DSc, The Old Barn, Mill Street, Islip, Oxford OX5 2SY.

Turner, J. A., MA, DPhil, 31 Devereux Road, London SW11 6JR.

Turner, Professor Ralph V., MA, PhD, History Department, Florida State University, Tallahassee, Florida 32306 U.S.A.

Tyacke, N. R. N., MA, DPhil, 1a Spencer Rise, London NW5.

Tyerman, C. J., MA, DPhil, Exeter College, Oxford OX1 3DP.

Tyler, P., BLitt, MA, DPhil, University of Western Australia, Nedlands, Western Australia 6009.

Ugawa, Professor K., BA, MA, PhD, Minami-Ogikubo, 1-chome 25-15, Suginami-Ku, Tokyo 167, Japan.

Underdown, Professor David, MA, BLitt, DLitt, Dept of History, Yale University, P.O. Box 1504A, Yale Station, New Haven, Conn. 06520, U.S.A.

Upton. A. F.. MA. 5 West Acres. St Andrews, Fife.

Vaisey, D. G., MA, FSA, 12 Hernes Road, Oxford.

Vale, M. G. A., MA, DPhil, St John's College, Oxford OX1 3JP.

Van Caenegem, Professor R. C., LLD, PhD, Veurestraat 47, B9821 Gent-Afsnee, Belgium.

Van Houts, Elisabeth, DLitt, Girton College, Cambridge CB3 0JG.

Van Roon, Professor Ger, Dept of Contemporary History, Vrije Universiteit, Amsterdam, Koningslaan 31-33, The Netherlands.

Vann, Professor Richard T., PhD, Dept of History, Wesleyan University, Middletown, Conn. 06457, U.S.A.

*Varley, Mrs J., MA, FSA, 164 Nettleham Road, Lincoln.

Vaughan, Sir (G) Edgar, KBE, MA, 27 Birch Grove, West Acton, London W3 9SP.

Veale, Elspeth M., BA, PhD, 31 St Mary's Road, Wimbledon, London SW19 7BP.

Véliz, Professor C., BSc, PhD, Dept. of Sociology, La Trobe University, Melbourne, Victoria 3083, Australia.

Vessey, D. W. T. C., MA, PhD, Dept of Classics, King's College London, Strand, London WC2R 2LS.

Vincent, Professor J. R., MA, PhD, Dept of History, The University, 13 Woodland Road, Bristol BS8 1TB.

Virgoe, R., BA, PhD, University of East Anglia, School of English and American Studies, Norwich NR4 7TJ.

Waddell, Professor D. A. G., MA, DPhil, University of Stirling, Stirling FK9 4LA.

*Wagner, Sir Anthony (R.), KCVO, MA, DLitt, FSA, College of Arms, Queen Victoria Street, London EC4.

Waites, B. F., MA, FRGS, 6 Chater Road, Oakham, Leics. LE15 6RY.

Wakelin, M. F., Royal Holloway and Bedford New College, Egham Hill, Egham, Surrey TW20 0EX.

Walford, A. J., MA, PhD, FLA, 45 Parkside Drive, Watford, Herts WD1 3AU.

Walker, Rev. Canon D. G., DPhil, FSA, University College of Swansea, Swansea SA2 8PP.
Walker, Professor Sue S., MA, PhD, History Department, Northeastern Illinois University, Chicago, Illinois 60625, U.S.A.
Wallace, Professor W. V., MA, Institute of Soviet and East European Studies, University of Glasgow, Glasgow G12 8LQ.
Waller, P. J., MA, Merton College, Oxford OX1 4JD.
Wallis, Miss H. M., OBE, MA, DPhil, FSA, 96 Lord's View, St John's Wood Road, London NW8 7HG.
Wallis, P. J., MA, 43 Briarfield Road, Newcastle upon Tyne NE3 3UH.
Walne, P., MA, FSA, County Record Office, County Hall, Hertford.
Walsh, T. J., MA, PhD, MB, BCh, LittD, (Hon.) FFA, RCSI, 5 Lower George Street, Wexford, Ireland.
Walton, J. K., BA, PhD, Dept of History, Furness College, The University, Lancaster LA1 4YG.
Walvin, J., BA, MA, DPhil, Dept of History, The University, York YO1 5DD.
Wangermann, Professor E., MA, DPhil, Institut of Geschichte, Universität Salzburg, A-5020 Salzburg.
Wanklyn, M. D., BA, MA, PhD, Dept of Arts, The Polytechnic, Wulfruna Street, Wolverhampton, West Midlands.
Ward, Jennifer, C., MA, PhD, 51 Hartswood Road, Brentwood, Essex CM14 5AG.
Ward, Professor J. T., MA, PhD, Dept of History, McCance Bldg., University of Strathclyde, 16 Richmond Street, Glasgow G1 1XQ.
Ward, Professor W. R., DPhil, 21 Grenehurst Way, The Village, Petersfield, Hampshire GU31 4AZ.
Warner, Professor G., MA, Arts Faculty, The Open University, Walton Hall, Milton Keynes MK7 6AA.
Warren, A. J., MA, DPhil, Vanbrugh Provost's House, 1 Bleachfield, Heslington, York YO1 5DD.
Warren, Professor W. L., MA, DPhil, FRSL, Dept of Modern History, The Queen's University, Belfast, N. Ireland BT7 1NN.
Wasserstein, Professor B. M. J., MA, DPhil, Dept of History, Brandeis University, Waltham, Mass. 02254, U.S.A.
Wasserstein, D. J., MA, DPhil, Dept of Semitic Languages, University College, Belfield, Dublin 4, Ireland.
*Waters, Lt-Commander D. W., RN, FSA, Jolyons, Bury, nr Pulborough, W. Sussex.
Wathey, A. B., MA, DPhil, Downing College, Cambridge CB2 1DG.
Watkin, The Rt Rev. Abbot Aelred, OSB, MA, FSA, St Benet's, Beccles, Suffolk NR34 9NR.
WATSON, Professor A. G., MA, DLit, BLitt, FSA (Hon Librarian), University College London, Gower Street, London WC1 6BT.
Watson, D. R., MA, BPhil, Dept of Modern History, The University, Dundee DD1 4HN.
Watt, Professor D. C., MA, London School of Economic, Houghton Street, London WC2A 2AE.
Watt, Professor D. E. R., MA, DPhil, Dept of Mediaeval History, St Salvator's College, St Andrews, Fife KY16 9AJ.
Watt, Professor J. A., BA, PhD, Dept of History, The University, Newcastle upon Tyne NE1 7RU.
Watts, D. G., MA, BLitt, 34 Greenbank Crescent, Bassett, Southampton SO1 7FQ.

Watts, M. R., BA, DPhil, Dept of History, The University, Nottingham NG7 2RD.

Webb, Professor Colin de B., BA, MA, University of Natal, King George V Avenue, Durban 4001, S Africa.

Webb, J. G., MA, 11 Blount Road, Pembroke Park, Old Portsmouth, Hampshire PO1 2TD.

Webb, Professor R. K., PhD, 3307 Highland Place NW., Washington, D.C. 20008, U.S.A.

Webster (A.) Bruce, MA, FSA, 5 The Terrace, St Stephens, Canterbury.

Webster, C., MA, DSc, Corpus Christi College, Oxford OX1 4JF.

Wedgwood, Dame (C.) Veronica, OM, DBE, MA, LittD, DLitt, LLD, Whitegate, Alciston, nr Polegate, Sussex.

Weinbaum, Professor M., PhD, 133-33 Sanford Avenue, Flushing, N.Y. 11355, U.S.A.

Weinstock, Miss M. B., MA, 26 Wey View Crescent, Broadway, Weymouth, Dorset.

Wells, R. A. E., BA, DPhil, Dept of Humanities, Brighton Polytechnic, Falmer, Brighton, Sussex.

Wendt, Professor Bernd-Jurgen, DrPhil, Beim Andreasbrunnen 8, 2 Hamburg 20, West Germany.

Wernham, Professor R. B., MA, Marine Cottage, 63 Hill Head Road, Hill Head, Fareham, Hants.

*Weske, Mrs Dorothy B., AM, PhD, Oakwood, Sandy Spring, Maryland 20860, U.S.A.

West, Professor F. J., PhD, School of Social Sciences, Deakin University, Victoria 3217, Australia.

Weston, Professor Corinne C., PhD, 200 Central Park South, New York, N.Y. 10019, U.S.A.

Whaley, Joachim, MA, PhD, Gonville and Caius College, Cambridge CB2 1TA.

White, Rev. B. R., MA DPhil, 55 St Giles', Regent's Park College, Oxford.

White, G. J., MA, PhD, Chester College, Cheyney Road, Chester CH1 4BJ.

Whiteman, Miss E. A. O., MA, DPhil, FSA, Lady Margaret Hall, Oxford OX2 6QA.

Whiting, J. R. S., MA, DLitt, 15 Lansdown Parade, Cheltenham, Glos.

Whiting, R. C., MA, DPhil, School of History, The University, Leeds LS2 9JT.

Whittam, J. R., MA, BPhil, PhD, Dept of History, University of Bristol, Senate House, Bristol BS8 1TH.

Wickham, C. J., MA, DPhil, School of History, The University, P.O. Box 363, Birmingham B15 2TT.

Wiener, Professor J. H., BA, PhD, City College of New York, Convent Avenue at 138th Street, N.Y. 10031, U.S.A.

Wilkie, Rev. W., MA, PhD, Dept of History, Loras College, Dubuque, Iowa 52001, U.S.A.

Wilks, Professor M. J., MA, PhD, Dept of History, Birkbeck College, Malet Street, London WC1 7HX.

*Willan, Professor T. S., MA, DPhil, 3 Raynham Avenue, Didsbury, Manchester M20 0BW.

Williams, D., MA, PhD, DPhil, University of Calgary, Calgary, Alberta T2N 1N4, Canada.

Williams, Daniel T., BA, PhD, Dept of History, The University, Leicester LE1 7RH.

Williams, Sir Edgar (T.), CB, CBE, DSO, MA, 94 Lonsdale Road, Oxford OX2 7ER.
Williams, (Elisabeth) Ann, BA, PhD, Dept of History, Polytechnic of North London, Prince of Wales Road, London NW5.
Williams, Gareth W., MA, MSc(Econ), Dept of History, Hugh Owen Building, University College of Wales, Aberystwyth SY23 3DY.
Williams, Professor Glanmor, MA, DLitt, University College of Swansea, Swansea SA2 8PP.
Williams, Professor Glyndwr, BA, PhD, Queen Mary College, Mile End Road, London E1 4NS.
Williams, Professor G. A., MA, PhD, 66 De Burgh Street, Cardiff CF1 8LD.
Williams, J. A., MA, BSc(Econ), 44 Pearson Park, Hull, HU5 2TG.
Williams, J. D., BA, MA, PhD, 56 Spurgate, Hutton Mount, Brentwood, Essex CM13 2JT.
Williams, Patrick, BA, PhD, 30 Andover Road, Southsea, Hants. PO4 9QG.
Williams, P. H., MA, DPhil, New College, Oxford OX1 3BN.
Williams, T. I., MA, DPhil, 20 Blenheim Drive, Oxford OX2 8DG.
Willmott, H. P. MA, 13 Barnway, Englefield Green, Egham, Surrey TW20 0QU.
WILSON, Professor C. H., CBE, LittD, DLitt, DLitt, DLitt, FBA, Jesus College, Cambridge CB5 8BL.
Wilson, Sir David., MA, LittD, FilDr, DrPhil, FBA, FSA, The Director's Residence, The British Museum, London WC1B 3DG.
Wilson, H. S., BA, BLitt, Dept of History, The University, York YO1 5DD.
Wilson, R. G., BA, PhD, University of East Anglia, School of Social Studies, University Plain, Norwich NR4 7TJ.
Wilson, Professor T., MA, DPhil, Dept of History, University of Adelaide, Adelaide, South Australia.
Winch, Professor D. N., PhD, BSc(Econ), FBA, University of Sussex, Brighton BN1 9QN.
Winks, Professor R. W. E., MA, PhD, 648 Berkeley College, Yale University, New Haven, Conn. 06520, U.S.A.
Winstanley, M. J., BA, MA, Dept of History, Furness College, The University, Lancaster LA1 4YG.
Winter, J. M., BA, PhD, Pembroke College, Cambridge CB2 1RF.
Wiswall, Frank L., Jr., BA, JuD, PhD, Meadow Farm, Castine, Maine 04421 U.S.A.
Withrington, D. J., MA, MEd, Dept of History, University of Aberdeen, King's College, Old Aberdeen AB9 2UB.
Wolffe, B. P., MA, DPhil, DLitt, Highview, 19 Rosebarn Avenue, Exeter EX4 6DY.
Wong, John Yue-Wo, BA, DPhil, Dept of History, University of Sydney, N.S.W., Australia 2006.
*Wood, Rev. A. Skevington, PhD, 17 Dalewood Road, Sheffield S8 0EB.
Wood, Diana, BA, PhD, 8 Bartlemas Close, Oxford OX4 2AE.
Wood, I. N., MA, DPhil, School of History, The University, Leeds LS2 9JT.
Wood, Mrs S. M., MA, BLitt, St Hugh's College, Oxford OX2 6LE.
Woodfill, Professor W. L., PhD, 762 Creston Road, Berkeley, Calif. 94708, U.S.A.
Woolf, Professor, S. J., MA, DPhil, University of Essex, Wivenhoe Park, Colchester CO4 3SQ.
Woolrych, Professor A. H., BLitt, MA, Patchetts, Caton, nr Lancaster.

Wootton, Assoc. Professor D. R. J., Dept of History, Dalhousie University, Halifax, Nova Scotia, Canada B3H 4H8.
WORDEN, A. B., MA, DPhil (*Literary Director*), St Edmund Hall, Oxford OX1 4AR.
Wordie, James R., MA, PhD, 6 The Knapp, Earley, Reading, Berks. RG6 2DD.
Wormald, B. H. G., MA, Peterhouse, Cambridge CB2 1RD.
Wormald, C. Patrick, MA, 60 Hill Top Road, Oxford OX4 1PE.
Wormald, Jennifer M., MA, PhD, St Hilda's College, Oxford OX4 1DY.
Wortley, The Rev. J. T., MA, PhD, History Dept, University of Manitoba, Winnipeg, Manitoba R3T 2N2, Canada.
Wright, A. D., MA, DPhil, School of History, The University, Leeds LS2 9JT.
Wright, C. J., MA, PhD, 8 Grove Road, East Molesey, Surrey KT8 9JS.
Wright, D. G., BA, PhD, Dip Ed. 9 Victoria Park, Shipley, West Yorkshire BD18 4RL.
Wright, Professor E., MA, Institute of United States Studies, 31 Tavistock Square, London WC1H 9EZ.
Wright, Rev. Professor J. Robert, DPhil, General Theological Seminary, 175 Ninth Avenue, New York, N.Y. 10011, U.S.A.
Wright, Professor Maurice, BA, DPhil, Dept of Government, Dover Street, Manchester M13 9PL.
Wrightson, K,. MA, PhD, Jesus College, Cambridge CB5 8BL.
Wroughton, J. P., MA, 6 Ormonde House, Sion Hill, Bath BA1 2UN.

Yale, D.E.C., MA, LLB, FBA, Christ's College, Cambridge CB2 3BU.
Yates, W. N., MA, Kent Archives Office, County Hall, Maidstone, Kent ME14 1XH.
Yorke, Barbara A. E., BA, PhD, King Alfred's College of Higher Education, Sparkford Road, Winchester SO22 4NR.
Youings, Professor Joyce A., BA, PhD, Dept of History, The University, Exeter EX4 4QH.
Young, J. W., BA, PhD, 11 Gordon Avenue, Leicester LE2 1AA.
Young, K. G., BSc(Econ), MSc, PhD, 11 Fawley Road, London NW6.
Young, Mrs Susan H. H., BA, 78 Holland Road, Ampthill, Beds. MK45 2RS.
Youngs, Professor F. A., Jr., Dept of History, Louisiana State University, Baton Rouge, Louisiana 70803, U.S.A.

Zagorin, Professor P., PhD, Dept of History, College of Arts and Sciences, University of Rochester, River Campus Station, Rochester, N.Y. 14627, U.S.A.
Zeldin, T., MA, DPhil, St Antony's College, Oxford OX2 6JF.
Zeman, Zbynek A. B., MA, DPhil, St Edmund Hall, Oxford OX1 4AR.
Ziegler, P. S., FRSL, 22 Cottesmore Gardens, London W8.

ASSOCIATES OF THE
ROYAL HISTORICAL SOCIETY

Abela, Major A. E., MBE, 21 Borg Olivier Street, Sliema, Malta.
Addy, J., MA, PhD, 66 Long Lane, Clayton West, Huddersfield, HD8 9PR.
Aitken, Rev. Leslie R., MBE, 36 Ethelbert Road, Birchington, Kent CT7 9PY.
Ayrton, Lt-Col. M. McI., HQ Mess, The School of Signals, Blandford Camp, Dorset DT11 8RH.
Ayton, A. C., BA, Dept of History, The University, Hull HU6 7RX.

Begley, M. R., 119 Tennyson Avenue, King's Lynn, Norfolk.
Birchenough, Mrs F. J., 6 Cheyne Walk, Bramblefield Estate, Longfield, Kent.
Bird, E. A., 29 King Edward Avenue, Rainham, Essex RN13 9RH.
Blackwood, B., FRIBA, FRTPI, FSAScot, DipTP, Ebony House, Whitney Drive, Stevenage SG1 4BL.
Bottomley, A. F., MA, Eversley School, Southwold, Suffolk IP18 6AH.
Boyes, J. H., 129 Endlebury Road, Chingford, London E4 6PX.
Bratt, C., 65 Moreton Road, Upton, Merseyside L49 4NR.
Bryant, W. N., MA, PhD, College of S. Mark and S. John, Derriford Road, Plymouth, Devon.
Butler, Mrs M. C., MA, 4 Castle Street, Warkworth, Morpeth, Northumberland NE65 0UW.

Cairns, Mrs W. N., MA, Alderton House, New Ross, Co. Wexford, Ireland.
Carter, F. E. L., CBE, MA, FSA, 8 The Leys, London N2 0HE.
Cary, Sir Roger, Bt, BA, 23 Bath Road, London W4.
Chandra, Shri Suresh, MA, MPhil, B½ Havelock Road Colony, Lucknow 226001, India.
Chappell, Rev. M. P., MA, St Luke's Vicarage, 37 Woodland Ravine, Scarborough YO12 6TA.
Clifton, Mrs Gloria C., BA, 13 Fontaine Road, London SW16 3PB.
Cobban, A. D., 11 Pennyfields, Warley, Brentwood, Essex CM14 5JP.
Coleby, A. M., BA, Dept of History, The University, Sheffield S10 2TN.
Condon, Miss M. M., BA, 56 Bernard Shaw House, Knatchbull Road, London NW10.
Cooksley, P. G., 4 Ellerslie Court, Beddington Gardens, Wallington, Surrey SH6 0JD.
Cox, A. H., Winsley, 11a Bagley Close, West Drayton, Middlesex.
Creighton-Williamson, Lt-Col. D., 1 The Pines, Westend Lane, Hucclecote, Gloucester GL3 3SH.

d'Alton, Ian, MA, PhD, 30 Kew Park Avenue, Lucan, Co. Dublin, Ireland.
Daniels, C. W., MEd, Culford School, Bury St Edmunds, Suffolk IP28 6TX.
Davies, G. J., BA, PhD, FSA, 16 Melcombe Avenue, Weymouth, Dorset DT4 7TH.
Davies, P. H., BA, Erskine House, Homesfield, Erskine Hill, London NW11 6HN.

Davis, J. M., BA, MA, MSc, 1 Hamilton Road, Harrow, Middlesex.
Davis, Virginia G., BA, PhD, Dept of History, The University, Hull HU6 7RX.
Denton, Barry, 10 Melrose Avenue, Bants Lane, Northampton NN5 5PB.
Downie, W. F., BSc, CEng, FICE, FINucE, MIES, 10 Ryeland Street, Strathaven, Lanarkshire ML10 6DL.
Dowse, Rev. I. R., 23 Beechfield Road, Hemel Hempstead HP1 1PP.

Edgell, The Revd H. A. R., SB, StJ, Horning Vicarage, Norwich NR12 8PZ.
Elliott, Rev. W., BA, 8 Lea View, Cleobury Mortimer, Kidderminster, Worcs. DY14 8EE.
Enoch, D. G., BEd, MEd, Treetops, 14 St David's Road, Miskin, Pontyclun CF7 8PW.

Firth, P. J. C., 59 Springfield Road, London NW8 0QJ.
Fitzgerald, R., PhD, BA, 32 Kynaston Road, Enfield, Middlesex EN2 0DB.
Foster, J. M., MA, 3 Marchmont Gardens, Richmond, Surrey TW10 6ET.
Franco de Baux, Don Victor, KCHS, KCN, Flat 2, 28 St Stephens Avenue, London W12 8JH.
Frazier, R. Ll., BA, Dept of History, The University, Nottingham NG7 2RD.
Freeman, Miss J., 5 Spencer Close, Stansted Mountfitchet, Essex.

Granger, E. R., Bluefield, Blofield, Norfolk.
Greatrex, Professor Joan G., MA, The Highlands, Great Donard, Symonds Yat, Herefordshire HR9 6DY.
Green, P. L., MA, 9 Faulkner Street, Gate Pa, Tauranga, New Zealand.
Grosvenor, Ian D., BA, 69 Church Road, Moseley, Birmingham B13 9EB.
Gurney, Mrs S. J., 'Albemarle', 13 Osborne Street, Wolverton, Milton Keynes MK12 5HH.
Guy, Rev. J. R., BA, Selden End, Ash, nr Martock, Somerset TA12 6NS.

Hall, P. T., Accrington and Rosendale College, Sandy Lane, Accrington, Lancs. BB5 2AW.
Hamilton-Williams, D. C., BSc, SRN, MRSH, 6 Faraday Avenue, East Grinstead, West Sussex RH19 4AX.
Hanawalt, Professor Barbara A., MA, PhD, Dept of History, University of Minnesota, Minneapolis, M.N. 55455, U.S.A.
Hawkes, G. I., BA, MA, PhD, Linden House, St Helens Road, Ormskirk, Lancs.
Hawtin, Miss G., BA, PhD, FSAScot, FRSAI, Honey Cottage, 5 Clifton Road, London SW19 4QX.
Henderson-Howat, Mrs A. M. D., 8 Dove House Close, Wolvercote, Oxford OX2 8BG.
Hendrie, A. W. A., BA, ACP, Sandy Ridge, Amberley Road, Storrington, West Sussex RH20 4JE.
Hillman, L. B., BA, 18 Creswick Walk, Hampstead Garden Suburb, London NW11 6AN.
Hoare, E. T., 70 Addison Road, Enfield, Middlesex.
Hodge, Mrs G., 85 Hadlow Road, Tonbridge, Kent.
Hope, R. B., MA, MEd, PhD, 5 Partis Way, Newbridge Hill, Bath, Avon BA1 3QG.

Jackson, A., BA, 14 Latimer Lane, Guisborough, Cleveland.
James, T. M., BA, MA, PhD, Plot 8 Three Ways, 36 Hermitage Court, Boley Park, Lichfield, Staffs. WS14 9ST.
Jarvis, L. D., Middlesex Cottage, 86 Mill Road, Stock, Ingatestone, Essex.
Jennings, T. S., GTCL, The Willows, 54 Bramcote Road, Loughborough LE11 2AS.
Jermy, K. E., MA, Cert. Archaeol., CEng, FRSA, MIM, FISTC, AIFA, 5 Far Sandfield, Churchdown, Gloucester GL3 3JS.
Jerram-Burrows, Mrs L. E., Parkanaur House, 88 Sutton Road, Rochford, Essex.
Johnston, F. R., MA, 20 Russell Street, Eccles, Manchester.
Johnstone, H. F. V., 32 Jolliffe Road, Poole, Dorset BH15 2HD.
Jones, Rev. D. R., MA, HQ 4 Armoured Brigade, British Forces Post Office 17.
Jones, Dr N. L., Dept of History & Geography, Utah State University, UMC 07, Logan, Utah 84322, U.S.A.

Keir, Mrs G. I., BA, BLitt, 17 Battlefield Road, St Albans Herts. AL1 4DA.
Kennedy, M. J., BA, Dept of Medieval History, The University, Glasgow G12 8QQ.
Kilburn, T., BSocSc, MA, 2 The Cottages, Chesterfield Road, Two Dales, Darley Dale, Derbyshire DE4 2EZ.
Knight, G. A., BA, PhD, DAA, MIInfSc, 17 Lady Frances Drive, Market Rasen, Lincs. LN8 3JJ.

Land, N., 44 Lineholt Close, Oakenshaw South, Redditch, Worcs.
Lazarus, D., JP, P.O. Box 449, East London 5200, S. Africa.
Leckey, J. J., MSc(Econ), LCP, FRSAI, Vestry Hall, Ballygowan, Co. Down, N. Ireland BT23 6HQ.
Lee, Professor M. du P., PhD, Douglass College, Rutgers University, NB, NJ 08903, U.S.A.
Lewin, Mrs J., MA, 3 Sunnydale Gardens, Mill Hill, London NW7.
Lewis, J. B., MA, CertEd, FRSA, 93 Five Ashes Road, Westminster Park, Chester CH4 7QA.
Lewis, Professor N. B., MA, PhD, 79 Old Dover Road, Canterbury, Kent CT1 3DB.

McIntyre, Miss S. C., BA, DPhil, West Midlands College of Higher Education, Walsall, West Midlands.
McKenna, Rev. T. J., P.O. Box 509, Quean Beyaw, Australia 2620.
McLeod, D. H., BA, PhD, Dept of Theology, The University, P.O. Box 363, Birmingham B15 2TT.
Mayhew, G. J., BA, DPhil, 29 West Street, Lewes, East Sussex BN7 2NZ.
Meatyard, E., BA, DipEd, Guston, Burial Lane, Church Lane, Llantwit Major, S. Glam.
Metcalf, D. M., MA, DPhil, 40 St Margaret's Road, Oxford OX2 6LD.
Morris, A. R., BSc(Econ), MA, Woolpit End, Duke of Kent School, Ewhurst, Surrey GU6 7NS.
Munson, K. G., 'Briar Wood', 4 Kings Ride, Seaford, Sussex BN25 2LN.

Nagel, L. C. J., BA, 61 West Kensington Court, London W14.
Newman, L. T., MSc, DIC, CEng, 27 Mallow Park, Pinkneys Green, Maidenhead, Berks.

Noonan, J. A., BA, MEd, HDE, St Patrick's Comprehensive School, Shannon, Co. Clare, Ireland.

Oggins, R. S., PhD, Dept of History, State University of New York, Binghamton 13901, U.S.A.
Osborne, Irving, M., BEd, Adv.DipEd, FRSA, FCollP, 169 Goodman Park, Slough SL2 5NR.

Pam, D. O., 44 Chase Green Avenue, Enfield, Middlesex EN2 8EB.
Paton, L. R., 49 Lillian Road, Barnes, London SW13.
Paulson, E., BSc(Econ), 11 Darley Avenue, Darley Dale, Matlock, Derbys. DE4 2GB.
Perry, E., FSAScot, 28 Forest Street, Hathershaw, Oldham OL8 3ER.
Perry, K., MA, 14 Highland View Close, Colehill, Wimborne, Dorset.
Pitt, B. W. E., Merryfield House, Ilton, Ilminster TA19 9EX.
Powell, Mrs A. M., 129 Blinco Grove, Cambridge CB1 4TX.
Priestley, Captain E. J., MA, MPhil, 7 Inverleith Place, Edinburgh EH3 5QE.

Raspin, Miss A., London School of Economics, Houghton Street, London WC2A 2AE.
Rees, Rev. D. B., BA, BD, MSc(Econ), PhD, 32 Garth Drive, Liverpool L18 6HW.
Reid, N. H., MA, Wingate, Church Brae, Limekilns, Fife.
Rendall, Miss J., BA, PhD, Dept of History, University of York, York YO1 5DD.
Richards, N. F., PhD, 376 Maple Avenue, St Lambert, Prov. of Quebec, Canada J4P 2S2.
Roberts, S. G., MA, DPhil, 23 Beech Avenue, Radlett, Herts. WD7 7DD.
Rosenfield, M. C., AB, AM, PhD, Box 395, Mattapoisett, Mass. 02739, U.S.A.
Russell, Mrs E., BA, c/o Dept of History, University College London, Gower Street, London WC1E 6BT.

Sabben-Clare, E. E., MA, 4 Denham Close, Abbey Hill Road, Winchester SO23 7BL.
Sainsbury, F., 16 Crownfield Avenue, Newbury Park, Ilford, Essex.
Saksena, D. N., 46 Vigyan Vihar, I.P. Extension Pt II, New Delhi 110 092, India.
Scannura, C. G., MA, 1/11 St Dominic Street, Valletta, Malta.
Scott, The Rev. A. R., MA, BD, PhD, Sunbeam Cottage, 110 Mullalelish Road, Richhill, Co Armagh, N. Ireland BT61 9LT.
Sellers, J. M., MA, 9 Vere Road, Pietermaritzburg 3201, Natal, S. Africa.
Shores, C. F., ARICS, 40 St Mary's Crescent, Hendon, London NW4 4LH.
Sorensen, Mrs M. O., MA, 8 Layer Gardens, London W3 9PR.
Sparkes, I. G., FLA, 124 Green Hill, High Wycombe, Bucks.
Starr, C. R., 63 Abbey Gardens, London W6 8QR.

Teague, D. C., ARAeS, MIMM, 1 Fisher Road, Stoke, Plymouth PL2 3BA.
Thomas, D. L., BA, Public Record Office, Chancery Lane, London WC2A 1LR.
Thomas, Miss E. J. M., BA, 8 Ravenscroft Road, Northfield End, Henley-on-Thames, Oxon. RG9 2DH.

Thompson, L. F., Colne View, 69 Chaney Road, Wivenhoe, Essex.

Tracy, J. N., BA, MPhil, PhD, Dept of History, National University of Singapore, Kent Ridge, Singapore 0511.

Tudor, Victoria M., BA, PhD, 33 Convent Close, Hitchin, Herts. SG5 1QN.

Waldman, T. G., MA, 620 Franklin Bldg./I6, University of Pennsylvania, Philadelphia, Pa. 19104, U.S.A.

Walker, J. A., 1 Sylvanus, Roman Wood, Bracknell, Berkshire RG12 4XX.

Wall, Rev. J., BD, MA, PhD, 10 Branksome Road, Norwich NR4 6SN.

Ward, R. C., BA, MPhil, 192 Stortford Hall Park, Bishop's Stortford, Herts. CM23 5AS.

Warrillow, E. J. D., MBE, FSA, Hill-Cote, Lancaster Road, Newcastle, Staffs.

Weise, Selene H. C., PhD, 22 Hurd Street, Mine Hill, New Jersey 07801, U.S.A.

Welbourne, D. J., 57 West Busk Lane, Otley, West Yorkshire LS21 3LY.

Westlake, R. A., 140 Wyld Way, Wembley, Middlesex HA9 6PU.

Wickham, David E., MA, 116 Parsonage Manorway, Belvedere, Kent.

Wilkinson, F. J., 40 Great James Street, Holborn, London WC1N 3HB.

Williams, A. R., BA, MA, 5 Swanswell Drive, Granley Fields, Cheltenham, Glos. GL51 6LL.

Williams, C. L. Sinclair, ISO, The Old Vicarage, The Green, Puddletown, nr Dorchester, Dorset.

Williams, G., FLA, 32 St John's Road, Manselton, Swansea SA5 8PP.

Williams, P. T., FSAScot, FRSA, FFAS, Bryn Bueno, Whitford Street, Holywell, Clwyd, North Wales.

Wilson, A. R., BA, MA, 80 Apeldale Road, Wood Lane, Bignall End, Stoke-on-Trent ST7 8PH.

Windrow, M. C., West House, Broyle Lane, Ringmer, nr Lewes, Sussex.

Winterbottom, D. O., MA, BPhil, Clifton College, Bristol BS8 3JH.

Wood, A. W., A.Dip.R, 11 Blessington Close, London SE13.

Wood, J. O., BA, MEd, 'Avalon', Les Croutes, St Peter Port, Guernsey, Channel Islands.

Woodall, R. D., BA, Bethel, 7 Wynthorpe Road, Horbury, nr Wakefield, Yorks. WF4 5BB.

Worsley, Miss A. V., BA, 3d St George's Cottages, Glasshill Street, London SE1.

Young Assoc., Professor B., MA, PhD, Dept of History, Illinois Wesleyan University, Bloomington, Illinois 61701, U.S.A.

Zerafa, Rev. M. J., St Dominic's Priory, Valletta, Malta.

CORRESPONDING FELLOWS

Ajayi, Professor J. F. Ade, University of Ibadan, Ibadan, Nigeria, West Africa.

Berend, Professor T. Ivan, Hungarian Academy of Sciences, 1361 Budapest V, Roosevelt-tèr 9, Hungary.
Bischoff, Professor B., DLitt, 8033 Planegg C. München, Ruffini-Alee 27, West Germany.
Boorstin, Daniel J., MA, LLD, 3541 Ordway Street, N.W., Washington, DC 20016, U.S.A.
Boyle, Monsignor Leonard E., OP, Biblioteca Apostolica Vaticana, Vatican City, Rome, Italy.

Cipolla, Professor Carlo M., University of California, Berkeley Campus, Berkeley, Calif. 94720, U.S.A.
Constable, Giles, PhD, School of Historical Studies, The Institute for Advanced Study, Princeton, N.J. 08540, U.S.A.
Crouzet, Professor F. M. J., 6 rue Benjamin Godard, 75016 Paris, France.

Duby, Professor G., Collège de France, 11 Place Marcelin-Berthelot, 75005 Paris, France.

Garin, Professor Eugenio, via Francesco Crispi, 6, 50129 Firenze F, Italy.
Gieysztor, Professor Aleksander, Polska Akademia Nauk, Wydzial I Nauk, Rynek Starego Miasta 29/31, 00-272 Warszawa, Poland.
Giusti, Rt Rev. Mgr M., JCD, Archivio Segreto Vaticano, Vatican City, Italy.
Glamann, Professor K., DPhil, DLitt, The Carlsberg Foundation, H.C. Andersens Boulevard 35, 1553 København, V, Denmark.
Gopal, Professor S., MA, DPhil, Centre for Historical Studies, Jawaharlal Nehru University, New Mehrauli Road, New Delhi-110067, India.
Guenée, Professor Bernaerd, 8 rue Huysmans, 75006 Paris, France.

Hancock, Professor Sir Keith, KBE, MA, DLitt, FBA, Australian National University, Box 4, P.O., Canberra, ACT, Australia.
Hanke, Professor L. U., PhD, University of Massachusetts, Amherst, Mass. 01002, U.S.A.
Heimpel, Professor Dr H., DrJur, Dr Phil, former Direktor des Max Planck-Instituts für Geschichte, Gottingen, Dahlmannstr. 14, West Germany.

Inalcik, Professor Halil, PhD, The University of Ankara, Turkey.

Klingenstein, Professor Grete, Paniglgasse 19 A/31, A-1040 Wien IV, Austria.
Kossmann, Professor E. H., DLitt, Rijksuniversiteit te Groningen, Groningen, The Netherlands.
Kuttner, Professor S., MA, JUD, SJD, LLD, Institute of Medieval Canon Law, University of California, Berkeley, Calif. 94720, U.S.A.

Ladurie, Professor E. B. LeRoy, Collège de France, 11 Place Marcelin-Berthelot, 75005 Paris, France.
Leclercq, The Rev. Dom Jean, OSB, Abbaye St-Maurice, L-9737 Clervaux, Luxembourg.

McNeill, Professor William H., 1126 East 59th Street, Chicago, Illinois 60637, U.S.A.
Maruyama, Professor Masao, 2-44-5 Higashimachi, Kichijoji, Musashinoshi, Tokyo 180, Japan.
Michel, Henri, 12 Rue de Moscou, 75008 Paris, France.
Morgan, Professor Edmund S., Department of History, P.O. Box 1504A Yale Station, New Haven, Conn. 06520-7425, U.S.A.

Peña y Cámara, J. M. de la, Avenida Reina, Mercedes 65, piso 7-B, Seville 12, Spain.
Prawer, Professor J., Department of Medieval History, Hebrew University, Il-Jerusalem, Israel.

Slicher van Bath, Professor B. H., Gen. Fouldesweg 113, Wageningen, The Netherlands.

Thapar, Professor Romila, Dept of Historical Studies, Jawaharlal Nehru University, New Mehrauli Road, New Delhi-110067, India.
Thorne, Professor S. E., MA, LLB, LittD, LLD, FSA, Law School of Harvard University, Cambridge, Mass. 92138, U.S.A.

Van Houtte, Professor J. A., PhD, FBA, Termunkveld, Groeneweg, 51, Egenhoven, Heverlee, Belgium.
Verlinden, Professor C., PhD, 3 Avenue du Derby, 1050 Brussels, Belgium.

Wang, Professor Juefei, Nanjing University, China.
Wolff, Professor Philippe, Edifici Roureda Tapada, 2ª,7, Santa Coloma (Principality of Andorra), France.
Woodward, Professor C. Vann, PhD, Yale University, 104 Hall of Graduate Studies, New Haven, Conn. 06520, U.S.A.

Zavala, S., LLD, Montes Urales 310, Mexico 10, D.F., Mexico.

TRANSACTIONS AND PUBLICATIONS

OF THE

ROYAL HISTORICAL SOCIETY

The publications of the Society consist of the *Transactions*, supplemented in 1897 by the *Camden Series* (formerly the Camden Society, 1838-97); since 1937 by a series of *Guides and Handbooks* and, from time to time, by miscellaneous publications. The Society also began in 1937 an annual bibliography of *Writings on British History*, for the continuation of which the Institute of Historical Research accepted responsibility in 1965; it publishes, in conjunction with the American Historical Association, a series of *Bibliographies of British History*.

List of series published

The following are issued in collaboration with the distributor/publisher indicated:

Annual Bibliography of British and Irish History
All titles   Harvester Press
Bibliographies of British History
   All except 1485-1603, 1714-1789   Oxford University Press
   1485-1603, 1714-1789   Harvester Press
Camden Series
   Old Series and New Series   Johnson Reprint
   Third and Fourth Series*   Boydell and Brewer
Guides and Handbooks
   Main Series*   Boydell and Brewer
   Supplementary Series*   Boydell and Brewer
Miscellaneous titles   Boydell and Brewer
Studies in History
   All titles   Boydell and Brewer
Transactions of the Royal Historical Society
   Up to *Fifth Series*, Vol. 19   Kraus Reprint
   Fifth Series, Vol. 20 onwards*†   Boydell and Brewer
Writings on British History
   Up to 1946   Dawson Book Service
   1946-1974   Instititue of Historical Research

Members' entitlements

Fellows and Subscribing Libraries receive free copies of new volumes of series marked*.

Corresponding Fellows, Retired Fellows and Associates receive free copies of new volumes of this series marked†.

Terms for members' purchase of individual titles are listed below.

Methods of Ordering Volumes

Institute of Historical Research—an invoice will be sent with volume.

In all other cases pre-payment is required. If correct price is not known, a cheque made payable to the appropriate supplier, in the form 'Not exceeding £   ' may be sent with the order. Otherwise a pro-forma invoice will be sent.

LIST OF TITLES
ARRANGED BY DISTRIBUTOR

BOYDELL & BREWER

Address for orders: P.O. Box 9, Woodbridge, Suffolk IP12 3DF.
Camden Third Series: All titles now available; a list can be sent on
request. Prices range from £10 for original volumes to £30 for the
largest reprinted volumes. (£7.50-£22.50 to Members).
Camden Fourth Series: The following titles are available price £10.
(£7.50 to Members) unless otherwise indicated:

1. Camden Miscellany, Vol. XXII: 1. Charters of the Earldom of Hereford, 1095-1201. Edited by David Walker. 2. Indentures of Retinue
   with John of Gaunt, Duke of Lancaster, enrolled in Chancery, 1367-
   99. Edited by N. B. Lewis. 3. Autobiographical memoir of Joseph Jewell, 1763-1846. Edited by A. W. Slater. 1964. £25.00.
2. Documents illustrating the rule of Walter de Wenlock, Abbot of Westminster, 1283-1307. Edited by Barbara Harvey. 1965.
3. The early correspondence of Richard Wood, 1831-41. Edited by A. B.
   Cunningham. 1966. £25.00.
4. Letters from the English abbots to the chapter at Cîteaux, 1442-1521.
   Edited by C. H. Talbot. 1967.
5. Select writings of George Wyatt. Edited by D. M. Loades. 1968.
6. Records of the trial of Walter Langeton, Bishop of Lichfield and Coventry (1307-1312). Edited by Miss A. Bearwood. 1969.
7. Camden Miscellany, Vol. XXIII: 1. The Account Book of John Balsall
   of Bristol for a trading voyage to Spain, 1480. Edited by T. F. Redda-
   way and A. A. Ruddock. 2. A Parliamentary diary of Queen Anne's
   reign. Edited by W. A. Speck. 3. Leicester House politics, 1750-60,
   from the papers of John second Earl of Egmont. Edited by A. N.
   Newman. 4. The Parliamentary diary of Nathaniel Ryder, 1764-67.
   Edited by P. D. G. Thomas. 1969.
8. Documents illustrating the British Conquest of Manila, 1762-63. Edited
   by Nicholas P. Cushner. 1971.
9. Camden Miscellany, Vol XXIV: 1. Documents relating to the Breton
   succession dispute of 1341. Edited by M. Jones. 2. Documents relating
   to the Anglo-French negotiations, 1439. Edited by C. T. Allmand. 3.
   John Benet's Chronicle for the years 1400 to 1462. Edited by G. L.
   Harriss. 1972.
10. Herefordshire Militia Assessments of 1663. Edited by M. A. Faraday.
    1972.
11. The early correspondence of Jabez Bunting, 1820-29. Edited by W. R.
    Ward. 1972.
12. Wentworth Papers, 1597-1628. Edited by J. P. Cooper, 1973.
13. Camden Miscellany, Vol. XXV: 1. The Letters of William, Lord Paget.
    Edited by Barrett L. Beer and Sybil Jack. 2. The Parliamentary Diary
    of John Clementson, 1770-1802. Edited by P. D. G. Thomas. 3. J. B.
    Pentland's Report on Bolivia, 1827. Edited by J. V. Fifer, 1974.
14. Camden Miscellany, Vol. XXVI: 1. Duchy of Lancaster Ordinances,

1483. Edited by Sir Robert Somerville. 2. A Breviat of the Effectes devised for Wales. Edited by P. R. Roberts. 3. Gervase Markham, The Muster-Master. Edited by Charles L. Hamilton. 4. Lawrence Squibb, A Book of all the Several Offices of the Court of the Exchequer (1642). Edited by W. H. Bryson. 5. Letters of Henry St John to Charles, Earl of Orrery, 1709-11. Edited by H. T. Dickinson. 1975.

15. Sidney Ironworks Accounts, 1541-73. Edited by D. W. Crossley. 1975.
16. The Account-Book of Beaulieu Abbey. Edited by S. F. Hockey. 1975.
17. A calendar of Western Circuit Assize Orders, 1629-48. Edited by J. S. Cockburn. 1976.
18. Four English Political Tracts of the later Middle Ages. Edited by J.-Ph. Genet. 1977.
19. Proceedings of the Short Parliament of 1640. Edited by Esther S. Cope in collaboration with Willson H. Coates. 1977.
20. Heresy Trials in the Diocese of Norwich, 1428-31. Edited by N. P. Tanner. 1977.
21. Edmund Ludlow: A Voyce from the Watch Tower (Part Five: 1660-1662). Edited by A. B. Worden. 1978.
22. Camden Miscellany, Vol. XXVII: 1. The Disputed Regency of the Kingdom of Jerusalem, 1264/6 and 1268. Edited by P. W. Edbury. 2. George Rainsford's *Ritratto d'Ingliterra* (1556). Edited by P. S. Donaldson. 3. The Letter-Book of Thomas Bentham, Bishop of Coventry and Lichfield, 1560-1561. Edited by Rosemary O'Day and Joel Berlatsky. 1979.
23. The Letters of the Third Viscount Palmerston to Laurence and Elizabeth Sulivan, 1804-63. Edited by Kenneth Bourne. 1979.
24. Documents illustrating the crisis of 1297-98 in England. Edited by M. Prestwich. 1980.
25. The Diary of Edward Goschen, 1900-1914. Edited by C. H. D. Howard. 1980.
26. English Suits before the Parlement of Paris, 1420-36. Edited by C. T. Allmand and C. A. J. Armstrong. 1982.
27. The Devonshire Diary, 1759-62. Edited by P. D. Brown and K. W. Schweizer. 1982.
28. Barrington Family Letters, 1628-1632. Edited by A. Searle. 1983.
29. Camden Miscellany XXVIII: 1. The Account of the Great Household of Humphrey, first Duke of Buckingham, for the year 1452-3. Edited by Mrs M. Harris. 2. Documents concerning the Anglo-French Treaty of 1550. Edited by D. L. Potter. 3. *Vita Mariae Reginae Anglie*. Edited by D. MacCulloch. 4. Despatch of the Count of Feria to Philip II, 1558. Edited by S. L. Adams and M. J. Rodriguez-Salgado. 1983.
30. Gentlemen of Science: Early correspondence of the British Association for the Advancement of Science. Edited by A. W. Thackray and J. B. Morrell. 1984.
31. Reading Abbey Cartularies, Vol. I. Edited by B. R. Kemp. 1986.
32. The Letters of the First Viscount Hardinge of Lahore to Lady Hardinge and Sir Walter and Lady James 1844-1847. Edited by Bawa Satinder Singh. 1986.
33. Reading Abbey Cartularies, Vol. II. Edited by B R. Kemp. 1987.

Provisionally accepted by the Society for future publication:

Charters of Hugh of Amiens, archbishop of Rouen (1130-64). Edited by T. G. Waldman.
Correspondence of William Camden. Edited by Richard DeMolen.

Early Paget Correspondence. Edited by C. J. Harrison and A. C. Jones.
Letters of J. A. Blackwell concerning events in Hungary, 1848-9. Edited by
  A. Sked.
Supplementary Documents of the English Lands of the Abbey of Bec. Edited
  by Marjorie Chibnall.
Letters to Sir Reynold Bray. Edited by De Ll Guth and Miss M. Condon.
Clifford Letters, c. 1500-39. Edited by R. W. Hoyle.
The Short Parliament Diary of Sir Thomas Aston. Edited by Judith Maltby.
Journal of Gilbert, second earl of Minto, 1847-1859. Edited by K. Bourne.
Financial Memoranda of the reign of Edward V. Edited by Rosemary
  Horrox.
Jean Creton's Prinse et Mort. Edited by J. J. N. Palmer and Mrs L. Finlay.
Indentures of retinue in peace and war, 1292-1461. Edited by N. B. Lewis
  and M. Powicke.
Early Eighteenth Century Parliamentary Diary. Edited by E. Cruickshanks.
John Howson's Answers. Edited by K. Fincham and N. Cranfield.
Parliamentary Debates, 1698-9. Edited by D. Hayton.
Collection of several speeches by Lord Treasurer Cecil, 1608-10. Edited by
  Pauline Croft.
Thomas Starkey's Dialogue between Pole and Lupset. Edited by T. F.
  Mayer.
William Latymer's Life of Anne Boleyn. Edited by M. Dowling.
Sir Arthur Kaye's Diary and Speeches. Edited by D. Szechi.
Minutes of the Rainbow Circle, 1894-1924. Edited by M. Freeden.
The Diary of A. H. D. Acland, 1871-1924. Edited by Lady Acland, with
  Lord Briggs.
Extracts from the Registers of Privy Council, 1603-1610. Edited by L. M.
  Hill.
The Oxford and Temple Book: Newdigate Family Accounts, 1618-1621.
  Edited by V. Larminie.
Stafford Lawsuit. Edited by C. Rawcliffe and M. Condon.
The Plumpton Letters. Edited by J. Kirby.
Correspondence of Swedish Ambassadors in England, 1655-6. Edited by
  Michael Roberts.
Correspondence of Henry Cromwell. Edited by P. G. I. Gaunt.
Memoranda on Spain, 1738. Edited by P. Woodfine.
The Derby Diaries, c.1870-1885. Edited by J. Vincent.
Letters of Elizabeth I to Foreign Powers. Edited by E. I. Kouri.

Guides and handbooks

Main series
1. Guide to English commercial statistics, 1696-1782. By G. N. Clark,
   with a catalogue of materials by Barbara M. Franks. 1938. (*Out of
   print*).
2. Handbook of British chronology. Edited by F. M. Powicke and E. B.
   Fryde, 1st edn. 1939; 2nd edn. 1961; 3rd edn. 1986. £25.00.
3. Medieval libraries of Great Britain, a list of surviving books. Edited by
   N. R. Ker, 1st edn. 1941; 2nd edn. 1964. £8.00.
4. Handbook of dates for students of English history. By C. R. Cheney.
   1981. £5.00.
5. Guide to the national and provincial directories of England and Wales,
   excluding London, published before 1856. By Jane E. Norton. 1st edn.
   1950; 2nd edn. 1984. £12.00.

6. Handbook of Oriental history. Edited by C. H. Philips. 1963. £5.00.
7. Texts and calendars: an analytical guide to serial publications. Edited by E. L. C. Mullins. 1st edn. 1958; 2nd edn. 1978. £8.00.
8. Anglo-Saxon charters. An annotated list and bibliography. Edited by P. H. Sawyer. 1968. £8.00.
9. A Centenary Guide to the Publications of the Royal Historical Society, 1868–1968. Edited by A. T. Milne. 1968. £5.00.
10. A Guide to the Local Administrative Units of England. Vol. I. Edited by F. A. Youngs, Jr. 1980; 2nd edn. 1981. £25.00.
11. A Guide to Bishops' Registers to 1646. Edited by D. M. Smith. 1981. £15.00.
12. Texts and Calendars: II: an analytical guide to serial publications 1957–1982. By E. L. C. Mullins. 1983. £15.00.
13. Handbook of Medieval Exchange. Edited by P. Spufford. 1986. £19.50.
14. Scottish Texts and Calendars. Edited by D. and W. B. Stevenson. 1987. £15.00.
15. Supplement to N. Ker's Medieval Libraries of Great Britain. Edited by A. G. Watson. 1987.

Supplementary series

1. A Guide to the Papers of British Cabinet Ministers, 1900–1951. Edited by Cameron Hazlehurst and Christine Woodland. 1974. £4.50.
2. A Guide to the Reports of the U.S. Strategic Bombing Survey. Edited by Gordon Daniels. 1981. £12.00.

Provisionally accepted by the Society for future publication:

A Handbook of British Currency. Edited by P. Grierson and C. E. Blunt.
A Guide to the Records and Archives of Mass Communications. Edited by Nicholas Pronay.
A Guide to the Maps of the British Isles. Edited by Helen Wallis.
A Guide to the Local Administrative Units of England. Vol. II. Edited by F. A. Youngs, Jr.
Handlist of British Diplomatic Representatives, 1508–1688. Edited by G. Bell.

Miscellaneous publications

Domesday Studies, 2 vols, Edited by P. E. Dove, 1886. £3.50. (Vol. I out of print.)
The Royal Historical Society, 1868–1968. By R. A. Humphreys. 1969. £1.25.

Transactions, Fifth Series

Vol. 20 onwards. Price £8.50. (£6.38 to Members).

Studies in History is a series of historical monographs, preferably of no more than 90,000 words, intended to help solve the increasing difficulties encountered by historians in getting their books accepted for publication, especially young scholars seeking first publication. Those interested in submitting works for consideration by the Editorial Board should write to the Editorial Assistant, c/o The Royal Historical Society, University College London, Gower Street, WC1E 6BT, from whom further details can be obtained. No typescripts should be sent until asked for.

1. F. F. Foster: *The Politics of Stability: A Portrait of the Rulers in Elizabethan London.* 1977. £19.60 (£14.00 to Members).

2. Rosamond McKitterick, *The Frankish Church and the Carolingian Reforms 789-895*. 1977. £19.60 (£14.00 to Members).
3. K. D. Brown, *John Burns*. 1977. £19.60 (£14.00 to Members).
4. D. Stevenson, *Revolution and Counter Revolution in Scotland, 1644-1651*. 1977. (Out of print).
5. Marie Axton, *The Queen's Two Bodies: Drama and the Elizabethan Succession*. 1978. £17.50 (£12.50 to Members).
6. Anne Orde: *Great Britain and International Security, 1920-1926*. 1978. £19.60 (£14.00 to Members).
7. J. H. Baker (ed), *Legal Records and the Historian* (Papers read to the 2nd Conference on Legal History, held at Cambridge in 1975). 1978. £19.60 (£14.00 to Members).
8. M. P. Costeloe: *Church and State in Independent Mexico: a study of the Patronage Debate, 1821-1857*. 1978. £19.60 (£14.00 to Members).
9. Wendy Davies: *An Early Welsh Microcosm: Studies in the Llandaff Charters*, 1978. £19.60 (£14.00 to Members).
10. Bernard Wasserstein: *The British in Palestine: The Mandatory Government and the Arab-Jewish Conflict, 1917-1929*. 1978. £21.00 (£15.00 to Members).
11. Michael McCahill: *Order and Equipoise: the Peerage and the House of Lords, 1783-1806*. 1979. £21.00 (£15.00 to Members).
12. Norman Etherington: *Preachers, Peasants and Politics in Southeast Africa 1835-1880. African Christian Communities in Natal, Pondoland and Zululand*. 1979. £19.60 (£14.00 to Members).
13. S. A. G. Rizvi: *Linlithgow and India: A Study of British Policy and the Political Impasse in India, 1936-1943*. 1979. £21.00 (£15.00 to Members).
14. David McLean: *Britain and her Buffer-state: The Collapse of the Persian Empire, 1890-1914*. 1979. £17.95 (£12.80 to Members).
15. Howard Tomlinson: *Guns and Government: The Ordnance Office under the later Stuarts*. 1979. £21.00 (£15.00 to Members).
16. Patricia Crawford: *Denzil Holles, 1598-1680: A study of his Political Career*. 1979. £19.60 (£14.00 to Members).
17. D. L. Rydz: *The Parliamentary Agents: A History*. 1979. £19.60 (£14.00 to Members).
18. Uri Bialer: *The Shadow of the Bomber: The Fear of Air Attack and British Politics 1932-1939*. 1980. £17.50 (£12.50 to Members)
19. David Parker: *La Rochelle and the French Monarchy: Conflict and Order in Seventeenth-Century France*. 1980. £19.60 (£14.00 to Members).
20. A. P. C. Bruce: *The Purchase System in the British Army, 1660-1871*. 1980. £17.50 (£12.50 to Members).
21. Stephen Gradish: *The Manning of the British Navy During the Seven Years War*. 1980. £19.60 (£14.00 to Members).
22. Alan Harding (ed.): *Lawmaking and Lawmakers in British History* (Papers presented to the Edinburgh Legal History Conference 1977). 1980. £19.60 (£14.00 to Members).
23. Diane Willen: *John Russell First Earl of Bedford*. 1981. £17.50 (£12.50 to Members).
24. Roy Schreiber: *The Political Career of Sir Robert Naunton, 1589-1635*. 1981. £17.50 (£12.50 to Members).
25. W. M. Mathew: *The House of Gibbs and the Peruvian Guano Monopoly*. 1981. £21.00 (£15.00 to Members).
26. D. M. Schurman: *Julian S. Corbett 1854-1922, Historian of British Maritime Policy from Drake to Jellicoe*. 1981. £19.60 (£14.00 to Members).
27. Scott M. Harrison: *The Pilgrimage of Grace in the Lake Counties 1536-7*. 1981. £17.50 (£12.50 to Members).

28. Angus MacKay: *Money, Prices and Politics in Fifteenth-Century Castile.* 1982. £17.50 (£12.50 to Members).
29. D. Duman: *The Judicial Bench in England 1727–1875: The Reshaping of a Professional Elite.* 1982. £19.60 (£14.00 to Members).
30. J. R. Wordie: *Estate Management in Eighteenth-Century England.* 1982. £21.00 (£15.00 to Members).
31. M. Doughty: *Merchant Shipping and War.* 1982. £19.60 (£14.00 to Members).
32. N. Jones: *Faith by Statute: Parliament and the Settlement of Religion 1559.* 1982. £19.60 (£14.00 to Members).
33. James Barros: *Britain, Greece and the Politics of Sanctions: Ethiopia 1935–1936.* 1982. £19.60 (£14.00 to Members).
34. J. Davis: *Heresy and Reformation in the South-East of England 1520–1529.* 1983. £17.50 (£12.50 to Members).
35. A. J. Pollard: *John Talbot and the War in France 1427–1453.* 1983. £17.50 (£12.50 to Members).
36. E. W. Ives and A. H. Manchester (eds.): *Law, Litigants and the Legal Profession.* 1983. £19.60 (£14.00 to Members).
37. J. Ashworth: *Agrarians and Aristocrats.* 1983. £21.00 (£15.00 to Members).
38. Joyce L. Malcolm: *Caesar's Due: Loyalty & King Charles 1642–1646.* 1983. £21.00 (£15.00 to Members).
39. L. W. Brady: *T. P. O'Connor and the Liverpool Irish.* 1984. £21.00 (£15.00 to Members).
40. J. A. Guy and H. G. Beale: *Law and Social Change in British History.* 1984. £17.50 (£12.50 to Members).
41. R. Holmes: *The Road to Sedan: The French Army 1866–70.* 1984. £21.00 (£15.00 to Members).
42. R. G. Little: *The Parlement of Poitiers: War, Government and Politics in France 1418–1436.* 1984. £17.50 (£12.50 to Members).
43. Ronald W. Zweig: *Britain and Palestine during the Second World War.* 1986. £26.00 (£19.50 to Members).
44. W. J. Murray: *The Right-Wing Press in the French Revolution.* 1986. £29.50 (£22.00 to Members).
45. Michael B. Young: *Servility and Service: The Life and Work of Sir John Coke.* 1986. £28.00 (£21.00 to Members).
46. Douglas Fermer: *James Gordon Bennett and the New York Herald.* 1986. £29.50 (£22.00 to Members).
47. Steven G. Ellis: *Reform and Revival: English Government in Ireland, 1470–1534.* 1986. £29.50 (£22.00 to Members).
48. D. J. Sturdy: *The D'Aligres de la Riviere: Servants of the Bourbon State in the Seventh Century.* 1986. £29.50 (£22.00 to Members).
49. Andrew Porter: *Victorian Shipping, Business and Imperial Policy: Donald Currie, the Castle Line and Southern Africa.* 1986. £29.50 (£22.00 to Members).
50. J. H. Denton and J. P. Dooley: *Representatives of the Lower Clergy.* 1987. £25.00 (£18.75 to Members).

DAWSON BOOK SERVICE

Address for orders: Cannon House, Folkestone, Kent.
Writings on British History to 1946. Prices on request.

HARVESTER PRESS

Address for orders: 17 Ship Street, Brighton, Sussex.
Annual Bibliography of British and Irish History (Editor: D. M. Palliser)

1. Publications of 1975 (1976)
2. Publications of 1976 (1977)
3. Publications of 1977 (1978)
4. Publications of 1978 (1979)
5. Publications of 1979 (1980)
6. Publications of 1980 (1981)
7. Publications of 1981 (1982)
8. Publications of 1982 (1983)
9. Publications of 1983 (1984)
10. Publications of 1984 (1985)
11. Publications of 1985 (1986)

Prices on request.
Bibliography of British History: Tudor Period, 1485-1603. Edited by Conyers Read. 1st edn 1933; 2nd edn 1959; 3rd edn 1978. Price £28.00.
Bibliography of British History: The Eighteenth Century, 1714-1789. Edited by S. M. Pargellis and D. J. Medley. 1st edn 1951; 2nd edn 1977. Price £18.95.

INSTITUTE OF HISTORICAL RESEARCH

Address for orders: University of London, Senate House, Malet Street, London WC1E 7HU.
Writings on British History, 1946-1948. Compiled by D. J. Munro. 1973. Price £20.00.
Writings on British History, 1949-1951. Compiled by D. J. Munro. 1975 Price £20.00.
Writings on British History, 1952-1954. Compiled by J. M. Sims. 1975. Price £20.00.
Writings on British History, 1955-1957. Compiled by J. M. Sims and P. M. Jacob. 1977. Price £20.00.
Writings on British History, 1958-1959. Compiled by H. J. Creaton. 1977. Price £20.00.
Writings on British History, 1960-1961. Compiled by C. H. E. Philpin and H. J. Creaton. 1978. Price £20.00.
Writings on British History, 1962-1964. Compiled by H. J. Creaton. 1979. Price £20.00.
Writings on British History, 1965-1966. Compiled by H. J. Creaton. 1981. Price £20.00.
Writings on British History, 1967-1968. Compiled by H. J. Creaton. 1982. Price £20.00.
Writings on British History, 1969-1970. Compiled by H. J. Creaton. 1984. Price £20.00.
Writings on British History, 1971-1972. Compiled by H. J. Creaton. 1985. Price £25.00.
Writings on British History, 1973-1974. Compiled by H. J. Creaton. 1986. Price £25.00.

JOHNSON REPRINT

Address for orders: 24–28 Oval Road, London NW1 7DX.
Camden Old and New Series. Prices on request.

KRAUS REPRINT

Address for orders: Route 100, Millwood, N.Y. 10546, U.S.A.
Transactions: Old, New, Third, Fourth, Fifth Series Vols 1–19. Prices
on request.

OXFORD UNIVERSITY PRESS

Method of ordering: through booksellers.
If members have difficulty in obtaining volumes at the special price, refer-
ence should be made to the Society.
*Bibliography of English History to 1485. Based on the Sources and Literature of
English History from earliest times by Charles Gross.* Revised and expanded
by Edgar B. Graves. 1975. Price £48 (£36 to Members).
Bibliography of British History: Stuart Period, 1603–1714. 2nd edn. Edited by
Mary F. Keeler, 1970. Price £35.00 (£26.25 to Members).
Bibliography of British History: 1789–1851. Edited by Lucy M. Brown and Ian
R. Christie. 1970. Price £38.00 (£28.50 to Members).
Bibliography of British History: 1851–1914. Edited by H. J. Hanham. 1976.
Price £58.00 (£43.50 to Members).
In preparation
*Supplement to Bibliography of British History: 1714–89. Edited by S. M. Pargellis
and D. J. Medley.* Edited by A. T. Milne and A. N. Newman.